Full Circle
Escape from Baghdad and the Return

Saul Silas Fathi

Saul Silas Fathi
27 Broadlawn Drive
Central Islip, NY 11722-4616

Tel (631) 232-1638 / Fax (631) 232-1638
www.saulsilasfathi.com
fathi@optonline.net

DEDICATION

I dedicate this book to the memory
of my mother Salha Ani,
the wisest woman in my life,
and to the dear memory of my brother Yeftah,
who taught us, and all those who knew him,
to laugh at life's adversities.
And to my father,
who inspired me throughout my life
and instilled in me the love of reading books.
This book is a tribute to those
who escaped hatred, tyranny and oppression,
and to all those who perished trying.

ACKNOWLEDGEMENT

I owe deep gratitude to Marianne Rogoff
and Janie Franz for their assistance in typing,
editing and researching this manuscript
and for their valuable advice
and dedication to my story.

Especially, I owe sincere thanks to my wife
and life-long friend Rachelle
for her patience, support
and understanding that my story had to be told.

Finally, I am indebted to my wonderful
and thoughtful daughters:
Suzanne, Sandra and Sharon
(and granddaughter Danielle),
whose love sustained me through
the arduous journey of writing these memoirs.

INTRODUCTION

Full Circle: Escape from Baghdad and the Return chronicles a prominent Iraqi Jewish family's escape from persecution, through the journey of one family member, a young boy, who witnesses public hangings and the 1941 Krystallnacht (Farhood) in Baghdad. After a dangerous escape from Iraq as part of a Sephardic Schindler's List, this ten-year-old begins a lifelong search for meaning and his place in the world. This journey takes him to the fledgling nation of Israel, then to Brazil, and eventually to the United States, where he serves in the US Army in Korea, works in top-level positions with three Fortune 500 companies, starts several businesses, and volunteers to assist the FBI after September 11. This chronicle strives to explore questions of meaning such as: Does hardship taint the lure of adventure for any young man? What sustains hope? Does a persecuted Jew ever feel at home anywhere? This young man's journey and subsequent identity crisis interfaces with historical happenings in the world and brings an understanding of the culture and contributions of Sephardic Jews.

There has been much written about the Jewish population in Germany and Europe and what they suffered, but little about Sephardic Jews who have also been persecuted in other countries, especially in Iraq, a country of which we as Americans have some familiarity, but know very little about.

FULL CIRCLE
Escape from Baghdad and the Return

By Saul Silas Fathi

"Our parents were risking their lives to try to save Yeftah's and mine. There had been no other choice for them. Staying in Baghdad could mean that we would witness our father's hanging since he had been falsely accused of treason against the Iraqi government. He was accused not only of being a Zionist but also of being a Communist, just as every other wealthy and prominent Jew here had been labeled. Being thus accused was a double insult in the eyes of the citizenry. One charge offended their nationalism; the other, their religion. It was sure to arouse the hatred and outrage of the entire Muslim population."

About the Author: Saul Silas Fathi

Saul Silas Fathi was born to a prominent Jewish family in Baghdad, Iraq, on May 8, 1938. At age 10, he and his younger brother were smuggled out of Baghdad through Iran and eventually reached the newly formed state of Israel. He began writing a diary at age 11 and had several stories published in Israeli youth magazines.

Saul enrolled at the Israel Air force Academy of Aeronautics, a 4-year program, where he earned his high-school diploma and became certified in electrical engineering. In 1958, he worked his way to Brazil where he nearly starved. Through perseverance and luck, he started his own electrical business and earned a patent for climate-controlled windows used in the building of Brasilia, Brazil.

In 1960, he came to the U.S. on a student exchange visa, studying sculpture at the Brooklyn Museum of Art and American history and public speaking at the New School of Social Studies. After 8 months, Saul volunteered to serve in the U.S. Army for three years, having been promised a college education and U.S. citizenship at the conclusion of his duties. After Basic Training in Fort Benning, Georgia, he was sent to helicopter school at Fort Bragg, North Carolina, and there enrolled at the University Of Virginia. Within a few months, Saul was shipped to South Korea where he served as Chief Electrical Technician with the 1st Cavalry Division, 15th Aviation Company, the famed helicopter division in the Vietnam War.

Back in the U.S., Saul battled the immigration department while studying at the University of Virginia, finally earning a Bachelor of Science degree in electrical engineering. This launched an impressive career as a high-level executive with several Fortune-500 companies. Later, he founded and managed three high-tech companies of his own over a 20-year period.

Saul retired in 2003 and began writing his memoirs, Full Circle: Escape from Baghdad and the Return. Today, he lives in Long Island, New York, with his wife Rachelle and has three U.S.-born daughters and one granddaughter. He is also a certified linguist, fluent in English, Hebrew, Arabic, and Portuguese.

Saul Silas Fathi   27 Broadlawn Drive   Central Islip   NY   11722-4616   FAX/Tel (631) 232-1638
fathi@optonline.net   http://www.saulsilasfathi.com

TABLE OF CONTENTS

FULL CIRCLE:
ESCAPE FROM BAGHDAD AND THE RETURN

Section One: IRAQ

Section Two: ISRAEL

Section Three: BRAZIL

Section Four: USA/Korea/USA

Section Four: Back To The U.S.A. (II)

SUPPLEMENTARY COMPANION:

The earliest and only surviving family photo,
Berta (l), Yedida (r), Saul (1 yr), 1939 (1)

Mother's grandparents and their extended family,
Baghdad, 1908 (2)

Shaleh (Zadok) and Neomi, my mother's grandparents,
Baghdad, ±1910 (3)

Oldest photo of my mother (far right),
Baghdad, 1932 (4)

Section One

My Life in Iraq

1938 – 1948

The Jewish Diaspora and the Jews in Iraq

Upon the rivers of Babylon, there we sat and wept:
when we remembered Zion
On the willows in the midst thereof we hung up our instruments.
For there they that led us into captivity required of us the words of songs.
And they that carried us away, said:
Sing ye to us a hymn of the songs of Zion.
How shall we sing the song of the Lord in a strange land?
If I forget thee, O Jerusalem, may my right hand be forgotten.

From the Douay-Rheims version

My father Silas in Basra, Iraq, 1929 (5)

Saul's father Silas, Basra, Iraq, 1930 (6)

Chapter One

My Father and Mother Meet and Marry

My father, Silas (also called Saleh) Fathi, was born in 1903 in Baghdad. His mother, my Grandmother Khatoon, was widowed when my father was only twelve years old. His older brother Joseph fled to Israel, leaving Grandmother Khatoon to manage alone. My father, therefore, grew up to take life very seriously and to be responsible at a very young age.

Father studied hard and graduated as a civil engineer from Bombay University on a British Scholarship. In 1930, he was brought back to Iraq to plan, expand, and develop the Iraqi railroad system. He was appointed "Railroad Master" in the southern port city of Basra, at Margeel. His assistant and second in command was a handsome blond Jew named Yehuda Ani. Although Father and Yehuda both were native Iraqis, they had been assigned these prestigious jobs by the British.

During a summer holiday, Yehuda's youngest sister Ruth went to visit her brother in Basra. Ruth was a beautiful young teenager, with blonde hair and deep green eyes. At the office, she was introduced to my father, who, it is said, was immediately smitten by her.

Blushing at his attention, she quickly informed him, "I'm only fourteen years old, but I have a beautiful older sister."

Father, a dashing bachelor, sensed that an "arrangement" was about to be set in motion. He nodded his head with a smile and apologized.

Ruth turned to Yehuda, "Would it be appropriate to introduce Salha to your handsome boss?"

Salha, who had been born in 1914, had just graduated high school and was ready to find a husband, yet Yehuda was reluctant to arrange a meeting. He feared that he might be opening himself to some embarrassment by letting his boss become familiar with his family.

Two weeks later, Salha paid Yehuda a visit in Basra and naturally was introduced to my father. According to my mother's recollection years later, it was love at first sight.

Yehuda could not believe it. "This man is a notorious lady's man, a sworn bachelor," he told his family. "He is just playing at being serious."

As it turned out, however, he wasn't. He, too, had felt the strong attraction and was permanently transformed. He was ready to make a life-long commitment.

Though Father was quite serious and his intentions were most noble, my mother was not permitted to go out on a date with him unless she was chaperoned by at least two of her sisters. Since they were not there in Basra, she had to return to Baghdad without being able to spend more time with my father. They did begin exchanging love letters. Four months later, they were engaged and were wed a month later.

Mother, in later years, often described the magnificent wedding and all of the people that attended. The wedding guests were not only close friends and relatives, but also many of Father's prominent friends: Arabs, Hindus, and British officers.

Mother and Father moved to Basra and lived in real luxury. After my sister Berta, whom we called Baby, was born in 1935, Father asked his superiors for a transfer to the Baghdad office so that they could be close to my mother's family.

Over the course of the next fifteen years, they created a large family of eight children. My sister Yedida, called Aziza, was born in 1937, and I was born the next year. My family called me Shaoul or Shoolee. My brother Yeftah (Fathi or Lincoln) was born in 1940. Brother Avram (Abraham or Ebraheem) came in 1941, with sister Hannah (Izdeehar) following two years later. Sisters Pirha (Farah) and Judith were born in 1945 and 1948, respectively.

Years later, Mother told my own daughter Sandra, "It's not good to have so many children. The more you have the more troubles and headaches. And the more abandoned you feel at old age." After a brief pause, she continued, "So when will you have a child?" My daughter, having just gotten married, may have heeded her advice. Seven years after that conversation, Sandra still has only one child, the most loveable Danielle.

Even so, Mother mourned the one child she lost in childbirth, Amal. Soon after Hannah was born, Mother was pregnant again.

Though Father gave Mother more attention when she was pregnant, as was proper, he never took her out in public when she was pregnant. Father was a member of elite British and Hindu clubs and often dined out with Mother when she was not pregnant. But each time she became pregnant, she was forbidden to go with him. Father, however, was no exception. No man in Iraq would dare to show up in public with a pregnant wife.

Mother was jealous out of her mind, not knowing what Father was doing—or with whom. She especially hated being left behind with a houseful of children. On Father's nights out, he'd get home at four am, wash, dress, and head for his office, never sleeping in his own bed.

As was also the custom, Mother always gave birth at home with the assistance of her Cousin Noor. Cousin Noor was a professional midwife. She was held in high regard by everyone in the city. On the expected day, my brothers and sisters and I were sent to play outside or to stay with our grandmother. Father would come get us and tell us whether we had a new baby brother or sister.

This time, we went to Grandmother Khatoon, father's mother. We played and wondered whether there would be more girls than boys in the family. When father came to get us, he had such a long, sad face.

"Is anything wrong, Silas?" My grandmother asked.

"No, really, nothing is wrong," he said. "Just get the children ready."

Grandmother, in her way of knowing, knew that something awful had happened. "Tell me, please," she urged. But instead of asking the obvious question about my mother's health, she asked, "Is the baby alright?"

With some hesitation, Father answered, "Our baby is dead. She was born dead. They couldn't revive her."

They had named her Amal (Hope, in Arabic), a name they had picked out months before. Years later, it seemed portentous to me that in the midst of the World War II, with Jews rounded up and tortured the world over, Hope had died that year. But at our young ages, except for my sister Berta, who was thirteen, we didn't feel a great deal of sorrow about Amal's death.

On the way out the door, Berta asked Father, "And, mother, how is she doing? Is she ok?"

Father's face softened as he looked down at Berta. "Yes, your mother is fine, thank God. We have to hurry now and get home so we can take Amal to the cemetery."

Berta begged, "I want to go with you, this time. Please Dad."

Father was firm. "No, you're too young for this. Besides, who is going to look after your brothers and sisters?" That ended the argument. Berta was the oldest, and she had to be responsible.

For weeks after that, we would find Mother in her bedroom, crying quietly. She would take out Amal's beautiful clothes, which she had sewn, and her infant shoes, from a drawer and look at them. Then she would neatly refold them and put them back in the drawer. Mother finally managed to shed her grief many months later when she donated Amal's possessions to a total stranger. She had met a poor, expectant Arab woman at the vegetable market and realized that having her beautiful clothes dress a poor baby would honor Amal's memory.

Chapter Two

Farhood: Krystallnacht in Baghdad, June 1, 1941

The treatment of Jews in Iraq during the early part of the twentieth century had been relatively positive. The British under the 1917 mandate saw the value of having Jews work with them and later with the newly formed monarchy. They realized that the Jews, who were already holding prominent positions in government and commerce, understood the Iraqi culture and knew both English and the local dialects.

In Iraq, Zionism, or the encouragement of Jewish identity and culture, was permitted from World War I to the early 1930s. However, with the rise of pro-German and pro-Nazi sympathizers in Iraq, restrictions began to be leveled on Jews. In 1933, the Iraqi government forbade the teaching of Hebrew and restricted its use to the Holy Scriptures and in prayers. Extra permits and licensing fees were levied on Jews; and sometimes an extra bribe had to be made in order for Jews to ship or receive goods, without their merchandise sitting in a customs dock indefinitely. Many Jews also were fired from their government jobs.

By the mid 1930s, Nazi-inspired policies became more widespread. Arab boys in Baghdad were often sent to Germany to attend Hitler Youth events. Public high schools stopped teaching French, the language of diplomacy, and began to teach German. Junior high school boys were encouraged to join the Futuwwa, paramilitary programs based on the Hitler Youth groups. Finally, in 1938, no Jews were permitted to attend the public high schools, nor were Jews permitted to leave the country. The Jewish community restricted its own movements to known safe places: work, school, and the marketplace.

Though the Balfour Declaration after World War I favored British support for the establishment of a Jewish homeland in Palestine, the British in Iraq could do nothing about the growing Arab support of Arab Palestinians and anti-Zionist hate. Nazi anti-Jewish propaganda found its way into Iraq and was actively distributed. German-backed anti-Jewish radio broadcasts filled the Iraqi airwaves, and short-wave radio receivers could pick up anti-Jewish broadcasts from Germany. Hajji Amin al Hussayni, the Grand Mufti of Jerusalem (1920-1937) under the British mandate, had fled to Iraq after authorizing terrorist attacks on the British and the Jews in Palestine, and was welcomed by the Iraqi Prime Minister, Nuri Al Sa'id. In response, Hussayni and his old friend, Fawzi Kawakchi, spent a year agitating the Iraqi populace against the monarchy, the Regent Abd Al-Ilah, the British, and, of course, the Jews. They used Iraqi radio as their primary propaganda tool.

It was in 1938 that Iraq and the rest of the world heard the awful news of Krystallnacht in Germany. Called "Crystal Night" or the "Night of Broken Glass," two-days of violence swept through a large Jewish community. German soldiers systematically marched from city block to city block, burning, looting, and killing. One hundred Jews were murdered. Thirty thousand were rounded up and moved to concentration camps. Seven thousand Jewish owned businesses were destroys and two hundred synagogues were burned.

With growing pro-Nazism in Iraq and the rise of hatred of the Jews there, the Jewish community feared open violence would reach their people as well. When World War II began in late 1939, Iraq's treaty with the British stipulated that Iraq would officially and politically side with the Allies. This served only to fan the flames of Arab nationalism that found sympathy with Nazism and anti-Jewish sentiment within the country.

In early April of 1941, an Arab nationalist, anti-British revolt was brewing within Iraq. Pro-Nazi military officers, known as the Golden Square, launched a successful military coup and set up Rashid Ali el Gaylani, another Nazi sympathizer, as Prime Minister. The British sent the legal Regent and the Prime Minister, along with Jamil Al-Madfa'ii, Ali Jawdat Al-Ayubi, and Da'ud Pasha Al-Haydari, to Jerusalem.

Gaylani opened diplomatic relations with Germany and invited Dr. Fritz Grooba, the former German ambassador, to return to his post with a complement of aides and Nazi military personnel. Grooba encouraged attacks on British air bases in an effort to remove the military power behind the legal Iraqi government.

When forces from the coup attacked these bases on May 1, British planes bombed rebel positions the next day, crippling them and bringing a rapid defeat.

Rebel forces attacked Meir Elias Hospital on the pretext of searching for British pilots who were supposed to be hidden there. They looted the hospital, set it on fire, and rounded up hospital physicians and administrators. The President of the Jewish Community, Sassoon Khedhouri, enlisted the aid of the Inspector General of Police, Husam Al-Din Jum'a, to release the hospital staff and restore order to the hospital.

By May 29, 1941, Al-Gaylani, Husseini, Fawakchi, and other rebel forces realized that their coup had failed. They fled to Iran and Turkey, and Husseini was welcomed in Germany. In the wake of the escape of the rebel leadership, Yunis Al-Sab'awi, the Minister of Economics, appointed himself as the Military Governor of Baghdad.

The next day, May 30, the Mayor of Baghdad Amin Al-Asima, Arshad Al-Umari, Husam Al-Din Jum'a, and other government officials signed an armistice with the British, declaring an end to the revolt. Though it looked as if all hostilities were ending, another, much darker horror was about to be unleashed on the Jews of Baghdad.

The same day that the armistice was signed, Al-Sab'awi called the President of the Jewish community and told him that all Jews were being restricted to their homes May 31 to June 2. Then, Al-Sab'awi instructed the Katayib Al-Shabab, a paramilitary youth group, to mark all of the Jewish houses and stores in red paint. Then, Al-Sab'awi sent a message to the radio station, urging the Arab public to massacre the Jews. Fortunately, the broadcast was prevented, and Al-Sab'awi was sent to the border.

Nevertheless, the Katayib Al-Shabab and others who had been incited by anti-Jewish propaganda carried out Al-Sab'awi's plan. Farhood, Iraq's own Krystallnacht, began in the evening of June 1, 1941. It was the Feast of Shavuot (Pentecost), a harvest festival held on the fiftieth day after the end of Passover. What would have been a celebratory holy day turned into a nightmare.

View from the roof

By the end of May 1941, my family was enjoying our evenings up on the roof since the heat of the summer months was upon us. My sisters and I usually played with dominoes. Since I was only three and Yedida was only four, we didn't understand the real rules of playing with the tiles, though Berta did, who was six. Instead, we laid them out in long lines and pretended we were building railroads like our father did. But for the last few nights, our sense of play was muted by worried looks between our parents. Father had also told us yesterday that we couldn't go out and play; we had to stay in our rooms. We had wanted to go with Mother to buy treats for Shavuot but couldn't. In fact, Mother had not left the house and neither had Father gone to work. We thought it was because of our holiday coming. We would all go to the synagogue, but we had not done that either. We had only eaten a light meal, and Father had offered prayers.

So, on the evening of June 1st, I wondered why we had celebrated a holiday alone and why no one wanted to play with me. We were put to bed early but none of us could sleep. We watched the stars as usual, trying to make patterns from the shapes of their lights. It was then that Berta sat up in her bed and said, "Father, why is the sky orange down by the center of the city?"

Father and Mother immediately jumped out of their beds and stood near the edge of the roof, facing the downtown area of Baghdad. We all got up to stand with them and look. Normally, Father would have told us to get back to our beds, but he didn't tonight. His eyes were transfixed on the glow emanating from the city's central district where the Jewish and Muslim communities abutted each other.

As we watched the glow crept toward us, spreading from block to block. On the night wind, we caught a faint wailing cry welling up from where we saw the orange light. Mixed with that wail were crashes and booms. Mother began to weep, and Father's jaw was clenched tight as he held onto Mother. As we watched the orange glow expand, we could see smoke against the growing light and an occasional lick of flame. The smell of burning wood was on the wind.

Father gathered Berta, Yedida, and me, along with my baby brother Yeftah, who was already there whimpering, into our parent's big bed with him and Mother. We clung to each other as we watched the fires and destruction creep closer hour by hour into the long night.

"That must be Sooq Ha-rage and Sooq Le-sfa-feer," Father said, "the markets."

After awhile, we could hear screams and distinct curses. "They've come to Bab-el-shar-gee and Taht-el-takya," Father whispered. These were wealthy Jewish neighborhoods. Father held us tighter and began to pray softly.

I was afraid, but I wasn't sure of what exactly. All I could see was that this orange glow was alive and growing and it brought pain. I squeezed closer to my father and my sisters. Around two o'clock, crashing and pounding stopped and all we could hear was the soft wail the seemed to come from everywhere now. After a little while, my parents' muscles seemed to relax and I fell asleep.

I woke the next morning to screams and renewed crashing in the streets nearby. The destruction in the city was clearly visible now. We could see people struggling with men wielding knives. We saw Jews on faraway rooftops jumping from their roofs to their Arab neighbors' roofs. Their neighbors quickly ushered them inside where they could hide.

The British army, which had now taken control of Iraq by then, remained just outside of Baghdad and was totally disengaged allowing the atrocities against the Jews to continue unabated.

The wave of destruction continued until about mid-afternoon. It was then that the Kurdish division of the military, ordered by the Regent, moved into the city, sweeping the neighborhoods, rounding up those responsible for this pogrom. By about two o'clock, Kurdish troops were beginning to take up posts in front of prominent Jewish homes. One soldier was stationed in front of our own door.

Aftermath

By Sunday afternoon, there were 180 Jews dead, 240 children orphaned, and 2,120 wounded. Countless numbers of women and girls had been raped and kidnapped. Babies had been disemboweled before their parents' eyes. Rioters broke into marked Jewish-owned stores, especially those on Shorja Street, looting and destroying. Two thousand homes had been plundered and 2,375 shops had been looted. The property damage was estimated at £3 to £3.5 million.

The Jews weren't permitted to bury their dead themselves. The dead were collected by the government, and eventually, all were buried in one mass grave.

The Iraqi government severed all diplomatic ties with Germany. Al-Sab'awi was arrested and hanged on July 20, 1941. But no apology was ever made to the Jews who had been terrorized. Neither was any restitution given for property loss or recompense for loss of life.

Hussayni fled to Berlin, where he met with Hitler himself, and continued to incite Arabs to persecute Jews, only returning to the Middle East after World War II. Later, during the Israeli War of Independence in 1948, it was he who would call on the Palestinians to leave their homes and join the Arab forces "to re-conquer it back and finish the Jews."

This marked the genesis for the Palestinian refugee saga.

Chapter Three

My Life on the Other Side of the River

As children, we never really knew you had to work to earn a living. We thought money somehow appeared magically. Once I asked my younger brother Yeftah, "I wonder where Father gets all the money to buy us things?"

Yeftah looked at me as if I were an idiot and said, "Simple. All you have to do is go to the bank and get as much as you want."

Despite where the money came from, we assumed that there was always plenty of it in the bank. We had more than enough to cover all of our needs, many of our wants, and provide a beautiful house for us to live in.

By Iraqi standards, Father was not considered wealthy. He was only a well educated and much respected government official. In reality, though, we lived in a ritzy neighborhood where very few Jews lived. Our street was special and somewhat restricted to the general public.

Directly across from our house was a huge estate, surrounded by a ten-foot black wrought iron fence. Restricting access was a manned guard booth. It was the private residence of the former Prime Minister Saleh Jah-burr. Many servants bustled around the house and grounds. At least twice a month, black limousines stopped at the guard booth, were waved through the gates, and drove up the driveway. At a winding walkway, immaculately dressed men and women emerged from the limousines and made their way past well-manicured lawns and elaborate landscaping to the guesthouse.

Mr. and Mrs. Jah-burr had several children, mostly boys between the ages of six and fifteen, who were always richly dressed. Occasionally, they would come out to play in the street, and we would join them in a game of marbles or make-believe soccer. Sometimes, we'd ride our bikes with them.

In all of our encounters with the Jah-burr children, there had not been a hint of prejudice or hatred. Nevertheless, Mother whispered to us, "Stay away from them. Who knows what will they accuse you of next." But she seemed to realize that children would naturally find other children to play with so she added, "Keep to yourselves. And, if you have to, let them always win. And don't let your father know you played with them."

At the far end of the street lived the present Prime Minister Noory El-sah-eed. His residence was just as impressive as that of Saleh Jah-burr. Though it would seem that they had much in common, we never saw them mingle. Over the years, it became obvious, too, that they actually tried to outdo each other in their house maintenance, grounds keeping, and upgrades. However, Noory El-sah-eed held the office of prime minister eight times over a twenty-year period.

The El-sah-eed children, however, were very different from the Jah-burr's. They wouldn't play with us because we were Jews. They had been indoctrinated from birth to hate us. If we passed them on the street, they would call us names and shout, "Jews! Traitors! Go away from here, dirty Zionist."

When that first happened, we ran home and told our mother what they had said to us. We didn't know what it meant and asked her about it. "Oh, that doesn't mean anything. Don't even think about it," she answered. "They are jealous of us, of our hard work and success. It's always been that way." But she added seriously, "Don't mess with them. And don't ever answer them back."

We heeded her advice. We made a conscious effort not to get close to the El-sah-eed home, either on foot or on our bikes.

Summer nights

In the summer, like most of the Iraqis, we slept on our flat roof so that we could breath fresh air and escape the heat. Our beds would be brought up to the roof, equipped with very fine, white nets to keep the mosquitoes out. We stretched out on our beds, looking up to the beautiful, clear, starry night skies, and we would wonder. Each of my brothers and sisters pointed out favorite stars. We'd count some and then try to impress each other with our knowledge.

Father and Mother often allowed us to join them in their bed on the roof. It wasn't just for when we were afraid after having a nightmare. Their big bed was a cozy place where they shared knowledge and family stories and imparted our religious history and traditions. Father and Mother recited poetry and told us about history and science. They made a point to explain the plight of the Jews and how our ancestors had been brought out of Israel in bondage to Babylon 2600 years ago. They told us that many other Jews had emigrated to other countries and lived well for a time. Then, they were expelled from their homes, finding yet another country in which to live, but never really feeling at home.

Those cozy family times always ended with a pledge that someday we would return to our old homeland, Israel. There, we would live in freedom and pride, without any fear.

Afterwards, we were tucked into our own beds. My brothers and sisters and I continued to study the heavens and point to the brightest stars. Our imaginations had been stimulated, and our hearts had been filled with a longing for something that we didn't quite understand. The historical hope of the Jews for a Promised Land began to take root in our young hearts though at that time in our lives, it was cast as a magical place, an Eden where milk and honey really flowed from the ground. We had not experienced the oppression first hand that would etch that longing and hope across our souls and drive us toward Israel.

As we looked up at the stars one night, one of us mused, "I wonder what is out there."

"Oh, it's just another star like our Earth," said one of my brothers.

"But with better people," one of my sisters said.

"Who love each other," another added.

"With one religion that unites them all," said Berta the eldest.

When we finally stopped talking, we could hear the approaching trains in the distance. How they whistled as they pulled into the railroad station not too far from our house! I loved that sound and never got tired of hearing it.

Seeing the sights

Sometimes, on our Sabbath, if we didn't accompany our parents to the synagogue, my sisters Berta and Yedida and I would wander off and walk towards the railroad station to see who was coming and going. Sometimes, we'd touch the train cars and dream of long trips to other places where we could experience freedom. (I am retired now, and in my office/study in the basement of my house, my walls are decorated with photographs of trains and locomotives).

Sometimes, we visited the National Museum in Baghdad, one of the most important museums in the world. At the gated entrance stood two gigantic sculptures of lions, one on each side. Inside, there were displays of some of the oldest historical artifacts in existence. Excavated at sites within the region and researched by foreign archaeologists, the museum had acquired 170,000 historical objects. Some of them dated to the time of King Hammurabi, almost 4,000 years ago and some even older to around 70,000 years ago.

The wealth of these precious objects made my family, and all Iraqis, very proud of its magnificent history. Here were objects and histories engraved in stone that marked the places where philosophy, law, geometry, mathematics, and the first writing and literacy were developed. When we saw objects like a cuneiform-incised stele from Babylon or the Warka Vase, a limestone vessel with carved scenes of Uruk dating back 3,000 years, we could see in our mind's eye our ancestors writing on the clay tablets that recorded contracts and mercantile inventories or building the great edifices from which the artifacts had been taken. We Jews were especially proud of this heritage because it authenticated many of the events and historical figures mentioned in the Torah.

Servants

Since Mother was busy raising eight children, she needed help keeping her household running smoothly. Father's position in the community deemed it fitting to hire servants, and his income made it possible. We, therefore, had two servants.

Our cook did just about everything. She was a pleasantly plump Christian woman with blonde hair and a beautiful fair complexion. Though she was deaf from birth and could not speak, she was able to communicate with my mother using sign language and facial gestures, which Mother deciphered perfectly. Sometimes, they disagreed on the choice of food for the day. Mother always felt sorry for her and let her win the argument.

Our cook arrived every afternoon. She first attacked the stack of dirty dishes left over from breakfast and the evening before. When they were washed, dried, and put away, she would begin preparing food. In the evening, and before my father came home, she left with a "care package" Mother always prepared for her. It was enough from all of the cooking she had done all afternoon to feed her family. She never forgot to wave goodbye to us children or kiss us on the forehead. We loved her and her wonderful gourmet cooking.

Years later, when Mother and Father fled to Israel in haste, Mother never forgave herself for not saying goodbye to our cook. We never knew what became of her. Mother always wished that maybe she had moved into our house with her children and made them some of our favorite foods. It was comforting to think that someone who had taken care of us would also be taken care of by the house we had lived in.

Our second maid was Daisy Shammah. She was known for her off-color repartee. It was said that I was the only one who could ever come close to matching her juicy curses and utterances. When she caught me using some of those words and phrases, she pinched my arm or my thigh, making me cry. I'd beg for her forgiveness and promise to wash my mouth out with soap, as she always demanded.

When this happened, Mother didn't dare intercede. This was perfectly acceptable behavior for anyone's maid. It was her duty to educate the children in proper social conduct. Pinching me was her method.

At times when Daisy had finished her normal chores earlier than usual, Mother often asked her to bathe us in the bathtub. She would gather up her apron and her dress and tuck them into the top of her underpants, so as not to get her clothes wet. Of course, she assumed that we were too little and naive to take notice of her panties and exposed thighs. But I did notice—and so did my brother Yeftah, who is a year and a half younger than I am. We'd pretend to close our eyes as she applied soap lather to our necks and faces, but we'd catch a glimpse of Daisy's uncovered legs and wonder at what lay beneath her cotton under things. Sometimes we just couldn't hide the fact that we were partially aroused, so we refused to stand up to be dried off. She made us stand anyway, and there we would be revealed. She'd smile knowingly. Then, to our embarrassment and misery, she'd spank our naked behinds to teach us a lesson. That was enough to endure, but we never knew for sure if she told our mother about what had happened and continued to happen, as we grew older.

Nightlife

Many of the high level Jews in Baghdad frequented the British Officers Club and the Indian (Hindu) nightclubs. One Hindu nightclub was my father's favorite and he went there quite often. On those nights, he would be driven home around 6:00 pm and eat his dinner at the table, with my mother catering to his every need. Then, he'd take an hour-long nap. When he awoke, he'd shower and put on a perfectly pressed white shirt, a good suit, a dapper tie, and his best pair of shoes. Thus, immaculately dressed, he would go alone to his favorite nightclub. It was evident that he wasn't dressing up to meet business acquaintances. Mother never complained because this was how every man in Baghdad behaved. It was indeed a man's world.

Once a month, he showed his generosity and humanity by taking Mother and all of us along. On these occasions, he walked about ten meters ahead of us, with Mother and us children trailing behind him. As a sign of respect as we approached the gates of the nightclub, the gatekeeper, who was an old bearded Sheikh Indian with a turban, always greeted us with:

"Welcome, Company, I am so happy to see you all." My father would only nod a short acknowledgment, as if he were embarrassed to be with his wife and so many children.

The nightclub was in a large courtyard, open to the starry night sky. Hundreds of electric light bulbs were strung high above the grounds of the nightclub. As we were led to our seats close to a small stage, some of Father's friends often recognized us and waved or came over to our table to greet us. They showered Mother with compliments and told us children how big we had grown or how well behaved we were or how pretty my sisters were.

We were served exotic foods and drinks by the most attentive of waiters (no waitresses). From the stage, the club was entertained by Hindu dancers and singers, accompanied by a group of musicians seated in the back of the performing area. The music was exotic and exquisite, but the dances were sensuous and graceful. On occasion, the Hindu singers sang songs that were familiar to the patrons of the nightclub. When that happened, people left their tables and joined others to sing those old songs. After a few hours, father would go behind the stage to complement some of the performers and offer them a generous tip. (Mother always suspected there was more to it.)

At the close of the evening, we would file behind Father, who led us between the tables of the now crowded nightclub, through the gate, down the street, and back to our home. On the walk home, Mother often said, "We had such a good time all of us together. It's not only fun, but is most educational. You learn about other cultures and languages."

It all seemed like such an innocent and enriching experience to Mother and to us children. We all envied Father going there to spend his evenings among these interesting people who knew how to have a good time. Years later, Mother learned that Father took us all there on what was called Family Night. It was very different from the kind of entertainment that was presented each night. The patrons were also very well behaved. Nightly, Father had drinks with his male friends, who yelled crude catcalls at the nude performers writhing in suggestive dances. Instead of going to an elegant club to unwind with a drink and cultural stimulation, Father was going to the equivalent of a strip club and flirting with the dancers.

This was the way of all men in Baghdad, no matter what religion or ethnicity. Young boys were often introduced to the delights of the flesh, not through dating girls one's age, but through clubs like the one Father frequented and the charms of women in the Mee-Dan or the Red District of Baghdad. Those encounters also trained young men in how to keep this life from the women who mattered to their hearts, like mothers, sisters, and, eventually, wives.

I was never aware of the existence of the Mee-Dan while I lived in Baghdad. I was only ten when I left Iraqi. Boys went there when they were older. I did find out about it later in Israel when I talked with older friends who had also emigrated from Iraq. They know the Mee-Dan very well.

One of my best friends told me about his experience: "You were too young and naive to taste the good life in Baghdad. You had to be at least fourteen years old and be accompanied by an adult. I remember when I was fourteen, my brother took me to the Mee-Dan. I saw dozens of beautiful women sitting or standing at the gate, calling out to us and motioning us to come closer. They flashed their beautiful breasts at us and smiled enticingly, and some even moved their bodies in sinuous motions that aroused me. I was shy, but my brother pushed me toward them and encouraged me with words. When he left me alone, I was uncertain of what to do. I was lured inside by the youngest of the women. That was my introduction to sex and to the keeping of secrets."

Neighbors

While we lived in Baghdad, we had some very interesting neighbors. One Muslim neighbor, Mrs. Abd-el-razack, was always borrowing something from us. She was not exactly poor, since she lived in the same exclusive neighborhood as we did, but she just seemed to run out of
some kind of food all the time. She'd come asking for rice, sugar, flour, or bread, saying to my mother, "My son-in-law is about to visit us. We have to impress him. What can you lend us?"

Mother always smiled as if she understood and promised to find something. Of course, Mrs. Abd-el-razack never returned what she borrowed.

Chapter Four

Father's Military Friends

British soldiers

Father had admired the British since his college days in India. He especially appreciated the British military presence in Iraq, which had been present since his childhood. Some of the British officers—Bob, Tage, and Ridley—later became Father's loyal friends. He always felt indebted to these men and other British soldiers, who always treated Jews fairly. Father felt that without their support, he and his family might not have survived.

In the middle of World War II, Bob, Tage, and Ridley, were assigned to duty with Allied Forces in Asia and the Middle East. Father knew he would never see his friends again, especially with the uncertainties of war and the changes that might happen in the region. He soon missed these friends terribly and began to feel regret that he hadn't properly thanked them for their friendship and their looking out for him and his family.

For several years, Father frequently used his high-level contacts in business and the government to inquire about the fate of these friends. Through these contacts, he found the addresses of some of the soldiers' family members in Europe. He wrote long letters to them, asking if they had news about these men he had become so close to. He also told them how grateful he was that these men had been stationed in Iraq.

Throughout his life, Father remained a great supporter of the British and Americans.

Iraqi military friend

Doctor X, a Jewish friend of ours, had graduated from a prominent medical school in Baghdad. Doctor X spent only a few years practicing medicine in the community before he was drafted to serve into the Iraqi Army. It was unusual for Jews to serve in the military since the Arabs in power generally questioned the loyalty of Jews. Normally, Jews were excused from military service. Doctor X, nevertheless, was given the rank of lieutenant and was sent to a training camp near Karbala. There he underwent basic orientation and was soon assigned to examine Iraqi soldiers for various skin disorders and sexually transmitted diseases.

Because he was a Jew among thousands of Muslims, he avoided touching a soldier with his bare hands. He always wore gloves and was aided by an 18-inch, polished, wooden ruler. When he examined a soldier who had disrobed, he used the long ruler to lift the soldier's penis and genitals and then bent down to look at them closely. This procedure always embarrassed the soldiers. Doctor X always maintained a serious, detached expression throughout these exams, though in private he couldn't suppress his laughter. He told me years later that at the end of each day, he went home always feeling depressed since he felt totally inadequately "equipped" compared to these young soldiers.

One day, Doctor X finished his task early and decided there was no harm in going upstairs to catch some badly needed sleep. While he was resting, a soldier was brought in on a stretcher. It was an emergency, but Doctor X could not be found. Subsequently, Doctor X was brought up before a military tribunal. The judge scorned him for what he considered irresponsible behavior and deducted a good part of his pay as punishment. Doctor X found out later that the money he had paid as a fine was pocketed by the tribunal judge. Six moths later, our friend was discharged from the military, and he gladly returned to private practice.

Chapter Five

Lost Hannah, Yeftah the Dishes Breaker, Pirha with a Bird's Heart, Berta's Lesson

My seven brothers and sisters made growing up in my family quite challenging. Luckily, we didn't have to worry about having adequate food or clothing like some large families often had to struggle with scraping together. Instead, my siblings were adventurous, impish youngsters who often pulled me into their exploits, getting me into trouble right along side of them. We would often fight about something as all brothers and sisters do. Sometimes, though, I would be struck by the beauty of their spirits or the fragility of their lives.

Lost Hannah

My sister Hannah is five years younger than I am. She was always curious and found routine activities boring. One Friday afternoon, my mother took five-year-old Hannah with her when she went on her customary shopping trip to the open market. Mother was skilled at bargaining and enjoyed haggling over the prices of fruits and vegetables. Hannah, however, always found that activity rather dull and cast her eyes about for something much more interesting. A musician had brought a monkey to the market and was playing a lively fiddle tune to which the monkey frolicked and danced. The music quickly drew a crowd of children, who laughed and clapped their hands as the monkey cavorted. Hannah moved closer into the crowd to get a better view of the monkey and the fiddler and soon was absorbed by the cluster of children. She was having a great time.

When Mother's current bargaining was done, she turned to make some comment to little Hannah. But, her daughter was nowhere to be found. Mother looked right and left but couldn't see Hannah's face among the customers in the marketplace.

Mother began shouting out Hannah's name. Soon her shouts turned to anguished cries. "Hannah, where are you?" she called. "Come to Mamma, Hannah."

An old Arab man with a cane in his hand took pity on my mother. He walked up to her and asked her to describe her daughter to him, so he could search the marketplace with her.

My mother, in her normal innocence, described my sister. "She's five years old and about three feet tall. And, she has a face full of scars." Little Hannah had suffered bad scaring from chicken pox.

The old man put his arm around Mother's shoulders and assured her. "Don't worry, lady. I will find her for you."

By this time, my mother was crying uncontrollably. She was worried sick, wondering what had happened to her child. Had she been kidnapped? Was she only lost and scared? What had really happened to her? How would Father react?

The old man's voice could be heard all over the marketplace. Heads turned toward the sound as he cried out the alarm. "Hannah, Hannah, has anyone seen a small girl with a face full of scars?" he asked over and over again. Though the situation was deadly serious, many of the customers in the marketplace began to laugh at the old man and his unusual question.

Suddenly, Hannah pushed her way through the crowd to the old man. She looked up at him and said, "I'm the little girl with the scared face. I am lost. Will you take me to my mother?"

The old man took Hannah back to Mother who was delighted to finally find Hannah alive and well. She thanked the old man and gave him a generous tip as a reward. Then, she turned to Hannah and slapped her across the face. "That's for scaring me to death," Mother explained.

Yeftah, the dishes breaker

My brother Yeftah was a very active, spoiled little brat who was always scheming about something. He would do anything to get attention.

Sometimes when he asked for his daily allowance, Mother would disagree with him about his accounting, since he always seemed to think he was owed more. Yeftah would then give her an ultimatum. "If I don't get the ten cents in one minute, it will become twelve cents you owe me."

Mother would laugh at him and say, "We will see."

Five minutes later, Yeftah would say, "It's fifteen cents now. Nothing will help you get out of this, Mother. You owe me fifteen cents."

Mother would laugh again and attempt to appease him by offering the original ten cents, which had been in dispute. But Yeftah would screech at the top of his lungs, "I refuse to accept anything less than my last offer. You owe me 15 Cents", Yeftah asserted with a commanding voice.

This would go on for hours, with his owed amount increased every few minutes. When it looked like no money was going to cross his palm, he would start throwing our china plates on the floor. Yeftah always knew that he would have to settle the allowance with mother well before father got home from work. And, perhaps, Mother knew that, too, because she always gave in and paid him the last amount he demanded.

Another time Yeftah became the center of attention was when he was at school. He had begun new science classes and was learning about basic physics and chemistry. He was taught that all humans need air and water in order to exist. If any one of those things isn't present in sufficient quantities, human beings will die. That concept must have really penetrated his brain because he woke up one night screaming, "There's no oxygen in the room! We're all going to die!" he shouted, throbbing with fear.

Roused from her bed, Mother came into his room and sat on the edge of

Yeftah's bed. She tried to reassure him. "It was only a dream, Yeftah," she said. "There's plenty of air to breathe."

That incident, however, followed Yeftah for life. Whenever he misbehaved, Mother always said to him, "Ah, it must have been the lack of oxygen that affected your brain. That's why you're so mischievous."

A year later, Yeftah contracted typhoid and almost died from an extraordinarily high fever. He was convinced that the absence of oxygen had somehow been the source of his illness and thus had done him in.

Still, it was Yeftah's rambunctiousness that got me into trouble most of the time. When our family had moved into a very modern apartment house in the center of Baghdad, Father was so proud of the conveniences in the house, especially the fully equipped bathroom. Yeftah got it into his head to use the shower curtain rod as a trapeze and spent all of five minutes climbing around the shower stall and doing pull-ups on the rod before it all collapsed, taking part of the shower plumbing with it.

We all heard the crash and came running into the bathroom. Father was furious. "You've broken the most modern toilet in Baghdad!" he shouted. We all laughed and left Yeftah alone to face Father.

Father had every reason to be angry. Yeftah's behavior had turned into an expensive repair, and it showed no respect for the comforts that Father's work had brought to the family. Yeftah was punished continuously for a week as Father set rules and tasks for him to do. Father appointed me as my brother's watchdog, making sure Yeftah obeyed all of Father's rules, which seemed to grow more numerous each day. If Yeftah disobeyed any of those rules, I suffered, calling down my own punishment from Father.

Of course, Yeftah was always hatching out ways to get out of doing what Father wanted. One way was to bribe me with some of his beautiful marbles. They were exquisite agates and I wanted them, so I was easy on him administering his punishment.

Pirha with a bird's heart

My sister Pirha is eight years younger than I am. She was a tiny little thing, with a delicate beauty. Ever since she had been born, she would episodes of shortness of breath. When she would have this breathing difficulty, Father would try to explain her condition to us. "The poor little girl has a bird's heart," he would say. "It's very small and has trouble doing what it's supposed to do. We hope she can survive."

Throughout her life, she was often accused of being Father's favorite daughter as I was accused of being Mother's favorite son. She denied it vigorously as did I, but in truth we both might have been favorites for very different reasons.

Forty-five years later, Pirha found out that a leaky heart valve was the cause of periodic breathing difficulty. It was repaired in a complicated open-heart surgery at Hadassah Hospital in Jerusalem.

Berta's lesson

Berta is the oldest child in our family and is three years older than I am. As a child and as a grown woman, she dressed elegantly and often spoke her mind with as much pride. She was always capable of standing up for herself.   One day she and I had a fight over her sandwich. It was an Italian hero, filled with fresh tomatoes and pickled mango. Those heroes were our favorites, and we ate them with great delight.

It was after school and Berta had used her bus money to buy the hero at one of the Hindu stores on our way home. She was sitting on the steps eating her sandwich, and I was lusting after all that delicious goodness. I asked her to share it with me. She adamantly refused. Though she was older, I was physically stronger so I tried to grab it out of her hands. Berta did a good job of keeping the sandwich out of my grasp, but I persisted, making it difficult for her to keep me away from her food and definitely foiling her own plans for enjoying her sandwich. Finally, out of sheer frustration, she reached into her school bag and drew out a newly sharpened pencil. Berta then stabbed me in the chest with it. The pencil broke as it hit my ribs.

It didn't hurt that much, and it wasn't a deep wound. But I cried anyway in order to scare her into giving me some of her sandwich. It worked. She was terrified that she had almost killed me and asked me to swear not to tell our parents. I was silent, sniffing for effect. When she offered me one third of her sandwich, I agreed.

She learned that day that it was so much better to share since it would have cost her much less if she had done so from the beginning. All I hoped for was one bite.

As we ate, I told her a story we read about in school, "The Greedy Mouse" (Originated in ancient Persia). It was about three mice friends who went out into the forest to look for food. They had not eaten anything in days; they were all very hungry. They decided to split up in three directions, to improve their odds of finding something to eat. The first to find food was to call up to his friends to join him in the feast.

Well, when one of them stumbled upon a big piece of cheese, instead of sharing it with his friends, he decided to keep it all to himself. In order not to get caught, he hid it away in a narrow hole in the trunk of a tree. He dragged his big chunk of cheese inside and began to gorge on the delicious cheese. There he stayed for days, eating to his heart's content.

In the meantime, his friends were looking for him, fearing he fell prey to some larger animal. They mourned the loss of their good friend.

When their friend had finally finished eating the entire block of cheese, he was ready to go out of his hole and join his friends, and to pretend to still be hungry. His overindulgence had produced quite a round little body. He was twice the size he once was and he couldn't get out of the hole in the tree. Now, his punishment was to wait till he lost enough weight to get out of the hole. Since he couldn't get out to forage for more food, he had to go hungry for many days and risk death in the process. The moral of the story, I told Berta, was that one must share with his fellow men (and animals).

Chapter Six

Uncle Khadoory and his Son,
Aunt Marcel the Teacher, Etc…

Uncle Khadoory and his son

It was said that Uncle Khadoory was the best-dressed man in town. Typically, he would come home from work, catch a two-hour nap, shower, and eat something. Then, off he went for most of the night to nightclubs, night tennis courts, or movie theaters. Unlike other men of his stature and generation, he took his lovely wife along and left his children with the live-in maid.

He was a heavy drinker when he went out to nightclubs. Sometimes, he would become violent and say terrible things. The family's biggest worry, though, was that he might reveal the whereabouts of some of his colleagues and relatives who had fled the country illegally. To be privy to an illegal venture as the smuggling of Jews out of Iraq—even in the slightest capacity—was a crime that was punishable by death. This was the family's constant worry.

On one of these occasions when Uncle Khadoory returned from a nightclub with his wife, the maid told them that their little son Edmond had been crying for hours. "No matter what I tried to bribe him with," she said, " he kept crying and refused to fall asleep."

My aunt went into the child's room to see why he was so upset. She felt guilty about always leaving him home with the maid. She gathered Edmond into her arms and smothered him with kisses. As she kissed his face, she noticed that his eyes were truly red from crying. She went to the medicine cabinet in the bathroom and found the eye drops. She came back to Edmond's room and administered drops in both of his eyes. Then, she tucked him back into his bed.

Suddenly, Edmond started crying in earnest and furiously rubbed his eyes. My aunt noticed that his eyes had become even redder. She put more eye drops into his eyes, making sure every spot was covered perfectly. She repeated this process three or four more time during the night.

For my aunt, it was a night she would remember the rest of her life. Edmund cried hysterically all night. My aunt didn't bother to wake Uncle Khadoory who had already passed out from drinking and who needed a night's rest in order to go to work the following morning.

When my uncle did wake up the following morning, he washed and shaved as usual, then sat down to have his breakfast. My aunt then told him of her sleepless ordeal. Before he left for work, he went in to check on his son and kiss him goodbye. It was then that he discovered a small, brown bottle sitting on his son's night table. This was the bottle his wife had used to treat Edmond's red eyes. In horror, he read the label and screamed. It was not eye drops. It was iodine in the same brown colored bottle. As a result, Edmond had become permanently blind.

My aunt and uncle were afraid to go to the authorities for fear of punishment so they didn't report the unfortunate accident. They also didn't risk taking the child to the hospital. Needless to say, guilt would follow them the rest of their lives.

Years later, the family immigrated to Israel like so many others in the early 1950s. Edmond didn't let his handicap stand in his way of success. He became a Professor of Philosophy at the Hebrew University in Jerusalem. Eventually, he married and had two children of his own.

Aunt Marcel, the teacher

Aunt Marcel, one of my mother's sisters, was the second oldest of twelve children. She was single, attractive, and very much sought after by eligible men. She, however, was choosey and remained unwed until she traveled to Palestine in 1947.

While in Baghdad, she had a reputation for being a superb teacher. She had keen knowledge of her subjects and was a strict disciplinarian. She was particularly in demand as an after-school tutor for the children of wealthy Jews and Arabs. To our family's delight and amazement, she had been engaged by the wife of the former Prime Minister Saleh Jah-Burr, who lived across the street from us. Aunt Marcel tutored his three children, who were all at different school levels. She was treated with great respect and earned more than just a comfortable income. She also was showered with expensive gifts.

Aunt Marcel was the most educated of her six brothers and five sisters. Her involvement with the social elite meant, indirectly, that no one could touch or harm our families. She actually interceded on behalf of Jews in jail who had been falsely accused of various crimes and was successful in freeing them, thus saving their lives.

Later in Israel, she met an enterprising taxi owner, Rahameem, who had the foresight to purchase old and dying groves from the Palestinians. She married him, and they became very wealthy, eventually acquiring numerous real estate properties all over Israel and buying more taxis to expand his already lucrative business.

However, Marcel and Rahameem had a great intellectual gap between them, which they could never bridge. I guess no amount of business savvy could compete with intellectual brilliance. They sued each other in court many times, using their children to testify on one or the other's behalf. During one such court appearance, her youngest son Benny told the judge, "Your Honor, my father beats my mother. But I love them both." He thought his testimony would keep his parents together. Ultimately, it did no good; their marriage ended in divorce.

Rahameem was a devoted vegetarian. At age 80, he met and married an Ashkenazi woman. They both lived to be over 96 and died in a retirement community. However, long before Rahameem died, he had the good sense to share his riches with his three children, so that he could see them settled and happy in his lifetime. It was rumored that he had a great amount of currency, gold, and silver buried in a 55-gallon tank in his enormous backyard.

My mother's family and their relationship with father

Because my mother was the first to marry in her family and because she and her siblings were orphaned early in their lives, her sisters looked up to my father and mother for moral and other support. My father practically adopted Mother's brothers and sisters as his own children.

Though Mother's siblings seemed to get poorer as time went by, they enjoyed the warm regard of a large, close-knit family, with many aunts, uncles, and cousins who cared about them. They lived in a huge rented house where the landlord stayed on the premises. The family shared a common shower and bathroom with the landlord, as well as one spacious hall in the center of the house.

Every morning when everyone was getting ready to go to work, they found it almost impossible to stand in line to use the bathroom. While the shower and bathroom were occupied, they stood in the big hall, with a pot of hot water in one hand and shaving gear in the other. It was comical to see grown men shaving and washing in public. But this was perfectly normal for them. On weekends, my uncles put on their best suits, white shirts, and ties and headed to outdoor restaurants and nightclubs.

My aunts appeared at our house every week to help out. They assisted Mother in dressing us children, feeding us, and washing us. Because Mother was curious and wanted to know everything, they whispered their tales from the week before to her. They told her all of the news and local gossip and whatever escapades their brothers had been involved in and who each aunt had her eye on.

At the dinner table, we all gathered together on our best behavior. Each one of us tried to impress Father with our accomplishments for that week. He spoke to everyone and made each of us, especially Mother's relatives, feel welcome and comfortable. Mother sometimes felt that her young sisters were being too cute and were flirting with Father. She would get up from the table and go into the kitchen, where she shed tears of jealousy. She couldn't deal with her sisters' need for attention. Father usually sensed that some-thing was afoot. He would excuse himself and go to the kitchen to reassure Mother and bring her back to the table.

Aunt Ruth was the main source of Mother's insecurity. Whenever Aunt Ruth was in the house and Father was home, Mother always felt uneasy. After all, it had been to Aunt Ruth that he had been introduced first and he had wanted her then, before he had found out she was so young. Mother often compared herself to Aunt Ruth and felt that she had come up short. Aunt Ruth was stunningly beautiful, with dreamy green eyes, but Mother had a beauty of her own. She did not have to worry about Father chasing after one of her sisters. He was discreet enough to keep his female interests away from the family.

Aunt Saiida

Aunt Saiida and I liked doing things together. One day she decided to peel an apple in one long continuous peel. She told me to hold the end of the peel as she pared it away from the meat of the apple. I was to just hold it and not to let it break. I had to keep the peel fairly close to the apple in order to keep the peeling from breaking of its own weight. The apple peel grew longer and longer, and I marveled at how long it was growing. Suddenly, Aunt Saida's knife slipped and removed a good chunk of my thumb. She took me to the hospital, and I had stitches put into my thumb. She was terrified that Father would become angry at both of us and that Mother would be disappointed in her for not taking care of Mother's favorite son. Therefore, she made me swear not to tell either of my parents how it had happened. I kept my promise.

Aunt Khatoon

Aunt Khatoon was our favorite aunt. She was one of the oldest girls in my mother's family and became responsible for her brothers and sisters after their parents died. She cooked for them, washed their clothes, and sent them to school.

Often, she complained of having a splitting headache. When that happened, she tied a brightly colored bandana around her head, rather like the sweatbands that athletes today wear. She had many of them in different colors and materials. It seemed like such a festive way to mark an ailment.

Uncle Joseph

My father's only brother was our Uncle Joseph. He had a mistress when he lived in Iraq. Her name was "Salma," and she was a Muslim woman. She followed Uncle Joseph to Palestine when he escaped in the mid-1940s. She never married but lived in Ramlah, where many Muslims lived, and continued to be Uncle Joseph's mistress. Eventually, Uncle Joseph married a Jewish woman and fathered a daughter named Hanina and a son named Yehuda.

Chapter Seven

Cousin Sabah, the Schemer

One of my best friends was my cousin Sabah Aslan. (later named Yeg-Al in Israel). When he was a child of three, during the pogrom of 1941, a bomb landed in his backyard. He was so traumatized by the event that he was unable to utter a single word for several weeks. From that day on, Sabah lisped, sometimes uncontrollably.

Children made fun of Sabah's lisping, teasing him cruelly. It was no wonder then that Sabah hated school. He devised elaborate schemes to avoid going there. Most children try to fain illness so their parents will keep them home. Sabah, however, didn't want to stay at home or involve his parents. He wanted to be on his own and explore his favorite parts of the city. On his way to school each morning, Sabah's brain would start working, creating plans and devising situations that would send him back home. Of course, he would delay going home for several hours.

One of Sabah's best tricks was to find the deepest, muddiest ditch and sit in it. When he arrived at school, covered with mud, the teacher would always send him home with a note for his parents. On his way home, he usually stopped at the local flea market.

Sabah used this and many other tricks to stay out of school for months. His teacher and his parents finally caught on and put a stop to his shenanigans.

Since he had to stay in school, Cousin Sabah decided to make the best of it. His calculating mind found ways to trick the teacher and his fellow students. I was privy to his secrets and was able to share the jokes with him. Being with him was always fun.

When our class was learning mathematics and basic geometry, we had to understand and use various units of measurements: length, height, width, depth, weight, etc. Our teacher set us tasks to measure different objects in the class-room. Sabah thought up a clever way to win some money. He stayed after school and measured everything he could find in the classroom. He wrote down the lengths or weights of these objects and took the data home. There, he memorized the weights or dimensions that he had collected.

The following day, our teacher gave us a quiz that challenged us to guess the measurements and weights of the same objects Sabah had already measured the night before. Sabah, of course, scored the highest. He continued to do well as the measurement unit progressed, sometimes even outscoring the teacher himself. Nevertheless, our teacher proudly told the entire class, "Students, learn from Sabah. He is a fine example of a good student. He does his homework. He is destined for greatness." Sabah would flash a big smile. Then, he would look left and right and bow his head in pride. The students were jealous and resented all the attention he received.

Later, during recess, he pestered his classmates, urging them to challenge him. "Do you want to bet me what the length of the blackboard is?" he dared them. Some boys just couldn't resist the challenge. After all, it was only a guess. Nobody knew exactly, right? The boys offered their guesses and Sabah countered with his answer. Of course, when they measured the blackboard, Sabah's guess would be correct, and he would always win the bet.

Sabah's little con game had fringe benefits for his close friends. He never lacked pocket money for candy and other goodies. Everyone wanted to be his pal. I was glad that I already was. These incidents bonded us together and made us cohorts in many other adventures.

Chapter Eight

Growing up in Baghdad

Growing up in Baghdad, in some respects, probably was no different from growing up in any other city in the world. My brothers and sisters and I pulled mischievous pranks on our friends, tried to fool our parents, and became socialized to the customs of our city and country. However, the landscape of the country and the culture prevalent among Baghdad's people were unique to the region. There was no place else like it in the world. As children, we thrived there.

Buying "on account"

My sisters and I had observed that Mother had a routine when she went shopping. She had favorite vendors at the marketplace and frequented specific shops, where she had become known to the storeowners. This wasn't remarkable. What was noteworthy, however, was that most of the time she wouldn't use any money. She would select her items and the proprietors would put her purchases "on account." They always smiled and nodded their heads, then wrote a note of her purchases in an account book.

Sometimes, this would accumulate over several weeks. When neither Mother nor Father came to pay what was owed, the store owners reminded them of their past due accounts and Father or Mother would promptly pay with polite apologies.

My sisters and I thought this was grand. We could buy things and Father would have to pay for them eventually, but he would never know that it was us who had bought anything. So on the way home from school, my sisters and I would go into a store and select all kinds of candy and goodies. Then we waved at the storeowner as we exited and shouted to him, "Put it on account." Like with our mother's purchases, the storeowner pulled out his booklet and wrote it all down. *Did he write in the right amount, or did he cheat us?* We didn't care. We knew Father would pay without question.

We used to laugh outside on the sidewalk, remarking about how we had outwitted the storeowner and our parents. "This is great!" we'd say, "Mother and Father will never find out how so much was owed." We naturally assumed that there was no way Father would discover that the goodies that we had bought had not been purchased by Mother. Father would just pay what the storekeeper showed him he owed. We thought we had a foolproof system so we continued buying "on account" for many months.

Much later, we discovered that both Mother and Father had known all along what we had been up to. The storekeeper had not just written down the items purchased and the date, but he also wrote down who bought the items. Since he didn't remember our individual names, he wrote "children."

Father and Mother kept their secret as we had thought we had kept ours. Occasionally, Father would come home and make an announcement to Mother at dinner. "I was at the market today to pay for the groceries," he would say. "You've been shopping there quite a bit."

Mother would smile knowingly and flash her bright eyes at him. "What can I do about it?" she would answer then add for explanation, "You have a lot of mouths to feed." (She said, "You have" as if we were Father's possessions only.)

We were never confronted by our parents about this mischief. And, we most definitely never admitted it.

Horse-drawn carriages

Though Baghdad was a modern city with automobiles and taxis, it still had quite a few horse-drawn carriages around, a remnant from its colonial days. The carriages in general use were painted black and looked a bit worse for wear. The horses, generally, were old and tired, and couldn't do more than plod along the street. The carriage driver, however, tried to keep them moving by using a long leather whip.

More elaborate carriages were still in operation. They were beautifully appointed ones, with leather seats and comfortable cushions. They had doors on both sides, with candle lamps in front. Great care was taken to keep their paint fresh and bright and to embellish them with hand decorated designs. The horses for these special carriages were retired Arabian racehorses. When they paraded through town, they were a sheer delight to watch.

Berta and I used to run behind the regular carriages and hitch a ride on the back axle to save our bus fair money for treats. Most of the time, we could do it without the carriage driver noticing. Berta soon became a "lady" and stopped accompanying me on these treacherous journeys.

My brothers, Yeftah and Avram, were eager to replace her. Since I was their oldest and most experienced brother, they followed my instructions to the letter. Despite their adherence to my rules and techniques, occasionally a carriage driver noticed us and flicked his long whip toward the back of the vehicle. The whip stung like the devil and left a cut on our necks or faces. Sometimes it was so deep it scarred. To avoid more pain, we'd jump off the carriage, and then invent some story to explain our cuts to our parents.

Usually, we'd come home and say, "Some kids jumped us outside the school. What could we do?" Our parents never found out what we had done.

Even with the treat of the whip, we couldn't stay off those carriages. A few days later, we'd be back running after another horse-drawn carriage.

Mother sews dresses for us

My mother developed a personal hobby. She bought a Singer sewing machine and learned to sew. She also bought a book of pattern designs, which tried to copy when she sewed. Unfortunately—at least for us boys—the patterns were all designs for girls. Mother eagerly sewed skirts and dresses for her children. It worked out quite well for the first two daughters. When I came along, Mother didn't have any instructions or patterns for boy's clothes. Therefore, I was dressed in girl's dresses until I was four or five years old.

Years later Mother always denied this fact, but I had dozens of photos to prove it. I resented it bitterly. One day, I ripped up all of the family photos of me dressed in girl's dresses, except for one. It was a family photo of me, my sisters Berta and Yedida, Father, and Mother pregnant, expecting Yeftah's birth. To this day, an enlargement of the photo hangs on our wall with me wearing a dress.

Mother and the shoemaker

Mother used to take us to a private shoemaker, who owned a tiny shop with a small display window. In it, the shoemaker showed off several dozen different styles of his personal designs. He only showed the left shoe or the right since he could not afford to make both shoes just for display. Mother let us try on several types of shoes that we liked, but somehow she always managed to convince us to choose something else of her own selection.

Since a new child was born every couple of years and we children kept growing and needing new shoes, Mother always looked for ways to economize. She would take three or four of us at once to get a better quantity discount from the shoemaker. But, her most annoying frugal shopping habit was to buy each of us oversized shoes. When we were fitted for shoes, she stuck her finger into the back of the shoe to give us growing room and would order that larger size.

"They grow big so fast," she explained to the shoemaker, who only smiled, never answering.

We protested and threatened never to wear those shoes, but she always won the argument. Otherwise, we didn't get new shoes. So, the orders were finalized and a partial payment was made. The shoemaker then set to making our over-sized shoes. A few weeks later, our shoes would be finished, and Mother would go back to the shop to pick up the shoes and pay the remainder she owed.

It was months before we had the courage to wear those over-sized shoes to school.

Public urinaries in Baghdad: Boys only

Throughout Baghdad, there were small unpretentious Urinaries (bathrooms) tucked among shops, businesses, and public squares. Each urinary was a small place, with a few toilets and a male attendant, who maintained order and cleanliness. The attendant usually had an open metal can where he expected the clients to deposit tips. These Urinaries were strictly for boys and men. I always thought girls don't have the same need.

Whenever we went for a walk on the beach or went shopping with Mother, there was always a problem when one of my sisters needed to use the bathroom. There just were no public bathrooms for women and girls.

Once my sister Yedida wanted to go so badly she asked my mother to request permission for her to use the boys' urinary. Mother was ashamed to ask the old man who was the attendant.

"I can't do that," Mother exclaimed. "Girls can hold it longer than boys, so hold it."

Yedida was twisting in agony, crossing her legs and trying to walk. Finally, Mother had to give her some money to buy something from a restaurant so that she could use their bathroom. Even then, Mother had to stand outside the bathroom door to make sure that no man entered while her daughter was there.

In Baghdad, as it is throughout the Arab world, the phrase "equal rights" had not been heard yet. This was yet another example of how females were second-class citizens, always discriminated against.

The Turkish bath

Twice a month, it was customary for every family of means in Baghdad to go bathe in public at the steamy, Turkish Bath. There were several in the city. Each was a huge facility divided into the men's section on the left and the women's section on the right.

Since I was a small boy, Mother took me with her to the women's side. Mother said it was safer. Though we were relatively modest at home, the public baths were not places for shyness. The Bath was my early introduction to nudity. Women of every age, shape, and ethnicity walked around and bathed completely naked. They washed their breasts and their private parts without any regard to my presence or that of other young boys there, too.

Though I was very young, I drew it all in. Yet, deep within me, I felt that there was something mysterious happening here, but it was something I couldn't quite grasp. As I got older and continued coming to the Turkish Bath with Mother, that sexual mystery began to be deciphered in the only way boys coming of age do. I could hardly wait for the day after our visit to the Turkish Bath when I would meet my friends, and we'd share our impressions of the Bath with each other. Our favorite topic always centered on the size of the boobs we saw, and, of course, we always exaggerated.

I always tried to keep a serious expression on my face so that Mother would not suspect how much fun I was having. When we left the Turkish Bath, Mother sometimes put her arm around my shoulder and commented, "It was fun, wasn't it, Shoolee?"

I could barely croak out, "It was OK, Mom," and tried to keep the enthusiasm out of my voice. The prevailing opinion at the time was that it was safer for a boy to be at the women's section than at the men's. It was years later before I understood why that would be the case.

Summer wonder: The miracle island

Every summer, Baghdad experienced an astonishing, geological phenomenon. As the great Iraqi rivers, the Tigris and the Euphrates, receded, the riverbed was exposed, surrounded by shallow waters, which allowed tens of thousands of citizens and visitors to walk or swim to a small "island" that formed in the middle of the rivers.

Thousands of electric lights were strung all over the island. Big bonfires were set up to broil fish that had just been caught in the shallow waters and were smothered with all kinds of spices. People gathered around the fire, playing drums and the oud (an ancient guitar-like instrument introduced by the Turks during the Ottoman Empire). Other people began singing and clapping their hands and some beautiful, young girls moved in the sensuous undulations of Middle Eastern belly dance, swaying their hips and shimming their shoulder.

The festivities went on all through the night for several months every summer. It was like a Middle Eastern Disneyland that was free for all to enjoy. As the summer months ended, the water rose gradually and covered these islands. Then seagoing vessels and oil tankers navigated once again through the rivers, passing under the great British-built bridges that I loved so much.

Summer vacation in Mosul

Almost every summer, my family looked forward to our vacation in Mosul. Father worked during the week but visited us on Saturdays. So it was Mother who gathered us at the train station and helped us get our belongings onto the train. Sometimes, one of mother's sisters came with us.

Our destination was a resort in Mosul, several hundred miles away in the north of the country near the Turkish border. The train ride, therefore, took several hours. We passed through beautifully cultivated fields, lush green pastures, and thousands of palm trees. Shepherds, tending their flocks, waved to us.

At stopovers, we bought little sweets, dates, yogurt, and drinks from the local peasants who wore colorful headwear and long dresses. The women, wearing black veils over their faces, carried huge, flat baskets full of foodstuffs and drinks on their heads. They paraded these wares close to the train car windows so that we could see what they had and be enticed to buy.

When we finally arrived in Mosul, we got off our train and took either taxis or horse-drawn carriages to the resort. There, we settled in, ate some fruit, and then rushed to the mud and mineral water spas. Most of the guests were women and children our age of all faiths.

There was not a trace of prejudice and hatred here. We mingled together with other children and played for many hours. Mother loved the mud pools and could always be found there, covered with a black volcanic substance that smelled of acid or burning tar.

On Saturday, Father joined us and brought goodies from home. Always dressed in his English-tailored suits and polished shoes, he seemed out of place when everyone else was half naked in bathing suits or in summer shorts and tops. Food was always served early in the evening at the spa, and with Father present, it seemed more festive. While we all shared news, some older people often began playing Arabic music on instruments they had brought along while young people began to belly dance to our delight. It was an added bonus to our vacation time there.

We remained at the spa for several weeks. When we returned to Baghdad, we went back to our old routines. We all reminisced for months about all the fun we at the resort and the many friendships we had forged.

Chapter Nine

Brushes with Danger

My bout with the bees

Every day, my father was chauffeured to his office and brought back in the afternoon to rest and eat lunch. After a two-hour nap, he washed, dressed up once more, and went back to the office for another few hours of work. In the evening, he was brought back to have a light dinner, freshen up, and go out. On some occasions, he took mother along.

One day, I showed my father how a large number of honeybees were constructing a beehive at the top of the stairway. He looked at the bees with great concern and warned me never to go anywhere near them. He reminded me of this everyday as he left the house.

One evening, Father decided to go out with Mother. He asked my eldest sister Berta, who was only three years older than I was, to look after my sister Yedida and me.

As usual, Father bribed Berta with extra money if she promised to keep a keen eye on me especially. No sooner than the door had closed on my parents, my curiosity about the bees overwhelmed me. How could such little creatures be so bad and frightening that I had to avoid them? I was indignant about being told to stay away from them as if I were a baby. I thought to myself that I was bigger than bees and I could look at them, if I wanted to.

Both of my sisters were engrossed in a game of dominos in their room when I decided to sneak out and face the challenge of the bees. But I wasn't going to do it without a proper weapon. I took a broom with a long handle and brought it with me to the stairway. I stood exactly under the beehive and tried to sweep the bees away with the broom, but I couldn't reach the hive. It was too high up. I decided to aim the broom at the beehive and kill all of those buzzing bastards.

I swung the broom time and time again. Finally, I hit the beehive so hard that it came tumbling down directly toward my face. Hundreds of bees covered my face and my neck and stung me again and again. I screamed at the top of my lungs and fainted with fright.

When my sisters finally arrived to see what I had done this time, they found me unconscious on the floor, with hundreds of bees feasting on me. They began screaming, too, and brought towels to chase the bees away. Then they rushed to our next-door neighbor who owned a telephone and immediately called an ambulance.

I was taken to the hospital a couple of miles away where I was given several shots to counteract the bee venom. Hours later, I woke up in the hospital and realized what had happened. My face was so swollen that you couldn't see my eyes. I was more scared of my father's punishment than of the pain from the bee stings. Berta assured me over and over again that Father would feel sorry for me and not punish me for disobeying his commandment.

When my parents came home from their night out, our neighbor met them at the door and told them what had happened. Of course, they rushed to the hospital to see me. However, the first thing they said to me was, "How could you do this? Didn't we warn you about the bees?" Father had an urge to slap me, but Mother held him back, as usual.

This encounter with the bees was not an isolated incident. I seemed destined to repeat it again and again in Israel and once in the U.S. when I was thirty.

Drowning in Baghdad

During the summer months, my father often woke all of us up early in the morning, around 5 am, and got us ready a short car trip to the riverbank. He helped us dress and even prepared our favorite sandwiches and cold drinks, filling a big basket with goodies. On these days, Mother stayed home and rested. We tiptoed one by one through the house onto the street, where Father's car and the chauffeur waited.

The trip to the river took only a few minutes, passing some of Baghdad's most luxurious homes, what we called the castles of the elite. Horse-drawn carriages slowly made their way in their lane on the road, taking people to work, to school, and to the food market. We passed by the most modern theater in Baghdad, which had been recently built in Western style. Then, we took a short, sandy, winding road to the beach. There, we met with some of my father's business friends and members of the nightclubs he frequented.

We rushed to take off our outer clothes and run into the shallow waters, jumping and splashing all around. A close friend of my father's, a British Officer named Ridley, always brought his huge dog with him. We thought the dog was the greatest because he liked to frolic in the water with us. He was the best swimming animal we had ever seen. He would even catch up with us and surpass us far into the deep water. As a precaution, the adults took turns watching the kids and giving us swimming lessons. Another adult usually swam with us but swam farther away and would periodically turn back and yell something to us and wave his hands. We were never to swim out into the deeper waters without an adult being nearby.

On one of these delightful morning swims, I decided to go after the dog and catch a ride over it to compensate for my poor swimming skill. However, the more I chased the dog, the further he swam away from me. I was exhausted and began to scream for help. But, I was a long way from the beach; no one could hear me. I began to sink below the surface. When I touched the river's floor, I pushed my body up with all my remaining strength. When my head was above the water, I screamed, "Help!" and sunk again.

Some of my brothers and sisters, who had stayed on the beach, playing in the sand, heard my cry. They ran to Ridley and pointed to where I had been in the water. They began to cry out that I had already drowned.

As luck would have it, Ridley was an excellent swimmer. He dove into the water and swam out to where the children had pointed. He jackknifed deep into the water and fished me out of the bottom of the riverbed, pulling me by my long hair. I was unconscious. Ridley brought me back to the beach and dumped me onto the sand. He lifted me by my feet, upside down, to drain the water out of me. I came to, surrounded by dozens of onlookers, including my frightened and angry father.

My only thought was worry over what would await me at home from my father. I had rushed into the deep water, following Ridley's dog, and I had disobeyed Father's repeated orders about swimming without an adult in the deep water. Out of respect to his friends, my father would not hit me or punish me in any way in their presence. He would wait until we were alone in our house. I pretended to be really hurt to solicit his pity.

But that day was truly my lucky day. Not only did I escape drowning, but also I escaped Father's wrath because he had to rush to work. By the time he returned from the office, he had calmed down.

I am Electrocuted!

I was a curious boy who was determined to find out how "magical things" worked and why. When I was about seven years old, I noticed that when Mother or Father inserted appliance chords into the electric sockets, the appliances made noises and performed some function. This was fascinating. How did that happen? What made it do this? But Father had always warned me never to touch any of the outlets.

Nevertheless, I decided that someday I would investigate this phenomenon. One evening when my mother and father went out to the Hindu nightclub, leaving my sister Berta to baby-sit me. I decided this was the time to follow my curiosity about electricity. Without my sister noticing, I took a hairpin out of a drawer in her room and planned to stick it into the electrical outlet. "What could happen?" I wondered. "Will it spin like the other appliances or even light up like a light bulb?"

The 220-volt wall socket was about knee-high. I reached down and stuck the hairpin into one of the holes. Immediately, I received such a shock that I was thrown about ten feet away and landed on my head.

Hearing the crash of my fall, Berta came running into her room. "What did you do?" She knelt down beside me and started slapping me and screamed at me, "Wake-up! Wake-up!"

When I wouldn't wake up, she ran out to the neighbors, as she always did in an emergency, frantically asking them to come help. I ended up in the hospital, nearly dead. Everyone came to visit me and brought gifts and goodies, including my parents, who were in shock. Poor Berta was blamed again for not being responsible and letting this happen to me.

A few days later, I was discharged from the hospital and driven home. I had missed a few days of school, which was nice, and I was served my meals in my room. I thought I had gained everyone's sympathy and understanding by this time.

When my father returned from his office in the evening, he came in to my room and said to me, "How many times have I warned you never to touch electricity?" It was more than a rhetorical question. It was an indictment of my wrongdoing. Father didn't let me answer the charge. He just slapped me once on the face and twice on the buttocks. "I hope you learned a lesson, young man," he said as he left the room. Mother stood at the door, feeling sorry for me.

A few days passed, and Father and I never spoke. I sensed that my father was feeling a bit guilty for smacking me.

Finally, at dinner one night, Father asked me, "How was school? Does anyone know what you did?"

"Yes, Dad," I answered. "Everyone knows what happened. Someone must have spread the word." I looked down at my plate and admitted, "The teacher punished me, too. He gave me an assignment to write 500 times: 'Electricity is dangerous. I will never touch electricity again.'"

I wondered quietly, *did he rat me to the principal?* But I didn't dare ask.

Father looked at me sympathetically. "If you're so curious about electricity," he suggested, "maybe you should study to be an electrician when you grow up."

And that's how it came to be. I finished high school and at an air force academy studied electricity and electronics. It became my career for the next forty years.

Chapter Ten

Flying Kites and Pigeons

Flying kites on the roof

When Father dismantled the beds and reassembled them on the roof for the summer months, he set up brass poles on the four corners of the beds and hung a fine, white mesh net over them. While we enjoyed the cool summer breeze blowing from the river, the netting spared us from the nasty bites of the mosquitoes. On the roof, there were many things we did to entertain ourselves. We played marbles and dominoes. We even did homework or read. But, our favorite past time was flying kites.

We either bought the kites at the store or designed and made them ourselves from all kinds of materials. Several rolls of string were purchased and tied together to make each kite string thousands of feet long. When we flew our kites, they could be seen from all of the rooftops from all over Baghdad. Sometimes, the sky would be filled with kites flying from many different roofs. It was an awesome scene.

The best time we had was when we engaged in kite duels with children from another neighborhood. We maneuvered our kites and tried our best to entangle it with another child's kite, pulling it down. To ensure our winning, we devised a trick that worked every time. We broke a glass or a bottle into fine, tiny pieces and used glue to attach the pieces to the farther edge of our kite strings. When we entangled an opponent's kite, our string would shear the other string in seconds, making his kite seem to mysteriously fall from its great height to the ground.

Whenever we did this, we had to make sure that the other boy didn't recognize our kite and lead it back to us. Otherwise, we risked being searched out and beaten up the following day.

We flew several different kites every few days to confuse our identities. Nothing made my brothers and sisters laugh louder and longer than when we vanquished our opponents in the kite duels.

Flying pigeons from our friend's roof

One of our father's Arab friends had an older son who had an intriguing hobby. He cultivated, bred, and flew pigeons. He was an expert on all aspects of pigeon biology and behavior. He had over fifty pigeons of various colors and sizes, including their eggs that had not yet hatched.

We used to knock on his door every now and then and ask if we could join him on his roof. He never said no (out of respect to his father). It was mostly just my brothers Yeftah and Avram and I. We climbed the stairs to the roof and crossed to the handmade shack where his pigeons were housed. Most of the pigeons were usually inside this shack, making their annoying cooing noises. We wondered if it were just noise or actually their language and they were communicating with each other. We didn't know.

Some of the birds sat on the ledge of the roof, waiting for a command from their master, our friend. He took us inside the shack and pointed out all of the changes that had occurred among his pigeon population since our last visit, especially the new arrivals. Some of the pigeons were in the back in nests, sitting on eggs. Our friend told us never to bother the brooding pigeons. But, he let us hold some of the other birds gently in our hands so that we could admire their beauty. The colors around their necks were magnificent. Sometimes he clipped their wings until they were properly trained.

We went out onto the roof, and he showed us what he used his pigeons for. He took a small piece of paper on which he had written something and inserted it in the mouth of one of his trained pigeons or tied it to one of his legs. He then took the pigeon into his hands, and while stroking its feathers, he actually talked to them in a language we didn't understand. Sometimes he just whispered something into the pigeon's ear and then threw it up into the air. The pigeon flew far up and away where we could no longer see it. The bird seemed to know his destination.

Our friend then smiled enigmatically and explained, "I told him to go to my friend Ebrahim who lives on the other side of the bridge, in Bab-el-shargi, miles away. You noticed I gave him a note in white paper. He will come back with an answer from Ebrahim in red or green paper. That was the proof he actually went there."

It was really fascinating. We asked endless questions, which must have appeared childish to him since he was twice our age. "But, what if Ebrahim is not there to respond?" I asked.

He would smile that strange smile of his. "Then he will wait there till Ebrahim is free to answer. He will not return empty-handed."

Sure enough, about an hour later, we spotted the pigeon in the distance, way up in the sky, flapping his wings rapidly to come back home. We got excited and clapped our hands, rooting for him and calling out to him at the top of our lungs. The bird finally arrived and ignored our extended hands and went directly to his trainer. There, in his mouth or tied to his leg, he brought back a different colored note, which he read out loud to us. It was always a funny note.

If our friend didn't get tired of us, he sometimes repeated the same episode again, using another pigeon and another note. This time, the pigeon was instructed to go to a different address, to Iben-allah-wee. We laughed easily together and shared some drinks and sandwiches that we had brought with us. It made for a fun afternoon.

We were pleased to note that neither the pigeons nor their handler nor their young admirers ever asked what anyone's religion was. There was never any hint of prejudice. We were all just pigeon fanciers.

Chapter Eleven

Schools for Boys and Schools for Girls

My sisters and I went to schools on the other side of the bridge, where the majority of the Baghdad population lived. Our schools, however, were Jewish-managed schools for Jewish children. There were separate schools: some for boys and some for girls. Since it was too far to walk in the morning and again back home, my parents gave us money for bus fair. My sister and I, however, preferred to use the money for a higher purpose. We'd use it to buy candy, sandwiches, and soda from a kiosk on the other side of the bridge, not far from the school district.

We got up an hour earlier each morning, grabbed something to eat on the run, and walked all the way to our schools. Sometimes, if we were lucky, we hitched rides on the back of a horse-drawn carriage and sat on the rear axle. The hardest thing was coming back home from school. We had to be motivated to walk that great distance. In the mornings on the way to school, we were eager to get across the bridge and buy treats and usually spent our entire allowance then. Unfortunately, when we walked home, we had no money left and therefore had no incentive to walk all that way. We had to encourage each other to keep walking.

My school: Mas-Ouda Salman

At Mas-Ouda Salman, we boys faced a lot of rules and received punishments if we broke any of them. We could be punished for being a few minutes late, or not preparing homework, or even for talking in the classroom. Our punishment sometimes was to stand inside the trashcan in a corner of the classroom, facing the wall for the entire day. If your crime was more serious, the teacher would administer a few lashes across your palms with his favorite, well-polished, wooden ruler before you were told to stand in the trash can in the corner. In the cold winter days, this was a particularly harsh punishment. We were told that this was fashioned after the British Education System. Though we admired the British, this was one form of punishment we abhorred. What shame we felt after having to stand inside the wastebasket in the corner with our backs to the class, and then turning around at the end of the day to face our classmates!

Sometimes the punishment was even worse. The teacher would give us a sentence or two to write 500 to 1000 times for homework, with a note to be signed by one of our parents. My sisters and I figured out a way to keep our parents from ever finding out we had punishment homework. We copied and copied our mother's signature, which was easier than Father's, until it was a fair forgery. Then, we would sign the notes for each other.

Berta's school: Gan Menachem Saleh Daniel

Berta went to Gan Menachem Saleh Daniel, a girls' school for the elite of the Jewish community. Since it wasn't too far from my own school, Berta and I occasionally met for lunch to split what was left of our bus fare money. After school, having spent every penny on food, drinks, and goodies, we walked hand-in-hand back home over the long bridge. It took over one hour of brisk walking to get home. We always arrived nearly exhausted, swearing never to it again.

Naturally, the following day we repeated the same thing all over again. We must have thought bus money was a waste. Now and then, we would be lucky enough to flag down a neighbor's car and ask for a ride home. When we did that, we always insisted on being dropped off a safe distance from our house so that our parents wouldn't find out. And they never did.

Chapter Twelve

High Holy Days and Religious Training

High Holy Days, Yum Kippur

During the High Holy Days, especially Yum-Kippur (the Day of Atonement), our family donned our best clothes and newly shined shoes. Mother and the older women also put on a head cover. Then, it was customary to walk to the nearest synagogue because we couldn't ride anything on that day.

At the synagogue, men and women sat in separate areas and used different prayer books. The Rabbi entered the space in procession, followed by the older men. They canted their prayers in beautiful, sad melodies. Invariably, the men started crying, wiping their eyes and their wet cheeks with their handkerchiefs. The prayers were in Aramaic, lamenting the plight of the Jews since the destruction of the great temple in Jerusalem and the many problems the Jews had experienced since then. Then the prayers usually got very personal as we remembered our deceased family members.

It was customary for the grownups to fast, taking no food or drink since the night before, and many didn't brush their teeth. Therefore, their mouths often smelled foul.

Late in the afternoon before sunset, the Rabbi and some of the men sounded the sho-far (ram's horn) as Jews had done for thousands of years. When the service was ended, we filed out of the synagogue, shaking hands with friends and wishing each in a whisper, "Next year in Jerusalem." This was the universal yearning of Jews everywhere since the days of their exile and their dispersal throughout the world: to return home to Jerusalem.

Keepers of the cemeteries

The Jewish cemeteries in Iraq date back hundreds of years. They survived the rule of the Romans, the Persians, the Mongols, the Turks, the British, and the Iraqi monarchy. To the credit of all of these ruling nations, they never desecrated nor bulldozed over the graves of our ancestors as did occur repeatedly in Eastern Europe.

Though the ruling authorities did not desecrate our cemeteries, there still was the possibility that citizens and visitors might do so. Therefore, in order to prevent any looting or vandalism, each minority group in Iraq took the responsibility to guard and maintain its own cemeteries. The Jewish cemeteries were no exception. As a matter of fact, entire families dedicated themselves to this duty and lived on the cemetery grounds. The cemetery caretakers were typically some of the poorest people in the community. For this act of selfless service, the Jewish community donated money, clothes, and food to these families in order to support this work. Most of the donations and contributions were taken in the synagogue on Saturdays and the High Holy Days.

I remember well as a child that Mother would remind us at each meal to leave some food on our plates. "You must leave something for the poor," she always said. This act of generosity was her way of trying to instill in us a sense of responsibility and generosity to our fellow human beings. It was a way for each of us to give something each day and to be grateful for what we had. By simply leaving something for the poor, we learned not only about generosity and thankfulness, but we saw how to avoid gluttony. This was a far cry from American mothers during the same time who urged their children to clean their plates because there were starving children in China or Africa or some such place.

Eating fish

It was customary in Jewish homes to eat fish at dinner every Friday. One day Father came home early and brought us a surprise. Father had his chauffeur open the trunk of the car, and we saw a huge fish flopping around. Father had purchased it from a fisherman on the river.

The driver immediately took a water hose and began filling the little cement pond in our courtyard. With father's help, they struggled with the huge fish and dumped it into the water. After a stunned few seconds, the fish began swimming beautifully. My brothers and sisters and I threw some breadcrumbs into the pond, and the fish swiftly ate them all.

The following day, several helpers showed up at our house to clean the fish and cut it up. They made all of the preparations to fry it in a huge pan. The sight of all of the blood and the smell of the fish made me sick and haunted me for the rest of my life. I would never again be able to eat fish.

That day and many Fridays that followed, I sat at the dinner table with my family and looked for something to eat that didn't contain fish. I usually ended up eating only bread and jam and some fruit. After a few weeks of this, Father began to feel that I wasn't grateful for the food he put on the table. He decided to punish me by sending me away from the table back to my room without anything to eat until I learned to eat fish like everyone else. Father repeated this lesson every Friday, explaining to the rest of the family, "Being hungry is the only way he is going to learn to eat fish. It's very healthy and necessary for growth."

I would always be hungry, but everyone was forbidden to sneak food in to me. No one was even allowed to come to my room to keep me company or to show me any sympathy.

My mother, fortunately, couldn't go to bed knowing that one of her children went to bed hungry. Around midnight, she sneaked out of bed, made me a couple of sandwiches and some orange juice, and tiptoed to my door with a tray. She set the food outside my door and knocked lightly to make sure I was aware of her tender motherly care. Not being aware of this, my brothers and sisters wondered how I could go hungry every Friday. Pretty soon, they began to suspect that Mother was sneaking me food because I was her "favorite son," an injustice they felt and uttered at me all their lives.

In spite of this punishment, I never learned to eat fish (and neither did any of the three daughters I had when I was a father myself). Father never knew why I couldn't eat fish. "I don't know how you survived all these years without supper," he often commented. I never said a word.

Years later in Israel, he said, "You should have learned to eat fish by now. It's a miracle you survived."

Mother smiled and said nothing. We both kept the secret. When I was married, fish would not be allowed in our house. And when I owned a boat and returned home with the catch of the day, we would give the fresh fish to our grateful neighbors.

Chapter Thirteen

Shifting Sands: Changes in the Arab Treatment of Jews

Even over my brief childhood, my family became aware of changing attitudes of Arabs toward Jews. Though our neighbors and the storekeepers treated us well, it was the fickleness of the ruling regimes that made our lives unpredictable and dangerous. With growing Arab nationalism and the horror of Farhood, the pogrom of 1941, ever in our memories, we couldn't expect our lives to remain peaceful for very long.

Cinema Balash (Free Cinema)

Though Iraq gained its true independence in 1933 and established a ruling monarchy, it was heavily influenced by the British. At first, this helped insure the stability of the monarchy by offering protection, advice, and expertise to leaders who were unfamiliar to rule and to the Iraqi people. Economically, the uninterrupted continuity of the oil flow was not possible without the British Navy, which protected oil shipments and oversaw the oilfields.

During World War II, German interests in the country were also vying for the region's oil. They were so few and had not developed a foothold in the country that they had little influence with the Arabs. However, growing Arab nationalism and a festering hatred of Jews drew German sympathizers even though Iraq had declared its alliance with the Allies.

In order to reassure the local population, the British organized outdoor movies, called the Cinema Balash, which the public attended free of charge. People came to these events and simply stood on their feet, shoulder to shoulder, as they watched newsreel footage projected on a white painted wall under the open skies. The films typically depicted Allied soldiers, especially the British, in great victories over the Germans and Italians on every front. The moviegoers invariably clapped their hands and cheered the victorious armies. While we watched, peddlers sold us cold drinks, sweets, and muffins. These evenings were always great fun.

Arab failure in the Israeli War for Independence

When the United Nations divided a portion of Palestine into the state of Israel, the British, in truth, abandoned their last colony in the Middle East. As the tiny country was being organized, it faced an added threat from the armies of five Arab nations, including forces from Iraq. A day after Israel was proclaimed a nation, these armies declared war on Israel on March 15, 1948, and descended on Palestine to take it back for the Arabs. The small, ill-equipped country had only Israeli freedom fighters from its underground to mount any kind of defense.

However, these brave fighters overcame these Arab forces.

Upon the return of the Iraqi army, defeated and humiliated, the government tried to appease their Arab population by blaming their defeat on the Jewish Zionists "spies." They turned their anger toward Jews within their own country. Zionism or Israeli sympathy became a treasonable offense, punishable by death. The government began compiling lists of the richest and most prominent Jews in Iraq. These Jews were rounded up and jailed for treason. Their property and possessions were confiscated, and many Jews were sentenced to public hanging, a spectacle the Arabs enjoyed.

The hanging of our friend Yehuda Saddik

Prominent Jews were not only accused of being Zionists, but were denounced as spies and Communists. These charges were almost always false, but were convenient, particularly nasty labels to place on Jews, making them much more susceptible to scorn, hatred, and reprisals from the local population. The hanging of Shafiq Addas, the richest Jew in Basra, in 1948 signaled the beginning of a new anti-Jewish wave of persecution.

Father's friend, Yehuda Saddik, a handsome 23-year-old man, was one of those rounded up early. In his jail cell, he was told that if he denounced Zionism and Communism in public, he would be pardoned. Mr. Saddik did just that in a loud and clear voice. Though this confession had served the government's purpose, it still ordered his execution anyway.

The newspaper showed photos of Mr. Saddik and the scheduled public hanging. Father took me down to the city square to witness the execution.

"No matter what happens, you are not to show any emotions," Father said to me. "No crying, no shouting, nothing, until we get back home. Can you do this? Do you promise?"

I was only ten years old when I watched my father's friend die before my very eyes. When Father and I got home, we were both so distressed that the subject of Mr. Saddiq's hanging was never mentioned again between us. Sometimes, though, I heard him talking to my mother about it, but he would change the subject as soon as I came into the room. Mother had always objected to his taking me there to witness the hanging. She thought I was too young. Still, she did understand Father's reasoning. He was preparing me for the realities of life as Jew in an Arab country, and I had to be grown-up. This experience also prepared me for the great escape that would come soon.

Father is blacklisted

A few months later, my father's name appeared on the blacklist. He couldn't continue to work in a government job so he stopped going to work. Not knowing how long he could live without being discovered, Father wondered how long it would be before he was hanged like other Jews. Since Jews were forbidden to leave Iraq, Father wondered how he could escape. It was becoming urgent that if father and our whole family could not escape, at least some of us should find a way to Israel where we would be safe.

Chapter Fourteen

Listening to the Radio in the Closet

Preparations for escape

An aunt, who lived on the other side of the bridge, gave us shelter in a place known as Bab-el-shargi. We were treated well. My aunt housed and clothed all of us and sent us children to nearby schools.

We stayed there three months until my father found and rented a place that was safe for us to live in. It was unlike our beautiful house in Sal-hee-yah. It was a five-story apartment building in the middle of Baghdad. We had an apartment on the third floor. My parents had their own bedroom, but they also kept my infant sister Judith there. My four sisters were in another bedroom and my two brothers occupied yet another bedroom. The smallest bedroom in the house was mine alone. I didn't have to share it with anyone. I was their first-born son; I commanded respect.

Our next-door neighbor was another Jewish family who had three children. One son had cerebral palsy. His mother and my mother became close friends. It was important for Mother to have someone to talk to, and it was also important for us to have children to play with.

Another neighbor, Salima Sigawi, had muscular dystrophy. It was a crippling affliction that affected all of her children, too, except her youngest daughter. The girl was a knockout and was the only teenager in the apartment building worth looking at. About fifteen of us boys were in love with her.

In our self-imposed exile on the other side of the bridge, we grasped for hope and news of Israel and its dream of statehood. The only way we could find information was to listen to Kol Yisrael, the Voice of Israel's broadcast on the short-wave radio. If we were ever found out, it was treason, punishable by death. My father gathered us all together inside a closet, with blankets thrown over our heads to muffle the sound. He turned the knob on his Zenith radio and tuned the fading signals arriving from the Haganah, the Israeli underground military movement, which became the precursor to the IDF, the Israel Defense Force that consolidated all of the individual fighting groups. We listened for hours every day, but had to limit our listening sessions to fifteen or twenty minutes at a time so that Iraqi authorities couldn't trace the signal. During those breaks, Father came out of the closet and motioned us into the living room where he tried to explain in simple terms what we had just heard and what it would mean regarding our fate as Jews and the fate of Israel. Everything hung in the balance. There was no guarantee Israel would survive fighting all its neighboring countries at once.

These secret radio sessions brought particular hope to my family. From them, Father and Mother decided that they must save some of their children by smuggling them out of Iraq to the promised haven in Israel. Unfortunately, as their plans evolved, not all of us could leave. Father chose his two oldest sons, my brother Yeftah and me. I was ten years old, and Yeftah was only eight and a half. Father made contact with some members of the Zionist underground, begged them to take his young sons, and paid them dearly for their help. Father told Yeftah and me that we would be leaving one day soon but we did not know when. We were not to discuss this matter with anyone, even other family members.

Chapter Fifteen

Escape from Baghdad!!!

[*When the Iraqi army returned from the war with Israel in 1948, defeated and humiliated, they tried to appease their Muslim population by blaming their defeat on the "Jewish Zionist spies." They began compiling a list of rich and prominent Jews, looting their possessions, jailing them, and hanging many of them in the main public square. My father took me there once to witness one of these hangings. Details can be found in previous chapters*]

A few months later, my father's name appeared on a blacklist of Jews. Not knowing his fate, Father wondered if he would be hanged like other Jews had been. He decided that he must save some of his children by smuggling them out of Iraq to the new state of Israel. Father chose my brother Yeftah and me. I was ten years old, and Yeftah was only eight and a half. Father contacted some members of the Zionist underground, begged them to take his young sons, and paid them dearly for their help. He told Yeftah and me that we would be leaving one day soon but we did not know when.

One hot summer evening around 8 o'clock, I was in my room, with the door closed, doing homework. I heard a soft knock at the door.

"Come in," I said, as I looked up from my textbook.

It was my father, still dressed in his usual English-tailored suit and conservative tie. His normally smiling face looked grim as he sat on the edge of my bed. As he looked at me, I knew something of the gravest importance was about to be said.

"Saul, my son," my father began, in quavering voice, "it's time to get ready. You know what I am talking about." He cupped my face with his soft clerk's hands. I could see, for the first time in my life, a single tear welling in his eye. It was so rare a site that that tear was burned into my memory. We had always been taught not to show emotion, and father was a strict observer of that custom. "This is the day we have all been waiting for," Father explained. "You and your brother are leaving tonight. You will be joining a small group of people, starting a long journey toward the state of Israel, our promised land, the land of our forefathers."

Even though I had been preparing for this day for many months, I was stunned that it had to be now, without any warning. And, I was petrified about the journey and the dangers ahead. Still, I tilted my head up and tried not to show how I felt. "Really, Dad? Tonight? So soon?" I said.

"Yes, Saul, tonight," he answered as he stood up and paced the floor in front of me, laying out my next duties. "You had better change your underwear and put on some clean clothes, just as if you were going to school." He moved about the room, pulling out clothes for me to wear. "Your mother has already packed everything you and your brother will need. It's just outside."

My father put his arm on my shoulder and guided me to the bathroom. For the first time in years, he stood there and watched me as I brushed my teeth and washed my face, nose, and ears. He smiled as if he were proud of me.

Then he picked up a towel and vigorously dried my wet face and hair, pulling me against his chest in the process. It was a rare, tender moment, making me feel safe and loved. Father didn't express his affection openly, but all of us children knew he loved us very much.

"Let's get you dressed," Father said, pushing me away gently and combing my hair. "Hurry now. Mother is preparing your brother. I bet he's ready by now." Father rushed me back to my room and helped me dress. "You must keep warm and dry. Keep this nice sweater on all the time. And your brother, too, make sure he does the same."

He left me alone to go check on the progress in my brother Yeftah's room. Mother had already dressed him and was now in the kitchen preparing sandwiches for the road. I could see her from the doorway of my room as she whispered to my sisters and youngest brother Abraham. They were all gathered around her in the kitchen, sensing that what they were witnessing was an extraordinary event in the annals of our family.

Our parents were risking their lives to try to save Yeftah's and mine. There had been no other choice for them. Staying in Baghdad could mean that we would witness our father's hanging since he had been falsely accused of treason against the Iraqi government. He was accused not only of being a Zionist but also of being a Communist, just as every other wealthy and prominent Jew here had been labeled. Being thus accused was a double insult in the eyes of the citizenry. One charge offended their nationalism; the other, their religion. It was sure to arouse the hatred and outrage of the entire Muslim population.

While the whispering was going on in the kitchen, my father signaled to me to follow him quietly. He led me to his bedroom, where we were rarely allowed. He pointed to the bed. "Sit down, son. I have something very important to tell you." He sat down beside me and continued. "As you may know, we paid a great deal of money to the Arab guides who will lead you and the others across the border into Iran. Of course, we don't know these people very well. That is why they are not to be trusted. We don't know what to expect from them. They could take our money and lead all of you into a trap. If that should happen, you would all be caught and shot on the spot. Then, the authorities would seek out the families of everyone who attempted to flee and execute them as well."

I shrugged, pretending to be brave. *So what,* I thought, there are things worse than death, like living in fear here in Baghdad, where we are hated as Jews. We can't even be citizens here, even after our people have been here for 2,600 years."

My father smiled. "You know our history well, son. I'm proud of you." He patted my shoulder, then added soberly, "We will have no contact with one another till we meet again someday in the land of Israel, God willing. It may take years. But we need to know that you and your brother made it across the border." He then reached into his jacket pocket for something. He opened his hand out to me. "Look, here are two beautiful glass marbles. One has your name inscribed on it, and the other one has your brother's. These are not for you to play with. You must keep them hidden. One is for you, and one is for your brother. When you make it safely across the border, I want you to give them to one of the Muslim guides, saying to him, 'Here, take these marbles back to my father, Silas Fathi; he'll reward you handsomely if you do." When the marbles are brought back to us, we will know that you are safe, that, at least, you have crossed the Iraqi border alive."

I was puzzled and asked, "But, Dad, what if only one of us makes it alive across the border?" Father stood up suddenly. Then just as suddenly, he pulled me against him, burying my face into his stomach.

Finally, Father said, "Then, my dear son, give the guide only one marble to bring back to us." Father pushed me away to look at me. "You will have to give one of these marbles to your brother, to keep in his pocket, so that whoever survives will be able to give his marble to the guide. But, don't give the marble to your brother just yet. He is so little. He can't keep a secret like this. But, you are older. You're a man now. You have a great sense of responsibility. I know I can count on you." Father offered the marbles to me again. "Here, keep them inside your jacket pocket, and put your handkerchief over them."

I was ten years old, yet Father thought I was a man of great responsibility for I truly became my brother's keeper. I nodded as I took the marbles and all of the responsibility that they represented and put them into my pocket for safekeeping. Beaming with newfound pride, I looked at my father and said, "O.K. Let's get going."

Father and I walked to the front door where Mother and my sisters and brothers were waiting for us. Suddenly, I had a thought. I ran back to my room, closed the door behind me, and pushed the night table beside my bed away from the wall. It seemed fitting to mark the occasion in some way so I wrote in neat letters on the wall: "I left my room today, perhaps forever, August 12, 1948." I restored the night table to its original position, covering the note on the wall, and dashed back to join the rest of my family near the front door.

Father announced, "O.K., this is where we say goodbye. We can't go with you to the car. Someone may see us and get suspicious." Yeftah and I nodded and began hugging and kissing first Mother, then our sisters Berta and Yedida, who were choking and crying, with the palms of their hands over their mouths.

Father gently pulled us away from these prolonged goodbyes. "Enough now," he said. "You must go." He handed each of us a small valise and then said his last goodbye. "God be with you. And, don't worry about us; we will join you someday. Be strong now."

Father opened the door and gently pushed us out into the evening air, closing the door quickly behind us. As it shut, it forever separated us from this house and our family and a part of our lives in a country we would never see again. We were alone; just two little boys in the dark night. But we were also emissaries of hope for a future the rest of our family might never know. In the darkness, we could just make out the nondescript car waiting for us. I took my brother's small hand in mine as I took a deep breath and walked briskly toward the waiting car.

A door opened and someone reached for us, pulling us into the laps of two young men in the back seat of an already crowded car. When we settled on bony male knees, we turned to look at the men who had us firmly in tow. To our surprise, two familiar faces grinned at us. It was our Uncle Moshe, who was nineteen, and Uncle Salman, who was only seventeen. To stifle any surprised cries of recognition, they put their hands gently over our mouths, but kept grinning at us. Inside the silent car, we sat, surrounded by familiar arms, as we sped through the city, making stops in the dark, picking up others like us who were hoping for a way out of the country.

After a few hours when other cars fell in line behind us as we traveled in caravan through the city, I realized there were actually three cars involved in the escape plan, not just ours. The three drivers maintained about 100 yards distance apart, but they remained within sight.

The trip and the dark night seemed to last forever. Yeftah pretended to be asleep in Uncle Salman's lap. I kept my eyes open, looking through the car window, trying to figure out where we were. It was difficult to see anything. There were no streetlights; only the light of the moon and the stars were visible. Our driver, an Arab, who never spoke a word during the entire trip, smoked one cigarette after another, and some of us to coughed and choked. Though we were all trying very hard not to make any noise as we tried to breathe in that smoky atmosphere, no one dared complain.

I craned my head around and tried to see who else was with us in the car. I saw two other children. One was about three years old. The other was an infant. Like my brother and me, they were held in the laps of two adults, who were most likely their parents and who kept the children's mouths covered with their hands. The family was snuggled under one blanket, leaving only the children's heads visible. In the front seat was man of 35 or 40. It seemed to me he was cold since his arms were wrapped around his wife's shoulders as they trembled uncontrollably. Now and then, on the slightest noise from the back seat, he looked over the seat and glared at us.

Uncle Moshe made a gesture to me to try to sleep by closing his eyes and tilting his head into the palm of his hand. I obeyed and tried to settle into his shoulder to sleep. Suddenly, I felt a kick on my leg. It was Yeftah, seeing if I really were asleep. I reacted like we always did, by kicking him back harder.

"Ouch!" he yelled.

The driver turned around and demanded total silence. Properly chastised, we nodded. The three-year-old looked at me and smiled, then he looked at Yeftah and made a face, sticking his tongue out and wiggling it. The boy knew he could get away with doing anything in our particular predicament. But I could tell my brother was having a hard time controlling his anger at the boy's antics. Yeftah was a person of action and revenge. Kicking the kid would have been a real treat for him, but it would have to wait for another time and place. Yeftah probably was plotting his own sweet revenge.

After almost eight hours of speeding through the city and the countryside, constantly on the alert for the police or border patrols that may have noticed us, we arrived in Basra, Iraq's main seaport. When the car stopped in front of a house, we were rushed one by one into the basement, which seemed uninhabited. There, eighteen of us—men, women, and children—lived in hiding in cramped quarters for sixteen days and nights. Food and water had been stockpiled in advance of our arrival so we did not get thirsty nor did we starve. Sanitation, however, was difficult to maintain, because there was only one toilet. We changed our underwear daily, but kept the same clothing on since many of us had little luggage with us.

We waited and worried. The adults feared that the longer we stayed in one spot, the easier it might be for the police or the patrols to find us. We lived each day in whispers among our own kin, not risking play or childhood interactions. I took care of Yeftah as father had told me to, but I wondered after all this time whether we would actually be able to leave Iraq. Maybe all of this was a big mistake and we'd all be sent back to our families. Maybe, then, I remembered that my father had been falsely accused of treason, and I knew that our little house was no longer safe. *But what of father, and mother, and our sisters and little brother? Were they safe?*

Then, one night unlike any other of those in that basement-hiding place, an Arab guide met with us. He told us to be completely quiet throughout the entire journey that night as we crossed the river into Iran. He made it plain what would happen if we were not quiet. "If the border patrol notices you crossing the river," he said, "they would shoot you and sink our boats. Don't say I didn't warn you."

One by one, we grabbed our small bags and bundles and filed into the waiting cars that would take us to the river. After a very short ride, we all scrambled out of the cars and ran to the river and waded in, up to our knees, to two small rowboats that were waiting for us. We climbed onboard as the unshaven Arab boat owners silently motioned for us to lay down in the bottom of the boats, which had been lined with bed cushions. It was dark and deathly still, except for the lapping of the water against the sides of the boats, the dripping of wet clothing as we came out of the water, and the little stirrings as people squished down onto the cushions.

I looked around for my brother who was nearby on the shore. Even fidgety Yeftah could sense the danger we were in and kept as still as he could. Without uttering a word, I pulled him closer to me and held his hand as we waded to one boat and boarded it. Down on the cushions next to us was the woman with the three-year-old boy and the infant. She again kept her hands over their mouths to make sure they didn't speak or cry. Just one little sound could endanger us all. Her husband lay next to the children and some other members of the group. We were packed liked apples in a box with little room to move. From the cessation of the muffled sounds, the other boat had just finished loading its passengers as well.

When everyone was on board, our boat owner signaled with his hand to the other boat. They began to row, slowly at first, then faster. With each labored stoke, we moved farther into the river and away from our native country, Iraq. Just on the other side of the river was Iran, our safe haven, where we would stop until we could make our way to the new state of Israel. O, Israel, the land of our forefathers, the hope of freedom and autonomy in a brand new land! Our first step toward that Promised Land and freedom wasn't far away now. It was just at the water's edge, just at the last dip of the boatman's oars, just a prayer away. I noticed some of the women were moving their lips in silent prayer and kissing the holy necklaces on their chests. It wasn't far, not now.

Then, as we came to the middle of the river, it happened. Maybe it was the fear in the air that the infant had sensed or its mother's own tension, or maybe it was just hungry or needed a diaper change. Out of its muffled little mouth came cries of discomfort. The boat owner waved his hand, trying to get the baby's mother to shush the unhappy child. Soon, others in the group began to whisper to the mother, "Hey, quiet. You're going to have us all killed." The whispers soon rose and profanities were used, creating more noise than the little child's cry.

Spurred by the fear in the voices of the others in the boat, the baby's father reached over and covered the mouth of the three-year-old. The mother then used both hands to silence her infant, with a hand over its mouth and another on the back of its neck. The baby's cries stopped, and it was quiet again. All we heard was the rise and fall of the oars.

Then suddenly, we heard the sound of rifles and a volley of bullets whizzed over our heads. The sides of the boats were thumped dully as bullets embedded in the wood. The border patrol must have heard the baby or the adult voices. They had found us and were intent on shooting in the direction of the sounds they had heard. But instead of maintaining our silence, members of our group started yelling and praying, "God, not here! Don't let them kill us now!" That only helped the border patrol correct their aim. The more the adults screamed and yelled, the more bullets hit the boat and passed over our heads.

The owner of our boat yelled at us, "I'll throw all of you into the river. You're going to have me killed and my boat sunk!"

That stunned the adults into silence. Everyone then huddled together, crying and praying in silence. We were trying to save ourselves, unaware of the fate of the other boat containing the other half of our group. We couldn't see anything in the darkness but the pale moonlight bouncing off the waves.

When our boat finally came near the far bank of the river, we all scrambled out into the water, running toward the shore, and collapsing onto the sand. We were alive and safe, and very grateful to be out of the nightmare on the water. Minutes later, the group from the other boat joined us.

Someone came down to the river from an open-bed truck nearby and told us to load up. We all climbed in and sat on the floor of the truck like cattle. Within minutes, we all were dashing through the desert toward the interior of Iran, away from the border patrol and the gunfire. One of the men from the truck looked back through the rear window and counted the number of people in the truck bed. He made a note in a little pocket notebook and tucked it away inside his shirt.

Suddenly, we heard a cry from the infant's mother. She was screaming and holding up her baby, "Oh, my heavenly God, my baby is not breathing! My baby is not breathing! He is dead! My baby!"

Her husband crawled rapidly across the truck bed toward her. He took the baby and shook it from side to side, confirming his wife's fear. "My beautiful baby is dead!" he cried. "Oh, God! Oh, God! What have we done?"

Everyone sat up and moved toward the poor parents. "You choked him too hard," said one of the men.

"I'm sorry for you," said another.

The three-year-old little boy put his hand on his infant brother's stomach, and said, "Wake up, Joseph! Wake up. We are free! We are safe!" But the child did not awaken.

By now, everyone was crying, feeling ashamed and guilty for what they had said earlier in the boat. Saving their own lives had been foremost in their minds, and blame was easy to cast when faced with their own possible deaths.

The Arab guide said nothing, but looked as if he had seen a lot of tragedy in this refugee business.

The mother snatched her baby back from her husband. She sat rocking the infant, murmuring to her dead child, "My baby! My baby! I'm so sorry. I will never forgive myself. Oh, forgive me. Forgive me."

Many of us clung to those close to us or held their hands. We felt the family's loss as if it had been one of our own relatives. We had all become one family in the life and death reality of refugees. Yet, we felt helpless. There was nothing we could do for this family to comfort them, and I as a child could only stare at their dead baby and hold onto Yeftah's hand. I felt that Yeftah's little fingers in mine had suddenly become quite large and heavy and almost more than I could be responsible for. But, I knew that I could not let anything like what had happened to that baby happen to him.

After about an hour of driving, the truck suddenly stopped, and the guide ordered us all to get out. The tailgate was lowered, and the men jumped out first to help the rest of us down. The infant's father was helped down, so that he could assist his wife, who still clutched her dead child tight to her bosom. When we were all out of the truck, the guide motioned for the driver to leave us.

As the truck drove away, we stood in the total darkness in the middle of the desert. Some of the group just sat down on the sand, wondering aloud if we had just been brought out here to be abandoned. The infant's mother sat on the ground with her legs folded under her. She put the baby in her lap and slowly rocked backward and forward, as if in prayer, murmuring unintelligibly.

The guide then spoke to us reassuringly. "You are safe now. Don't worry. You will be the honored guests of our friends, the Bedouins, who will offer you food and drink and a place to sleep for tonight."

In less than an hour, several men appeared silently out of the darkness. They were the Bedouin friends the guide had told us about. These men shook hands with some of the grownups in our company and told us in Arabic to follow them on foot. As the group moved out, the Bedouins conversed quietly in Farsi among themselves. We all were beginning to finally feel safe, but were still in shock about our ordeal and what had happened to the infant.

We walked about twenty minutes in complete silence, which seemed very unusual to our hosts, who were enjoying each other's good company. We soon came to a cluster of tents amid some cows, lambs, and camels. Children were everywhere, running and playing. Yeftah and I felt comfortable because kids could play and make noise and just be kids. We were greeted by the women of the tribe, who all wore colorful, long dresses, and some wore black veils over their faces.

We were motioned to enter a huge tent and sit on the floor, which was covered with colorful mats, like something out of a tale from long ago. We did as our hosts requested, all of us, except the parents of the infant, who were standing outside of the tent, sobbing and talking to their baby.

The guide frowned in sadness as he looked at the young family. Then he left to seek out one of our hosts. The guide whispered in the Bedouin's ear, probably telling him what had happened to the baby. The Bedouin then approached the parents, offering his condolences. He called to his teenage son and whispered something in his ear. The boy ran into another tent, brought a shovel and began to dig a hole in the ground, about a hundred yards away. He returned and told his father that the space was ready. His father approached the parents again and tried to convince them that they should bury their child there.

The mother cried out, "No! Please don't make me leave my baby here in the desert. Please, I can't!"

Her husband hugged her and begged her to listen. "It's the only thing we can do. I love him, too. But, we have to go on. We have to save ourselves and all these people. I beg you."

The three-year-old joined in. "No, please, Daddy, don't let them do this. I want to keep my brother with us. Let's take him with us to Israel."

Adults from our group came out of the tent and began to beg the couple's forgiveness, urging them to bury their child in this land that brought them closer to freedom. The mother continued to wail in mourning. But after a long time, she finally relented, and we all marched silently to the gravesite. The father jumped into the newly dug grave, and reached up for their infant son still wrapped in his blanket, taking him from his wife. He kissed the baby on the forehead and laid him flat in the grave, face up, and then climbed out. He clung to his grieving wife, with their three-year-old son between them, his small face buried in his mother's dress. All of them were sobbing and so were others in our group, and even some Bedouin women were crying quietly.

One of the men asked of the group, "Does anyone know the kaddish?" This was the Jewish prayer for the dead.

A woman stepped to the edge of the grave and began to pray. When the words *"el malleh ra-ha-meem"* (God is full of mercy) were uttered, everyone joined in with her, crying. When the prayer ended, the Bedouin boy motioned for all of us to leave, and he began shoveling the sand back into the grave.

We walked solemnly back toward the tents. The rest of the Bedouins were all sitting around a fire pit where a sheep was roasting, skewered on a rotating spit. The meat smelled wonderful. One of the Bedouin women began to sing a lullaby, and her children joined in. We were all served chunks of lamb in pita bread, and drank water from a military jerry can. Then they served hot tea and fruits and urged every one of us to help ourselves. The grieving family huddled together, eating slowly, without saying a word.

For about two luxurious hours, we sat eating and listening to the singing and the quiet talk around the fire. The stars were very bright in the night sky, far away from city lights, and Yeftah and I marveled at them.

The guide, having thanked our hosts and giving him a hearty farewell hug, confided to a man from our group, "I must leave now. You're in good hands. You all go to sleep in the tent, and tomorrow morning a truck will come to pick you up and take you to Ah-bah-dan. There you will board a train to Tehran."

On hearing that, all of us were full of apprehension. Our hosts had been very gracious, but they had only promised to care for us for one night. We were far into the desert, without our own food and water. Would the Bedouins move camp in the morning and leave us alone out here? Would anyone really come for us in the morning? Who would lead us after the guide was gone? Nevertheless, no one dared to question him.

As the guide was leaving, I pulled my brother close to me and whispered in his ear, "O.K., give me the marble that I gave you. I have to give it to this man before he leaves so he can take it back to father."

Yeftah put his hand inside his pocket and felt under three layers of clothing, but was surprised that no blue marble was there. "I can't find it," he said meekly.

"What do you mean you can't find it?" I asked him, anger and shock welling in me. "You must find it. Otherwise, Father will think that only I made it here alive and that you are dead. He will think I did not take care of you."

Yeftah searched all through his clothing, but couldn't find his blue marble. "It must have fallen out in the boat. I was holding it in my hand when we made the crossing, when they were shooting at us. I'm sorry."

The guide was leaving right then, and I didn't have much time. I had to let Father know that we both were safe. Quickly, I made a decision. I took a pen from the inside pocket of my jacket and wrote "Yeftah" next to my name on my marble. I hoped the ink will hold.

Then I ran after the guide and grabbed his arm. He turned. I said very quietly to him, repeating my father's words, "Take this marble back to my father, Silas Fathi, as a sign that my brother and I both survived. He will reward you handsomely when you bring this to him."

The guide took the marble, examined it closely, and understood. He nodded and said, "I will take it to him within three or four days. I promise." He gave me a small smile, then turned and slipped away into the night. Still, I wasn't sure I could trust him.

Reluctantly, one by one, we filed into the big tent that our Bedouin hosts had prepared for us to sleep in. There were some knitted mats and straw mats on the floor, but no pillows. Families and relatives bunched together, folding our jackets under our heads for pillows. Some rested their heads on their small suitcases, and some actually slept on them; fearing they might be robbed in the night. It was hard to fall asleep in this atmosphere of uncertainty and mistrust. The grownups kept talking, advising everyone who could not fall asleep to do so. Finally, late into the night, we all managed to sleep a little.

In the early hours of the morning, we were awakened by a scream from one of thee women in our group. "No! No! Leave me alone!" she yelled.

One of the Bedouin men was standing over her with a drawn dagger in his hand. He was not trying to kill her, but was trying to remove the jacket and sweater from under her head. Some of the men of our group jumped to their feet and tried to subdue the Bedouin. He waved his dagger violently to the left and right of the men's faces, threatening to slash them. Even though he was outnumbered four to one, he kept them at bay. Finally, one of the men offered a compromise, giving the Bedouin his own sweater. The Bedouin accepted it reluctantly and left the tent in anger.

Everyone was awake by then, all of us frightened and hungry. No breakfast, however, was offered by our hosts. It was as if we had somehow broken some social or moral code, but we didn't know what we had done. We all gathered our belongings and left the tent, looking for the promised truck.

Around 6:30 AM, we spotted a truck on the horizon. We waved and called out to the driver. Within minutes, he stopped about fifty feet from us. The driver and another guide got out and motioned us to load into the truck.

Suddenly, three tall Bedouin men came running out of their tents, daggers in their hands, shouting, "We have given you food and shelter and got nothing back from you. Give us some clothing and jewelry."

That was the unspoken taboo we had broken. We did not know that Bedouin hospitality was meted out in a reciprocal format. They gave to us; they expected a gift for their generosity. I suppose if we had given to them first, they would have felt obligated to give us an equal gift. Everyone else in the chain of people who had helped in our escape had been paid. We did not know that the Bedouins had not been paid by our guides. The Bedouins were not thieves, and we weren't ungrateful guests. We had both not known what the customs and social rules were. That didn't stop us from being frightened or some of us from feeling that we had been robbed.

Two Bedouins posted themselves by the truck and kept us from climbing into the back. They pointed to some of the men of our group and ordered them to take off their jackets. Our friends were trembling with fear, but took out the belongings from their pockets and handed their jackets over to the Bedouins. As each man did that, he was allowed to climb into the truck. During all of this, the driver went to one of the tents and spoke with our Bedouin host. We could hear their loud interchange.

When we were finally all on the truck, the guide counted heads, like our other guide had done. We were now seventeen. The infant's mother looked out of the truck toward the hole in the ground where her son had been buried the day before. She began to cry again, quietly this time. Her husband put his arm around her and comforted her once more.

The driver finally emerged from the Bedouin tent. He appeared to be giving the host something, perhaps money. He walked to the truck, looked us all in the face, and without uttering a word, began to drive. We had no idea of what he had just done nor where he was taking us. We knew the city's name but had no idea in which direction it was since no one knew the local geography. After this last altercation, we had no idea if the driver would take us where we were meant to go or dump us in the desert somewhere to get rid of his troubles.

It was several hours more before we arrived at a train station outside of an Iranian town named Ah-bah-dan. We climbed out of the truck, making sure we had left no personal belongings behind. The driver and the guide helped us form a line by having us all hold hands as they led us to the back of the train. The guide pulled several train tickets out of his pocket and handed them to the infant's father, who appeared to be the leader among us. The driver and the guide shook our hands and assured us that someone would meet us at the end of the line at Tehran. The driver and the guide then left us at the station.

When it was time, we filed into the rear of the train, which was nearly empty. Only a few merchants with their live chickens, some in wooden crates and some strung up on leashes were on board. We were all smiling now. We were happy to have survived all of our ordeals. But, the adults kept admonishing us every time Yeftah and I talked as if our speaking aloud would somehow affect how we were treated. We held our belongings in our laps, trying not to make eye contact with the Iranian peasants. The infant's father appeared to be taking charge of the group, which was reassuring to us because we all seemed to need a leader. We also were glad that he was finding a way to put his own grief in perspective and taking on this responsibility. Everyone spoke to him with a great deal of respect and sympathy.

We spent nearly ten hours on the train. All of us heard horror stories about similar trips by others who had preceded us. Those stories were now passed around our group. One was particularly heart wrenching. Some months earlier, during the winter, the same train had been stopped because of a massive snowstorm. Emergency crews could not reach the train in time. Many perished, freezing to death or dying of thirst and hunger. We were told to count our blessings so far, and also to remember the benevolent Shah, who was friendly to Israel and the Jews, in our prayers.

Yeftah and I thought of our parents. We missed them very much. Did father escape from his sentence? How would Mother and our sisters and little Abraham survive without Father? Did our Arab guide bring them the one marble? Did my father understand that we both were safe? Was the Arab able to convince him?

Upon arrival in Tehran, our group was greeted by several well-dressed men, some dark and some blond, with baskets of fruit beside them on the ground. They bent down and picked up a piece of fruit and offered it to us. "Have some," they said. "They are washed."

We were ushered into waiting cars and driven about forty-five minutes out of town to a gated camp. With fear in our hearts and memories of news reports of Auschwitz and Dachau, we all thought, *This is a concentration camp.*

But it was not. It was a refugee camp where young children from all over the world had been gathered for an organized trip to Israel. We were divided into several tents and wooden barracks, with beds and clean sheets. One of our new guides was a beautiful young girl with a khaki hat, who spoke fluent Arabic, Iranian, English, French, and, of course, Hebrew. She was a mad-ree-kha, an instructor. She told us that we were safe there and explained where the showers and the mess hall were. There was plenty of food and drink available, with three meals a day, a break in mid-morning and another in mid-afternoon. We were not, however, allowed to venture outside the camp. There were scheduled games, dances, and Hebrew lessons to fill our days until we made the voyage to Israel.

During the next three months, our numbers kept swelling. Every day, a new group of children arrived. They were mostly displaced children who had lost their families in the Holocaust. Each one could write a detailed book of the adventures he or she had experienced in their short lives. We played together and learned to understand one another, even though there were over thirty different languages spoken among us. We played outside with balls and jump ropes, and we learned to hold hands in a circle and dance the new Israeli national dance called the Horah. We also learned Hebrew songs and sang the Israeli national anthem, "The Hatikvah" (The Hope) every morning, standing at attention outside of the mess hall.

We were constantly assured that our parents would someday join us in Israel. Some of us wrote tearful letters to our parents, even though we knew there was no way we could mail them since many of our parents were under sentence like my Father. We gave them to the mad-ree-kha, and she kept them all.

Finally, the day of our relocation arrived. We were driven to the airport in several buses and put on an unmarked Constellation airplane. As the plane took off, all of the one hundred and fifty passengers clapped their hands and sang our favorite Hebrew songs. We all thought, *Are we finally 100% safe? What if we get shot down over Arab land? What if we run out of fuel? What if? What if?* A thousand worrisome thoughts swept through our minds. But, our guides, especially the young blond girl with the hat, kept reassuring us that everything would be all right. They said that we were now flying on an Israeli airplane, headed to Israel, but we would not be flying over any Arab country. The flight time would only be four to five hours, depending on several factors. She didn't explain what those were.

We touched down in Lud Airport (later renamed Ben Gurion Airport). We were still singing, laughing, and clapping our hands. We impatiently awaited the stewardess' direction to disembark. When we finally stepped off the aircraft and our feet touched Israeli soil, we all kneeled down and kissed the ground.

We young Jewish children were home at last...
It had only taken 2,600 years.

Section Two

My Life in Israel

1949 – 1958

Silas Fathi, Baghdad, Iraq, 1948 (7)

Chapter Sixteen

Aunt Ruthi, the Fortune Teller

Settling in

Our young uncles, Shlomo and Moshe, who had accompanied us when we had escaped from Baghdad, took us to live with our Uncle Yehuda and Aunt Ruthi. Uncle Shlomo and Uncle Moshe stayed with us while they found work and a place of their own. The most educated of our uncles, these young men worked the orange groves, digging ditches and transplanting trees.

Uncle Yehuda owned a restaurant in the middle of Sha-Ah-ra-yim, the Yemenite village in Rehoboth. Being the eldest uncle in our family in Israel, he became responsible for my brother and me while our family was still in Baghdad. For nearly two years, we could not safely make any contact with our Iraqi family. My father was on a list of prominent Jews in the country, who had been sentenced to be hanged. We worried every day and prayed for him, along with all the other enslaved and persecuted Jews still in Iraq. *Was our father still alive or had he been hanged in public?* Every day we asked this question.

At the same time, our parents were probably worrying whether their two oldest sons had safely made it across the desert into Iran and all the way to Israel. The blue marbles system that Father had created to report our safety had not been foolproof. We were only able to send one marble back with both our names scrawled on it. We didn't know if they had received it or whether both names were legible. Did they think that only one of us had survived?

Aunt Ruthi took care of us day-to-day. We slept in her home, ate her meals, and wore the clothes she gave us to wear. We attended primary school in Rehoboth, learned Hebrew, and made friends.

Yeftah and I spent a restless few months in Rehoboth. Uncle Yehuda and Aunt Ruthi tried to be our parents and hoped to make us forget the family we left behind.

Aunt Ruthi's profession

For over thirty years, my Aunt Ruthi was a famous fortuneteller in Rehoboth, the fifth largest city in Israel. She became a rich woman and always remained independent. She lived in a beautiful house, which the Israelis called a villa. It was private, hidden away in an orange grove, with a big backyard full of flowers, trees, and vegetables. She paid a gardener to help keep everything looking nice, and my aunt loved working in the rich scented soil and bringing seeds to life. It was her own little Garden of Eden.

Her husband, Eliahu, owned a fish store and barely made enough money to feed his six children. Eliahu never liked Aunt Ruthi's profession. He was ashamed of it, but reaped the benefits of her success. He lived in luxury and prestige because of her.

A long time ago, Aunt Ruthi had read her own future. She predicted that she was going to be competitive, strong, and independent by being a palm reader. Except, instead of reading hands, she read coffee grounds. This was an art she learned from an old unmarried Egyptian poet who lived next door with his sister.

The Israelis called the bitter brew *fin-Jan*. Aunt Ruthi served it in a very small cup. The coffee was dark black, thick, and very strong. After you drank it, she turned the cup upside down over the saucer. The coffee grains left mysterious images on the inside wall of the cup. Aunt Ruthi would gaze at it very seriously and tell your past and future—and whatever else you might wish to hear.

I remember seeing her single, lonely clients come for encouraging news that they would meet someone to love. And then there were the married husbands, in love with beautiful young women who weren't their wives, who came to Aunt Ruthi, begging to know how such complicated relationship would be resolved.

While my parents lived in a shack in Ramah, I was sent to live with my aunt's family for a few weeks because I was suffering from bronchial asthma, which, incredibly, my parents believed was all in my head. Though the climate was the same, they imagined I would feel better living in a plush villa.

During the years I lived in Israel (1949-1958), I saw Aunt Ruthi build up quite a clientele. People came to the house from morning to night. Sometimes they wore disguises, either because they were ashamed of something they were about to reveal or because they didn't want anyone to recognize them in such a place. My aunt's house was a perfect place for hosting this secret section of society.

At the time, fortune telling was seen by most people as equal to astrology or the interpretation of dreams, both suspect arts that preyed on innocent and vulnerable people. Aunt Ruthi's clients wanted to believe everything she told them. They came so they could be amazed by how she could guess secrets that no one else knew and some they didn't even know themselves. Aunt Ruthi was an excellent judge of character and could read people's faces, carefully watching how the eyes, wrinkles, and lips reacted to her every word. She had different lines delivered for every grimace, smile, or tear.

Aunt Ruthi kept a beautiful jeweled box on a small table near the living room door. In this box, her clients left their payments. After each session, I liked to imagine counting all the Lyrot (later, shekels) her clients left behind in that box. I noticed that the more positive expectations she gave them, the bigger her tip. As years passed and so many predictions came true, Aunt Ruthi even began to believe them herself.

When her children (Miriam, Ezra, Mazal, Anat, Tamir, and Eitan) came home from school during working hours, they knew not to disturb her and her guests. When I was living with her, we children entered the dimly lit house and went straight up to our rooms. My cousins were never that interested in their mother's business life, but I was curious all the time about its mysteries and ways. Here was a married woman who didn't have to depend on her husband to pay for a luxurious home; she managed it all on her own earning power. This was unusual, as only those of third and fourth generation born in Israel before all the wars were able to reach such status.

One day, I learned that one of Aunt Ruthi's business secrets was that she never declared her fortune telling income to the state. Therefore, she never paid taxes on all of this money and was able to keep more of it.

Dissatisfied customer demands refund

Once a dissatisfied customer came by the villa. She demanded that Aunt Ruthi give her back the money she had paid for a fortune telling session. I heard the woman say, "Nothing you told me came true. You're a fraud. You're ignorant. You know nothing."

Aunt Ruthi was steadfast and refused to give the woman a refund. The client threatened to go to the police and expose her for not paying taxes. My Aunt the Fortune Teller told her, "Go ahead. Your fate will be even more hopeless." (Implying she will cast a spell on her.)

When Uncle Eliahu heard this, he begged his wife to refund the money and spare herself from going to jail or having to pay a big fine.

Aunt Ruthi told him, "Don't worry, I am not going to jail."

A few days passed before a police car showed up. The tall officer in uniform was very impressive with all his medals and citations pinned to his chest. I was surprised when Aunt Ruthi greeted him like an old friend. He was the Chief of Police of Rehoboth, and he was one of her most admiring clients. My cousins and I knew the story of his affair with a woman young enough to be his daughter. How he wished that Aunt Ruthi could unravel his future.

That particular day, he sat down to his usual double-cup of coffee. This time, however, it was the Chief of Police who turned the cup upside down, looked inside, and, with a smile, began to tell his fortuneteller's own fortune. "Look what I see," he remarked. "Someone paid off your tattletale to shut her up. The taxman will never darken your door. You must have some secret admirers, Ruthi." My aunt and he smiled in conspiracy and slowly nodded their heads. I guess in secret societies, people have to look out for each other.

The mysterious case of the disappearing cat

Though Aunt Ruthi could handle the most disgruntled customer, she had a problem with felines. Beware my aunt's wrath if you were a cat found in the great fortuneteller's presence! My aunt was just like my mother in this way. My mother didn't like animals of any kind. I suppose this reaction was due to their upbringing.

I remember the time some stray cats wandered into Aunt Ruthi's backyard. We kids had fun feeding and petting them. From our own rations, we sneaked out bowls of milk to the cats. But soon, Aunt Ruthi found out. Broom in hand, she would try to chase the cats away. But, none of us children knew that she was driving them away.

Every day, we returned home from school to find fewer cats in the yard. One little cutie boldly hung around, refusing to be intimidated, even by such a fierce witch as my aunt.

"They just up and go," Aunt Ruthi told us, then she revealed a bit of her true feelings. "It's okay. Let other people take care of them."

One day, we saw Aunt Ruthi chasing the cats out of the yard and wondered where the poor animals would go. We were distraught that the little cutie we had all grown fond of would be chased away to starve if we took no action. We children all got together and decided to hide the little brown-and-white cat we had named Cutie under one of our beds, out of the way of the sweeping broom. When Aunt Ruthi was busy with her clients, we took food and milk from the kitchen and brought it to the little cat, hidden in one of our rooms. We liked watching her sharp pink tongue slurp the white liquid into her kitten mouth.

Cutie wasn't so happy being confined under the bed all day. While the children were at school, she hauled herself out to wander around outside. She enjoyed the fresh air of the big garden and meandered among its blooms. A cat in the garden was not Aunt Ruthi's favorite sight! When Aunt Ruthi saw the cat there, she took Cutie on a bus to the next town and let her go in the wilds of some other neighborhood. Aunt Ruthi was certain that a little cat could never find her way back, with no tracks or scents to follow.

When we came home from school, we ran into the bedroom to play with Cutie, a pastime that had become our favorite part of the day. But on this day, the cat was nowhere to be found. My cousin Eitan had a sneaking suspicion his mother might have had something to do with Cutie's disappearance.

Eitan asked his mother if she had seen any cats around that day, and she was happy to report that they lived in a highly refined home without animals around messing things up. Eitan feared the worst. He began to cry and admitted his feelings for our little Cutie.

"I swear I didn't see her today," Aunt Ruthi lied blithely. "She must be wandering around the neighborhood. They don't like to be kept confined, you know." She used all her most conniving ways to convince us this was the truth. But we knew her too well, and we didn't buy her story. To me, she looked guilty.

Every day thereafter, we came home and looked under the bed and in the garden for our dear little Cutie. We put bowls of milk under draping leaves hoping to lure Cutie back, but every day there was no Cutie to come home to.

Two weeks went by and we were deep in mourning. Then one afternoon, when we were passing through the garden path on the way into the house, we heard a sweet meow coming from the trees in the backyard. To our amazement, Cutie had somehow found her way back to Aunt Ruthi's house! She was hiding among the trees because she knew the "enemy" lurked nearby. Pushing aside leaves and branches, we discovered our kitty and embraced and kissed her.

Thereafter, we vowed, we would donate all our food to her, because, of course, we had to be allowed to keep her now. Aunt Ruthi was a superstitious woman, and she saw in this return an Omen.

"You see, she must have gotten lost, the poor cat. But, by the will of God, she found her way back to us," she said to her happy children as we all surrounded Cutie. My cousins were allowed to keep their loveable kitten after all.

Aunt Ruthi moves to the US

When Aunt Ruthi was fifty years old, she moved to the US to join her daughter Miriam, who had married and immigrated to America. Though Uncle Eliahu was still alive, he and Aunt Ruthi didn't get along well anymore and had many fights. She used to say "all he knows is how to father children." I guess to her he had outlived his usefulness so she left him in Israel.

Aunt Ruthi was so rich she could buy another grand house when she settled in Miami, within walking distance from Miriam and her family. The house was like a castle for that neighborhood and that era.

Even though she had moved halfway around the world, don't think her loyal clients couldn't find her. Old El Al flight attendants tracked her down and went all the way to a new continent to have their futures told by Ruthi the Witch, their nickname for her. It wasn't long before she had a booming business in the United States, doing what she loved. She lived in her new country the same way she did in the old one, by relying on instincts as ancient as Babylon. She studied human nature by coffee fortune telling. She started charging $100 a session (no more counting shekels). And clients were always showering her with gifts: porcelain figurines, crystal vases, and other objects that she collected over the years.

Aunt Ruthi takes up painting

In old age, Aunt Ruthi took up a new hobby, oil painting. She was good, though not great, but she sold some of her works to her fortune telling clients for over $500. What I loved most about her was that she never gave up, especially when she set her mind to something. She really knew people. She knew how to read them. She could see their secrets in a cup of coffee. A lot of psychoanalysts would give their right arms to know how she did it. But that was her secret, and none of us ever knew.

Chapter Seventeen

Stealing oranges with Yeftah

On very hot afternoons, Yeftah and I often felt bored and very broke since we no longer had an allowance and had no opportunity to buy on account as we had done in Baghdad. We were growing boys, away from the close watch of our parents, and we wanted some action!

One day, we walked outside of our usual boundary of the town's main street, Hertzl Street, and found ourselves in the midst of vast groves of oranges and lemons. That was when Yeftah had an idea.

"Why don't we steal some fruit? There're so many, no one will notice," he said. "We can go into town and sell them to restaurants and get ourselves a little pocket money."

It sounded good, but something bothered me. "What if we get caught?"

My eight-year-old brother waved his hand in a dismissive gesture and then poked his finger at my forehead. "Think a little with that big brain of yours," he said. "Would I let us get caught?"

I shrugged and pushed his hand away. Though two years younger than I was, he always had schemes that he was able to pull off. "Okay," I agreed. "What's the plan?"

Yeftah had it all figured out. "I'll go inside the fence and pluck the oranges and lemons. You sit here on the sidewalk and watch for anyone coming," he instructed. "If you see anyone, warn me by singing this song, 'Watch out for the wolf; he is coming to bite you.' If I hear you singing, I'll stop stealing fruit and go hide in the trees. As soon as you stop singing, I'll go back to work."

I liked his plan. It seemed foolproof. "Okay, but you must pay attention and act quickly when you hear me sing," I said.

Yeftah agreed without further word and climbed under the fence, slipping into the thick citrus grove. I watched as he took off his shirt and tied the ends of the sleeves, forming a sack.

Soon, I could hardly see him, but I could hear his stealthy movements as he began shaking the trees to save the effort of climbing. He piled oranges in his makeshift sack, laid open upon on the ground.

After awhile, a car passed, and I became afraid so I began to sing, but not loud enough for Yeftah to hear me. He merrily continued to pile up fruit. His shirt was nearly full. I began singing impromptu lyrics, "Let's get going to the park; we have enough to eat and drink. It is getting late. Let's go, let's get going…."

Yeftah paid no attention to me, deeply intent on his work.

Though the car had passed without incident, I suddenly heard horses galloping toward us from the far end of the grove.

I sang, "Someone is coming. Let's go. We have enough. Hurry up."

My brother either thought I was bluffing or he was too greedy to leave before grabbing as much as he could carry because he never even paused in his picking. He ignored me and continued piling oranges and lemons into a grand pyramid of fruit. It was then that Yeftah decided to climb the nearest orange tree to get more fruit.

We were in deep trouble. The horsemen were the guardians of the groves. I watched one gallop toward Yeftah. My heart was pounding. It was too late to warn him, and he wouldn't listen to me anyway. I hid behind a pole along the side of the road as I watched the guard confront my brother.

"Young man, what are you doing?" the guard said to Yeftah in a stern tone my brother jumped down from the tree, startled.

Then the man's voice softened. "You could have asked me for some. I would have given them to you."

Yeftah spoke quickly and earnestly, "I am sorry. But, it's not for me." The little storyteller had begun one of his elaborate excuses. "It's for my sick aunt who can't afford to buy them. I just wanted to help."

The guard got off his horse and looked at Yeftah closely. Then he looked at how many oranges my brother had piled onto his shirt. He turned on Yeftah. "I don't believe your story. Who is your aunt?"

Yeftah hesitated then said quickly. "Her name is Ruth. You don't know her."

"Ruth what?" the man demanded. "What's her last name?"

Everyone knew everyone in that town so Yeftah didn't want to let the guard know who Aunt Ruthi was so he hesitated answering.

"Tell me her last name or I am calling the police," the guard threatened.

"Ah, ah," Yeftah stammered, thinking wildly for some name, but all that came out was Aunt Ruthi's real name. "Ruth Sofer. Her name is Ruth Sofer."

"Ruth Sofer is your aunt?" the man asked. "Does her husband have a fish store in the market?"

Yeftah nearly fainted. He knows Aunt Ruthi! *How can I get out of this?* Yeftah wondered, and frankly so did I.

"Yes, that's her, my aunt Ruth. She is very sick, waiting for me to bring the oranges."

The guard broke into loud laughter. "Your Aunt Ruth the Fortune Teller is not sick. I was just there with my girlfriend, and she read our futures with great energy and health. Your Aunt Ruth is not sick, young man, and besides, she is so rich she could buy the entire grove!" He continued to laugh.

Yeftah realized that he was in very deep trouble now. So what does he do? He decides to share the blame by pointing out his accomplice, me, his loving brother. "Ask my brother. I am telling the truth," Yeftah said, pointing his finger at me hiding by the side of the road.

The guard still didn't believe him so Yeftah tried another tactic. "Okay, you can have your oranges back. Just let me go."

I felt sorry for my brother even though he had talked me into this scheme. I crawled under the fence and joined my brother. I was, after all, just as guilty, especially since I was the elder.

The orange grove guard stood, grasping the horse's reins with one hand and holding a long whip in the other. I looked at the whip and was scared. I didn't want to be whipped, so I begged for mercy. "Please let us go," I groveled. "Just this one time. We will never do this again."

Yeftah looked down at the earth and nodded in agreement.

The man just laughed at us, more and more, louder and louder. "Go ahead, take what you have this time. Maybe your aunt will give me a discount the next time I visit her."

Yeftah grabbed his shirt full of citrus and handed it to me. As we crawled under the fence, we waved to the man and his horse as he mounted. "Thank you," I called and Yeftah just stamped his feet.

We walked a mile back to town in total silence. Then that little thief began trying to pin the blame on me. "You didn't sing loud enough," he said. "I didn't hear you."

"Yes, I did," I insisted and then remembered just how narrow an escape we had made. "I think we should just forget about it."

Yeftah continued his silence; obviously he was deep in thought. Finally, he told me what he was thinking. "Let's not take the oranges to Aunt Ruth. Let's go to Uncle Yehuda and offer them to him and his customers at the restaurant. He will pay us for them."

Why did I think I should trust another of his foolproof plans? But I did. Yeftah always had a very convincing way about him.

When we arrived at our uncle's restaurant, I stood outside with the oranges while Yeftah went in and turned his charms on Uncle Yehuda. "We have some very nice oranges and lemons for your customers," Yeftah said. "Are you interested?"

Uncle Yehuda's eyes, so full of wisdom, looked directly into Yeftah's. The old man had to know these were stolen fruit. How else could a boy come up with such a prize? He had to play it safe. Slowly, he answered, with a wry grin, "Only if you are willing to go into the kitchen and turn them into juice."

Yeftah believed he had fooled our uncle and motioned me to come in. I was filled with shame, but I followed my brother into the kitchen. We didn't say a word as we squeezed all the oranges into huge pitchers. Then we squeezed all the lemons into a smaller pitcher, stirring them well. We emerged into the restaurant and put all the pitchers on Uncle Yehuda's table, where he and a group of friends sat playing cards.

"Here is the juice," Yeftah said. "Freshly squeezed and delicious."

Uncle Yehuda laughed good-naturedly and reached for some coins on the table. He put them into Yeftah's right palm.

"Go have something to eat," he said. "And I hope your poor sick Aunt Ruth is feeling better soon."

We couldn't walk out of the restaurant fast enough. Totally mystified, Yeftah shouted at me, "How did he know?"

"He knew all along that they were stolen," I said.

"He played us for fools!" Yeftah answered.

We went straight to Aunt Ruthi's house, praying that the grove guard had not told her of our escapade. We never knew if she found out about our afternoon of stealing and lying and making juice as punishment. If she knew, she never said anything to us about it, and we chalked it all up to experience.

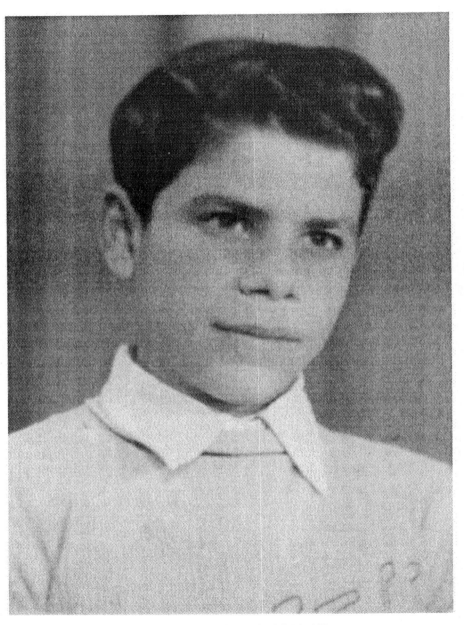

Saul age 13, Israel, 1951 (8)

Chapter Eighteen

Little Runaways

After about six months with Uncle Yehuda and Aunt Ruthi and some more embarrassing deeds, my brother and I decided to run away and hitch a ride to Tel-Aviv. Authorities of the *Sukhnut* met us, and listened to our tale. We told them we were orphans, without anyone to look after us, and that we wished to live among other displaced children of the big war. We felt neglected living with our aunt and uncle, with little sympathy for our plight. The officials promised to take care of notifying Aunt Ruthi.

I don't know if they believed us or just went along with our desire to live with other children our own age. They sent us to Tiv-On, a children's camp in a beautiful region on the Mount Carmel range near Haifa. There were hundreds of acres of green forests around us and lush grass to play in. We felt serene and safe.

Life at Tiv-On

At Tiv-On, we met children from Rumania, Czechoslovakia, Turkey, Syria, Poland, and North Africa. We had been gathered from around the world, displaced children, victims of wartime and ancient animosities, but we were treated gently and lovingly here. With no other family around, we connected ourselves to each other as brothers and sisters. Over thirty languages were spoken, but very little Hebrew, yet somehow we managed to understand one another

We also learned of each horrific story they had to tell of being separated from family and friends and smuggled into Israel as we had been. The kids were near our ages, between eight and twelve years old. We were all so young, yet we had already lost our innocence and childhoods forever.

Our days were spent studying, playing, singing, dancing, and practicing sports. On the playground, we learned games from all of the other children. On Friday nights in Tiv-On, we gathered around big fires, linked our hands, and danced until the early hours of the morning. We sang the songs of Israel, old Russian songs translated into Hebrew. But our hearts were all sad. We felt lost, alone, and guilty. We wondered, *Are we having too much of a good time while our families are being held hostage in Baghdad? Will they ever be allowed to join us in Israel?*

We all shared the yearning to see our families once again and to know they had somehow survived, but some children already knew that that was just a dream. Many children had no kin. In fact, they slept with nightmares from having watched their parents, siblings, and other loved ones let into the gas chambers in the concentration camps of Europe. Some came to Tiv-On weighing less than ninety pounds, their bones bulging from their legs, arms, and chest.

The *madrekhim,* or supervising teachers, knew everyone's story. They were kind and sympathetic as they took on the role of substitute parents.

My brother and I, in contrast, were lucky. We were very healthy, physically and mentally, and required little attention from the *madrekhim.* All of us children, however, found peace in each other's company.

We told the other children about the good times we remembered, growing up in Baghdad. Some of them told us their stories, of how lucky they had been in their lives before the war and during their escape. A number of children had been sheltered by Christian neighbors and therefore saved. People stepped up, even knowing they faced mortal punishment if discovered, because it was the right thing to do.

After three months of bonding together, the *madrekhim* led us out to stand in a long line. They were doing a roll call, and we had to answer, "Present," as our names were called, which we did. This was something that had never happened before. We listened carefully as we heard then that we were about to be divided and sent to more permanent quarters to different kibbutzim far away.

We didn't want to be separated. We all bunched close together, holding hands, as if to beg to stay together. Everyone was crying. Unfortunately, we were powerless. Our fate had already been decided by others. We were to be divided among several kibbutzim, based on age, ethnicity, and each kibbutz's willingness to absorb a certain number of children.

We were handed papers listing our names and destinations. The move would take place the next morning when buses arrived to take us to the kibbutzim.

We knew in our hearts that we would probably never see each other again. We were all sad and angry. Nevertheless, we had no choice. We were mere children at the mercy of the large forces of history. We were told that we should stop crying and to put these feelings aside. "You have survived so much in your young lives," the *madrekhim* told us, "you will surely survive this separation. Keep in mind that we will still all be in Israel, safe and secure, in our ancestors' promised homeland."

Right then, as young boys and girls, we wiped our tears away with our sleeves and vowed to be people of courage.

The next morning, we boarded buses, each marked with a separate destination. Yeftah and I, along with thirty other children, climbed into a bus with the sign for Kibbutz Ma'anit. We sat by a window and waved to our friends, who were heading off to other places. No bus moved until all of the children were aboard.

Our *madrekhim* at the camp were not so brave themselves as their own tears fell when they waved goodbye to us. The buses, in a line on the winding dirt road, slowly pulled away, one by one. At the end of the road, each bus veered off in a different direction. We wanted to feel happy again and tried to look forward to our next home. Someone began singing a Hebrew song we had learned at Tiv-On, a song that was sung by the Red Army soldiers during World War II. It made us feel connected to something larger than ourselves.

Life in Kibbutz Ma'anit

Two hours passed, then the driver announced that we had arrived at Kibbutz Ma'anit. We looked for a big sign, but there was none. With our small suitcases and other belongings, we stepped off the bus. The kibbutz office was near the gate entrance where the officials waited to greet us.

"Welcome. Welcome," one woman said and opened her arms toward us.

"Smile a little," said a man in the back "This is not a funeral."

We tried to smile, but it didn't come easily.

"That's better," he said. "You are going to have a lot of fun. You will work a little and learn many things. This is your home now. You are safe here." The man looked us over, then continued. "My name is Murdi. I will be your supervisor and teacher and a substitute father. Come to me with your problems or anxieties. I can help you."

The woman then said, "Follow me."

We followed her and Murdi to a large mess hall where we were offered milk and sandwiches made of dark bread, margarine, and jam. That was a good beginning. We devoured everything.

Then, we were given papers to fill out, written in Hebrew, of course, which was fast becoming our new Mother Tongue.

"This is only a formality," Murdi told us. "Fill out what you can; leave blank what you cannot. Especially, tell us your name, your date of birth, your last address, and the name and address of a relative, in case of an emergency."

All of the kids looked at each other in amazement. *What last address? What relatives? Don't you know where we've come from?* Everyone wrote his or her name and age and left the rest of the page blank.

Murdi glanced at each page as he piled them on his desk. "It's okay," he said, smiling kindly. "I understand."

We were shown where we would sleep, a wooden barracks with bunk beds for eight children. There were drawers for our clothes and shelves for our personal belongings. The baths were public, with no toilets or showers. We had to take our clothes and walk about a hundred yards to them, just as we had done in Tiv-On.

Some girls chose to room with the boys, which was okay with Murdi. Yeftah and I didn't have to stay together, which was a delight to him. He wanted to be with kids his own age and not under his brother's watchful eyes. This left me feeling freer to focus on my own growing needs and not to worry so much about him.

At dinner, we entered the crowded mess hall in a single line with our trays in our hands. We picked up what we wished from the selection of food. If you had a problem eating what was cooked, you could help yourself to bread, jam, and margarine. There was always plenty of fresh milk.

On our first night, we were introduced to other teachers and *madrekhim*. They spread out among us, sitting with groups of children, at least one per table.

Hebrew was spoken here, becoming our common way of communicating. We were eager to learn it and speak it well. Knowing Hebrew meant that you were more accepted among the Jewish people here in Israel and were less of an outsider. Our teachers told us that we should try to lose our accents as soon as possible.

"We are in Israel now," our teachers said, "in our country, with our own unique, Biblical language."

Everyday thereafter, we spent four hours in the classroom and another four hours at work. The rest of the day was ours to do as we pleased. Our work was assigned to us by our *madrekhim*. Some children cleaned the cowshed; some the chicken coops. Others worked in the fields or picked fruit and vegetables.

Life in Ma'anit had its routines and pleasures and surprises, even as we all missed our families and wondered what they might be doing or whether we'd ever see them again. Everyday, we cleaned ourselves up after our work and had an early dinner. Then, we all set about playing a game—dominos, backgammon, marbles, or even spin-the-bottle. Sometimes, we would build a bonfire to dance and sing around.

My horse Malchik

I worked under the banana trees. I learned to drive a flatbed wagon drawn by a horse and park it as close to the tree as possible. Standing on the flatbed, I could cut off bunches of green bananas and pile them up high on the wagon bed. It was fun, but physically challenging. Who knew that I was destined to live in a place with such fringe benefits: all of the bananas I could eat!

My horse's name was Malchik. I don't know who had named him. He was golden brown and very old and very gentle. I loved him. Before Malchik, I had never touched an animal of any kind, much less ride and care for one. I surprised even myself when I learned to gallop!

After a day's work, I'd take Malchik to his stable where I'd hose him down, brush his hair, and feed him. You might think that a horse's favorite food would be hay, but my Malchik preferred watermelon! I made sure he had plenty of both hay and watermelon by bartering with my newfound friends. I would give them bananas in return for fruit, eggs, watermelons, and vegetables.

Malchik and I shared a beautiful, happy, and mutually beneficial relationship. My horse carried me where I needed to go, and I rewarded him with food, drink, and lots of kind strokes.

Letters from the heart to my parents

We loved our teachers and trusted them with our deepest, personal problems. It was Murdi who suggested one day that we write letters to our families and loved ones, even though there was no way to deliver them. It was good to vent our anger, express our love, and even whine a little. Writing down all our feelings helped ease our longings.

I began writing a diary and swore to make a daily entry, no matter what. Slowly but surely, the pages filled. Yeftah and I both wrote letters to our parents, but we addressed them to my Uncle Yehuda in the hope that someday he would be able to hand them to our parents. I also wanted him to know of our longings, and I asked him to visit us at the kibbutz. Many children had relatives, who visited them on the Sabbath. We gathered each Friday at the entrance, waiting for a visit or a letter. But no one ever visited us or wrote any letters. *Did everyone assume we were safe? Or did they think we were ungrateful and here having a great time? Did they forget we existed?*

Once in awhile, we were given bus money to go visit our relatives and spend a few days with them. During one visit to Uncle Yehuda's restaurant, I was appalled to see my tearful letters stacked on top of the refrigerator, unopened. I took them and hid them in my coat pocket, still hoping to show my parents someday. I felt so unloved.

When I shared these feelings with my brother, he told me to let it alone. But then, Yeftah always took matters more lightly than I did.

Concentration Camp survivor

On Friday nights, we celebrated *Oneg Shabbat* (the pleasure of the Sabbath) in the mess hall, singing and dancing. One older woman played lively piano tunes while another accompanied her on the violin. We especially enjoyed the heartfelt melodies from the accordion, which was played by a tall, very skinny, young *madrikh*. He liked to wear his shirt unbuttoned, which showed his skin and bones. His blond hair was wild and never combed; he would just run his fingers through it and let it fall over one eye.

Whispers circulated about this *madrikh*, about who he was, what he had been through to bring him to Ma'anit. It was rumored that at sixteen, he had witness his beloved mother being led away from him to the gas chambers in Treblinka. He was allowed to live because he was strong and healthy enough to work in the Nazi factories, making weapons. Though the Americans had freed his camp and ultimately saved his life, he felt that the Allies should have bombed the concentration camps and the railroads leading to them. The prisoners would indeed have been killed, but millions more would have been spared, he believed. If Hitler had not invaded Russia and attempted to defeat England, the world would have stood back and let the Nazi dictator solve his Jewish problem through more and more mass murder.

At night, many of us cried with sympathy for this *madrikh*. We tried to imagine how it was possible for him to survive such trauma.

Friends at Ma'anit

We lived at Kibbutz Ma'anit nearly a year and a half. During those days,

Yeftah and I made many friends. We learned to trust and to love children from
places we had not even heard of before. There were children from places and
experiences so different from our own, who began as strangers and ended up
becoming our brothers and sisters.

The *madrekhim* were able to truly become surrogate parents to the displaced
children of the world. We all experienced a deep sense of belonging there. We
were kept busy all of our waking hours. We learned to speak Hebrew, a new
language to many of us, a language as ancient as the land and the ways of our
people. We sang Hebrew songs together in one voice. Many children learned to
write Hebrew that first year together. Some of us were better at adapting than
others. The older, more self-assured ones or those with an easier upbringing
coped better. Sometimes, it depended on the reason the child was there in the first
place. The saddest among us were the ones who pretended that they had felt no
pain.

Aliza the "Saf-tah"

One girl was singled out by the cruel and insensitive children—there are
always a few in every group. Her name was Aliza and was born in Iraq. She was
thin and tall for her age and long braided hair. Word was circulating that she had
reached puberty, of which many of us were on the verge anyway. It made her an
adult and not a child among us, further separating her from the rest of us.

This cruel rumor came from some of the children who were in wonder and
awe of the mysterious concept of reproduction and birth. Some kids, out of their
own insecurities probably, needed a target, someone to vent their cruelty on. A
few boys and girls had noticed Aliza's frequent trips to the supply room, called
Afsa-ni-yah, and they began calling her *Saf-tah* (Grandmother).

The boys were too bewildered by their own changing bodies and personal
needs to consider they might be causing her pain by bestowing such public
attention to this intimate matter. The girls cringed and whispered among
themselves, curious about which one of them would be the next *Saf-tah*.

Aliza spent her free time alone, reading in her room with her door closed. A
girl who used to be her friend noticed her absence one day and knocked on her
door, asking her to come out. Aliza emerged red eyed. She had been crying in her
room. When she joined us for meals or work, she hardly ever smiled now.

I tried to treat her well and welcome her, though I felt I might be suffering
isolation from my friends. I sat with Aliza in the mess hall sometimes, and we
danced together on *Oneg Shabbat*. We liked talking walks in the tall, green
eucalyptus and "brush" trees, usually ending at our ritual spot under one special,
tall eucalyptus where we sat together talking. It was easy to talk to each other,
and we both listened sympathetically as we each revealed a little more of our
personal stories. We shared about our lives before we came to Israel and how we
came to be here. We pondered our futures as we lingered in the eternity of those
sweet summer moments.

On one particular afternoon, Aliza asked, "I see you writing in the library. It looks like letters. Are they letters?"

"Yes," I answered. "I like writing letters. It helps me pour out my heart."

"But, letters to whom?"

"My parents."

"But how can they ever read your letters? Do you know where they are?"

"No," I admitted. "I just write to them. But I mail them to my Uncle Yehuda in Rehoboth. Someday, I hope my parents will read them." I held that wish close to my heart. Then, I asked Aliza," Do you write letters?"

She shrugged and threw her arms in the air. "To whom? I have no one. I am alone in this country. I had an uncle, but he was killed in the War of Independence. When my parents sent me here, they thought he was alive, and would take me in and protect me."

She didn't know if her parents were alive or dead. I found out years later that they were never reunited. She lived in the kibbutz until she went into the Israeli Army at seventeen.

The sun was lowering over the treetops as we suddenly realized how long we had been gone.

"We might miss dinner!" I said.

"Or worse," she said, "new rumors will be sprouting in the kibbutz about us!"

"Well, enough talk for one day," I said and held my hand out to help Aliza stand. We walked in the twilight along the narrow pathway back to our barracks. No one saw us as we parted each time with a squeeze of hands and a friendly hug.

We spent many hours, even entire afternoons like this, and I remember them all well. Was Aliza what some might call my first love? Perhaps. She certainly shared my heart through those years at Kibbutz Ma'anit.

Drowning in Caesarea

Among the most enjoyable activities at Kibbutz Ma'anit were the field outings we took throughout our new country. In the ancient city of Caesarea, on the Mediterranean Sea, we explored the remnants of the Roman Empire and marveled at the engineering ingenuity that went into construction of the port. Antiquities from the Byzantine and Crusades periods had been uncovered there. A magnificent Roman amphitheatre of 4,000 seats, built by Hordus over 2500 years ago, was nearly intact. The great walls of ancient Caesarea could hold back high waves from the sea. Though these walls are underwater now, at the time I was there, its manmade strength was awe-inspiring.

The day we went to Caesarea was a typical hot summer day, and we were permitted to swim and dive in small groups. About two hours into this marvelous activity, I encountered a swirling cone-shaped phenomenon in the seawater, a whirlpool, which overpowered me and pulled me to the bottom. As I reached the floor of the ocean, I thrust myself with all my power to the top. When my head was above water, I shouted "Help" several times but was pulled back down again and again to the bottom. I swallowed the ocean's salty water and felt sure I was doomed to die that very day.

At that moment an old memory flashed before my eyes: I had nearly drowned in Baghdad when I was six years old and was saved by a British officer named Rudely. But I wasn't in Baghdad, and the British were not around to save me. I was drowning in Caesarea, struggling for air. Suddenly, I felt the hand of one of my beloved teachers, a loving lady from Czechoslovakia, pulling me from the undertow by my long, curly hair.

On the beach, I was placed facedown and helped to vomit out the water I had swallowed with a finger thrust into my throat. Then, someone lifted me by my feet into the air. All my friends from the kibbutz gathered around, watching to see if I was breathing normally. Once I was sure I would live, I felt ashamed and guilty for spoiling the field trip for everybody.

I didn't speak for the duration of the bus trip home as I realized that this was the second time I had beaten the angel of death in a drowning incident. Little did I know that this ill-fated brush with a watery death would happen again and again through my life.

Chapter Nineteen

Reunion with My Parents

In August 1950, about two years after our escape from Baghdad, my parents were permitted to register to immigrate from Iraq, as long they signed papers renouncing their citizenship and all claims and possessions. They also had to promise never to return to the homeland where they were born.

With heavy hearts, my parents, Silas and Salha, boarded a commercial plane to Cypress and then took another to Israel. On this journey, they brought with them two children, the same age as Yeftah and me. My parents had to find substitutes for me and my brother on their Iraqi ID cards, otherwise they would have to explain where we were and face severe punishment for our escape. They went to a local Jewish orphanage and made arrangements to "adopt" two kids our age and bring them along to Israel.

On their arrival, those boys were put in Kibbutz Hadassah and lived there happily. This act of kindness served to save my parents' lives, by acting as if these orphans were their missing children. They also saved the lives of those two Jewish boys who would otherwise have been forced to grow up as Muslims, in forced conversions much like their brethren, the Sephardic Jews of Spain, some 500 years earlier.

As our parents were flying from one country to another, my brother and I were doing our daily chores at Kibbutz Ma'anit. Later that day, we were called to the office. Murdi sat behind his desk with a big grin on his face. Then, he told us that our parents and siblings had arrived safely in Israel. Silas and Salha had found us by searching government archives that said we had been placed at this kibbutz. I hugged Yeftah very hard at the news, but I wasn't convinced Murdi wasn't joking.

"When? When will they come to see us?" I asked.

"Today, at 3:00 PM. They will come on the 3:00 PM bus."

Yeftah and I left the office, full of happiness and holding hands for the first time in months. I thought of asking my parents at the first opportunity, "Well, didn't I take good care and protect my brother as I promised you?"

A few minutes before 3:00 o'clock, our favorite teacher Murdi told the whole class that our parents were going to be here in Israel very soon! The whole class cheered and clapped their hands. We felt so many feelings all at once.

Yeftah and I ran to the fence and stood where the bus had to slow down along the curve in the road. As we waited, Yeftah kept jumping up and down.

"I wonder what they look like now. I wonder what they brought with them for us," he said.

At 3:10, we spotted a bus crawling in the distance on the dusty dirt road. We began jumping and waving.

"Here they are. I see them," I shouted, lifting my brother up above the fence so he could see them too.

"Where?" he shouted for a few minutes, until we spotted a man sticking his head out the window and waving back at us. It was our father!

Father didn't want to wait until the bus arrived all the way at the office. He called to the driver to please let him down right there where we were standing. The driver agreed! One by one, my mother, my father, my brother, and my sisters appeared. Our mother was carrying our new baby sister! Her name was Judith.

Yeftah pointed at each one of them and called their names. Berta, Yedida, Hannah, Avram, Pirha, Judith, Mother, and Father. They ran toward our fence until they could touch our fingers through the chain links and kiss each other. Yeftah climbed the fence, with father helping to pull him up. I ran over a quarter mile to the only opening in the fence and back that same quarter mile toward them. They ran to meet me along the way. What a glorious day!

We all spoke at twice the normal speed, mixing Hebrew with Arabic. Yeftah and I tried to tell them all that we had gone through, not pausing for a minute to hear their side of the story.

Before we left Iraqi, my father had been blacklisted along with other prominent Jews in Baghdad and destined to be hanged like so many others. We all had gone into hiding, and Father never showed up at his government job as head of the Railroad Systems. My family left their house without selling it and moved to an apartment on the third floor of a big apartment house, where we all stayed until arrangements had been made for Yeftah and me to escape to Israel.

My family remained there until they could leave by government decree. Beginning in the middle of 1950 until the end of 1951, the government urged Jews to emigrate. After that, those who didn't leave were held hostage for bargaining purposes.

Yeftah and I told our stories about farming and about all of the games and new songs we had learned. We told them of friends we had made. Often, Father said to slow down and speak clearly, but we couldn't. We were choking with excitement. Yeftah told them some of our adventurous tales, and we all laughed at his ten-year-old's sense of humor. The tale of stealing oranges was one of his favorites, and I had heard him tell it many times, but this time I did not deny him the pleasure of retelling it, as if for the first time.

Yeftah had gained weight, and Mother was pleased. "You both look so healthy. We did not expect this," she said as she kissed us both on our cheeks.

Our sisters got our attention by pulling all kinds of candies and goodies out of their pockets, which we grabbed and nearly swallowed without chewing.

"Where can we go to sit down and talk?" Father asked.

"Come, let us show you," we said. "This place is beautiful, full of green pastures, trees, hills, and animals."

We pulled them by their hands and took them to our barracks. "Here, this is where we live," I said. "Come in and sit on the beds."

For the next two hours, we all sat on the beds and talked and hugged and laughed. Father told us stories of their plight, many with much intrigue.

Tent Camp in At-Leet

"When we first arrived in Israel, we were sent to a tent camp south of Haifa. It was called At-Leet," he said.

The camp had been set up in a great hurry by the army for Jewish immigrants who were flooding the country from all corners of the world, especially from the Arab countries. There were some non-Jews who fled persecution, too, and settled in Israel.

My father continued, "Each family was assigned a large tent. Families with more than four children got two tents. We had army cots and set them up under the tents on the muddy fields of government or kibbutz property.

"Showers were communal. We all bathed together. We walked from our tents with our towels and soap in hand, a distance of some 500 yards. The showers were made of wood pillars wrapped in sheets of tent material and privacy was limited.

"The mess hall was a common room. We walked 500 yards to get there too and brought our own plates and utensils. If you didn't like the food they served, you could go to grocery stores nearby and buy what you liked with your own money. Most immigrants from the Arab world did not enjoy the food at Camp At-Leet. [It was mostly Ashkenazi food, the heavy rich peasant foods from Russia and Germany.] Black markets flourished, and the authorities overlooked it. Some people made small fortunes selling clothes, coffee, sugar, oil, and other precious commodities.

"We were there two months and it rained nearly every day. The mud was black and sticky, very wet, sometimes reaching up to my knees. All the time, we were petitioning the Israeli government to help find you boys, but it took two months before we were directed here to Kibbutz Ma'anit."

The blue marble

I was ecstatic that our parents were able to track us down. As I listened to the stories, amazed at all we had been through to bring us to this moment of unity here in a new land, I was still most curious about one thing.

"Did you get the one marble we sent?" I asked. "Did you read both names on the marble? Did you believe the guide that we both survived?"

Father and Mother said it was hard to trust the guide. They admitted that sometimes they lost faith that we were alive and cried in their bed. But then they looked around at all of us at that moment. Our family was all together in the same country!

"The important thing is that we are now all together," our father said. "Safe with our own Jewish people—back to our ancient home. I am so happy." Father then looked at all of us.

"No one can hurt us now."

Father tells of Flora and Haron

When my parents left Iraq, two of their closest friends, Haron and Flora and their family, were on the same flight. But they did not sit together, Father told us.

Haron and Flora had often came to visit our home when we lived in Iraq. Haron had worked at the American Embassy ever since he was a young man. He was a telegraph operator and could decipher secret messages sent in several languages. Anything about his duties at the embassy was always said in whispers. It was believed among those he trusted that Haron worked for the Americans in an intelligence-gathering capacity. He was at extreme risk of being hanged for treason if the Iraqi authorities found out. No proof or hard evidence was necessary. A suspicion was enough to impose the death penalty.

Sometimes, my father invited some close friends to our house in Iraq to talk over current events, especially, how World War II was being fought and won by the Allies. They would sit in the kitchen, with the door closed, and talk in whispers. Heron's name always came up in those conversations as the source of news, and sometimes he even joined the group while they were in mid-session.

So, when the Jews were permitted to leave Iraq in 1950, Haron and Flora sat on the airplane, apart from their friends because they feared that there might be Iraqi secret service members among the passengers. They did not want anyone harmed because of Heron's work for the Americans.

Upon their arrival in Israel, Father told us that Haron and Flora were treated as special guests and were whisked away from the airport. While my father could not find work in Israel for over two years, Haron was immediately hired by the American Embassy in Tel-Aviv. Haron and his family also stayed in a nice apartment in Ramat-Gan where most of the Iraqi Jews had settled. Father and Mother remained close friends with Flora and Haron and never betraying their life-long secrets.

Chapter Twenty

Life in Ramah

The bugs are biting

When my family found us at Ma'anit, Yeftah and I moved to the arrival camp, At-Leet, in northern Israel, where they were staying. We all slept under torn, leaky military tents, but we endured the hardship because we were all together.

In 1951, my family was transferred to Ramah, a suburb of the southern biblical town of Rehoboth. Ramah was another immigrant camp of around two hundred families. Nearby was the famous Bilu Square (which was more a circle than a town square).

Most families had three to five children. We had eight. At least twenty languages were spoken at Ramah, and its inhabitants wore a variety of colorful, ethnic clothing from countries all over the world. Most parents spoke only their own native languages, but the children spoke Hebrew at varying levels of skill. It was just enough so that we kids could understand each other.

Our housing was primitive: makeshift wooden structures erected over concrete slabs. The government saw this as a great improvement over the military, black, garment tents we lived in before in At-Leet. This was true. They were better, but we still were eaten alive by mosquitoes and the huge biting bugs that made homes in the cracks between the wooden panels.

Every day, we sprayed ourselves with all kinds of chemicals, but these bugs were impervious to our murderous desires. They kept on biting, even after we smeared on special lotions and covered up our exposed skin in the sweaty heat. These tiny animals were relentless, and the bites they left on our sweet, soft skin were painful. The younger children cried and begged for help. They couldn't sleep at night, and in the morning they were hardly rested enough for school.

Eventually, we drafted a plan. After spraying the walls with an experimental anti-bug solution we had concocted, we plastered the cracks between the panels. This reduced the biting, but not by much.

Our family had two dwellings. One wooden shelter housed my parents and the younger children, while I lived in the other one with my grandmother Khatoon and the older children. On Friday nights, I felt it was my job to make sure the kids were out of my parents' barracks, to leave them opportunity for intimacy. The young ones never understood the reason for my insistence that they clear the room, and I often had to resort to trickery and bribes to get them to come out. I knew instinctively that it was important for my parents to spend time alone. But sensuous delights were hard to come by at Ramah, even with my less-than-subtle attempts to make it happen for them.

As I grew older, I understood there were many stresses that worried their minds, but I wondered if the lack of privacy over so many months and years was a factor in my parents' deteriorating relationship and the root cause of my father's deep frustration and occasional volcanic outbursts.

Defending Avram

When we lived in the Ma'Abarah in Ramah, my brothers Avram and Yeftah and I, the boys of the family, took turn daily going to the ice factory and buying a block of ice for our primitive icebox. We had to cross a long field of sparse grass to get to the factory, which was about a half a mile from our house.

One day, as I was returning from the library, I noticed my brother Avram being attacked by two boys. They had toppled Avram's bicycle, and the ice block had fallen to the ground and was now covered with dust, quickly becoming mud.

I had taken boxing at my daytime school and had had private lessons in the evenings at a boxing gym so I felt pretty confident to handle two bullies. I rushed to Avram's aid and knocked the two boys on the ground. While I held them both down, Avram picked up the dripping ice block and put it on their faces. Though it was a hot day, the muddy ice against their faces was unbearable. They screamed for mercy. Finally, laughing, we let them up, and off they ran.

Avram put what was left of the ice block back on his bicycle and hurried on home. From that day on, Avram, nor any of us, were ever bothered again by these bullies when we went out on ice duty.

On top of Love Hill

I made many friends at Ramah. I was a natural leader, and I took it upon myself to organize a dance group, a theater group, and a hiking group. I had also inherited my father's voracious appetite for reading books on all subjects, and the lessons I learned from great literature taught me to assert myself and think big. The world was larger than we were, but that didn't mean it wasn't ours to investigate and play in. Though we had school here, there were no other organized activities as there had been at Tiv-On or Ma'anit.

Nobody seemed to mind. My peers were grateful that someone took the initiative to make the place and the whole situation more livable and even fun. But these outings were usually done in secret, with no adults knowing what we were doing.

In one of these gatherings, the teenagers decided to name the hill behind our housing complex Love Hill. None of us was mature enough to make love yet, but it was a romantic and cherished hideaway where we could distance ourselves from watchful parents, play music, and dance all of the popular Israeli dances. On warm nights on Love Hill, we played Spin the Bottle and enjoyed the new sensation of a kiss on the lips from a girl. This was our innocent introduction to adulthood following our not-so-innocent experiences of war.

We held meetings on Love Hill every Saturday morning around 11 o'clock.

To hide our tracks, we each took a different route to get there, walking separate dusty roads that all led up to the top of the hill. Total secrecy was our code of honor. Nobody ever betrayed the group or any individual. Sometimes, we met on Friday nights when the weather blessed us with warm breezes and bright moonlight to light the way. We carried our parents' records and heaped them on a pile. Someone brought a record player. I remember the night one of my friends showed up with a portable transistor radio, a new technology recently introduced into that country.

Later, we sat on the ground in a large circle, spaced close enough for our shoulders to touch. In the middle, a pile of broken tree branches was set ablaze in a bonfire. One person usually began a song and the rest followed. Invariably, we would end up dancing in the night air around the fire. All this created deep bonds between us. For some, the bonding went a bit further than dancing, but this too was natural and part of growing up.

We always ended our meetings with a smile and *shalom* or *le-hit-rah-ott* (see you later). For some, this meant sooner rather than later as some boys and girls walked around in a long circle after we all parted to come right back to Love Hill, never reaching home all night. It was not a secret, and I myself enjoyed the first thrills of young love on that ancient Israeli hilltop.

My friend and the exploding mine

My friend Gaddy liked to climb Love Hill on his fancy bicycle. We all envied him having that bike, which cost the equivalent of two month's earnings to buy. One day, he found an unexploded mine buried on the slope of the hill. He must have thought that since the last war ended four years ago, it would be safe to dig it up. As he reached into the earth for what he thought would be a great souvenir, the mine exploded, taking off his left hand, just above the wrist.

Bleeding profusely, Gaddy was taken to Kaplan Hospital where the doctors saved his life. We were shocked to hear this story, for by then we had all been walking up Love Hill from all directions for more than two years.

We visited Gaddy at the hospital where he told us his theory that the recent torrential rains must have exposed the mine. We had no idea our idyllic Love Hill could be hiding this buried danger. We wondered how many other mines were still buried there.

We never saw Gaddy on top of Love Hill again, but he continued to ride that fancy bike, steering with one hand and waving hello with his stump. We all used to poke fun at him as he rode his bike, holding on with one hand. We waved to him and tried to trick him into letting go of the handlebar to wave back. He would, and he would fall. That, of course, brought on loud, malicious laughter. It took him a few months, but Gaddy caught on to us, and learned to drive his bike without holding the handlebars. He never fell again.

Sometime after this, his brother told me he had a new hobby: Stamp collecting. I didn't think it was a happy substitute for biking up to Love Hill. But sometimes, life forces us to change in ways we could never imagine.

The shameful plight of Daliah and Raffi

Raffi was older and more mature than the rest of us. He was nineteen when we were fifteen and sixteen years old. Known as a lady's man, he especially liked chasing after girls younger than he was. He had a reputation that even all of our parents knew about, and they forbade their daughters from associating with him. Of course, this made him all the more attractive and didn't deter the blossoming girls from seeking his affections. Plus, he was tall, athletic, and handsome.

Daliah at sixteen years old was a dazzling beauty. Their mutual attraction naturally led them to the top of Love Hill. We whispered about what they were doing there, as Daliah was rumored to be sexually active. Raffi had bragged to us in great detail about the ways and wherefores of the act of love. My friends and I shared laughs and wonderment at all the possible positions two human bodies could assume in the heat of adolescent passion. The rest was provided by our boyish imaginations and our individual experiences walking in on our parents or sneaking looks in magazines or, in my case, reading the great erotic literature and studying *Kama Sutra* depictions from India and the Far East. On nights when we knew they were up on Love Hill, we fiercely guarded our own surging desires and eagerly awaited our turn to try it out with the girls of our dreams.

One day we heard the most amazing story: "Raffi and Daliah got stuck!"

Tightly embracing in the middle of a sexual encounter on top of Love Hill, the two at the end were unable to separate. I had heard of this happening to dogs or other animals, but I didn't know it was possible for humans to become so engorged as to be unable to retreat after penetration. A night wanderer had come upon the linked couple at the top of the hill some time around midnight.

Quickly realizing this was a private matter, he began to leave the hill when he heard Raffi call for help. The intruder came closer and understood the nature of the predicament. He ran to his house and called for an ambulance.

Raffi and Daliah, inseparable, had to be driven to Kaplan hospital where they were given relaxation shots. Eventually, one body became two once more. Naturally, the story circulated throughout Ramah camp and jokes continued for months, driving both of them away from our village.

The baths and the movies

My family lived at Ramah from 1951 to 1960. I left in 1958. During my adolescent years there, every afternoon after school or work, I would see boys and girls (and some adults) walking toward the communal bathhouse, towels wrapped around their necks or waists, underwear in hand, and carrying something clean to put on after. Some teenagers made it their primary interest in life to stand outside their homes and watch the girls go by. These same voyeuristic boys would also be the last to go take showers, as they seemed to need their own privacy.

The boys entered the bathhouse from one side, the girls from another. Of course, one boy had drilled a peeping hole in the wall that separated the two sides, and we all liked to have "juicy" discussions at school the next day, describing what we had seen, making things up when we had failed to get a good glimpse. The boy who drilled the hole was the best storyteller, but we never questioned the truth of his tales because we were happy to be privy to all the sexual intrigue he was able to conjure in our willing and lustful minds.

Once a week, the camp movie house showed a new feature. The new movie's title was posted each week outside on the electric poles. We never missed a movie, as it was a primary social place to gather. My group of friends and I liked to buy our tickets and enter the movie house at least two hours before the start of the movie, where it was cool and dark inside and the adults hadn't shown up yet.

There were no chairs or comfort whatsoever. We sat on long, rocky, wood benches. They didn't sell any popcorn in our movie house. Instead, we all brought sunflower seeds and consumed huge quantities, covering the floor with shells. The closer we got to the time of the movie's start, the closer people squeezed in next to one another, which was sometimes a pleasure if they were cute girls. At other times, it caused friction if it was a group of bullies. Rarely did anyone enjoy enough privacy to touch or kiss a date, but the hopeful possibility was enough to make us save up our money and return week after week.

Saul and friends atop "Love Hill",
Israel, 1953 (9)

Saul age 15 in Rehoboth, Israel, 1953 (10)

Chapter Twenty-One

My Father, Silas Fathi

With father at the *Moshavah*

One summer day, I was out walking with my father in the middle of town. In Hebrew, this part of the city is called *Moshavah*. We were starting to sweat, absorbing the intense summer heat as it soaked our clothes and parched our throats. We were near the Maccabee Sports Club, and I suggested we buy ourselves a refreshing, cold drink, *gazoz* in Hebrew. I was stepping toward a nearby vendor when my father pulled me gently by the arm.

"Don't buy from this kiosk," he said. "Look, he has enough customers. Let's cross the street and buy soda from that poor man. No one is buying anything from him. He is on the wrong side of the street. If we don't buy our drinks from him, he might soon go out of business."

I looked at my father strangely at first. The drink I wanted was right here, near at hand already, on this side of the street. But by the time we crossed to the other side of the street, I began to comprehend my father's position. I looked closely at the scene in the marketplace of the *Moshavah* and, sure enough, no one was buying from this lone fellow, who looked like he was probably struggling to support a wife and who knew how many children.

We ordered our *gazoz*, and they were promptly delivered. The man smiled through the gaps in his teeth and thanked my father with extra heartiness. I think he had been watching our conversation and subsequent agreement to cross the street and buy from him. Apparently, this wasn't the first time my father crossed the street to buy *gazoz* from this man.

This was an important lesson that my father had just taught me. It was important to share our wealth and blessings with those who had less, whenever possible. This was just one of the many profound lessons from my father, the honest, compassionate, intelligent, Silas Fathi.

Father tries his hand at Pita Bread business

Early on, when my father was struggling to find his next career after arriving as an exile in Israel, friends suggested he open a pita bread bakery. Pita is the common, flat, pocket bread of the Middle East.

Father had been a professional bureaucrat all his life, a "glorified clerk" as he put it. He wasn't a baker. At first, he refused to consider that pita bread might be a satisfying source of income. Eventually he relented after my Uncle Yehuda convinced him and two of their friends to go in on the business as partners. A few months later, the men opened their bakery after hiring a local Arab baker who was familiar with the techniques of baking pita bread.

Father rose each morning at 6:00 AM to go to his new job at the bakery. He hid inside the building, lest anyone from his more glamorous past should see his face and recognize him. He was embarrassed to be seen there and wore a big hat, which he tilted down to cover his face.

The business never flourished, and it wasn't long before the Grand Opening Pita Bread Bakery became a closed bakery. Through this unlucky venture, Father lost the remaining few dollars he had left to support his family, and his eldest children (myself among them) learned at a young age how to go out in the world and find paying work for ourselves.

Father's illness: Bleeding Ulcers

Israel's Department of Labor had no use for bureaucrats or glorified clerks. What the newly established country needed most during those early years of its formation were manual laborers. But my father was grossly unqualified for such tasks. After the pita bread debacle, he was unemployed for nearly two years.

He hated standing in line and asking for work. He had always been a proud and successful man. The loss of his country, his livelihood, and his formerly high status in the hierarchy of privilege and wealth took a toll on his health. He began complaining of unbearable pain in the stomach. The diagnosis came back as bleeding ulcers.

Though he loved smoking cigarettes, my father was used to being healthy. He walked miles every day and enjoyed swimming in public pools and riding ocean waves. Ever since his youthful days in India, he remained a faithful practitioner of yoga. I remember him throughout my childhood, getting up early in the morning and standing on his head for twenty or thirty minutes. Then he sat crossed-legged in lotus position and toggled his arms back and forth dozens of time. He believed in eating vitamin-rich nuts and almonds, which he consumed in large quantities.

"If you learn to eat a bird's diet," he liked to say, "you will live a long, healthy life."

His doctors wanted to operate to repair his bleeding ulcers, but this was something else outside of my father's experience. He was a stoic and a fighter, who believed he could right all wrongs, whether in the large world of wars, Diaspora, and politics, or in his own body. But after more months of severe pain and procrastination, he relented and checked into Hadassah Hospital in Jerusalem. There, his ulcers were operated on, and Silas Fathi was sent home with explicit instructions to quit smoking or die.

To our surprise and delight, he had the strength and wisdom to stop smoking. It had been a lifelong habit. He also went on a prescribed "baby diet," as he called it, which demanded that he eat more dairy and less meat. Soon, his health returned, and he was able to find work he felt was not beneath him at an Israeli Air Force base called Tel-Noff. There, he stayed until his retirement at age sixty-eight.

Father teaches high school students

When he retired from the Air Force, my father sought to fill his now-idle days with meaningful activities. He was never someone who enjoyed having free time on his hands. In his old age, he tutored high school kids in English. His five-year college education in India and his long association with the British Military in Iraq made him a master of high-level Oxford English.

Silas Fathi taught the next generation of children as he grew into his final role in life, as a mature and wise man, and continued to practice his yoga and eat his "bird's diet." He was always healthier than any of us, until cancer of the pancreas caught him and killed him within six months at age eighty-four. I still miss him and his hard-acquired wisdom very much.

Chapter Twenty-Two

My Brother Yeftah

Yeftah takes off his shoes at the movies

I had the pleasure of my brother Yeftah's company when we went to the movies. He wore those very uncomfortable pointed shoes that were in vogue in the fifties. Yeftah was in excruciating pain as we sat through the first hour of the movie because of those tight shoes. To get relief, he took his shoes off and immediately sighed in comfort.

At the conclusion of the movie, Yeftah struggled to put on his shoes. He could not get them on because his feet had swollen to twice their normal size. He began to curse in frustration. People had filed out of the theater, and it was almost empty. The theaterstaff was getting ready to start a new show, and there we were still as Yeftah tugged and tugged at those fashionable shoes. I began to laugh at his antics. Yeftah panicked, grabbed his precious shoes, and made his way out into the street in his stocking feet, hoping that no one would see him. He was lucky that not many people were there. But I sure was, and it was a night to remember!

Yeftah tells mother, "I want a pet."

While living in a *shikoon* in Ramah, my parents had a nice little backyard where Mother and my siblings had planted fruit trees and vegetables. One day, Yeftah came home with his usual single-mindedness. He addressed our mother, "Mother, I want to get a pet. I'll take care of it. You won't have to do anything."

Mother stared at him incredulously. She never liked animals and was so surprised that Yeftah would want one. "What kind of a pet?" she asked.

Yeftah answered quickly, "A little pet, a dog. I will take care of it myself."

Mother smiled and said slyly, "I already have eight pets. Don't give me another headache." She meant that she already had eight children, of course. We all laughed at that and thought that was the end of Yeftah's request.

A few days later, Yeftah showed up at the house with a huge Boxer dog, with overgrown yellow hair and enormous ears. Before Mother could greet him with a lashing of her tongue, he took it to the backyard and let it loose. He went inside, filled a pot with water, and took it out to the dog.

All of us came running to see the dog and watch Mother's reaction. We wondered how was he getting away with it. *How did he get mother to agree?* A few minutes later, Mother appeared in the backyard with Yeftah and the dog.

"Didn't I tell you to forget about a pet?" she said angrily. "Yet, you still went and got one? I promise you I will not lift a finger to care for him, feed him, or clean up after him."

"Yes, I know, Mother," Yeftah answered. "I told you I would take care of him. You won't even feel he's here. Just leave it to me."

And that was that, or so we thought. But, as time proved, when Yeftah was at school most of each day, someone else had to care for the dog. He begged mother, "Just give him water twice a day, that's all."

Mother did not promise Yeftah, but she felt sorry for the dog. *Why should he suffer from her son's stupidity; it's not his fault*, she reasoned. So, everyday she put out fresh water for the dog.

A little while passed and Yeftah began to forget to feed the dog. He considered it everyone's dog now and felt that each one of us should look after all of the dog's needs, including walking him once a day for exercise. We did care for the dog because we liked having a pet.

Though Mother was unhappy about having a dog, she absolutely hated to clean up after him when he defecated all over the backyard.

"You don't have to do this, Mother," Yeftah insisted. And, we all waited for him to say, "I'll do it." Instead, Yeftah answered, "It's good fertilizer. Just leave it there."

Mother wouldn't hear of it. She couldn't bear to feed us vegetables from a backyard full of dog droppings!

The dog must have wandered away

Mother decided to do something about the dog one day. When everyone was at school and father was at work, she took the dog by the leash and went for a long walk with him. In fact, she walked all the way to the next village, Ah-kier, and just let him go, with the leash still attached to his neck. She rationalized that someone would see him and feel sorry about such a beautiful, lost dog. The dangling lease, she thought, would make it easier for someone to catch him.

When we all came home from school, the first thing we always did was go to the backyard and pet the dog and make sure he had plenty of water to drink. This particular day was an especially hot, summer day. When we got out to the backyard, we couldn't find the dog. We wondered where he was. Mother would not utter a word as to his whereabouts.

When Yeftah arrived home, he did the same thing as we did. He went to the backyard and looked for the dog. He came back into the house and demanded, "Mother, where is my dog? What did you do to him? Did you give him away without consulting me?"

Mother shrugged and said with an innocent face, "No, I swear. I don't know where he is. Maybe he was unhappy here and ran away. Who knows?"

Yeftah laughed at her, knowing it was a lie. "Don't tell me this. He wouldn't run away. We all loved him and pampered him. Where would he go?"

This questioning and denial went on for hours. The sun was beginning to set and soon it would be dark. Yeftah was worried that something bad had happened to his dog.

"Tell me the truth, Mother. Where is my dog? What did you do with him? Tell me before something bad happens to him. He might get run over and be killed. Or someone might take him home and beat him up. There are lots of cruel people in this world. Tell me, please."

Mother looked at all our faces. We all wanted to know what had happened to the dog and whether he was all right. Mother was definitely outnumbered and stood to be accused of cruelty. "Ok, I took him to Ah-kier and let him loose there," she admitted. "He will be ok. There are lots of families with young children there. They will find him and take care of him. Don't worry."

Yeftah was furious. "How could you do this to my dog? He is my responsibility. He bothered nobody."

Yeftah looked us all in the eyes, and he himself looked like a lost puppy. We couldn't resist when he ordered. "Ok, all of you. Let's go look for him. If we're lucky, we'll find him alive."

Before Mother could stop us, we were all outside, running in all directions through Bilu toward Ah-kier. Before dark, my sister Judith found the dog, just crouching where Mother had left him near the high-traffic road, afraid to make a move. He figured one of us would be back to fetch him, and indeed we did.

From that day on, everyone contributed to the dog's upkeep, loving it more every day. Mother did not have to lift a finger to take care of him. We made sure of that. She might even have grown to like him a bit. It was possible.

I wish I could fly away like these birds

When we were young, Yeftah and all my other siblings and I used to sit on the balcony of our *shikoon,* clustered around Mother like a bunch of yapping puppies, asking her incessant questions about anything and everything. Mother used to look up in the sky for a flying bird. When she spotted one, she would lift her hands upward, and say, in total resignation, "I wish I could fly away like this fortunate bird. I wish I could get away from you all."

We always laughed at her gesturing and sighs though we knew that we had tried her patience. She was weary of our questions and our chatter. One by one, we slipped away, leaving her alone on the balcony.

Chapter Twenty-Three

My Beloved Librarian, Mrs. Newtoff

During the years I lived in Israel, Mrs. Newtoff was my guiding light. She taught me to love books. Just five feet tall, she walked with a cane, her back hunched over. To me, she was beautiful because of her intelligent and well-read mind. Thirty years later, my mother told me that Mrs. Newtoff still asked about me. "Where is Saul?" she often asked. "He's destined for greatness, you know." Mrs. Newtoff always sent me her love, no matter where in the world I was.

When I was a boy, each day after school I rode the only bike our family owned about five miles to the public library in the town of Rehoboth. Mrs. Newtoff was impressed by this teenaged immigrant boy who was so eager to learn. Each time I came through the door, she motioned for me to come and see her. This made me smile as she waited with a stack of books for me: history, poetry, philosophy, and the classics. She knew I wasn't interested in romance and entertainment. I liked Plato, Nietzsche, Dostoevsky, Spinoza, and Russell, the philosophers. My favorite poets became Tagore, Rachel, Gorky, Pushkin, Bialik, and Sappho. Byron, Hugo, and Joyce wrote the best novels. When I returned the books, Mrs. Newtoff often asked me to sit, and she would quiz me about the stories and the ideas in the books I read.

She knew that Einstein and Archimedes, to me, were the greatest scientists ever. Mrs. Newtoff asked, "What did Einstein mean when he said 'God doesn't play dice with the Universe?'" And I knew he meant that everything is controlled by forces outside of us, that nothing was random or accidental. Everything was predictable. Later on, Einstein changed his mind when quantum theory took root, but at the time everything he proposed made sense to me.

Madame Butterfly

One day, I saw a poster on the library door that announced the opening of a new movie house. The Summer Theatre Khen had no roof. It was open to the skies with modern, comfortable seats.

"What's the excitement about this theater, Mrs. Newtoff?" I asked.

She gently touched my arm and replied, "It will be an outdoor theater like those of ancient Rome and Greece, and the premier movie will be *Madame Butterfly,* Puccini's classic. Would you like to see it?"

I was surprised. "You mean, you and me together?" I asked.

She smiled. "Yes, if you don't mind going with an old lady."

I smiled back. "Oh no, Mrs. Newtoff, I would be honored. I would really enjoy that," I said enthusiastically. "How can we get tickets?"

"Leave that to me."

On the next Saturday night, I met my favorite librarian on the sidewalk near the new movie house. Hundreds of well-dressed people stood in line to buy tickets. Excitement was in the air. Mrs. Newtoff waved me to come closer. She took my arm as if we were a couple of lovers as she showed me the precious tickets. I hoped the other boys and girls in line wouldn't recognize my "date" as the librarian. I decided maybe they would think she was my mother, which would be embarrassing enough.

Inside, we found our seats and waited for the movie to start as music played. We looked up to see a clear, summer night with millions of stars shimmering above us.

As the movie unfolded, Mrs. Newtoff explained every scene to me, wanting me to understand the drama of opera. I was afraid the people around us would object, but no one did. Mrs. Newtoff was respected and feared. You didn't mess with her.

Madame Butterfly made a huge impression on me. Unlike most operas that are grand spectacles with lots of subplots and huge casts of characters, this opera was an intimate telling of a tragic love story with a small ensemble cast. The story was straightforward but full of passion. Pinkerton, a married but philandering Naval officer, takes a Japanese wife, Cio-Cio San, who falls in love with him. He abandons her and expresses his regret for leaving her in an extended aria in the second act. While he is gone, she bears him a son. Two years later, Pinkerton returns with his American wife and wants to take Cio-Cio San's son back with him. Cio-Cio San realizes that she now has nothing to live for and commits suicide. Pinkerton, of course, sings of his deep remorse over her death in the last act.

This was the first time that I had seen what that kind of passion could do to a man and how tragic love could destroy a life. During different parts of the opera, I thought I saw Mrs. Newtoff crying, and I tried to comfort her with a small squeeze of her hand. This opera was also my first exposure to a truly exotic culture, not realizing that my own culture might seem exotic to someone else. Like Puccini and those of his era, I became enamored with Japanese motifs, art, and culture. It was not surprising that years later I would choose a Japanese pen pal not only to find out more about Japan but also to draw closer to it through another person.

At the end of the film, Mrs. Newtoff and I left the theatre slowly as the throng of people filed outside. We stood near the bushes, and Mrs. Newtoff asked, with glittering eyes, "Well, young man, did you enjoy the story? Wasn't it wonderful?"

"Yes, thank you very much," I replied. "Please, let me pay you for my ticket."

"Pay me someday when you're a successful writer," she suggested. "I know you will be. God willing, I will be alive to see it."

When I got home, I decided not to tell my father where I'd been. He wouldn't find it manly that I had been to the opera, especially escorting an older woman. When I told my mother, she laughed and said, "That old lady is in love with you. She is *majnoonah* (insane). Don't be fooled by her age either; she is as strong as an ox. She will live to be a hundred, you will see."

Remembering her generosity and kindness, I smiled and whispered to myself, "I hope so. I really hope so."

Chapter Twenty-Four

My Dearest Uncles

Uncle Salman goes to Hebrew University

My uncle Shlomo (Salman) went to Hebrew university when he was twenty-two to get a degree in Middle East studies. He also worked as a newscaster at Kol-Yisrael, the Hebrew broadcast station in Jerusalem. The big news of the day when Uncle Shlomo was on broadcast duty was the threats by the new leader of Egypt, Gamal Abd El-Nasser, to wipe out the State of Israel by uniting Arab countries under one flag.

Most of our family had been living in Rehoboth, a biblical city twenty miles south of Tel Aviv. I was suffering from asthma and bronchitis in the midst of the stress and strain of our uprooted lives and had been advised by doctors to get away from the climate of Rehoboth and try living in Jerusalem. They thought the high mountain air might help to alleviate my wheezing symptoms and shortness of breath.

I found myself at fourteen, living with one of my favorite uncles. My uncle Shlomo was handsome and athletic, and everyone knew him to be really smart. He had a reputation of being a lady's man, with a personal aversion to marriage and permanent relationships.

I admired him for many reasons, but deep in my heart I felt I owed him for everything good that had happened to me. He and Uncle Moshe had guarded and protected my brother Yeftah and me during our escape from Baghdad when I was ten and Yeftah was eight. I realized later on that Shlomo had only been eighteen himself on that harrowing journey, yet we looked up to him as a wise adult. He took on that responsibility earnestly, protecting us with his very life and yet managing to keep up his good spirits and ours. He taught us to be optimistic and to be brave.

Now here I was living with my uncle, who was making his own life as a grown man. A college student, he rented a furnished room from a Yemenite woman in the old Arab outdoor market neighborhood, Mahaneh Yehuda. The woman served him dark, concentrated black coffee all day and night, supposedly to keep him awake and studying. Of course, as his guest I was invited to participate in the rituals of strong coffee and the stimulating effects of caffeine. I found the dark brew tasty and agreeable as the Yemenite brewer added exotic spices, such as cinnamon, cardamom, and cloves. And the thick coffee smell brought back fond memories of living with my Aunt Ruthi, who had become rich by reading people's futures in the ringed black stains left behind in their coffee cups.

Uncle Shlomo often locked himself in his room away from me for days at a time in order to study for his exams and stay focused on his work. I saw him a few minutes each day when he went to the bathroom or to shower. To get closer to him and seem more worthy of his attention, I used my free time to read his books: histories of the Middle East and the Arab nations, Arabic poetry, and philosophy. I started showing up at Hebrew University to listen in on his classes, to hear what the professors and his fellow students had to say about these books they were reading. They read many versions of history and tried to grasp the differing perspectives. They discussed these histories in the context of current-day politics and the motivations of modern world leaders.

My uncle and I started quizzing each other on our reading. Our good-natured competition caused us both to listen harder in class and to absorb the complex stories on more profound levels. I enjoyed being in this just-enough-older man's company as I felt my way toward my burgeoning manhood, absorbing his philosophy of no commitment when it came to women, trying to keep up with him in sports, and beginning to get glimpses into the underground world of espionage.

Many men in those times, in that place, were trained as spies to protect Israel from its many enemies and to secure for their families a safe country, free from persecution. We needed Israel to remain a secure land for the Jewish people. Too many Jews had been killed in our short lifetimes.

Two months later, I began to get homesick and returned to Rehoboth. My health was a little better, though my symptoms were not completely relieved. The doctor believed it was psychosomatic, my body's response to the sad environment of my parents' desperate situation and the level of poverty to which we had been driven. We had been forced to leave everything we owned behind in Iraq. We were grateful to be alive, for this chance to start over, but this did not mean it was easy for the refugees to stay healthy and forward-looking. Hard work, the connection of family, and our devout faith in God kept us going, as each one of us re-created our lives in our new country of Israel.

Uncle Shlomo eventually immigrated to New York, a city where many members of my family eventually settled. Even I ended up there after many adventures.

Uncle Abboody and Sham-ah, the crazy Yemenite dancer

Every day, my family and I passed by Sham-ah, a Yemenite woman who took long walks through the streets of Rehoboth. Sham-ah was around thirty years old and certifiably insane, but everyone knew she was harmless. She lived in her kind parents' house. When she was out on the street, she liked to sing as she walked and wobbled along the way to everyone's delight. She also had a very foul mouth, which made us all laugh. Teenaged boys always seem to enjoy hearing nothing better than a creative, string of curse words, and it was a rare pleasure to hear such language coming from the mouth of a woman.

Occasionally, Sham-ah paused to regale passersby in front of my Uncle Abboody store. She had decided she admired Abboody and liked to make fun of his extreme shyness. She often stationed herself on the sidewalk near his store to shout in the presence of all of his customers, "Abboody, you pretend to be shy, but you are the biggest fucker of them all."

My quiet uncle was duly humiliated. When Sham-ah was out front, Uncle Abboody retreated to the back room of his store to hide among the rotting vegetables and wait until "the she-devil," as he called her, had left.

Chapter Twenty-Five

Neighbors in Ramah

Boosey, our own Black Orpheus

When our family arrived in Israel in 1951, we were assigned a place to live in a Ma'Abarah (Transitory Camp) named Ramah, nestled between Rehoboth and Bilu, about forty-five minutes south of Tel-Aviv. My brothers and sisters and I were enrolled in schools in the center of the town and were slowly adapting to suburban life in Israel. We made many friends of all ethnic and social backgrounds. Among those my mother met and befriended was a most gentle Yemenite woman who had a grown son named Boosey.

Boosey was a black-complexioned, well-muscled man with an unpredictable temper. There was a secret joke among the people in the town about Boosey. They said among themselves that he could be seen even in the darkest night because he was blacker than night itself. Had he heard, Boosey would have killed anyone who had spoken about him in such a disrespectful manner.

He lifted weights to develop his imposing physique and kept it toned by his part-time manufacturing business. Spread out in his backyard, Boosey spent hours in the hot sun making concrete bricks in this labor-intensive enterprise. Through this, he earned extra money to spend on the young ladies who flocked around him. He always seemed to have money enough to eat in the best outdoor restaurants.

On Saturdays, he strutted and preened, showing off his muscles at the Maccabee Swimming Pool. The girls were always impressed, and many young boys secretly wished they would grow up to look like Boosey. Often, he climbed the poles on all four corners of the pool and made graceful dives from each perch. This really was not permitted because it was unsafe—at least it was unsafe for the average diver. It also wasn't a good example to set for some of the more daredevil youngsters who admired Boosey and might want to copy his risky dives into the pool.

Boosey reveled in exploring and pushing the limitations of his body and then crowing about his skill or bravery. Though the lifeguards at the public pool shook their fists at him, Boosey just laughed. No one could tell him what to do or where to go.

Partly because of his defiance of authority and his physical strength, everyone wanted to be Boosey's friend. Like the hero in the film, *Black Orpheus*, Boosey gave you a sense of safety and security because he probably could fight anyone who got in his or his friend's way. He also seemed invincible, capable of spitting in a bully's eye or the authorities. He was like a Superhero, bigger than life and able to tackle anyone and anything, including ideologies and uncertainty. At first, we all thought of him as our very own Joshua.

But, there was another side to Boosey. He could be laughing and joking one minute, and the next, he would be taking a swing at somebody. Sometimes, no one knew what had changed the atmosphere and triggered Boosey's anger. Frequently, he got into loud arguments and fistfights. These weren't just two men trading a punch or two. When Boosey got angry enough to hit someone, he kept at it until either he was exhausted or someone pulled him off the other guy. Sometimes, Boosey's rage put the other man in the hospital, and Boosey would end up in jail overnight, much to his mother's embarrassment. These incidents began to occur with regular frequency, and the violence escalated.

One day his mother, whom he loved very much, went to see a dentist about an abscessed tooth. The dentist apparently misjudged the amount of Novocain he gave Boosey's mother to treat her tooth. The woman's heart stopped, and the dentist could not awaken her. She died right in the dentist chair.

Boosey was devastated by his mother's death. He brooded over what had happened in the dentist's office and was determined to make someone pay. After his mother's funeral, Boosey decided to pay a visit to the dentist and settle accounts with him. I doubt that Boosey even talked to the dentist. He just beat the hell out of him. The dentist was so badly hurt that he was hospitalized for nearly three months and was never able to practice his profession again.

That incident occurred at about the time I left Israel to see the world. When I returned sixteen years later for a visit, I asked about Boosey and what had become of him. I then was told one chilling story after another of his notorious, and often illegal, escapades.

One of them was about his latest business enterprise. He had become a major gambler and a pimp, with a stable of prostitutes. He also had a criminal gang that carried out his illegal schemes. Moving to Elat to be close to the hotels there, he preyed on their international clientele whom he fleeced or supplied with ladies of the night.

One day in a nightclub in the heart of Elat, he got into an argument with a member of his own gang. The shouting quickly turned to something worse and guns were drawn. His underling stuck his gun in Boosey's face and pulled the trigger, killing him instantly.

Though Boosey had lived and died on his own terms, death seemed to follow him wherever he went. He had met a violent end as he had so often delivered his own brand of violence to others. No one envied him, as far as I know. However, new stories about his life still pop up from time to time, embodying him like some legendary gunfighter of the old American West or a notorious gangster of the Prohibition Era.

The street beggar

There was a male beggar near our school in Iraq. Every boy and girl felt sorry for him and felt obligated to give him a donation so that he could have something to eat.

Years later, in Israel, we found out that he now was living in a most luxurious home in the best Tel-Aviv suburb. The people who knew him from Iraq acknowledged him with a wave of the hand or a nod of the head, yet they always wondered how he had become so prosperous. *Had he saved all those coins we children and others had given him and became wealthy? Was he rich and just begged on the street for some strange reason? Or did he find some business in Israel that he was especially good at and therefore had remade himself?* We never knew.

The news of David Parizat

It was rumored that David Parizat was a leader in the Zionist underground movement in Iraq. But to us children, he was a heavy, redheaded man with a freckled
face who was always laughing and joking. One of the jokes he liked to play with children was to pull them off the ground by their ears like poodles.

My youngest brother Avram was one of his victims. Avram was hard of hearing most of his life, and he blamed it on Mr. Parizat and so did my mother. Father, the gentleman that he was, would never say a word to him, but suffered his child's pain silently. Mr. Parizat was far more prominent and much richer than my father, yet they remained fast friends.

Like every other Jew remaining in Iraq after WW II, Mr. Parizat had immigrated to Israel within that narrow window of opportunity, those ten months in 1950-51. Leaving all his assets and possessions untouched, with only two suitcases of clothing, like every other Iraqi Jew who wanted to escape from Iraq, Mr. Parizat had to sign a government-printed statement: "The undersigned is hereby forfeiting all his rights, his assets, claims, and his citizenship forever and ever, and shall not be allowed to return to Iraq for any reason whatsoever."

In Israel, like my father and others, he did not posses any needed skills, as far as the labor department was concerned and was unemployed for a long time. He had to beg for food, clothing, and shelter for himself and his family. He lived in a suburb of Tel-Aviv, Ra-Mat-Gan, where many of the Iraqi Jews settled. It was sometimes called the New Baghdad. (Ironically, forty years later, this settlement was targeted by scud missiles sent from Baghdad during the Gulf War.)

Now and then, Mr. Parizat and my father met by chance and sat on a bench in the city's public park, reminiscing about their lives and intrigues in Baghdad. They seemed to remember only the good things with great nostalgia and longing.

"Would you ever consider going back?" my father often asked him.

"No, I'm not returning," Mr. Parizat would say, "but I would give ten years of my remaining life just to visit there."

A few years later, Mr. Parizat began working for the electric company (a government owned entity) and was taught to climb poles to perform repairs by soldering loose wires.

Once like a minor god in Baghdad, a leader of his community, David Parizat, a most learned and prosperous man, was now a laborer, climbing poles, forty to fifty feet in the air. By this time, my father was working for the Israeli Air Force in a senior position, down in the southern part of Israel, and was fairly content. It was almost as if their positions in society had been reversed.

One day, my father received a phone call from Mr. Parizat's wife, which shocked him. "David has fallen off the electric pole and died," Mrs. Parizat told him. "Will you come to the funeral? It's on Friday afternoon, before sundown."

Of course, my parents attended the funeral and cried plenty. They returned to Mr. Parizat's home to sit Shiv-ah, a mourning period of seven days and nights, where friends and relatives visit the deceased's home and offer their condolences. They also tell favorite stories about the deceased person's life and experience. This was no exception. There were plenty of stories to tell.

When my parent's came home, they told us all that had happened at the funeral and at the Parizat home. To those of my siblings who didn't remember David Parizat, my parents described him as "the one that used to pull you off the floor by you're ears."

"Oh, the one that made Avram deaf," my baby sister Judith acknowledged.

My mother and Mrs. Parizat remained in close touch, sometimes meeting in Tel-Aviv. Father made sure Mr. Parizat's children were going to school and not wanting for food or clothing.

About six months later, when Mother went to visit Mrs. Parizat, her friend told her the real events around David Parizat's tragic death. "You know, David didn't die from accidentally falling off that pole," she practically whispered. "I was going to donate his clothes to charity and so I emptied his pockets before putting them in a box. There in one of the pockets, I found a farewell letter to me and the children in David's handwriting, saying that he was tired of this life, that he loved us all, and that he hoped we would forgive him this action."

Mother and Mrs. Parizat began to cry, hugging each other. "How tragic! How terrible!" my mother said. "Do the kids know?"

"Yes," Mrs. Parizat said, "but we didn't change the accident report for fear that the government would cut off our survivor's benefits. David actually went to work as usual, climbed a pole, and touched the hot wire. He fell on the concrete sidewalk and died on the way to the hospital."

Israeli youth is stabbed

In the mid-1950s, a rare stabbing took place in our city of Rehoboth. A Yemenite youth had an argument (we never knew what about) with an Ashkenazi young man and stabbed him to death. The uproar that followed caused some ancient wounds—hatred between the Ashkenazi and Yemenite groups—to surface. There was fear in the city that more killings would follow in revenge for the Ashkenazi death.

Menachem Begin was the head of the opposition party, Heirut, (later changed to Likkud) in Israel at the time. Begin was eventually elected to be one of Israel's most beloved Prime Ministers, as he was a revered advocate for peace. The great man came to Rehoboth in the midst of the turbulence following the stabbing to give a speech, calling for restraint.

The rally was the largest ever seen in our city and was attended by all immigrant and *Sabra* (Israeli-born) communities. Begin pointed out that we were all Jews. We were living here together in our own small country after a 2000-year struggle to claim a Jewish homeland. "We must be united as one nation, committed to the defense of our country. No one standing here today is the enemy," he said.

The emotional applause that followed this declaration galvanized the entire rally. We began hugging and kissing each other, strangers united in a show of love and common heritage, regardless of our ethnic backgrounds and apparent differences.

Begin's speech succeeded in defusing the dangerous polarization that had been fomenting for weeks. Everyone went home that day feeling peaceful, a relief from the fear of more potential violence. That was Begin's greatness: his ability to bring people together and form bonds of respect based on our common humanity.

Chapter Twenty-Six

Working to Support the Family

Berta, Yedida, and I

Our family began to settle into a life at Ramah, in the south of Rehoboth. We children were registered for school in town and had to walk three to four dusty miles to get there every day. It was always hot, even in the bright early morning sun. Even so, the harsh afternoon heat made walking home always a chore.

Soon after we arrived, Father became sick with a stomach ulcer. His having trouble finding a job to feed his large family probably made his condition worse. Certainly, it was no wonder he had an ulcer since he had been living in forced exile for two years, trying to be strong and supportive to his frightened wife and brood of children.

Berta, Yedida, and I were the three eldest children in a family that needed to be fed, clothed, and sheltered. I was thirteen, Yedida was fifteen, and Berta was seventeen. We took our elder status seriously. As custom dictated, we left our regular school and went out to work to support the family. We had no experience or qualifications, but we were able to land jobs as laborers in the fields, mostly banana farms, where on many days the black Israeli mud was sticky thick and ankle-deep. Carrying the heavy bunches of bananas after a successful morning of picking them down from their high perches in the tall trees was backbreaking work. The pay was minimal but enough to keep our brothers and sisters in school and save our anxious parents from more worries.

After a day spent sweating dirt through all our pores, Yedida and I rushed home to take cold showers, change from our ragged clothes, and eat food on the run as we rushed out to attend night classes so we could still graduate. Our parents held schooling in high regard and felt added shame because we three children had to forgo school to make money just for basic bread and butter. My older sisters and I earned our keep during the day and went to school at night, because it mattered. We did this for nearly a year.

Our sister Berta, who worked in the banana groves with us, was accepted to a teacher training school at night to become qualified as a kindergarten teacher. She was so proud the first day she welcomed a herd of eager five-year-olds into her own classroom.

Hatzor: Israel Air Force Academy of Aeronautics

In high school, we were introduced to a unique opportunity conducted by the Israeli Air Force. It was a four-year program in aeronautics skills. Four hours each day, we could work on Air Force planes, inspecting, maintaining, and repairing them. It was the hands-on hard labor of mechanics. After work, we could study for four hours in the classroom, earning a small income in the process.

I came home and enthusiastically recounted the deal to my parents and begged them to allow me to participate. Father was immediately in favor, but Mother hesitated. Four years was a long time to be away from the family. She was worried about separating us again.

I finally convinced her to let me at least try and studied hard to pass the entrance exams, which I did. And so, I worked from 1952 to 1956 for the Israeli Air Force Academy of Aeronautics at a military base in Hatzor, specializing in aircraft electronics. My cousin Sabah, now called Yeg-Al, studied at the academy with me and excelled at aircraft mechanics.

At Hatzor, the workforce boys were trucked to the base daily. We sat in the back of a pickup truck on very uncomfortable, long wooden benches. Most of the boys, who were young and full of restless energy, engaged in all kinds of wrestling and shenanigans as the truck bumped along on the ride. I sat on a separate bench and read books. They began referring to me, some mockingly, some with awed and ignorant respect, as "The Philosopher."

The truck was crowded and the drive was long, so to make an adventure of the daily grind, two or three boys defied the rules and sneaked out each day to ride on the tailgate. It was all good fun—until the day a bus rear-ended our truck and two boys, best friends from childhood, fell off the truck and were killed—on the spot. We absorbed a bitter lesson as we attended their sad funerals and listened to the rabbi read Kaddish, the prayers for the dead.

After four years, we were issued impressive certificates of completion and given recommendations for jobs. These qualifications made it easier to secure prestigious positions, either in the government or the private sector.

Sukrer Power Station

The super secret underground power station, Sukrer, was bequeathed to Israel by the German company Telefunken, as part of a reparations agreement between the two countries after World War II. It was built to withstand attacks and air bombardment, with six-foot-thick reinforced concrete walls and ceilings.

My assignment was in the ultra-modern control room, where huge consoles were devised to monitor the production, distribution, and maintenance of the power. Millions of feet of wiring were used to accomplish this. Together with eight other technicians, I squatted under the consoles all day long to wire hundreds of instruments, closely following the detailed and complex original German Telefunken blueprints.

My fellow electricians and I rose up from under the consoles every few hours to stretch, get a drink, or smoke for a few minutes before returning to the intricate chores of wiring. At the end of each day, a supervisor oversaw our work and produced a report with critical comments, if any. Then, we boarded company buses that dropped us off at our homes. We were sworn to secrecy about exactly what went on at Sukrer (many of us never knew the full story, including me), and we never discussed our work with friends or siblings—or even amongst ourselves.

Where is Mr. Almuzninoo?

Sukrer Power Station operated day and night, around the clock, 24/7. Every night, someone had to clean up the day's wire debris left under the consoles in the control room. A nice old man with a mop and a broom, Mr. Almuzninoo, clocked in after our shift each day to clean the room and prepare it for the next morning. He worked until midnight.

One morning, the day shift supervisor got a phone call. "My husband didn't come home last night. Is he still there?" a worried Mrs. Almuzninoo asked.

The supervisor was perplexed, but didn't suspect anything amiss. "He should have been on the bus at midnight," he said. "Let me call you back."

The supervisor came into the control room and bent down to ask if any of us electricians had seen the cleaning man leave. No one had seen him. He went to the administrators and asked if they had given Mr. Almuzninoo any additional chores or duties.

"Negative," they answered.

The supervisor recruited three men and spread out in three directions, covering the entire power station. Tense searching found nothing wrong and no Mr. Almuzninoo. The three men met at the office an hour later, with no trace of the cleaning man.

The quest went on for three more hours, with increasing concern and no sign of Mr. Almuzninoo. The search group swelled to ten, then to twelve. But the old man could not be found.

The supervisor called Mrs. Almuzninoo and asked, "Did he get home yet? Has he ever done this before?"

To both questions, the frantic wife answered, "No."

He assured her that he would continue to look and would call her back. *Maybe he fell asleep somewhere,* he speculated.

The supervisor came to the console room again and asked, "Has anyone seen the cleaning man since yesterday?"

No one had, we repeated, but a few minutes later a technician came out from under the console.

"I didn't see him," he said, "but I think this is his broom." In his hand was a piece of a broom handle.

The supervisor crawled under that console then. When he scanned his eyes around the space, he found something. Looking further, he recognized it for exactly what it was. He let out a scream, "Oh, my God! Oh, no! Oh, my God!"

Everyone rushed to see what was going on. One by one, we were shown a pile of black carbon, with visible bones among the ashes. It was Mr. Almuzninoo.

The old man had gone into the console to clean the wire debris with a wet mop and was instantly electrocuted. Two hundred twenty thousand volts fired through his frail body. Parts of his wet mop and broom were still there.

It took me a while to truly comprehend that these remnants were once the humble man I waved hello to every day as I came to work and when I left. He was a man I barely knew yet respected for his reliability, ready smile, and easygoing demeanor.

There I was, The Philosopher, standing over a lifeless heap of carbon and bones that just the day before was a living man, the same as me. I pondered the mysteries of a universe that could randomly strike someone down like that, indiscriminately trigger sudden deaths and meaningless accidents. *How can a hearty man of flesh and blood be reduced to a pile of black dust?* I wondered.

We were all visibly shaken, grown men who couldn't very well cry tears at such senselessness. We could only stare in wonder and privately make our peace with the reality of death.

The supervisor told us to quit whatever we were doing and wait until he came back. He ran to the office to inform the management. Then, all hell broke loose.

Someone decided it would be best to send us home early while the management decided what to do and how to prevent this kind of tragedy from happening again. The supervisor and two other officers drove out to inform the old man's wife. As we all rode home on the bus, I pictured the scene at her door, her ears going deaf, refusing to listen as she tried to grasp the meaning of the words she was hearing. Her beloved husband was dead. *Did she believe in God,* I wondered, *and how would she feel about Him now?*

Following a heart-breaking funeral, Mr. Almuzninoo name came up in conversation from time to time. All he wanted was to have a steady job and do it well. He had been a humble, ordinary man, devoted to his family and work. *Are we more than a pile of carbon and pieces of bone once the life is sucked out of us? Where was that kind soul now?*

Weitzman Institute: Robert Oppenheimer and Ben-Gurion

I stayed on at the Sukrer Power Station and tended to business, then worked for the Israel Electric Company for a while before I was transferred to the Weitzman Institute in Rehoboth. There, I was trained to wire scientific control panels at the new physics research building. Again, it was work designated Top Secret as it was rumored to deal with atomic research and production of heavy water.

At the building dedication, I was in the fortunate position to be close enough to photograph David Ben-Gurion, Prime Minister of Israel, and one of the great scientific minds in the world, Dr. Robert Oppenheimer, father of the atomic bomb, who had managed the American scientific team, known as the Manhattan Project, that had developed the first atom bomb. To be in the presence of great men makes one believe it is possible to be a great man yourself, and I cherished that moment and all that it meant for Israel, and also for me, a young man who wasn't a great man yet, but believed in himself enough to imagine he could be one day.

Even at the time, I sensed the historic value of that photo. I have carried it in my wallet for forty-seven years. Its value to me personally is hard to put into words. Yes, there are heroes among us. Every now and then they present themselves, and I was there with them, in the same outdoor yard, at a crucial moment in the history of my country and the world. An enlargement of that photo still hangs in my basement.

The Israeli Navy needs me

During 1956, a disturbing incident occurred involving Israel and the Egyptian Navy. A small Israeli vessel was pursued by a larger, well-armed Egyptian Navy vessel. The Israeli crew feared their boat would be boarded by the Egyptians, and secret documents fall into the hands of the enemy navy. They began franticly shredding documents and tossed them into the sea.

The Israeli boat escaped capture, but the Egyptian Navy fished out the documents and were able to reconstruct the planned activity, much to the embarrassment of Israel. Hearing that, I decided I had been trained in the requisite skills to circumvent similar incidents in the future. I would devise a storage box with an electronic moisture sensor. A few drops of water reaching the documents would trigger a flame that would incinerate the document completely.

My father noticed that I was deeply engrossed in a project. Curious, he asked "What are you doing, son?"

"I am inventing a new apparatus," I said. "The Israeli Navy needs me."

He smiled and brushed away the idea that an eighteen-year-old boy could be of any help to the highly regarded Israeli Navy.

I worked on my project for about a month then was finally ready to test the device. A steel box contained sheets of paper, and a battery-operated electronic circuit was connected inside to a small water pipe that held the explosive powder. (I obtained the powder by prying open some gun shells.)

I stood over the box in my room and told my brother Avram to stand a few feet away. I began pouring drops of water into the tiny opening that led to the electronic trigger circuit.

In an instant, the gunpowder lit. The entire apparatus exploded and bits and pieces shot high into the air, exiting through the roof of our house!

The flying debris missed my head by about two inches. It's a miracle I was not decapitated!

I had miscalculated the size of the tiny escape hole intended to vent the initial gases. The pipe exploded like a hand grenade. Dozens of chunks of shrapnel lodged themselves in the delicate flesh all over my body.

It was a Saturday so my parents and brothers and sisters were home. At the sound of the huge explosion, they came rushing in to my now-roofless room. The smoke was still in the air when they found me splayed on the floor, in shock, alive, apologetic, and bleeding profusely from my arms, neck, legs, and stomach. My sister Hannah screamed bloody murder and ran to our neighbors who owned a telephone to call the police, just like she had done so often when I was a child and had gotten hurt through some foolish antics.

Within minutes, an ambulance showed up to take me, along with my father, to Kaplan Hospital in Bilu, a few minutes' ride away. At the hospital, the doctors gave me a shot and began removing the shrapnel embedded in my torso and limbs. To make sure they had found and removed every last metal scrap, they subjected me to a series of intensive X-ray exams. They assured me I was lucky to be alive. I looked into my father's impenetrable eyes, and I was certain he was grateful I hadn't been the unwitting victim of you own ingenuity. He also wanted to kill me—again—as he always felt after one of my near misses.

On the way home, it was total silence until we turned the street just before my house.

"I hope you learned a lesson," Father said. "The Israeli Navy *does not* need you." Emphasis on *does not* was tinged with sarcasm.

I still believed they did, but I dared not tell my father that.

Thirty years later, I was admitted to Huntington Hospital in Long Island, New York, for an unrelated, persistent stomachache. After I was X-rayed, the doctor asked my wife if I had been shot.

She laughed. "Of course not. He just has pain in the abdomen."

After lengthy interrogation and further extensive examination, it was determined that a sliver of steel shrapnel from the old incident in Israel was still stuck in a portion of the tissue near my liver.

Dare I tell them I was only trying to save the world?

This metal scrap was all that was left of my grandiose attempt to intervene in world events. The doctors decided to leave it there, as it was causing no harm. The stomachache was from other things, nothing of monumental interest. I learned to live with the pains and with my little piece of history that would remain inside me forever.

Tel-Aviv at the waterfronts: What's out there?

Sidelining my role in high-level military defense after the exploding electronic, moisture sensor, storage box incident, I enrolled in poetry and history courses at Tel Aviv University three times a week after work. "The Philosopher" wanted to feed his soul on something more than wires, war, explosives, and supporting his family. I often visited the Tel Aviv boardwalk after classes to look out across the water at the mesmerizing pink and orange Israeli sunsets. I stood leaning on the old, rusty handrails, straining my eyes to stretch as far as they could see into the distant horizon.

"What's out there beyond what we can see?" I asked myself. *"I want to go there someday and find out."*

My lifelong hunger for knowledge and the meaning of life was nourished at that corroded handrail. It grew as I read volume after volume of literature, history, philosophy, and poetry, and later as I traveled the wide world. I have lived in many places, reading books everywhere I went, always willing to experience the range of everything possible. I have never stopped searching and wondering, for the answer remains always just beyond the farthest horizon line.

The influence of James Dean

Like millions of youth around the world in that era of movie history, I was deeply affected by the young American actor, James Dean. I saw his popular movies *East of Eden* and *Rebel Without a Cause* more than once. As a young and impressionable deep thinker, I identified with his rebellious, non-conformist spirit.

I decided I would be more like James Dean. I would become an actor. I signed up for night classes in Tel Aviv, at a locally-respected acting school. The experience helped me to construct a more glamorous identity for myself, and the hours we spent re-enacting scenes from the great dramas of the past and imagining a meaningful new theatre of the present were enlightening and enjoyable.

One afternoon, the teachers took head shots of all the students and gave them to us to use as we pleased. I decided to send mine to Elia Kazan, director of James Dean's movies, and introduced myself as the next, bright contender for fame and glory.

I didn't hear back from Mr. Kazan. It was a few months later that James Dean was tragically killed in his racing car in 1955. Around the same time, my photo, along with a kindly letter from Mr. Kazan, were returned to me. I mourned James Dean's death for quite some time, along with everyone else in the world that identified themselves with him as beautiful outsiders. Eventually, I had to surrender my acting fantasies to pursue more practical career goals.

In Sinai, aftermath of 1956 war with Egypt,
soldiers burnt by napalm (11)

Saul age 16, with friend Carmella,
Tel-Aviv, Israel, 1954 (12)

Saul with friends in town park,
Rehoboth, Israel, 1954 (13)

Saul (far right) with friends and brother
Yeftah (bottom), Israel, 1954 (14)

Saul at acting school, Israel, 1955 (15)

With cousin Yeg-Al, Jerusalem, Israel, 1955 (16)

Saul in acting school,
Israel, 1956 (17)

Saul showing off his physique at
Tel-Aviv Beach, Israel, 1956 (18)

My father Silas Fathi, Israeli Air Force,
Tel-Nof, Israel, 1956 (19)

Prime Minister Ben-Gurion and Oppenheimer (father of the
atom bomb) at Weitzman Institute, Israel, 1957 (20)

Father Silas and brother Yeftah,
Israel, 1957 (21)

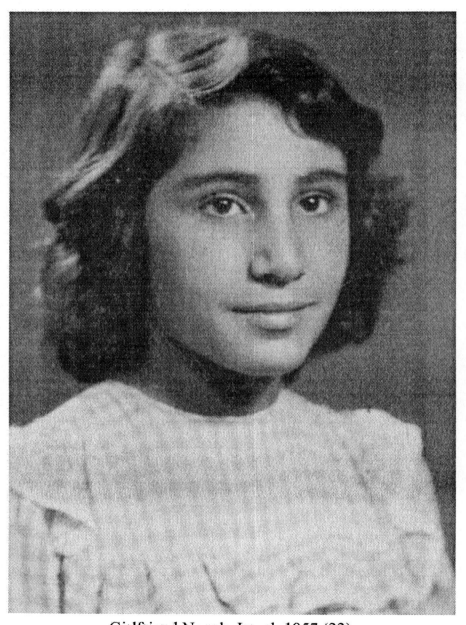

Girlfriend Nogah, Israel, 1957 (22)

Father Silas and brother Avram, Israel, 1959 (23)

Sister Yedida and Ezra's wedding,
Israel, 1960 (24)

Friend Carmella, Israel, 1960 (25)

Brother Avram in the 1967 Israel-Arab
War, Sinai, 1967 (26)

Hanah and Haiim's wedding,
Israel, 1967 (27)

Sister Pirha and husband Uri's wedding,
Israel, 1968 (28)

Chapter Twenty-Seven

Avram and Berta Grow Up

Avram goes to the Technion in Haifa

While I was serving in Korea with the U.S. Army's First Cavalry, my youngest brother Avram, back in Israel, had graduated high school and was accepted to the prestigious Technion University in Haifa. Avram was intelligent and did well in his studies, and he excelled in sports. Our parents saw his acceptance to this particular university as a dream fulfilled. One of their sons would be a college graduate and would graduate from a very noteworthy institution. Their only worry was their ability to afford his high tuition and the cost of his dormitory.

Avram worked very hard at his studies and kept his grades high so he qualified for loans from the Israeli government. But it wasn't a free ride. He found menial jobs that paid a little money so that he could sustain a few of his needs through four years of college. I learned later from my sisters that Avram had lived mostly on tap water and stale sandwiches that Mother sent to him on a monthly basis. He had persevered and had endured. But his hardships continued. He graduated owing thousands of dollars to the Israeli government, which he had to work years to repay.

We were all very proud of him. Nevertheless, Avram never forgot the hardships he had had to endure to get his degree. He harbored resentment toward our parents and the Israeli government for the financial burden he had suffered. As a consequence, he didn't speak of this to our parents for years.

Berta's wedding to Isaac: Splitting the family again

In 1956, when my oldest sister Berta began teaching kindergarten, she received an introduction to an American named Isaac Joseph, who was the nephew of Elias, my Aunt Roni's husband. When Isaac had come to visit his aunt and uncle in Israel, Roni and Elias had given him the opportunity to meet Berta. They seemed to like each other well enough.

Just after Berta and Isaac met, everyone around them decided he was a suitable match and began preparing for a wedding. Luckily, the couple had no objections. They were both looking for a change in their lives.

As my parents could not afford to rent a hall, the wedding was held in my Uncle Yehuda's house, which was the most spacious house in the family. The wedding was very modest, with less than fifty people attending, but it was still a beautiful celebration. Berta's was the first wedding we had experienced in our family.

The only thing that marred the event was the knowledge that Berta and Isaac would not be setting up housekeeping in Israel. Isaac had to return to the United States, and Berta was going with him, of course. It would be there that they would live and raise their family.

My parents had misgivings about Berta's leaving us and living in the far-away country of America. Memories of splitting up the family once before, I'm sure, must have filled their minds. Notwithstanding, they were very eager to see Berta, the oldest daughter, married and settled in her own household and able to raise her own children, free from want and danger.

In general, Berta and Isaac's marriage was a blissful one. Isaac prospered, and they had three children: Alex, Danny and Michelle, all born in New York City.

Of course, Berta's departure marked the beginning of a new phase in our family's history. She was the first to marry and move far away. It was the beginning of the separation and dispersal of our family out of Israel. It was hard for all of us, but especially for our parents, after they had fought so hard to get all of us there safe and sound.

Saul's sister Berta with husband Isaac in
Atlantic City, NJ, USA, 1959 (29)

Chapter Twenty-Eight

First Loves and Lovemaking

Introduction to love: Was this sex?

Ossnat was a stunning beauty with gorgeous skin, shining eyes, and a come-on smile that knew the effect it had on pre-pubescent boys alert enough to notice. We all noticed. She was a *Sabra* (Israeli-born) and had been taught not to associate with types like me: a poor immigrant. She was loved by many and admired from afar by even more. She went to my school, but we were not in the same class. At breaks, I waited at the end of the hallway just to catch a glimpse of her bright, dazzling face. She knew we all loved her, and she loved to tease. She never discouraged anyone from falling in love with her; she enjoyed torturing us as she added new names to her list of hapless admirers.

It was Ossnat's habit to stay behind in the classroom when everyone else was leaving and peek out the window of the door into the hallway. This gave her the advantage of already knowing which of us were there, hoping to catch a glimpse of her. It wasn't unusual that as many as three boys waited at the same time, pretending to eat our lunch or study notes as we lounged against the walls of the hallway. When she finally appeared full-bodied, she passed by each yearning boy and said hello in the most seductive way she knew how. And, believe me, she knew how.

After too many days of this, I grew tired of the competition around her. I decided to try a different tactic. I began to write her secret letters. *(I would give anything to get my hands on those letters now.)* During breaks when no one was in classroom, I sneaked into her homeroom and slipped my pronouncements in the drawer of her desk. Though I couldn't leave them anonymous nor could I sign them boldly for fear that they might get passed around the school, I did pencil my initials at the bottom of them. That way, I could deny that I wrote them, if I had to.

This went on for months. Under her spell, I was alert to her every move, but I was making no progress in gaining her attention. In the meantime, rumors flew around the school whenever she went on a date or to the movies with someone. I was jealous, especially when I heard the exaggerated descriptions of what went on at the movies as the object of my desire and my rivals for her love sat shoulder to shoulder in the last rows of the darkened theatre.

Then one bright day, Ossnat slipped a note under my bench, folded to the size of a matchbook. I could not wait for the break to read it. I raised my hand and asked permission to go to the bathroom. The teacher sent me on my way down the hall. In the little bathroom stall, I locked myself in and sat on top of the toilet. Hands shaking, I opened the note.

"I noticed your persistence in writing me your stupid letters. I guess you have really fallen in love with me. It's not my fault. I have many admirers, and I am willing to add your name to the long list. Don't keep after me. You don't stand a chance. But, if you want to discuss this over a falafel or a movie, I will accommodate you. Just say when."

I was simultaneously upset and excited by the rejection and promise contained in those words. I stayed in the bathroom until the class was over and avoided her eyes in the hallways for the rest of the day. Every now and then, I thought she looked in my direction, soliciting a reaction to her note.

Toward the end of the school day, I finally managed to write a reply: "Thanks for your generosity. Yes, I do want to discuss this. Let's meet tonight at the movie house at 7:30 pm."

Since there was only one movie house in the whole town of Rehoboth, there would be no mistaking our meeting place. I tucked my note in her bench and left in a hurry. I walked three miles home, ate a quick snack, washed up and changed my clothes. *If I am lucky,* I thought, as I entered fresh-faced onto the streets in the evening, *I will catch a bus on its way to the movie house.* There, my appointment with destiny awaited.

I stood around for about ten minutes, impatiently watching for a bus, then gave up and finally walked into town. At the theatre, I stood at the side of the building behind some trees, so no one I knew would see me and suggest we go see the movie together. I fidgeted with my money, not knowing if I was expected to be a gentleman and buy us both our tickets in advance.

What if she doesn't show up? I wondered.

I waited and saw no sign of her. I was beginning to get angry. *Did she set me up to play me for a fool?* I wondered. *Ossnat, the most popular girl in school, is never going to show up, not here, not now, not for me. It was an evil trick. She used me like a pawn in her love game.*

I was ready to give up when I saw her walking toward me from the other side of the movie house, still dressed in her school clothes with a small purse in her hand, looking like an angel.

"Hi Saul," she said. "Let's go." She pointed to a moonlit area in back of the movie house.

I was puzzled. I thought we were going to see the movie together, that we were going to have a date. "We have to hurry up and buy the tickets, the movie is starting now," I said, matter-of-factly.

She laughed, grabbed my hand, and motioned me to follow her.

What is going on here? I thought. *Is she setting me up for a beating or some other embarrassment?*

Though the moon was out, it was dark behind the theater. I couldn't see a thing. For some crazy reason, I followed her, feeling like an insignificant child or an obedient little dog being led to an unknown fate.

When we arrived at her chosen destination, I was shocked by her next move: She pulled me close against her and kissed me on the lips. Then she looked at me for a reaction. When I hesitated, she grabbed me again and kissed me, harder and longer this time.

"Forget about the stupid movie, let's stay here," she whispered in my ear.

I was beyond excited. I thought, *I better show her quick that I have experience in these matters, or she is going to go to school and mock my ineptitude to everyone.*

I pulled her gently toward me and kissed her sweetly on her lips, her cheeks, and her neck.

To my surprise (and pleasure!) the girl of my dreams, Ossnat, began loosening her blouse and her bra. Then she took my hands and placed them on her heavenly, forbidden breasts. I was lost, a novice who before this night had only imagined such a splendid thing could happen to a poor boy like me. I had no idea how far this might go. And I had no experience in taking initiative to move the process along.

Luckily, my girl knew what to do. Again, I was shocked (and pleased) when Ossnat, the stunning beauty I had worshipped from a distance and addressed without hope in so many love letters, reached her hands down to open my pants zipper and touched me there. Some instinct told me to do the same to her. She threw her blouse on the grass and pulled me down over her, where we thrashed and rolled around, all over each other's eager bodies.

Is this wrestling or sex? I asked myself. *It's both,* I concluded.

We explored each other's mouths and muscles and private places, there in the dark grass, for the duration of the movie.

Just before the movie ended and people began filing out of the theater, Ossnat said, "It's time to go. And, remember what I said in the letter: You don't stand a chance with me, but I am willing to add you to the list of my admirers." She smiled, and I melted, unable to answer. As she was leaving, she pointed a finger at me and added, "Not a word to anyone. I will deny it all."

She left me instantly, and I rearranged my clothes, my thoughts, and my feelings in the darkness, contemplating what had just taken place. I felt inept and such a fool, but maybe, a lucky fool. A fourteen-year-old, stupid, lucky fool!

During the two hours I took to walk home, I went over and over in my mind every action, taste, and sensation that had just happened. I wanted more, knowing I'd never get another chance with her, but grateful for this unexpected chance to experience what I had only heard about before this night. I never had another encounter with Ossnat, but there were others who taught me more.

Lilly in Bilu Square: A sexy beauty

Lilly was a knockout, the type of female known in those days as "a sex kitten." She was probably only sixteen or seventeen years old, yet every move she made was meant to seduce: the way she dressed, the way she smiled, the way she moved her body as she walked.

Her father was a Muslim, a dentist, member of a prominent family named Dajani, from the old Arab village of Ah-Kier, south of Rehoboth. He dated and married the sister of Shmuel Richtman, Jewish, who later became the Mayor of the city of Rehoboth.

They owned a restaurant whose location was the most traveled intersection in Bilu. Lilly ran things from behind the counter. Soldiers frequently hitchhiked to their bases from there. To extend their freedom a little longer, the young men gathered at Lilly's counter to sip soda or drink coffee for hours, savoring any glimpses they could get of her.

Between the ages of fourteen to eighteen, I was a student at the Israel Air Force Academy, going through their four-year program. I often sat at the counter with the other soldiers, hoping for the same as they did: a glimpse of beauty, and perhaps something more.

My friend, nicknamed "the cheap Persian," ordered a small soda. Of course, he got hungry like everybody else, so every time Lilly went into the kitchen, he pulled out a homemade sandwich from his briefcase and stole quick bites. He ate plenty but only paid for that single soda as he sat there nursing it all afternoon, just to be around the power of this woman. *Did he fool her? Or did she outsmart us all, consciously trading her beauty to lure us in and keep us there?* We were all under her spell.

When she was in her early twenties, Lilly was crowned "Miss Israel," making her the most beautiful girl in Israel. Many years later, we heard that she had moved to New York and had been arrested for running an illegal abortion clinic.

With Carmella in Tel-Aviv: At the daytime movie

I began writing short stories and poetry when I was eleven when my brother and I lived in the kibbutz. It was more like an undeclared diary, really. In it, I poured out my most sensitive inner thoughts, my longing for my parents and siblings, and my deep fear that maybe my father might not survive the ordeal of being a wanted man in Baghdad. *Was it possible that he would be hanged, like other prominent Jews in Iraq during the years of persecution?* I wondered. I had witnessed this atrocity myself, so this was not mere speculation or paranoia on my part. *Maybe... What if...* It was endless wondering.

But to whom could I confide in? Where could I confess worries? Other Jewish children with me at the kibbutz knew for certain that their parents and siblings had perished in the concentration camps of Europe. *How could I solicit sympathy from them?* I was ashamed of my own relative safety. I had not suffered nearly as much, compared to them. I felt guilty for my small, fearful emotions. I wrote because within the blank pages of my small notebook I was neither judged nor compared.

One day, when I was thirteen, two years after our family's reunion in 1951, while living in the Ma'Abarah in Rehoboth, Father pointed out something in the morning newspaper. He read several of Israel's many daily papers, but he favored one called *Ha-Ah-Retz*. He recommended articles for me to read whenever he came across something he thought would be of interest to me. That morning, he pointed out an article announcing a new weekly publication *Anakhnu,* which meant "We" in Hebrew. It was dedicated to youth growing up in Israel, written by them and for them.

I thought it was a great idea. I wrote the editor and told him my name and background and offered my services. "I could contribute an article or a story at least once a month," I wrote. With it, I enclosed my first fictional story about a birthday girl and a small snapshot of myself.

A month after sending in my submission, I was notified of my acceptance as a "young journalist," complete with an ID card and a welcome letter (I still have this ID card, fifty years later). My story was published the following week. My sister Pirha made sure the whole family was aware of it and was so proud of me that she handed dozens of copies of that issue to our neighbors and friends.

About four months later, I went with my girlfriend Carmella to Tel Aviv, for an interview with the editors of *Anakhnu.* They were pleased with my contributions and assured me I could count on some earning power when I reached sixteen. I was happy and proud at the prospect of a career as a writer and promised them I would continue to write.

After the interview, Carmella and I had the rest of the day to ourselves. It was really hot out, so we walked to the Tel Aviv oceanfront, took off our sandals, rolled up our pants legs, and sloshed around in the warm, lapping waves. It was a most pleasant and sensuous afternoon. We licked melting ice cream cones from the famous Persian Gleedah Masteek (chewing-gum ice cream), whose store was near the boardwalk.

We were excited by the day's happy offerings and decided to continue celebrating my flourishing career by going to see a matinee movie. We knew of a movie house that ran twenty-four hours, frequented mainly by bums and the unemployed. Some cowboy movie was playing, but we didn't care about the movie, we just wanted to get out of the heat and sit in a dark, air-conditioned theater where we could be alone. We wanted to touch each other and "make out" till the lights went up.

The movie started and soon we began touching and kissing, feeling safe in the absolute darkness. Suddenly, I felt a touch on my shoulder. It was a middle-aged man from the seats in back of us. "Hey mister," he said. "I came to see a movie, not to see you two in action." We said nothing, but quickly filed out of the theater. We were so embarrassed Carmella and I didn't talk for several hours.

Nogah, the good-hearted beauty

Everyone was aware that Nogah as a sexually active, beautiful teenager. All the boys wanted to be her friend and have her bestow upon them one of her generous "charitable acts." Those who knew her well enough to have received small portions of her gifts, called her "Nogah, the Good-Hearted."

I made an effort to get to know her better at a friend's private party. After my self-serving introduction and a bit of the story of my life, she flashed me her winning smile.

"You sound interesting," she said. "I would love to get to know you better."

My friends had told me that was her signal, the key to heaven's gates. I promised to get in touch, but no one in my family owned a telephone. A week or so later, I had the brilliant idea to go to a friend's house to use his telephone and call Nogah.

Happily, she told me where she lived and agreed to meet me at the Moshavah for ice cream at Kapulski's. That evening I treated her to her choice of ice cream cones. While tasting the delicious vanilla and chocolate, we strolled along the streets, talking. It was a pleasure to watch Nogah licking the sweet, sugary cream in the most seductive way. As I escorted Nogah home, I was ever hopeful that my moves were having the desired effect and that I would be duly rewarded before the night was over.

Her house was nestled between citrus and palm trees in an enormous yard. Part of the backyard had been converted into a parking lot for her father's many trucks. As we approached the house, she held my hand and directed me out back. "Come, let me show you what we have in our backyard," she told me, with a charming and sly smile.

I felt my heart beating hard within my chest. Beads of sweat formed along my forehead and neck.

It was a hot night, with millions of stars glistening in the Middle Eastern summertime sky. Nogah took me on a tour of her father's trucks and explained their functions to me one by one, trying to impress me with how rich they were (unlike poor me from the Ma'Abarah in Ramah). We walked among the fruit trees and palms, and she named each tree and told me how old they were and how her father had wisely bought all this land from Arabs during the years of the British Mandate of Palestine. All the while, she held my hand as if I were her little, kid brother, needing help to cross the street. We were nearly the same age (she was sixteen and I was fifteen), but she was light years ahead of me as far as life experience in the relationship category was concerned.

We took our time, strolling through the grassy yard where shadows cast by the moonlight provided sufficient cover for us to privately enjoy each other's desire as it built to bursting in the dark air of the evening. Nogah directed our path back to where the fleet of trucks was parked. There was a space of three to four feet between each one, and that's where we paused. I stood there with her, a little awkward, highly charged, fearful, excited, and ever so curious.

Nogah carefully surveyed the windows of her house with its threatening lights and watchful eyes, then decided we were safely invisible where we were. She began to touch my private parts, kissing me nonstop.

I was eager to show her this was not my first experience, that I was a man, so I reciprocated by opening her blouse, button by button. I at least knew the goal now, since my night with Ossnat behind the movie house. It was to remove the bra and set the stage for caressing her breasts. But of course I had a problem with

the bra, complex constructions that they are, because I had thought they employed snaps, like Ossnat's, which she had handled for me herself. But Nogah's
bra had buttons, many tight frustrating buttons. I fumbled to undo them, snapping
some off in the process. Several fell on the ground.

As things became heated and almost uncontrollable, Nogah thankfully took
charge, opened a truck cabin door, and pulled me inside. Expertly unzipping me,
she pulled my pants to my knees, and directed me down on top of her.

Everything about it was awkward. I was doing my best to provide what she
seemed to expect and thought I was conducting myself in a fairly manly way.
Suddenly, she pushed me off her. Before I knew what hit me, she straddled me
brazenly, saying, "I like it this way better."

Once I got used to this new reversal of position, I thought, *Okay, I could get
used to this.* I stretched back and enjoyed the ride, opening my eyes from time to
time to watch Nogah's face as she worked to please herself. When my eyes were
closed, I'm not exactly sure what went on, but memory tells me that I liked it.

When I finally sat up, a long while later, I had a feeling that I had lost a few
unaccounted-for minutes. *Did I black out? Where was I the last few minutes?*

I was anxious and near panic. I lacked experience, but I had learned enough
to know that there were consequences to "going all the way," and I was not
entirely clear whether we had or not.

"What's the matter, Saul? Was it all right?" Nogah asked me, wiping my
gleaming sweaty forehead with a handkerchief. "Did you like it?"

I hesitated, "Yes, it was wonderful. But, did I do anything wrong? Did we do
something we weren't supposed to do?"

She laughed her famous heart-breaking laughter. "Don't worry, Saul. You
will be surprised how many things a girl can engage in and still be a virgin," she
said, to my astonishment and relief.

I didn't say anything as we dressed ourselves and rearranged our clothes and
hair. I was weak-kneed, both strengthened and drained by the act of love. Now
that we were upright again and back in our clothes, I felt utterly unsure of what
the whole thing meant.

I said, "It's late, we should probably get going."

"Okay, I will see you around," Nogah said. "I like you, Saul. Hope to see you
again,"

There was no need for an answer. I headed out of the backyard as my lover
headed in the opposite direction toward her house. I watched from the shadows
as her mother greeted her at the door, and then closed the door behind her.

I walked home three or four miles, with gnawing feelings and plenty of
questions. *This Nogah, the Good-Hearted, will she laugh at me? Will she tell on
me? Did I do it right? Did I measure up? Did I make a fool of myself? Does she
really like me? If so, as what - a lover, friend, a brother?*

I had no answers, only more questions.

Chapter Twenty-Nine

Nagako Obata, my Japanese Pen Pal

The Israeli editor of *Anakhnoo* made a lengthy trip to Japan and wrote extensively about the youth of that country. To all of us living in Israel, we read about a people shrouded in mystery and with a fascinating history.

This was one of the lands written about by Marco Polo in his book *The Description of the World*, which was published in the 13th century. From his home in Venice, Polo had traveled at the age of seventeen (exactly my age at this time) with his father and uncle, who were merchants, to the court of Kublai Khan, the Emperor of China. Polo was bright and curious and had a knack for languages, ultimately speaking four fluently. This skill earned him an honored place as one of the Khan's ambassadors and took him to many lands on the business of the Chinese court. Among those countries he visited were India, Ethiopia, Madagascar, Ceylon, Siam, Java, and Burma. He was the first European to visit the string of islands that came to be known as the Japans.

Though Marco Polo had introduced the world to this country, it wasn't until 1854 that a treaty brokered by US Commodore Matthew Perry opened up this region for trade. The treaty also insured help for American ships that often were stranded off the Japanese coast because of foul weather and protection for people who were shipwrecked. These islands became vital stops for American ships to take on water, coal, and supplies as they traveled about the Pacific.

The Japanese islands, like many in the Pacific Ocean, were formed by volcanoes. There are 108 active volcanoes distributed among the four main islands (Hokkaido in the north, Honshu the main island, Shikoku the smallest, and Kyushu in the south) and several smaller ones. Okinawa is a part of the Kyukyu island group in the far south. This region is geologically active, and the country experiences frequent earthquakes.

For the most part, these islands are mountainous and have never been suitable for building cities inland. Therefore, the population has concentrated along the coasts, creating large cities with dense populations. While visiting one of those cities, the capital Tokyo, the editor of *Anakhnoo* was a guest of the Japanese Department of Education. Here, his Japanese hosts suggested that the youth of Japan and the youth of Israel should have an opportunity to correspond with each other to promote peace and understanding between the two countries.

Upon returning to Israel, the editor published impressions of his visit to Japan in a series of articles. One story detailed the Japanese Department of Education's youth correspondence idea. With that article, the editor included a list of names of Japanese students, twelve to seventeen years old, who wished to find pen pals in Israel.

I seized the opportunity to find someone to funnel my thoughts and ideas to. I wanted to be able to write to someone other than my family and friends, who might tease me for some of my intimate thoughts. I selected the name of a sixteen-year-old girl, Nagako Obata, who lived in Nagoya.

The letters

When we began corresponding, we exchanged personal photos and shared long introductions of ourselves and our lives, our friends, and our families. Then, we began to write about our nations, our histories, and our cultures. I wrote her about the holocaust in Europe and what was happening to Jews in other places of the world, including my home country. I told her in great detail of my escape from Iraq, my separation from my family, and finally our reunion. I shared with her the struggles of the Jewish people from around the world who were making a new nation in Israel. As a typical Japanese, she was totally ignorant of the history of Israel and the Jewish people.

She wrote about the history of Japan. I found out that the Japanese don't refer to their country as Japan. That is a Chinese word, *Jihpenkuo*, meaning "land of the rising sun," which was Europeanized to *Jipang* when Marco Polo wrote of his adventures there. The people of Japan refer to their country as Nippon, though it was once called *Yamato* or "place of mountains."

Nagako told me that rice was not native to Japan. It had come from China as had ink painting, Buddhism, and a system of law codes. But, a female Japanese writer had made a major contribution to the world when she wrote, *The Tale of the Genji*, in the 2nd century CE. It was the world's first full-length novel.

Japan also has the longest unbroken ruling bloodline in the world. An Emperor of Japan has held this position for 1400 years, though it is a title of respect but with no power in the government today. Military rulers have historically controlled the country. In the 12th century CE, the Minamoto family, members of a warrior class known as the *samurai*, came to power and set up a *shogunate*. Minamoto No Yoritomo was given the title *shogun*. A long line of shoguns followed for nearly seven centuries. These shoguns, though driven by a strict military code of honor, were not necessarily the gentlest of rulers. Some were ruthless and treated their subjects harshly. Others were firm but fair. By the mid-1400's CE, feuding warlords and a weakened shogunate plunged the country into civil war that lasted nearly one hundred years.

Bringing peace in the 17th century CE, Tokugawa Ieyasu unified the country but cut it off from the rest of the world. Europeans had been visiting Japan since the mid-1500s CE. Tokugawa dropped all contact with other countries except for China and the Netherlands. US Commodore Perry's arrival in 1853 and the treaty he negotiated the next year opened the country to trade and more Western influences. In 1868, political authority was returned to the imperial court and the age of the shogunate was over.

Nagako explained about Japanese religions. There were many and people didn't just practice one. Nagako was a Shinto. Shintoism and Buddhism are the most widely practiced. Shintoism, a traditional Japanese religion, recognizes the spirit or *kami* in everything. There are nature *kami* found in stones, trees, mountains, etc. Clan *kami* are guardian spirits of specific clans, usually a revered ancestor. There are also heavenly *kami* who live on the celestial plane as we think of Greek gods. And, there is even a *kami* of the rice paddies that is honored at plantings and harvests.

The Shinto religion has no sacred texts, but advocates purity in life and cleanliness when dealing with *kami*. It has been considered the religion of every day living.

Japanese Buddhism, in contrast, is practiced as the religion that honors the dead. Starting around the 5th century BCE in India, it spread throughout China and finally came to Japan during the 6th century CE. It took root among the more affluent and those who could understand the more esoteric precepts of the belief. Zen Buddhism originated in Japan in the 13th century CE. It was received by the samurai because of its meditation and riddles that were supposed to hold great truths. Zen also influenced the arts and certain sports like fencing, archery, judo, and karate. As Buddhism developed over the centuries, other sects appeared, but most Buddhists in Japan follow the rituals that honor the dead that are found in all sects.

Christianity, though introduced in 1549 by Francis Xavier, never really caught on. It would seem that the belief in one God would prohibit the multiple worship that Buddhists and Shintoists enjoy. However, many couples today are choosing Christian wedding services when they get married.

Nagako said that there were also a number of new religions, which might be more cults than beliefs, that have appeared in the past century. Minkan Skukyo or the folk religion, however, has never faded. Rituals for life stages or rites of passage, fortune telling, and the creation of amulets for good luck and protection are still alive and well.

My Japanese pen pal also told me heart-wrenching stories of the effects of the bombing of Hiroshima and Nagasaki in August 1945. Just a decade and a half previously, the United States had chosen to end World War II by unleashing the most potent weapon of its time. The first bomb, nicknamed Little Boy, was an untested uranium-fueled weapon that struck Hiroshima on August 6, 1945. This city was targeted because it was an important army depot and port, situated in an industrial region tucked among hills. Its location was vital, not only because of its military significance, but because the hills would focus the bomb's effect, increasing the blast damage. Nearly 140,000 people had died by the end of 1945. (Estimates to date say that nearly 400,000 people died from bomb-related illnesses.) Japan still refused to surrender.

Three days later, a plutonium bomb, dubbed Fat Man, was dropped on Nagasaki. This city was not considered part of the original lists of targets but was chosen because it had an arms factory and a medical college where the effects of the bombing could be documented and the terror of it appreciated. I found out later that this bombing might not have been scheduled at all. Poor visibility due to bad weather had made all of the other targets impossible to see. Some researchers suggest that the bomber crew may have released the bomb over Nagasaki, which was on the revised list, only because they were afraid of trying to land with the bomb on board. It had never been done before. There is also some speculation that this bomb was a test case to see how it would explode in a region that didn't have the hills to multiply its effect.

Nevertheless, over 40,000 people were killed instantly, and another 70,000 died in the years since as a result of radiation-related illnesses. It was also said that after the bombing that vegetation would not grow in these two cities for 75 years. There is an International Peace Park in Nagasaki today, filled with sculptures and lots of trees. It is green again, much earlier than it was anticipated.

Though the devastation was enormous for the Japanese, Nagako, like many of her people, did not blame the United States for this. The Japanese mourn their losses but add that it was the Japanese military who bombed the US first and started this war. This humility in the face of such horror is a lesson for us all.

Much later, I learned that these bombs were not originally created to be deployed in Japan. They, and the whole idea of making weapons with fissionable material, came from German scientists who had fled to America and worried that their counterparts in Germany would make a weapon before the US did. They persuaded Albert Einstein to sign a letter to President Roosevelt to inform him of the possible uses of nuclear fission in bomb building and clearly indicated that the real threat was Nazi Germany. It is ironic that these weapons that were created to fight evil in one arena of war were used in quite a different one altogether.

Family reactions and plans

My parents were delighted that I was polishing my English through this correspondence but were somewhat worried that this relationship would develop into something more. Occasionally, I asked Father for help in writing the English language, which gave him the opportunity to read some of Nagako's letters and my responses to her. He, in turn, may have disclosed to my mother and sisters the progress Nagako and I were making in our relationship.

Before long, Nagako and I were expressing to one another the hope and desire to one day meet and get to know each other better. Of course, this was an unattainable dream for both of us. Our countries were very far apart geographically, and we both came from lower-middle-class families where money for international travel was nonexistent.

We kept writing to each other for a period of two years, until I left Israel to see the world and ended up in Brazil. When I left Israel behind me, I also left my friendship and correspondence with Nagako. Now and then, when I felt lonely and miserable in Brazil, I thought of writing to her and pouring out my soul. But, I was afraid of the obligation to continue writing once I began again. So I didn't.

Nagako and I finally meet

After two years in Brazil, I went to the United States on a student visa. I spent eight months in this country and then volunteered to serve in the U.S. Army, where I was promised help with college tuition. Six months into my enlistment, I was ordered to report to Oakland, California. Soon, I was on my way to Korea.

Aboard the military ship, I could not resist the urge to get in touch with my old pen pal Nagako and sent her a short telegram: "Dear Miss Nagako: I am in the U.S. Army now, on my way to Korea, but will stop in Yokohama on ... for 24 hours. Could you meet me near the Officers Club there?" I signed it and indicated a return address for her telegram reply.

A few days later, midway between Hawaii and Yokohama, I received a telegram from Nagako. "Dear Mr. Fathi, I will meet you as requested."

Now, all kinds of feelings awakened. I decided this would make a good story to write my parents about and mailed it in Yokohama to dispel any doubt that I was there indeed. And so it was I came to Yokohama, the second largest city in Japan and a busy port. Here the first Western hotel and restaurant were built, as well as the first coffee shop and bakery. Yokohama also had the first water system and railroad in the country. Since 1859, when the port first opened, the city has exported raw silk, tea, and sea products and imported silk and wool textiles. The silk trade expanded in the late 1880s. Electricity followed in 1890 and a new hospital the next year.

The city was totally destroyed in the Great Kanto Earthquake in 1923, but soon rebuilt itself, becoming an industrial city, focusing on heavy chemicals, in the next decade. Then, in 1945, Yokohama was hit in repeated bombings, destroying almost half of the city. The port facility was commandeered by US occupying forces. It wasn't until 1951, when the port ownership was returned to Yokohama that rebuilding was undertaken in earnest. Not only were new piers built, but a passenger terminal and parks were added.

At the end of the occupation, Japan was considered a less-developed country. In twenty years, the country had moved to "developed" status, the first country in the world to do that. At the time I arrived in Yokohama, the city was bustling with activity and feeling its economy growing.

I met Nagako near the Officers Club, and we found a place right away to have lunch. She looked different now, bespectacled and skinny in a nice, conservative suit. I wore my Army uniform, with some citations pinned on my chest and my hat in my hand. Soon, I realized that although Nagako could write decent English, she could not carry on a conversation in English, and I did not know Japanese. She kept consulting her pocket English dictionary for words to complete a sentence. Everyone was staring at us, puzzled. Even the local prostitutes, I was told, spoke better English than she did. I asked myself, *Who was this woman?*

Writing Nagako notes

Two hours later, we were walking down a tree-lined boulevard, barely holding hands. I tried to spare her having to talk to me. I kept talking and describing how exciting it was to be in Japan, an impossible dream it seemed for me. I knew she understood everything I said, and she just kept on listening to me prattle on. When I had a problem explaining something, I stopped and wrote her a note, using all capital letters, and handed it to her. She would read those little notes and nod, understanding exactly what I meant. Then she scribbled a reply for me.

As evening came, I spoke to her politely, "Nagako, I must report back to my ship," I said. "I can see you again tomorrow for a couple of hours, if you're willing to stay over in a hotel. I am happy you came. I will continue writing to you from Korea. And, in a year, I will have R&R coming to me, a whole month. Maybe I can spend it in Japan."

She was teary-eyed, but she smiled. "I know. You go now," she said. "But I can't stay in hotel. Family waiting for me tonight. I must go. So, please write to me from Korea. I shall answer right away."

She walked me to the Yokohama port and came as close as she was permitted to my ship. We said our goodbye with a handshake and a brief hug. No kisses. As I boarded my ship, I stood and waved to her. Then, she walked away without looking back.

I wrote a detailed letter to my father about my meeting my pen pal and mailed it right away. When he received it, back in Israel, he read it out loud to my entire family as he did with all of the letters I wrote home. I was told later that my mother immediately reacted by saying, "I knew it! From the beginning, he was planning to meet this girl. Don't tell me otherwise."

Remembering that family story, I always chuckle. My mother was convinced I joined the US military in order to be sent to Japan to meet my pen pal! She was convinced I had planned this since the day I left Israel. Indeed, I could not convince her otherwise.

Chapter Thirty

Hiking with Menasheh in Northern Israel

One of my best friends growing up in Israel was Menasheh, a Jewish young man also from Iraq. He had studied with me at the Israel Air Force in Hatzor, and we continued to work together in the aeronautical industry upon graduation.

Hatzor

The modern settlement of Hatzor in central Israel, just one hour south from the coastal city of Tel-Aviv, lies next to ancient remains of a grand Canaanite city that had been built in the 18th century BCE. Over the next five centuries, it spread to cover 2000 acres and was ten times the size of the city of Jerusalem at that point in history. That early city thrived because it was on an important trade route to Mesopotamia and prospered by the sale of tin.

By the 13th century BCE, the city had been conquered by the Israelites under the military leadership of Joshua, who burned the city to the ground. At first, the Israelites camped in tents and huts around the city and didn't bother to build any new stone structures. King Solomon in the 10th century BCE rebuilt Hatzor as part of a larger building project that restored and built new structures throughout Israel. It included work in Megiddo and Gezer and continued construction of the temple in Jerusalem. The temple was destroyed by Syrian forces in 885 BCE and was rebuilt by Israelite kings Ahab and Omri. King Ahab constructed an elegant underground water system that was used when the Assyrians lay siege to the city. Unfortunately, the people of Hatzor needed more than adequate water to withstand the Assyrian onslaught. In 732 BCE, the ancient city was utterly destroyed. Only, during the last few hundred years had Hatzor been rebuilt.

Manasseh's new travel scheme

Menasheh and I occasionally dreamed up schemes to see the rest of the country. We were working in Rehoboth, a town 20 minutes south of Tel-Aviv, when we decided not to put out our thumbs and hitchhike by car or truck as we had in the past. This time, we were going to sneak a ride on a cattle train that was going to Haifa, a town at the northernmost limit of the railroad line. We found the train at the railroad station in the nearby town of Nes-Tzionah, one of a cluster of industrial towns and science centers in central Israel, south of Tel-Aviv. Quietly, we slipped into one of the rear train cars.

We were lucky not to be seen, but we weren't so fortunate in our choice of accommodations for the trip. The stench of cattle and horses in the cars was almost unbearable. We endured the horrid ride since we could not afford to pay for the trip on a regular passenger train or even by bus.

For nearly two hours, we spoke in whispers, trying not to spook the animals so they wouldn't give away our location. Finally, we arrived in the busy port city of Haifa. Called the "city of the future" by Theodore Hertzl, the father of modern Zionism, Haifa is built on the slopes of Mt. Carmel and sprawls into the Bay of Acco. The train slowed down before entering the station, and we jumped out onto the embankment, unnoticed by anyone and scurried away from the train tracks.

We found an Arab restaurant and sat in the fresh open air for lunch. We had some command of the language, but not enough to be considered fluent speakers. Therefore, we spoke clumsy Arabic when we accosted the owner and the waiter and placed our orders. We were delighted that we received exactly what we wanted. As it turned out, the owner spoke perfect Hebrew.

Mount Carmel

After our meal, we decided to do some sightseeing. The Mount Carmel range is rich in Biblical history. A symbol of beauty and fertility, Mount Carmel is full of springs and lush natural vegetation, including carob trees and ancient kermes oaks, and once sported swamps at the turn of the twentieth century.

It was here that the prophet Elijah had held a contest with the prophets of Baal to determine the true deity. Elijah had been trying to turn the Israelites back to God after they had begun worshiping Baal, the Canaanite god whose worship Jezebel, the wife of King Ahab, had brought with her. For their unfaithfulness, Elijah told them that God would bring a three-year drought to the land. Indeed, the drought occurred, and famine swept through the country. Finally, Elijah created one final test to convince the Israelites that God was real and had not forgotten them.

Elijah gathered 450 prophets of Baal on Mount Carmel and a group of Israelites, including King Ahab himself. Each group of worshipers offered a bull for sacrifice on an altar. The worshipers of Baal called on their god to send fire down to consume it, but after hours of loud praying, nothing happened. At sundown, Elijah prepared his bull, had it laid on his altar, and then had four barrels of water poured over the sacrifice, the altar, and into a shallow trench he had dug around the altar. He ordered that done three times. Then, he prayed in a quiet voice, and God rained down fire from the sky that not only devoured the sacrifice but the entire altar and consumed all of the water in the trench. Afterwards, Elijah announced that the drought was ended, and precious rain finally returned to Mount Carmel.

For centuries since, tourists and religious scholars from all over the world have come to the slopes of Mt. Carmel. They want to walk where the prophet Elijah walked and to see the cave where he lived.

As Menasheh and I hiked up the slopes of Mount Carmel, we decided to visit the magnificent gardens of the Baha'I shrine located there. We were treated with respect by the guide who told us about the Baha'I religion, which originated in Persia in 1844. This religion advocates the harmony of all religions and the unity of humankind as a single race. It supports compulsory education for all, a common language, universal peace, and racial, gender, and economic equality. It also recognizes the independent search for truth. God is revealed through divine messengers, which include Zoroaster, Moses, Jesus, Muhammad, Buddha, and Krishna.

We were told that the beautifully manicured lawns, trimmed shrubs, and lush flowers surrounded the tombs of not only of the founder of the Baha'I faith, Mirza Husayn'Ali Nuri, also known by the title, Baha' U'llah ("the Glory of God") but also its forerunner, Said Ali Mohammed, the Bab ("the gate"). This was the equivalent of having a Christian shrine to both Jesus and John the Baptist, who foretold Jesus' coming.

From the gardens at the top of Mt. Carmel, Menasheh and I could see the entire city. We took turns pointing out the large boats anchored out in the harbor and dreamed of distant voyages of our own someday.

Galilee

When we came down from the mountain, we bought some sandwiches and hitchhiked to Galilee. Even though the trip was only an hour and a half car trip, it took us over five hours because we had to keep waiting for cars or trucks to come along the road so that we could ask for rides.

At Galilee, we walked along the banks of the Keneret. Also called Lake Keneret, Lake Tiberius, the Sea of Gennesareth, and the Sea of Galilee, this was the place where Christians believe Jesus had gathered his disciples, men fishing on the calm waters of this fifteen-mile freshwater lake. Here, Jesus walked on the water of the lake out to a boat where his disciples were fishing. One of them, Peter, wanted to walk on the water, too, so Jesus told him to step out of the boat. According to the New Testament, Peter was fine as long as he kept looking at Jesus. But, the moment he began to doubt and started looking at where he was placing his feet down he went into the water.

On this same lake, Christians tell of another miracle when the disciples and Jesus were out in a fishing boat and a terrific storm blew up. The disciples were afraid that they would capsize, as the waves grew higher around them. Jesus stood on the deck of the little boat and quietly said, "Peace. Be still," and the storm suddenly stopped.

Flowing south from the Keneret is the Jordan River where Jesus met his cousin John the Baptist and asked him to baptize him in the river. John told Jesus that he should be baptizing him, but Jesus convinced him and John took Jesus into the river and baptized him. The river attracts Christian followers from around the world who each year come to be baptized in the same river.

The Keneret is a unique lake because the surface of the water is almost 700 feet below the level of the Mediterranean Sea. It is fed by several freshwater springs but has salty springs on the lake bottom and along its shores. There are hot mineral springs nearby. Evaporation and drought increase the saltiness of the water, but not enough to hamper the growth of its fish population. The lake has always had an abundant supply of fish in its waters, including sardines and tilapia. Periodically due to drought, the level of the Keneret drops to dangerous levels, threatening the very existence of Israel and Jordan, which depend on the lake's supply of fresh water.

Birds were everywhere the day we were there—in the water and along the beaches that surrounded the pear-shaped lake. We saw gulls and pelicans flying overhead. And, in the sandy shallows, we found turtles and crayfish.

Keneret

Though towns had sprung up along the shores of the Keneret, there are also Jewish settlements. Some of the first Kibbutzim were established in the southwestern corner of the Keneret. The first was Kibbutz Degania, which had been founded in 1910. The Haganah's strike force, the Palmakh, used Kibbutz Degania as a base in Israel's struggle for independence in 1948.

During the Ottoman rule from the 1517 CE to 1917 CE, the northern regions of Israel especially suffered through neglect. Absentee landlords owned the land and leased it to poor tenant farmers who were also heavily taxed. The forests of Mount Carmel were clear cut, allowing both swamps and deserts to creep into agricultural lands. By the 1800s, Western countries began to send ambassadors, missionaries, archaeologists, and economic investors to Israel. The Suez Canal stimulated trade and furthered economic development in the Middle East.

Zionism, or the desire for a Jewish homeland, also stimulated emigration to Palestine. At the end of the 19th century, Jews from Eastern Europe began to arrive and to establish settlements. Unfortunately, the Ottoman rulers were hostile to this influx of foreigners in the country. Settlers faced poor living conditions with inadequate transportation and communication. Swamps in the region bred mosquitoes that carried malaria, which soon began to take its toll on the people trying to make a home here. Further, the soil had been so neglected that it was a poor medium in which to grow much needed food so these outposts could become self-sufficient.

Though these conditions were difficult, they did not hamper the country's growth. From the early 1500s to 1914, the Jewish population swelled from 5,000 Jews in Palestine to 85,000. The 20th century, however, brought large numbers of Jews from specific regions to what would one day be the independent nation of Israel. Between 1919 and 1923, 35,000 Jews came from Russia, bringing communal and cooperative forms of agriculture and rural settlement, the kibbutz and the moshav. They also provided the labor for building roads and houses.

Some 60,000 Polish Jews came between 1924 and 1932. These people settled in the cities, mainly Tel Aviv, and influenced urban life by establishing businesses, construction firms, and light industry. Between 1933 and 1939 after Hitler came to power in Germany, 165,000 German Jews came to Palestine. These settlers were professionals and scholars, who broadened the cultural life and improved urban and rural amenities. Many of these early settlements or kibbutzim were established in Galilee and other regions of northern Israel.

Acco

From Galilee, Menasheh and I decided to hitchhike to Acco, north of Haifa, on the coast. That took a few hours as well. When we finally arrived, we explored the city's ancient sea wall, which had been fortified by the Ottoman governor of Acco, Ahmed Pasha, known as Al Jazzar ("the butcher").

Originally a city of the great seafaring people the Phoenicians, Acco, whose name means, "hot sand," was never occupied by Israelites in ancient times though it had been conquered by King David in the 10th century BCE. Acco fell to many other nations over the years because it was built on a peninsula with natural defenses. The Romans used the harbor in the 7th century BCE, and the Crusaders occupied the city in 1104. Then, in 1187, Saladin took the city, holding it for three years. Then, Richard the Lion-Heart took it back and held onto it until 1250 when the Egyptian Mamluks took it from him, only to neglect the city.

It remained abandoned for 500 years when the Turkish governor Al Jazzar began to fortify the great walls after he learned that Napoleon Bonaparte was on the march toward Acco. Napoleon intended to conquer city after city on his way to take India as a French colony. In 1799, Napoleon laid siege to the city, expecting it to fall quickly as it had done so often in the past. Instead, Al Jazzar had prepared his people for the long siege by laying in stores of food and tapping into an underground water supply.

Napoleon failed to take Acco and had to retreat to Egypt. In order to do that, he ordered his army to bury their equipment on the shores around Acco. He even sent his siege engines out on leaky boats to be sunk in the harbor. Among the military goods that Napoleon's army left were huge canons.

Menasheh and I touched the old French canons, still pointing at the port of Haifa, left there by Napoleon's armies two centuries before. We climbed on top of the ancient canons and sat there, eating our sandwiches and imagining the terror Napoleon's forces must have represented to the people behind those thick city walls.

We decided it was too late and too dark to go anyplace else that night. So, we slept among the ruins of Acco on the floor of some ancient building or square, using blankets we had brought with us. The temperature dropped quite a bit that night, and we could hardly sleep, even though we had all our clothes on and had a blanket apiece. We talked all night.

In the morning, we found a stream in a small ravine and washed our faces. We began hitchhiking again, this time back towards our town of Rehoboth. But, when we arrived in Haifa again, we decided to savor the moment a bit longer. We went down to the harbor and got a closer look at all of the ships anchored there. We stood, pointing out first a steamship, then a big cargo carrier, and finally a huge oil barge. We wondered where were they had all come from and where they were headed. We longed to stowaway on one of them to see the world.

The trip's conclusion

With a sigh, we started walking along the roadway, putting out our thumbs yet again. We got lucky and caught a ride with a military truck. The driver, a nice young soldier, had taken quite a chance by allowing us in his truck since we could have been enemy killers in disguise. It had happened many times already. The truck took us all the way south to Rishon Le-Tzion, saving us untold hours of exposure, standing along the road in the sweltering sun.

Rishon Le-Tzion

Rishon Le-Tzion, meaning "First in Zion," is the first permanent Jewish settlement by Zionist immigrants founded in Israel. Baron Rothschild also gave this community assistance by sending money to dig deep wells and to support its agriculture, citrus groves, and budding wine industry. Rishon Le-Tzion boasts starting the first Hebrew school and the first Hebrew kindergarten in Palestine. This city also is the site of the creation of the Israeli flag and its national anthem, "Hatikvah."

Once in Rishon Le-Tzion, Menasheh and I bought sandwiches and Gazoz, a fruity carbonated drink much like Fresca, and looked at our budgets. We found we had just enough money to get on the Dan bus that would take us back to Rehoboth. We decided to ride home in style and boarded the bus.

Rehoboth

Experiencing an uneventful ride, we finally pulled into the bus terminal at Rehoboth. Also called Rehovot, this town is a trade center for citrus growers and supports light industries like fruit packing, pharmaceutical manufacturing, cereal production, and plastics fabrication. Israel's first president, Chaiim Weitzmann, who had been elected in 1948 after Israel had declared its independence, lived in Rehoboth from the start of World War I until his death in 1952.

Rehoboth also is the site of the Weitzmann Institute of Science, a medical and biological research facility that was established in 1934. WEIZAC, one of the world's first computers, was designed and built at the Weitzmann Institute in 1954. The facility has also been a major cancer research center since the early 1950s. It also has recently constructed the world's first interactive science museum.

After an exhausting several days exploring our beloved Israel, Menasheh and I congratulated each other for such a wonderful, flawless adventure. We said our goodbyes and promised to do it all over again at another time.

My friend Eliahu Mesika (in military uniform),
Israel, 1958 (30)

Goodbye party, Haifa, Israel, 1958 (31)

Goodbye party on departing from Haifa,
Israel, 1958 (32)

Leaving Israel with cousin Yeg-Al, farewell in
Port of Haifa, Israel, 1958 (33)

Saul and cousin Yeg-Al leave Israel
aboard "Artsa", 1958 (34)

With cousin Yeg-Al in Barcelona, Spain, 1958 (35)

Last night in Israel "going away party" with all my friends,
Israel, 1958 (36)

Saul and Yeg-Al in Marceille, France, 1958 (37)

Chapter Thirty-One

Leaving Israel: September 19, 1958

I had been restless for months, feeling claustrophobic in the land of Israel. It seemed to me that there was nowhere for me to go, and I had no prospects for expansion. What compounded my situation was the fact that I kept meeting people who had come from other parts of the world. I longed to see something other than the buildings I saw every day. I wanted to see new places and new people. But most of all, I wanted adventure.

My sister Berta was in the United States. I had considered joining here there, but she had not encouraged me to come, nor was I able to obtain a visa from the American consulate. This, however, wasn't going to stop me from escaping what I thought was my dull life in Israel.

I looked into the prospects of immigrating to Brazil, a country with endless possibilities. It was a wild new frontier with an atmosphere akin to the pioneer America a hundred years ago. The Brazilian consulate required very little documentation, such as proof of birthplace and age, a clean police report, etc. This was 1958, and I was twenty years old, making parental consent unnecessary. I bought a one-way ticket on a passenger ship sailing to Barcelona, Spain. From there, I would figure out how to get to Brazil, some 8,000 miles away.

Two weeks before I left, I told my parents that I was tired of working and that I wanted to see the world before I settled down. "It may be only three or four months, and I will be back permanently," I told them. "My first destination is Barcelona, from there I will plan the rest of the trip." Of course, I failed to mention Brazil. I thought that they would think that Brazil was too far away and that I might not come back at all.

My parents, obviously thinking there was nothing they could do to change my mind, reluctantly went along with my decision to travel. On the eve of my departure, my family organized a surprise going-away party for me, partly I think because they wanted to somehow pass their blessing onto my decision to travel and partly because they wanted our last night together to be full of joy and laugher, and most of all—hope. They invited all of my friends and cousins who were close to my age to our house. There was plenty of food and drinks.

My cousin Sabah (Yeg-Al) surprises me

As friends and relatives began to arrive, the atmosphere turned from a sad farewell to a more festive event. The house filled with guests who came to congratulate me on my courage and adventurous spirit. To my utter surprise, one of the guests was my cousin Sabah the Schemer of my youth. Now, he was called Yeg-Al in Hebrew. My brother Yeftah had phoned him and told him about the party.

Soon after Yeg-Al arrived, he motioned me over to a corner of the kitchen, far from anyone else's ears. "Saul, I have a surprise for you," he said, with a glint in his eye. "I am going with you."

I was flabbergasted. "What are you talking about?" I asked. "You don't know where I am going. I don't even know where I'm going. No, you should stay here," I urged him.

Yeg-Al began with his usual stutter but soon the words flowed as his enthusiasm grew. "Saul, I checked things out," he said. "I know what you are up to, and I don't care. I want to go with you. My parents and brothers know my plans already. They don't mind. They will even be in Haifa at the boat tomorrow."

I began to grin. "How did you find out my plans?" I asked. "Who told you? My parents certainly don't know."

Yeg-Al looked amused. "Saul, you can't keep secrets from me, you know that," he said. "I spoke to some mutual friends, friends you confided in, that's all." He laughed. "Don't worry," he said in a whisper. "No one will find out from me." He then moved away to help himself to a cold drink, and I mingled with some friends.

Going to see the world, back in few months

"We are going to miss you, Saul," said my friend Carmella. "Who is going to lead us and organize us now?"

I smiled and held her hand. "Don't worry, Carmella. I will be back in no time, and we will continue as before," I said.

"You're going to see the world, huh?" asked Dvorah. "I envy you, I wish I could be so adventurous. My brothers would kill me."

I hugged her. Then, she added, "Well, don't forget to come back. We belong here, remember? After all, we all went through hell to get here. And now, you're leaving us."

I was beginning to feel melancholy, but I hid my feelings so no one could see. It was hard to part with such good, close friends. And, it was doubly so, leaving my parents behind to fend for themselves, to feed, clothe, and educate my younger brothers and sisters. Suddenly, I felt guilty. *Am I escaping the hardship?* I wondered. *Am I copping out?*

Someone put on a record on the record player. It was an old song, "Kalaniyot," sung by a preeminent native singer, Shoshannah Damari. Some of the guests joined in, singing, swaying side to side and sipping their drinks.

Mother was dressed nicely. With a perpetual smile, she served fruits and sweets to all of the guests. My father stayed in his room, reading. Occasionally, he came out to say hello to some of the guests. Then, he rushed back to his room and closed the door behind him. *Was he hiding his feelings?* I wondered. *Was he apprehensive? Does he know more than he lets on?*

My good friend Eliahu Messika and his young sister (in Army uniform), lingered by the door, standing apart because they didn't know many of the other guests. They motioned for me to come over to them, and I did. We shook hands and hugged lightly. "How long will you be gone?" Eliahu asked.

"Oh, just a few months," I told him, "until I feel I've had enough of the outside world. Then, I'll be back."

They both smiled and nodded. I wondered if they believed me.

I moved away from them, looking for other friends and relatives. The festivities went on until after midnight. People kept coming and going. I had to promise to write to so many of them that by the end of the night, I wondered if I did, would I have time to explore the world.

When everyone had finally left, my family and I sipped one final cup of tea together in the quietness of the house. Then, we all turned in to grab a few hours sleep.

I lay down on my bed, but spent the night thinking, without getting any sleep at all. I tried to distract my busy mind by reading, but that didn't work. I had a thousand worries and was certainly feeling guilt-ridden. *Do I have the right to leave my family now?* I asked myself. *Will they be ok as they bear their burdens alone? Will I ever see them alive again?*

I began to cry. Embarrassed, I got up and locked the bedroom door. I didn't want anyone to see me in my doubt, especially when everyone that night had said how brave and adventurous I was!

Leaving Israel aboard Artsa

In the morning, we all put on smiles and tried to create a festive mood. We ate breakfast and soon were on our way to Haifa, some three hours by bus. I sat by a window with Father next to me, but we talked very little. We both stared at the great pastures of the Moshavim and Kibbutzim along the way.

My closest friends and cousins accompanied us all the way to the port of Haifa. Yeg-Al's entire family came: His father Asslan, his mother Simkha, his brothers Jamil, Nuri, David, and his sister Saiida. On the dock, we found the boat, a "tin can" really, that Yeg-Al and I would be sailing with. It was a depressing cargo ship. But, to Yeg-Al and I, it was a symbol of liberty and freedom. We all stood in front of the ship and took a group photo. An hour later, Yeg-Al and I were onboard and were waving good-bye from the railing. More photos followed.

Our families stayed down on the dock, waving, as the ship began to move out slowly. Yeg-Al and I found our room and put our suitcases under our beds. We climbed to the top deck and sat down on the lounge chairs and let the cool breeze hit our faces. It was wonderful—until I remembered the faces of all of my family standing on the dock. Yeg-Al noticed me getting sad and tried his best to tell jokes and make me laugh. I tried, but I felt so guilty for leaving. I remembered my escape from Baghdad and the hardships and sacrifices my family had experienced during our two-year separation. *If I had only stayed in the Kibbutz and not joined the family upon their arrival!* I mused. *How different life would have been!*

The Mediterranean was unusually calm. We were headed to Genoa, Italy, then to Marseille, France, and from there to Barcelona, Spain. Slowly, I began to notice that there were luxuries aboard this ship. We spent all of the time between meals, sitting on the top deck and catching the breeze, or writing letters to our parents and friends. We got stamps through the captain's office and mailed them at our next stop.

Fortuneteller in Genoa: You're going far away

After four days on the open sea, we docked at the port in Genoa, Italy. We were told we could disembark, but we should not wander too far from the ship since it would be leaving the port in a few hours. Yeg-Al and I joined a friend we had made during the journey and left the ship to explore the city.

Located on the northwest coast, Genoa is Italy's main commercial seaport and has been influenced by many cultures through its long history. It is also a part of the Italian Riviera that stretches along the Mediterranean from the French border to Tuscany. We could see the foothills of the Apennines Mountains in the distance with low, heavy clouds shrouding their peaks. Not far from the ship, we found an outdoor café where we sat down and ordered coffee and Italian pastries.

Our new friend was a little older than we were and was a far more experienced traveler. He said that he had been in the Israeli Merchant Marines for several years and had been to Genoa more than a few times. He also told us about a palm reader, not too far from the port, who was amazing in predicting the future. I laughed, shaking my head as a non-believer, remembering my Aunt Ruthi and her clever observations of human behaviors.

But Yeg-Al was intrigued. "Let's go see her," he said. "We have time."

We made our way through the narrow medieval alleys that the residents call *carruggi*. The buildings were so tall and squeezed so close together you could barely find the sky. We passed ancient stone buildings next to modern, brightly painted shops. We could smell food frying and the pungent basil of pesto, the city's favorite sauce.

After many turns, we found the fortuneteller's place actually quite easily. We entered a darkened foyer of an apartment building, and there she sat behind a tiny square table, waiting for customers. Strings of beads decked her neck. Candles were lit around the space, making everything feel mysterious.

Our friend greeted her as he would have an old friend, and she motioned for us to sit opposite her. She scrutinized us sternly, trying to read our facial expressions. Suddenly, she grabbed Yeg-Al's palm and began to follow the markings on it with her finger.

Her English was good, though she had a heavy Italian accent. "You are young, yes? May be twenty, twenty-one?" she asked. "First time travel, yes?"

Yeg-Al was impressed and nodded with a smile.

"You are going far away. Very far away. But not alone. Two of you going together, yes? But I don't know which one." She looked at me, then at our friend. "Any way, don't worry. You will be ok, hundred percent. Don't worry."

Our friend was next. "You travel much, yes?" she asked. "You married, yes? But I see much trouble with wife. You not happy. Maybe divorce, yes? I don't know. Maybe not, maybe you fix, yes?"

Our friend was getting excited. "I told you she is good," he exclaimed. "Look how she guessed everything right. It's true. I am having trouble in my marriage, and we spoke of divorce. But my wife doesn't want to. She is ashamed. So maybe we will get back together. I will be back in few months."

Then came my turn. I reluctantly extended my right palm to her and rested it on the table. "Ah, you are the second man. You go with him far away, yes?" she pointed to Yeg-Al. I didn't answer, but Yeg-Al acknowledged her question. "You going far away," she continued. "Long time no return, long, long time. But don't worry, everything all right. You are successful. Make money, but you no go home very long time. This I see, yes? I'm sure"

I thought to myself, *Amazing, how accurate she is! How did she know I have no money for a return ticket? I am going one way. The future rests with my fate.*

We gave the fortuneteller two US dollars, and our friend gave her three packs of Kent cigarettes. He got away cheep. *Was he rewarded for bringing customers?* I wondered. But, the fortuneteller was happy.

As we walked away from her, Yeg-Al and our new friend were satisfied with their readings. I, on the other hand, was worried. *What did she mean, "Not go back home long, long time"?*

We returned to the Artsa, and soon it pulled out of the port on its way to Marseille, France, where we would board another ship to Barcelona. We passed the Lanterna, a lighthouse build in 1543 on a mass of rock in the harbor. It was a symbol of the city of Genoa, the birthplace of Nicolo Paganini, the famous violinist, and of Christopher Columbus, who I suspected had as much wanderlust as I did at that moment. This was also the port where many Italian residents emigrated to other countries. It was then that the fortuneteller's words echoed again in my mind: "Not go back home long, long time."

As the ship moved out to sea again, it was clear that something momentous was happening. Yet, what it was I had no idea. I was just keenly aware that we were at sea again, going somewhere I had never been before.

Marseilles, France

The Artsa docked in Marseilles a few days later. Yeg-Al and I gathered our belongings and hurried down the gangplank. We wandered along the dock until we found the Britagne, a grand passenger liner much like the Queen Mary. We quickly got on board and secured our rooms for the trip to Barcelona. The Britagne wasn't due to depart for 24 hours, so Yeg-Al and I decided to find a restaurant and get a coffee.

We found an outdoor café nearby and sat with our coffees, looking at the magnificent ship that would take us to Barcelona. The Britagne seemed to dominate the pier in this the oldest city in France. Marseilles, our second exotic port of call, was wreathed in romance and adventure. We walked along the Riviera and looked at dozens of magnificent statues and memorials. Artists were painting the pavements with colored chalks. Here along one of the coastal islands was the Chateau d'If, the legendary home of the Count of Monte Cristo. This was what I was longing for, new places to explore and new people to meet. And, soon, we would be in Barcelona. Then what?

As Yeg-Al and I made our way back to the ship, we fell into conversation with one of the ship's crewmen who had been sent ashore on a quick errand. We asked him about all of the places he had traveled. The man started naming off port after port, many I didn't even know what hemisphere they were in, much less what country. I asked him then what was the final destination for the Britagne this trip. The man flashed a smile and said the marvelous, magical word to me, "Brazil. Don't you know?"

Yeg-Al and I looked at each other and grinned. Brazil—where I had talked of going with my friends and who, in turn, had told Yeg-Al. Brazil—jungles and bustling cities. Brazil—the country of carnival, beautiful girls and festivities. This had to be fate. The wheels began to turn in our minds. *How could we get there?* We didn't have much money, and we only had one-way tickets to Barcelona.

Over the next several days, while we lounged in the deck chairs and looked at the blue water, we schemed and plotted. Yeg-Al, after all, wasn't called the Schemer as a child for nothing. Before we reached Barcelona, we had hatched a bold plan but an honest one. It was up to me, however, to put it into action.

We waited until we could get the captain of the ship away from other ears, and then we cornered him with our plan. "Sir," I said as Yeg-Al lurked behind me, "we have a business proposition for you."

"Oh?" he inquired, raising an eyebrow.

"Yes," I answered, then took a deep breath and launched right into it. "We are hard workers. We would like to work for you for passage to Brazil. We will work hard. You won't be sorry you hired us."

The captain tried to look stern, but we could tell he was amused. "And what can you do for me?" he asked.

Yeg-Al then piped up. "Oh, we'll do anything. We're hard workers. And we'll pay half the fare."

I frowned at him. It was my job to talk to the captain. "Sir, I had four years training in the Israeli army in electrical engineering. There must be lots of ways I can help on a ship this big."

The captain smiled slowly then. We showed him our passports and Brazilian visas. Though he didn't need any helpers, he agreed. We would begin our duties after we docked in Barcelona. Until then, we were still passengers, guests of the Britagne.

Barcelona, Spain

When the port of Barcelona came into site, though our days of leisure were over, we knew we really were starting our adventure there. We already had visas for Brazil. Everything was going better than we had expected. We were really going to see the world.

Yeg-Al and I left the ship when we docked in Barcelona briefly to celebrate. We found a restaurant and ordered a modest meal of the local cuisine. We couldn't believe that we were on our way to our dream destination and that we were also in a city that had once housed 4,000 Jews in the Middle Ages. They had been merchants and scholars. After the Jews had been expelled by Queen Isabella and King Ferdinand the same year their protégé Christopher Columbus discovered the West Indies, signs of Jewish settlement had all but disappeared. We had read in the newspapers in Israel that, decade after WW II, a Jewish community was forming again in Spain, here in Barcelona.

It seemed fitting somehow that on the verge of our own grand journey we would remember those Jewish ancestors who had come to a new land and lived and prospered here. *Where would our journey take us in Brazil? What would we find there? Would we prosper, too?*

Straits of Gibraltar

As the Britagne sailed along the coast of Spain toward the Straits of Gibraltar, Yeg-Al and I began our duties as members of the crew. I worked in the control room doing electrical testing and repairs. Yeg-Al worked on deck, mainly painting the rails. We were excited about our new jobs and were surprised that we had so much free time on our hands. When our duties were over, we'd go up on deck and dream about the life we would have in Brazil.

When our ship sailed through the Straits of Gibraltar, we marveled at the Rock of Gibraltar on our right, that unmistakable landmark that was said to once be a footing for the Colossus of Rhodes. One of the Seven Wonders of the Ancient World, it was a giant statue with one leg on Gibraltar and the other on the Mt. Acha in Ceuta in Africa. Another name for these large promontories was the Pillars of Hercules that mythology says were split in two by Hercules wielding his mace, forming the Straits of Gibraltar.

For centuries, this place marked the end of the Western world. Beyond were terrible unknowns, possibly dragons and sea monsters or fantastic lands. If you sailed beyond this point, you would fall off the edge of the world. That was before the world was discovered to be round and not flat, and therefore full of possibilities.

Yeg-Al and I were thrilled that we were following many courageous adventurers like Christopher Columbus, who ignored the dangers and sailed toward hope and riches. For us, it was Brazil.

Dakar, Senegal

Our first exotic port of call was Dakar, a major trading center in Senegal in West Africa, where we took on cargo that we were told was peanut oil and fertilizer. Though the city at this time was (and still is) a modern blend of African and European influences, it still is undeniably Africa.

As Yeg-Al and I walked ashore to explore the local markets, we couldn't help but marvel at the mix of cultures. People flocked to the markets on foot or rode horse-drawn cart. A few pushed through the crowds in a cars or small trucks. We saw men in t-shirts and khaki pants and women in colorful dresses and bands of cloth twisted atop their heads.

Walking among the merchants, eagerly calling out to us in French, I remembered that it was here that the French had secured the slave trade north of Dakar, gathering up able-bodied young men and women, and shipping them off to America from the very port where our ship was anchored. As I looked at these robust, energetic people, I couldn't imagine them being a commodity as the fish or the fruit they were selling.

I returned to the ship, deep in thought, marveling at the wide diversity in the world but also troubled by the cruelty that seemed ever present. That evening, Yeg-Al noticed my pensive mood. He teased me, calling me, "the philosopher." I smiled. Perhaps I was indeed.

Open Ocean

The Britagne had few passengers when we left Marseilles. But at each port, we were taking on more people and cargo. We saw so many places we had only read about. Each one seemed more exotic than the next.

Our work kept us occupied but not very busy. I loved my work in the control room. It was what I had been trained for and in the area that had always fascinated me even as a child when my curiosity had caused me to electrocute myself, back in Baghdad.

But, poor Yeg-Al hated his duties. It was physical labor and not very interesting. Yeg-Al had never been one to seek out the more difficult route when an easier one presented itself. Though he complained to me, he did his duties to the captain's satisfaction and thus we remained on board, working our way toward Brazil.

Each day as we saw only the vast ocean all around us, we wondered what was ahead. How soon would it be before we saw the shores of South America? Here was the land of opportunity for both of us. Here we could make our fortunes once we had tasted the delights of the native girls and their land.

Yet, all we saw for days was nothing but ocean. Soon Yeg-Al began to complain. "When are we going to see this great land you've been talking about?" he kept asking. "Does this ship even know where it's going? Maybe we'll be lost at sea and no one will ever find us."

I tried to console him by repeating what I had read about South America and the possibilities that Brazil offered. This seemed to always boost his spirits and mine, too. After all, it is our dreams that keep us going.

Rio de Janeiro, Brazil

Yeg-Al and I couldn't contain our excitement as the Britagne approached Guanabara ("Arm of the Sea") Bay. We caught sight of the famous Sugarloaf Mountain on the right, the imposing tip of a spit of land that forms the bowl-shaped harbor. When Portuguese navigators led by Amerigo Vespucci first discovered the shores of South America here in on January 1, 1502, they thought this was the entrance to a river; hence they named the city that grew up here Sao Sebastiao do Rio de Janeiro (San Sebastian of the January River).

The modern city of Rio de Janeiro sprawled along the bay, tall buildings alongside of famous pristine beaches like Copacabana and Ipanema, and edged up against the luxuriant tropical rain forests that covered the mountains that stood as a primordial backdrop to the busyness of human beings on the shores. Rio had grown here, thriving on businesses built on coffee, Brazil wood for shipbuilding, and trade, especially in gold and diamonds.

As we drew closer, our eyes were drawn to Corcovado Mountain, rising 2,300 feet above the harbor. At top it is the Church of the Redeemer, which serves as the base of a huge sculpture of Jesus. The statue was designed, not by an artist but by Brazilian engineer Heitor da Silva Costa and built between 1926 and 1931. French sculptor Paul Landowski completed the work on Jesus' face and the enormous hands of his outstretched arms.

Fellow crewmen aboard the Britagne told us that Jesus' open arms were protecting the city. To Yeg-Al and me, it felt more like a welcome, an embrace to come to this land of plenty. I took that as a good sign. It meant that Yeg-Al and I were destined to be here. This wasn't just a young man's dream. We were surely going to find adventure and make our fortunes.

But as the ship steamed closer to the busy shore, reality began to creep into my thinking. Yeg-Al and I had no money really. How were we to live? Where would we find work? We didn't speak the local language, Portuguese. At this nostalgic moment, I extended my arm to shake Yeg-Al's hand: "Cousin, I am glad you came along with me" His smile was tinged with fear of the unknown.

I looked up at the embracing arms of Jesus and wondered to myself, *what am I doing here?*

Then, the old fortuneteller's prediction came back to me, "Not go back home long, long time."

As fate proved, it took me sixteen years before I was able to visit my homeland again.

Section Three

My Life in Brazil

1958 – 1960

Chapter Thirty-Two

Discovering Brazil

Making the journey

I had been restless in Israel. I was twenty years old and kept meeting people who had once lived in fascinating parts of the world. All of their conversations about their homelands only intensified my desire to see more of the world. Though I was safe in Israel with my family, I wanted more. Perhaps it was due to all of the books I had been reading all of my life, the movies and operas I'd seen, or my early exposure to so many different cultures, but I longed to see new places and new people. But most of all, I wanted adventure.

I dreamed of going to the most exotic locale I could think of. For me, that was Brazil, a country on the frontier bursting with endless possibilities. Some of my friends had planned to travel there, and we had talked endlessly of what it would be like. It was easy to get a visa. As I came closer to making the decision to leave Israel, I made contact with someone a friend had suggested I contact in Sao Paolo, Brazil. While I dreamed about exotic travel, I wrote letters to this person in Sao Paolo. He assured me that if I ever made my way there; I could always look him up.

Finally, I decided to book passage as far as Barcelona, Spain. I thought that I could at least see the Mediterranean, and someday I could make my way to Brazil. On September 19, 1958, my dearest friends and many of my cousins joined my friend Yeg-Al and me at the port of Haifa where they shared their good wishes as we boarded a cargo ship to Genoa, Italy.

Italy's main commercial seaport, Genoa, was our first stop. Yeg-Al and I went with a fellow passenger through the city's narrow streets and passed both modern shops and ancient stone buildings to a fortuneteller who left me with a disturbing future. She had told me, "Not go back home long, long time"

I mulled over that prediction, but I shrugged it off. I had told my family in Israel that I would just be away a few months, just long enough to lose my wanderlust, and then I'd be back.

In Marseilles, France, we changed ships and boarded the Britagne, a grand passenger liner much like the Queen Mary. It was here that we had asked a crewman what the final destination of the Britagne was. He told us, "Brazil."

This had to be fate. But, we only had one-way tickets to Barcelona, Spain, and very little money otherwise. As we sailed from France to Barcelona, Yeg-Al and I plotted and schemed to find some way to stay on board and go all the way to Brazil, the land of carnival and jungles. Finally, we approached the captain of the Britagne and asked if we could work our way to Brazil for half fare. To our great surprise, the captain agreed.

As we passed the Straits of Gibraltar, Yeg-Al and I were thrilled that we were following many courageous adventurers like Christopher Columbus' crew, some of which had been Jews from southern Spain. They might have come from Barcelona itself.

We docked in our first exotic port of call—Dakar, Senegal in West Africa. This was where the French had opened up the slave trade, gathering up able-bodied young men and women, and shipping them off not only to America but also to Brazil to work on the plantations there.

I enjoyed working in the control room doing work that I had been trained for. But, poor Yeg-Al hated painting the rails and doing other kinds of physical labor. He complained, of course, but he did his work well enough to keep his passage on board.

Arriving in Rio de Janeiro

When we finally spied the famous Sugarloaf Mountain in the harbor at Rio de Janeiro, we both realized that we had actually done it. We had realized our dream. We were finally in Brazil.

It was October 9, 1958 when the ship steamed into Rio de Janeiro, a city built on coffee, gold, diamonds, and slaves. All of the passengers stood at the rails, pointing at the cityscape unfolding before them. Some pointed to the distant mountain where the enormous statue of Jesus stood atop Christ the Redeemer Church with its arms outstretched. The passengers were commenting on how that it looked as if Jesus' open arms were protecting the city.

To Yeg-Al and me, however, those outstretched arms looked more like a welcome. We took that as a sign that we were supposed to be there. Yeg-Al grinned at me and said, "Saul, we're going to make our fortunes here. We're going to be rich."

As I gazed up at the statue high on the hill, I wondered. We wouldn't be released from our work agreement on the ship until it had docked in Santos, the port of Sao Paolo, the next day. We would try to find the friend I had been writing to in Sao Paolo and then we'd figure out what to do with our lives. I already knew how light my own wallet was. How would we support ourselves? We didn't even speak the language.

That's when it occurred to me that I was in a strange and remote land where I really knew no one. I looked deep within myself and asked, **"What am I doing here?"**

Yeg-Al and I disembarked at Rio de Janeiro with the other passengers and bought a few small souvenirs from the local merchants near the harbor. Then we went back to the ship and spent a restless last night on board as we sailed on to our final destination of Santos, the port for the city of Sao Paolo.

Santos was built on an island in a natural harbor in 1535. It is about forty miles south of Sao Paolo, the largest city in Brazil, and our final destination. In the heart of the coffee trade, Santos grew to be a major port when the railway to the interior was completed in 1867. It exports fruit, cotton, and Brazilian beef along with its enormous shipments of coffee, and imports machinery for the growing industries in the region.

Much of the new apartment construction that was done in the 1960s was on unstable sand. These many-storied apartment buildings shifted on their foundations and have tilted every which way, making a strange cityscape.

Santos also has the longest public beach in the world and supports a vibrant tourist trade. Its Japanese immigrants urged Santos to become a sister city with Nagasaki in 1972.

When Yeg-Al and I awoke the next morning, October 10, 1958, we gathered our already packed bags and made our way down the gangplank onto the shores of Santos. Whatever our fortunes were, we would share them together.

Chapter Thirty-Three

Sojourn in Santos

Arrival in Santos, Brazil

On October 10, 1958, the Britagne entered the Brazilian port of Santos, just south of Sao Paolo. Yeg-Al and I, however, didn't know what the port city was called. We joined the remaining passengers and were rushed through customs it seemed. Our passports and visas were inspected briefly and quickly stamped. Suddenly, we found ourselves alone on the dock. Most of the passengers were picked up by private cars; others took taxicabs. Some waited to get on one of the buses that were beginning to line up just outside the port gates.

Yeg-Al and I had no clue where we were or how far we were from our destination, the city of Sao Paolo. While all of the other passengers were scattering, obviously knowing where they were and what to do, I pulled a small Portuguese-English dictionary from my inside jacket pocket. The dictionary also contained some maps of Brazil. I studied them intently, but I could not determine exactly where on the map we were really standing, and for that reason I couldn't judge just how far it was Sao Paolo.

I decided that the one person who would know exactly where we were was a cab driver. I hailed a taxi and immediately asked where we were. I was flabbergasted to find that the driver did not know a word of English.

Yeg-Al tried another cab and spoke just one word, "Sao Paolo." The cab driver gave us a long, winded answer in very rapid Portuguese. All we understood was the word for the Brazilian currency, *Cruzeiros*. But we couldn't understand exactly how many *Cruzeiros.*

Still unsure of where we were, we were forced to stay overnight in what we found out later was Santos. A uniformed guard came and asked us politely to leave the premises. As we dragged our suitcases along the pier and out past the metal gates, the guard locked them behind us. We stood and gazed around us at the various buildings crowding the harbor. Needless to say, nothing looked familiar and no building had a sign in English.

We started walking away from the pier, hoping to find someone who could speak English. Within thirty minutes, we were near a little city park with several benches. We decided we should go into the park and take a rest. We needed to think, to figure out what to do next.

Sleeping on park benches

It was early evening and not many people were in the park. We sat on a bench and discussed our predicament. We decided it was too late to do anything about it that day so we could get some sleep on the benches that night. In the morning, we might have better luck finding help.

Yeg-al took one bench, and I took another, some 20 feet away. We lined our suitcases on the bench, took off our jackets and converted them into pillows. So no one would steal our suitcase, we decided to sleep on top of them like my fellow refuges had done in the Bedouin tent in the desert of Iran when I had escaped from Baghdad as a boy.

We were a bit apprehensive, sleeping out in the open in a foreign city. We had no concept of what danger might lurk behind the dense trees in this park. We would not risk squandering the few dollars we had on a taxi that might take us to the wrong place. Besides, the air was clean and cool, and I remembered the adventure of sleeping out under the stars in Israel when I had hitchhiked with my friend. I told Yeg-Al all about those adventures as we tried to settle in for the night.

The homeless and prostitutes

Hours later, we were still talking. Suddenly, we noticed some homeless people sleeping on the benches not too far from us. Their bags and boxes were on the ground beside them. We wondered if they were going to mug us. *How could we sleep now knowing that desperate strangers were nearby?*

Just then, a good-looking young girl walked by and made a gesture. She had long, black hair, and her skin was a beautiful copper tone. Yeg-al came to my bench. "You know, she might be for hire," he said to me with a smile. "What else would she be doing at this hour in the park?"

I became serious. "Yeg-Al, don't you get funny ideas here. We could be lured into a trap, and, who knows, we could be killed for our money."

This didn't seem to phase Yeg-Al, who kept watching the girl as she walked the length of a fifty-foot path. She would turn often, stop, and look back at us. Her smile grew wider each time she paused to look at us. Then, she began pointing her hand to her crotch and grabbing herself.

Yeg-Al was getting excited. "You see? I told you," he said. "I wonder how much she charges."

"Don't even think about it," I said. "It's dangerous. Besides, we have no money for the taxi and you want to blow it on sex?"

The girl then sat down on a bench and continued to look in our direction. Yeg-Al was getting aroused. "I bet you it's cheap, real cheap here," he speculated. "There's a lot of poverty in Brazil. Aren't you horney after all these weeks on the endless ocean?"

Making up his mind, Yeg-Al got up and went over to the girl. She pulled him down beside her and rubbed two fingers together, the universal symbol of money. Yeg-Al stuttered and pulled two single dollar bills from his pocket and offered them to her. She realized then that he did not speak Portuguese, but she made him understand that that wasn't enough money. He reached again into his pocket and drew another single dollar bill. She reluctantly accepted it, got up, and led him behind the trees.

I was really concerned that this was a trap. I began to outline a fantastic scenario. I began to believe that one of the homeless characters near us was actually her pimp and that he might jump Yeg-Al when he had his pants down and steal all of Yeg-Al's money. We would both be in dire straights then with no money for a taxi to Sao Paolo and no money for food. But, Yeg-Al followed the girl and had sex, standing up behind a tree.

When he emerged, weak-kneed, he motioned for to me to come over. "She is terrific," he shouted to me in Hebrew. "Come over here and try her!"

I refused. I remained seated, guarding our suitcases.

Yeg-Al came back to my bench. "Go ahead," he urged. "I will stay and watch over our things. Don't worry. I am telling you she is terrific. She actually enjoys sex, not like these other prostitutes we had in Tel-Aviv."

He pushed me, toward the girl, who was now back on the bench, brushing her long hair. It was nearly midnight, but the moon shined full, making her look even more exotic and beautiful. But I was reluctant to go to her. I was afraid of catching a disease or something. And, I couldn't bring myself to be the second man to have sex with the same girl, without washing. I figured that I owed her something so I walked over to her and gave her two bucks and told her with my hands that I did not want anything for them. She was surprised, but she grabbed the money and quickly tucked it into her bra.

Yeg-Al called me a sucker and a few other choice names. We stretched out on our suitcases, but we did not dare to fall asleep. Surprisingly, no one bothered us.

In the morning, we went to the pond in the park and washed our faces and combed our hair. Then, we walked out of the park and hailed a cab. This time, I held up the piece of paper with the one address I had in Sao Paolo that belonged to the fellow I had been corresponding with when I was in Israel. I let the cabdriver read it. He nodded that he understood and told us with his fingers how much it would cost. He was counting in local Cruzeiros, which we did not have. I pulled out a ten-dollar bill and flashed it before his eyes. He nodded his head again in agreement, a wide grin on his face.

Within two hours, we were settling down in my friend's apartment in Sao Paolo.

Chapter Thirty-Four

The *Mukhtar* of Bom-Retiro, An Israeli aristocrat

History of Sao Paolo

Sao Paolo is an old city, having been inhabited in the 1500s by indigenous natives and then by Portuguese colonists a century later. The first white settler was a shipwrecked Portuguese sailor named Joao Ramalho who came ashore in 1510. He married a native woman, the daughter of a local chief, and started a family. Ramalho was of great help when Martin Afonso de Souza came with settlers and a Jesuit priest in 1553 to establish a village in the southern coast of Brazil. The priest, Manuel da Nobrega, established Sao Vicente farther inland to act as a base to house priests and teach the newly converted. When Fr. Jose de Anchieta and thirteen Jesuit priests began to build a more permanent structure at Sao Vicente, he called the building the Colegio Sao Paolo (the College of St. Paul). This became Sao Paolo.

African slaves flooded the region later to work on the coffee plantations that sprung up there. By the 19th century as the world demand for coffee grew, Sao Paolo began to experience a population boom. In 1870, a railroad connected the city with the port of Santos, drawing bankers and export businessmen into Sao Paolo.

In the 20th century, electricity fueled new industries and amenities in the city. Japanese immigrants began to arrive to work on the plantations after slavery was outlawed. They settled in the Liberdade district, which to this day has kept its traditional customs and culture, becoming one of the largest oriental centers on foreign soil. As immigrants from other countries and cultures arrived, they began to cluster together in distinct communities. There are Italian, Arab, Lebanese Christian, and Jewish neighborhoods still today.

In 1958, when I came to Sao Paolo, immigrant Jews lived in Bom-Retiro, another ethnic neighborhood of Sao Paolo. In ghetto-like concentration, Jews from all over the world lived and worked. These were the lost souls of another Diaspora, searching for a new start where they could enjoy freedom of religion and find work to feed their families. There were schools, places of worship, and charity organizations.

Jews in Brazil

When Jews were banished from Spain in 1492, some converted to Christianity but many settled in Portugal where Jews were treated fairly and given the rights and privileges as any Portuguese citizen. But just five years later, the Spanish Inquisition gained steam and targeted Jews everywhere. Jews were forced to convert to Christianity or die. Many became *Marranos*, or New

Christians, but secretly retained their Jewish faith. They honored Queen Esther and her holiday, Taanit Esther, because she had had to hide her faith in the palace of King Ahashverosh. Some Jews were offered a deal that said that if they went to Brazil and helped colonize the wild country there, they would be exempt from the Inquisition for one hundred years. Jews fled to Brazil by the shipload.

Then in 1598, officials from the Inquisition arrived in Rio de Janeiro to check up on the *Marranos* to see if they were still good Christians. Brazil now was under Spanish rule and with that came oversight by the Inquisitors. If any Jews were found to have relapsed into the faith of their fathers, they were shipped to Lisbon, tried, and executed.

During this time, the Portuguese and the Dutch began to struggle over control of Brazil. The Dutch gained northeastern Brazil, calling it New Holland, and established Recife as the capital. Just fifty years before, Portuguese Jews had transplanted the first sugarcane shoots from Madeira to Brazil and became very influential in the sugar industry. Unfortunately, when one of the community became prominent, they came under scrutiny by Portuguese officials. When the Dutch controlled the region, they invited Jews from the rest of the country and even from Holland to come and work in the sugar industry. Over 600 Jews sailed from Amsterdam to Recife in 1640.

Six years later, the Portuguese recaptured the Dutch-held regions and forced the Jews there to leave. Many went back to Holland. Others fled to the West Indies, and some even went as far as New Amsterdam, the Dutch city that became New York. Historians think that the failure of the sugar industry was not so much the growth of coffee in southern Brazil but because so many Jews had been sent back to Portugal and Spain that it totally disrupted the sugar trade.

It is thought that few descendants of the original Portuguese Jews remain in Brazil. Even though some of them are said to have monopolized the diamond trade in the south since diamonds were discovered in 1734, the Jews who came later during the twentieth century came from Eastern Europe and Syria. Even after World War II, Brazil, like so many other countries, refused to open its doors to Jews. Some Jews sought help from the Vatican and were issued papers saying that they were Christians. Even in the twentieth century, some Jews had to resort to being Crypto-Jews, or Jews hiding their faith.

Today, about 130,000 Jews live in Brazil in a total population of around 170,000. Rio de Janeiro has about 30,000 and Sao Paolo has 70,000 Jews. There are smaller communities in smaller towns throughout the country, including a healthy number in Recife.

Though Jews have been treated fairly well for the past two hundred years, anti-Semitism is still present in Brazil. It is mainly seated in southern Brazil, where the largest Jewish population is located and where there are large German communities. Anti-Semitism here, however, is not as pronounced as it is in Argentina.

The *Mukhtar* of Bom-Retiro

In the Jewish district of Bom-Retiro, there were a host of so-called commissioned advice-givers, consultants if you will, who knew the ropes and could direct you to where you wanted to go or help you find what you needed.

One of these was a notorious young Israeli in his mid-thirties. He sat in outdoor cafés from morning till night, wearing his ceremonial white suit and mirror-shined shoes, as he smoked imported cigarettes and sipped coffee. Like something out of a novel, he stood out in that crowded community, aloof and reeking of wealth, but with an air of something else, as if he enjoyed the desperation of humanity but was above it. He seemed to profit by it in ways we could not imagine.

Everyone knew him and many feared him. But all gave him respect; whether it was his due or their obligation, it was not certain. He was called the *Mukhtar* of Bom-Retiro, or the mayor of Bom-Retiro.

Somehow, this fellow came to know all of the newly-arrived immigrants, the number of their children, their professions, and, most importantly, their economic status. You might say he was a one-man racket, sort of a Godfather in the organized crime sense. He dispensed no information to help these new immigrants without strings attached and, most definitely, with a hefty commission. He made a fortune, but was both revered and despised.

When I was hungry and desperate, he offered to help me find a job. And the string? I would forever owe him 10% of my income as his commission for helping me. He would own me, in a sense, for life. I never took him up on his offer.

Chapter Thirty-Five

Hunger and the Church

A week after settling in Bom-Retiro, a district of Sao Paolo where many Jews from various countries had sought shelter, I became aware of a church that attracted hungry and destitute new arrivals. The church was a Christian Baptist church, run by a Jewish convert from Los Angeles, named the Rev. Emanuel M. Woods. The church was called *Salvacao de Israel* (Salvation Of Israel).

The door of the church was always open, 24/7, welcoming anyone who cared to come inside and help themselves to a modest hot meal or a bowl of soup. Rev. Woods and some of his assistants stood just inside the doorway every day and greeted everyone who came in. They encouraged visitors to go to the table and help themselves to food and drink. Of course, the price, like in so many missions in cities all over the world, was listening to an evangelical sermon geared at bringing one more lost sheep into the Christian fold.

Evangelism of Brazil and Dr. Billy Graham

In the nineteenth and twentieth centuries, Brazil appeared to be hungry for the Gospel. Nowhere else in the world, except Korea, had the Bible been so widely distributed. The receptivity of the Brazilian people and their desire to share their new conversion with their neighbors drew evangelists from Europe and the United States. Late in the nineteenth century, Baptist and Presbyterian churches began arriving and charismatic churches followed. By 1940, every Brazilian state had a Pentecostal church. This charismatic movement even infiltrated some Brazilian Baptist churches in the 1960s, causing fourteen of them to be expelled from the Baptist Convention of Brazil. It took thirty-five years for these churches to be reinstated and to become full members of the Baptist World Alliance.

Among the evangelists who found their way to Brazil was Dr. Billy Graham who had left the mountains of North Carolina to embark on a series of worldwide crusades. In 1960, Brazil was one of thirteen countries that hosted Dr. Graham's crusades. The sites included Brazil, the United States, West Germany, Switzerland, and nine African nations. Rio de Janeiro was the host of the Baptist World Convention that year. Dr. Graham spoke at the closing service to nearly 200,000 people. His books, his message, and his acclaim captivated audiences, drawing him back frequently to Brazil and other countries where he has spoken to over 210 million people in his worldwide ministry. His son, Franklin Graham, continues to preach around the world, including Brazil, sponsoring Christian events now called festivals instead of crusades.

This name change may have been due to sensitivity to how the word *crusade* might be perceived by Arab nations or other countries of the world. *Crusade* implies conquest of another country through their religious beliefs. That certainly wasn't the intention of most of these urban Christian missionaries. Dr. Graham, in particular, has tried to work with local religious leaders in a spirit of ecumenism. But, that hasn't always been well received by the world or even by Dr. Graham's denominational colleagues.

In 1963 at a crusade in San Paulo, Brazil, Dr. Graham invited a local Roman Catholic bishop to join him at the podium and permitted the bishop to bless the converts as they came forward. A part of his regular evangelism, Dr. Graham always referred new converts to local clergy, including Protestant, Catholic, and Jewish religious leaders. Dr. Graham justified this action as a means of bringing people of all faiths to Christ regardless of how they worshiped or what church they chose. He often wrote that this was an example of a great awakening happening within Christianity. By recognizing the value of all beliefs, he saw Christianity broadening but not losing its core worth. Unfortunately, many Baptists and other evangelical church leaders took issue with Dr. Graham's ecumenism and began to preach against him and question his salvation. This controversy, however, has never really tarnished Dr. Graham nor his mission. The Gallup Poll has named him one of the Ten Most Admired Men in the world over 37 times since 1955. He also has been the advisor of US presidents and heads of state around the world.

Jews and Christianity

For centuries Jews had either been forced to convert to Christianity or had voluntarily sought shelter in the Church in order to live. After the atrocities in Germany and in the Middle East during World War II, Jews sailed all over the world, looking for a new place of sanctuary and a new homeland. But every door was shut in their faces. No one seemed to want any more Jews. And so, some Jews sought help from the Pope himself, hoping that by claiming to be Christian converts (just as they had done in Spain and Portugal centuries before and even much earlier in Mesopotamia when they had been carried off as captives and had to claim to be a follower of the local religion), that they would be welcomed. The Vatican readily issued papers identifying hundreds of Jews as new Christians, and they were indeed embraced by countries such as Brazil. But in secret, these new converts still practiced the faith of their fathers, becoming Crypto-Jews, hiding their faith while appearing to be just like their Christian neighbors.

When I heard how Christian churches had set up missions in places like Bom-Retiro to once again try to force their faith on Jews, I was angry and deeply saddened. This was more of the same kind of intolerance Jews had faced in their long and ancient history. But now, the selling of religion took an ugly turn, I thought, preying on the desperation of needy families who only wanted bread to feed their hungry children.

Many Jews, like myself, had refused contracts with the consultants, who grew fat and rich on the desperation of others and sought to enslave those they helped by their perpetual ten percent commission. We struggled to find some kind of employment, though none of it was regular or paid very much. We sought to just stay alive one more day.

My epiphany

During one of the very lean times I experienced between employment, I overcame my resistance to handouts and agreed to tag along one Friday night with a nice Jewish family I had befriended. They came to the church often for meals. Joining this family, it felt somehow like my life had been in the Kibbutz at Friday night *Oneg-Shabbat*, when we ate, drank, danced, and sang in complete joy to be with each other and to practice our faith.

But, here, it was different: Most of the Jewish families who came felt embarrassed and could hardly manage a smile, including the innocent children. There was sickliness in them that spoke of more than just hunger and thirst. There was humiliation and hopelessness about them as if they had suffered greatly somewhere. There was no joy in being together or even of being in a free land. And, there was no shared belief because we were all not practitioners of this Christian faith.

Rev. Woods was always the epitome of honor, and he and his followers and helpers obviously believed in what they were doing, following in the steps of the old prophets and Jesus' disciples. But, it was not our belief, our rituals, our prayers, or even our songs.

The dinner that Friday began with a short prayer of thanks to Jesus, and then the minister blessed and welcomed the guests. After dinner, there were readings from the Old and the New Testament, but mostly the readings came from the prophets and disciples that followed in Jesus' footsteps and spread the new order, which evolved into Christianity. Rev. Woods exerted no undue pressure on anyone to convert, as far as I saw or anyone else could tell me, though he freely taught about his religion at every opportunity. I came to appreciate and praise the church's generosity in trying to help us in our pain.

To me, this particular Friday service filled a gap in my knowledge of the history of the Jewish and Christian religions. I began to see how Judaism had shaped Christianity and gave it a rootedness in a place and culture, though its practitioners would mold it to their times and their philosophies.

To the other Jews, these gatherings were more of an ugly attempt to convert them to Christianity by appearing to help them. They thought that this was worse that open anti-Semitism or other forms of hatred that could be seen. This was insidious because it wormed its way first into the empty bellies of these desperate people and made them feel obligated. Then it worked on their hearts and minds. Some of these Jews wondered if this was the Church's lifelong ten percent commission, the enslavement to another religion.

Some Jews there had converted already, mostly in appreciation for what the Church had done for them by saving them and their children from certain starvation. Some resisted to the end.

One in particular, a Bolivian Jew who converted, was disabled, making his way with a walker wherever he went. He had a beautiful young wife and two beautiful children, a girl and a boy, about five and six years old. Not only was he philosophically a convert, he was an ardent assistant to Rev. Woods and tried hard to convert others by speaking to them about Christianity in Yiddish. Outside the church, he was a man of considerable knowledge of the languages, customs, and laws of Brazil. He assisted some of the Jewish immigrants in obtaining permanent residence and citizenship papers. He also had clout at the U.S. Embassy and helped many obtain visitor visas to America.

For me, then, the Baptist church in Bom-Retiro had been an interesting place of scholarly and biblical learning to help me further appreciate my own faith.

Hungry, will I die?

I had been in Brazil several months and was hardly working enough hours at odd jobs to earn money for rent, laundry, and food. I was skipping meals so that I ate only twice a day instead of three times. When I was so hungry that I cried, I would sit in my room and write a paragraph in my diary, wailing about my troubles. Sometimes, I was afraid to fall asleep because I feared that I might not wake up in the morning. Sometimes late at night, I would gather sufficient courage to knock on my landlady's door and ask if she could spare a cup of coffee, the cheapest commodity in Brazil. I hoped each time that with the coffee, she would offer a biscuit or a slice of fresh bread, whatever she had. She always smiled, invited me in, and offered me something to eat with my cup of coffee.

Falling off the electric pole

I fell into a particularly fallow period where I couldn't even work enough to feed myself. I sought work anywhere and everywhere, but there just were too many people like me looking for a few jobs. I had been walking for days and asking if anyone would give me a job. I didn't want money necessarily. I just wanted to work long enough to pay for something to eat and something to drink.

One of the car maintenance garages took me up on my offer to work when I pleaded that I was a skilled and licensed electrician. The garage owner agreed to give me a special project. The neon sign for his garage had been knocked down by a strong wind a few weeks earlier, but no one was willing to climb up the twenty-foot pole to reattach it.

I gladly accepted the challenge when he offered me a sum of money that would feed me for three days. I picked up the ladder from the back room and placed it against the electric pole. With a few tools in my hand, I proceeded to climb fearlessly up the ladder as the garage owner held it steady beneath me. When I neared the top of the ladder, I examined the top of the pole and where the sign had been attached. I reached for the broken wires and pulled them closer to me so that I could splice them together.

Anxious to start, I had forgotten to turn the power off before I climbed the ladder. When I took the live wires in each hand, I received a 12,000-volt jolt. I screamed and plummeted down on top of the garage owner. The man not only didn't show me any sympathy but also yelled at me for hurting him and for failing to remedy the problem!

I lay on the sidewalk semi-conscious, barely hearing his screams. I twisted in agony and moaned. But all I could think was: *Is he going to pay me for the job?*

A large crowd soon gathered around me. A couple of men tried to pull me up from the sidewalk. It was a struggle since I was still so shaky, but they got me on my feet. One man extended this kindness by offering to take me to my home in his old car. I accepted. As the man helped me to his car, the garage owner called to me. He pulled out of his pocket a wad of *Cruzeiros.* There must have been hundreds of them. With a show of generosity, he offered me just one. For some reason, be felt sorry for me even though I had not completed the job. The man who owned the car closed my door and drove me to my apartment building. He even helped me up the stairs to my room.

Going to sleep: Will I wake up?

That night, hungry and aching, I sat on my bed and cried as I entered the day's excitement into my diary. I hadn't slept for days. I was in pain, and I needed to rest. But that night in particular, I was seriously afraid that I might die in my sleep. I was nearly 15,000 miles from home, without family or friends here. *Who would be the first to discover my body? How many days would pass before someone came? Would anyone be able to notify my family? Would they even know who my father was and where to write?*

I decided that, for the first time in my life, I must plan ahead. My father had often told me that every successful man had a plan for his life and that I should have one, too. But that night, I knew I was not a success. I was a singed, half-electrocuted young man who had no employment and no prospects for any. I definitely didn't have a career. I was hopeless.

All I could do in my circumstances was to write a brief Last Will and Testament. It would serve as an apology to my family for leaving them. As tears fell, I wrote:

"My dear parents, brothers, sisters, and friends, if you find me dead in the next few days, please do not mourn my passing: I am twenty-one. Perhaps I have lived the equivalent of three lifetimes by now. I see them all now: the painful childhood as a Jew in an Arab state, the early separation from the family, the wars, and the scars of the Ma'Abarah. If you can, please take up a collection from my good friends and bring my body back to Israel to be buried among my people.

"I have seen enough, and I feel peaceful. I hope to meet every one of you someday on the other side, free of pain, and with plenty of time to read a few more books. Don't be sad for me. So long."

I laid my pen down and leaned back into the bed, crying. I lay there sobbing late into the morning, when my eyes finally closed, and I fell asleep.

Suddenly, the next morning, I was awakened by a soft knock on the door. I opened my eyes, surprised that I was still alive. It was 4:30 a.m., and I was very curious about who was knocking on my door.

"Hello, Sal, are you awake? I have a job for you, if you are in shape to work," someone said through the closed door.

A job? I opened the door to fine one of the garage workers where I had fallen from the electric pole the day before. We shook hands, and I invited him in to wait for me on the bed. I put away my diary and grabbed some clean underwear and ran to the shower down the hall to clean up for this new job. I had no idea what it was but I felt that my fortunes had somehow changed for the better.

That day I began my real working career in Brazil. I was hired as a truck electrician, on a small salary and a commission. Within six months, I managed a department of three and was earning every week what the average Brazilian was earning per month. *Should I believe in miracles like Rev. Wood always talked about?* Something had definitely happened. Something had definitely changed. *Was it me or was it fate?*

I worked in this garage for six to seven weeks doing all kinds of odd maintenance jobs, crawling under huge trucks, changing oil, tracing wiring, etc. My boss, whom I loved for the opportunity to work at something close to what I had been trained for, noticed that my work clothes were always neat and clean. He called me into his office one day, black grease on his hands

"Sal, how long have you been with me?" he asked. I was petrified that this was a pre-cursor to being fired.

"Oh, six or seven weeks, Mr. Sebastiano," I answered beginning to wonder if my luck had just run out. "Anything wrong?"

"No, nothing is wrong," he said. "But, I was just wondering. How can your clothes be so clean and neatly pressed? Do you see my clothes? Are they clean? No! " He pointed to his greasy overalls and came closer to me. "You can't be working here and stay so clean." As he said that, he reached over and smeared his black greasy hands on my clothes, front and back. "Now, you will be normal like us, not afraid to be dirty."

I was startled. But I quickly realized what he meant. It really looked like I wasn't doing my job if I could stay so clean. And, it also set me apart as if I were somehow better than everyone else. Instead, now I looked like everyone who worked in the garage, including Mr. Sebastiano.

"You are right, Mr. Sebastiano," I said. "I understand, and I appreciate your confidence in me and the opportunity you've given me."

Mr. Sebastiano waved his hand. "No, thank you for your diligence. You can go back to work now."

From that day on, I made sure my work clothes were the greasiest of all of the people who worked there.

Saul in Brazil, 1959 (38)

Rev. Emmanuel Woods and family,
Sao Paolo, Brazil, 1960 (39)

Saul, Sao Paolo, Brazil, 1959 (40)

Chapter Thirty-Six

Working at a Syrian Restaurant

When I returned from my adventure along the Amazon, I showed up for work at the garage and found that I no longer had a position there. I had not expected the journey to take so long. Again, I had failed to tell those close to me that my life was taking a detour. As I had told my friends and family in Israel before I left for Brazil that I would not be gone long, here again I only wanted to see what wonders were out in the world. I truly thought that I would be back home in just a few months. This side trip to the interior of Brazil was like that. I had gotten caught up in the excitement of seeing new places and new people, and I truly thought that I would be back in a few days.

My employer, however, saw my absence as irresponsibility at the least. With so many new immigrants coming into the country and many of them not staying, he must have thought I had found my way back home. I couldn't fault him for firing me, yet I still needed to find a way to eat regularly.

I soon found temporary work in a restaurant owned by a Syrian Muslim. I manned a cigarette booth that also sold candy and magazines.

The owner was very understanding and kind to me, even though he knew I was an Israeli Jew. This was quite remarkable to me because Syria and Israel have suffered a long and deep cultural and religious hatred of each other. Bordering Israel's northern boundary, Syria has set itself against Israel since Palestine was under the British mandate.

To Jews, the Golan Heights, a territory in the northernmost section of Israel, belongs to Israel. Called the Bashan region in biblical times, the Golan Heights has cultural and religious ties to Israeli Jews. Baron Edmond de Rothschild bought 80,000 hectares of the Golan Heights in 1892 from Arab landowners. He began establishing Jewish settlements in the region soon after.

In 1920, the League of Nations designated the original British Mandate for Palestine to include the Golan Heights. However, in some obscure political payoff, Great Britain gave the Golan Heights to France in 1923 before the British took over Palestine.

The Golan Heights became part of the French Mandate of Syria-Lebanon, but wasn't officially part of Syria until 1941 when the French Mandate terminated and Syria gained its independence. When Israel was formed in 1948 by United Nations Resolution 242, Syria and other Arab nations refused to acknowledge the new country. Eventually, many Arab countries, including Egypt—but still not Syria—signed Resolution 242.

In 1957, Baron Rothschild deeded the land to the state of Israel. Jews were living in the region in a variety of settlements. Syria didn't want any Jews there and eventually tried to push out Jewish settlers living in the Golan in the 1973 War. Syria couldn't hold the territory yet still wanted the region back as a war settlement. This continues to be a source of animosity between these two peoples. Syrian Muslims are suspicious of Israeli Jews and vice versa. This has festered over the decades, creating open hatred between Syrians and Israelis.

Yet, here I was, an Israeli Jew, employed by a Syrian Muslim who offered me generosity and respect. The restaurant owner gave me leftover food to take back to my little apartment and often invited me to his home for dinner. I grew fond of him and his wife and children.

He and I shared long conversations about our homelands and what it had been like living in Syria and Israel. Somehow, here in this land where we both were foreigners, we found the common ground between Muslim and Jew. We both loved the land, the bustle of the markets, the local foods, the music, and the people there. We grew to respect each other regardless of our different cultures and religious beliefs. I prayed Israel and its Arab neighbors could get along as well.

But I still had much to learn about life and responsibility.

There were often lulls in between the rush of customers at the restaurant. Sometimes, even in the evening or midday rush, customers bypassed my cigarette stand. Not every customer needed cigarettes or wanted candy or a magazine. These idle periods drove me to distraction because I sat with nothing to do. I began to bring a book to work to read under the counter during these idle times with no customers.

The owner caught me one day. "You can't read books during your work here," he scolded me. "The customers will not want to disturb your reading, and they will avoid the cigarette stand. I will lose money."

I protested, "But I only do it when there are no customers."

He would not accept this excuse, and I wasn't mature enough to recognize that he was right. My friend and employer fired me on the spot, but with much regret he said.

Once again, I was on the street looking for work and wondering where my next meal would come from.

Death Row #2455: Caryl Chessman

The book that I was reading under the counter was Caryl Chessman's autobiography, "Cell 2455 Death Row." It was one of two books that I read in Brazil that were written by Chessman. The other was "The Cruel Face Of Justice." They had been translated into Portuguese and were both bestsellers in Brazil. Chessman's books told of his ordeal in prison after he had been convicted of a series of robberies and kidnappings and how he had fought the death penalty. The subject matter captured the interest of Brazilians, who believed Chessman was innocent.

Chessman's book and his case easily attracted sympathetic ears because of the harsh conviction he had been given for the crimes for which he had been imprisoned. A parolee from Folsom Prison, Chessman had been in and out of trouble most of his adult life. Mostly, it was simple theft or stealing cars, but never cases involving harm to other people. This time, 27-year-old Chessman conducted several robberies in the last two and a half weeks of January 1948. First, he stole a car and five days later began to hold up couples parked or driving along the Pacific Coast in California. He stopped them by using a red flashing light like police officers had in their cars. Thus, he was known as the Red-Light Bandit.

The robberies were almost laughable since he didn't seem to even be armed and were mainly crimes of opportunity. The money that he took was hardly worth the effort. Once, he only took fifteen dollars, and the most was only fifty. To show how ill-planned these robberies were, Chessman didn't even bother to cover his face. Only after the first couple of them did he think about putting a handkerchief over the lower half of his face, and even then it often slipped so that his victims could identify him.

What turned the tide against him and created the legal predicament he found himself in later was the fact that in two of the seventeen robberies, he decided to take the female companions of the men he robbed out of their automobiles and transport them to a secluded location. In both cases, he forces the women to perform oral sex on him. Chessman also attempted to rape and sodomize his last victim, Mary Alice Meza, though neither act was successful.

Though these acts were horrific, they weren't usually capital crimes. Any of his crimes would have rightly earned him consecutive sentences but not the gas chamber. What swayed the jury was the prosecutor's interpretation of California's Little Lindbergh Law, which had been passed in 1933, after the Charles Lindbergh baby had been kidnapped earlier. This law went into effect when there had been bodily harm to a kidnap victim. The prosecutor determined that two of the kidnapping charges had indeed resulted in bodily harm, especially in Mary Alice Meza's case. The jury thought there was merit in those charges, found him guilty on all counts, and did not recommend mercy. The Little Lindberg Law carried either a life sentence without the hope of parole or the gas chamber. For Chessman, it was an automatic death sentence.

Chessman spent the next twelve years on Death Row in cell 2455, trying to commute his sentence and even to get his conviction thrown out. He maintained that he was innocent. He had eight stays of execution as his lawyers pushed appeal after appeal.

While in San Quentin Federal Penitentiary, the new warden, Harley O. Teets, encouraged Chessman to write a book. Teets thought that Chessman's story would help young people turn away from a life of crime. The chief psychiatrist, Dr. David G. Schmidt, also tried to get Chessman to write about his life of crime. Schmidt thought that criminal psychologists would benefit from Chessman's book because Chessman had been the most intelligent and most completely criminal psychopaths the doctor had ever seen.

Ironically, Richard E. McGee, the California Director of Corrections, gave permission to Chessman to write his book, but he thought he would never finish it, much less get it published. Director McGee didn't realize the power of a newsworthy story no matter how poorly written. In Chessman's case, the book actually was quite well written, and New York publisher Prentice-Hall grabbed it up. The book immediately skyrocketed to the bestseller list. Chessman eventually wrote four books about his life. His first book sold a half million copies and was translated into eighteen different languages, including Portuguese.

Chessman eventually was executed on May 2, 1960. California governor, Pat Brown, strongly against capital punishment, could not help Chessman, though he had wanted to. The California Supreme Court had voted previously to prevent Governor Brown from commuting Chessman's sentence. There was nothing Governor Brown could do.

Many people all over the world felt that Chessman was innocent, including people in Brazil. Although I am against the death penalty, I supported the evidence against Chessman. This often led to many hot arguments in public places. When Chessman was executed, the world raged against the injustice it felt had been done in California. Mobs of demonstrators in countries in Europe and South America threw stones and bricks at the American Embassies in their countries, breaking windows and disrupting business.

I was amazed that so much empathy could be raised worldwide for one person. I found it ironic that this kind of universal outrage had never been voiced for the Jews who had suffered in Iraq or those millions who had died in the gas chambers in Europe. Only many decades after have people around the world expressed their horror and outrage at what could be done to other human beings.

Here in Brazil, Chessman's execution only fueled hatred towards the United States. It also increased support for Cuba's rebel Castro, who had found Communist supporters in Brazil.

Chapter Thirty-Seven

Working at Nilotex

Finding work

By now, I had been in Brazil for about a year and once again needed to find employment. I had thought about going to the United States but that had been foiled because the US State Department had denied my visa. Since I had to remain in Brazil for the time being, I decided to make as much of my life there as I could. I needed a normal job with a steady paycheck.

I prepared an impressive resume in English and had it translated into Portuguese. With that in my hand, I began interviewing.

One of the contacts I had cultivated in the *feira* (street markets) told me about a company called Nilotex, a silk lingerie manufacturer in the nearby town of Lapa. It was owned and run by wealthy, Orthodox, Hungarian Jews. I took the train to Lapa and secured an interview for a position as an electrician in the Maintenance Department.

The interview went well. I then took a written test administered by the personnel department, which I passed. Afterwards, I was introduced to the head of the Maintenance Department, Mr. Ghelermo. I was most surprised when he began speaking Arabic, not Portuguese, to me as he reviewed my resume. It turned out he was an Egyptian, a Coptic Christian. He, too, administered a written test to me on the subjects of electricity and electronics.

Mr. Ghelermo graded my test and then smiled. He told me that I had passed with a significant score and that I was hired. I was to report to work the following Monday.

I was very happy to have finally found my place in the world. Things were now looking up for me. I would be able to pay the rent on time, feed and cloth myself, and save some money in the process. As I was being escorted to the gate, Mr. Ghelermo began to talk about the prejudice the Jews and Christians were subjected to in Egypt and in other Arab countries. As I left him, he gave me a warm welcome to Brazil, the new land of opportunity. I knew then that I not only had bonded with him as employee to employer but as friend to friend.

When I got back to Bom-Retiro where my little apartment was located, I immediately knocked on my wonderful landlady's door and notified her of my good news. She was happy that I had found something steady and reliable but appeared to be worried a bit. I asked her what was troubling her, and she told me that she was worried that I might leave her apartment building and move to Lapa to be closer to my new job.

My landlady had kept me alive for all these months and patiently allowed me to pay my rent when I had the money. I certainly was not going to betray that care and trust for more convenient lodging. In spite of the difficulty and the cost of the daily train ride to commute to my job, I would not abandon my landlady and take lodging elsewhere now that I was assured of steady income. I reassured my landlady of my loyalty and told her how much that I had appreciated her care and concern for me while I had been in Bom-Retiro.

My first day

The following Monday, August 3, 1959, I took an early train and arrived at the gate of Nilotex at 7:45 am, a full, half hour early. I stood by the gate until someone from personnel came out to greet me and let me in. I was issued an ID patch, which was pinned to my shirt. The man from personnel then took me to the Maintenance Department and introduced me to some of the workers on the way to Mr. Ghelermo's office.

My day began with a tour of the factory so that I would know where everything was. I passed the old knitting and weaving machines, which were very noisy. Then, I went by the hundreds of machines that converted the silk bobbins into long, continuous sheets of silk. Conveyer belts transported the silk sheets to the Cutting Department where the material was cut down to precise size according to the requirements of the garment.

As I was being shown around, I couldn't help but notice the many young, beautiful girls operating the various machines at the factory. They appeared happy in their jobs and confident enough to look my way and smile. I had a feeling I would have a good time here.

In the afternoon, I was brought back by my guide to the Maintenance Department and was shown a pile of motors in need of refurbishing. I was given a toolbox and was shown where the Parts Department was located. I began testing and tagging the motors, indicating what was wrong with them and what was needed to fix them.

At the end of the day, I walked to the parking lot outside the factory gates and took the waiting bus to the train station. The bus was full of workers from Nilotex, mostly young, talkative girls in their teens.

I sat down next to a girl and immediately introduced myself. "They call me Sal. What's your name?" I asked.

She girl smiled, a bit surprised at my directness. "I am Maria," she said. "But don't confuse me with all the other Maria's in Nilotex."

I thought she was really cute but worried she might be too young to mess with. I estimated her age to be fifteen or sixteen. Worried a little, I wondered if she had older brothers.

The night shift

Sometimes, I had to work the night shift; rotating with the rest of the staff of the Maintenance Department. On those occasions, I became acquainted with the night watchman, a fat, old man, who stood on guard at the gates. He had no gun or other weapon except for a big stick that he carried with him everywhere. He, too, turned out to be Egyptian, except that he was Jewish. He spoke Arabic, French, English, and Portuguese.

I felt a kinship with him. He was like me, an educated man who found himself exiled in Brazil. The night watchman, however, was working to feed his extended family. He told me that some of the workers teased and mocked him because he weighed a lot. He told me that my boss, Mr. Ghelermo, was full of resentment and prejudice against the Jews, and to be very careful. The night watchman said that Mr. Ghelermo was no better than the Arabs. I listened, but I refused to let the old man poison my mind against my boss. Mr. Ghelermo had seemed sympathetic to the plight of the Jews around the world and had treated me fairly. I reserved the right to find out for myself what Mr. Ghelermo's treatment of Jews day to day really was.

During some of the night shift work, I was pleasantly surprised by the open sexuality of the Brazilian women who worked in the factory. During a 30-minute coffee break at 10:30 pm, many of these women would walk out of the factory and sit in the parking lot to have their snack and coffee. They preferred this to sitting in the cafeteria inside.

I took my dinner in the night air with these young beauties. Some of them even began flirting with me. I was younger than most of them and new there so I assume that that was part of my novelty. Then one night, when I got up to go to the men's room to throw away the wrappings of the dinner that I had brought, one of the women followed me into the bathroom. She immediately pressed her lovely body against mine, and it was clear what she wanted. Though there wasn't much time, foreplay was eliminated, and we moved directly to sex. Pushed against the wall in the corner of the men's room, we made love standing up, with urgency.

This soon became a pattern with a different young woman each time. Sometimes, these encounters were so frenzied and so brief, I had no time to remove my pants. Always, it was either standing up against one of the walls or sitting on the toilet seat with legs sprawled around each other. There was no pretending about social niceties and no commitments or promises. We just responded to desire that flamed during these nightly breaks. It probably was every young man's most envied sexual fantasy. But, it was entirely real.

"Is it cut off?"

I suspected that the women had been curious about me and had possibly shared their experiences with each other. I do know that they were very curious about what nationality and religion I was. Was I a Jew, an Arab, or a Christian?

During one of these night-shift encounters, a Catholic young woman startled me. I suppose she didn't want to offend me by asking outright what religion I subscribed to. Instead, with a cute giggle, she asked in her native Portuguese and pointed her finger at my pants zipper, *"E ta curtado?"* ("Is it cut off?").

She obviously wanted to know if I were circumcised. That would identify me generally as a Jew, though Muslims and converted Jews would also be circumcised.

I smiled at her and replied, *"Si, mais no esta curto."* ("Yes, but not too short.")

This conversation spread among the female workers of the factory like wild fire. Some of the girls teased me at coffee breaks by pointing to my zipper and saying, *"Curtado,"* (Cut off) and laughing their heads off.

I suppose it was my own fault for being quick witted. So, I bore their teasing with good humor. Instead of curbing the occasional trysts in the men's room, they actually increased because of all the talk. This certainly was one time when there was a definite plus side to being teased.

Chapter Thirty-Eight

My Adopted Family, the Molnars

Every day, I bought a ticket at the train station in Bom-Retiro and traveled to Lapa to work and then took the evening train home. The train was always crowded with passengers, both going to work and eager to get home. This was always a pleasant time for me. I often talked to the passengers to find out their stories, where they came from, how long they had been in Brazil, what kind of work they did. Slowly, I began to make friends.

One of the first friends I made was Julio Molnar. He lived in a modest house in Lapa with his parents, his wife, and their two small children. Sometimes, he drove a car to work, and at other times, he came on a bicycle. I met Julio on the train going to Sao Paolo one evening. We talked easily together and sought each other out when we took the train. Julio learned that I worked at Nilotex, which wasn't far from his home.

One Friday night after I had finished work, Julio rode over to the factory on his bicycle. He met me at the gate and invited me to dinner at his house. I was grateful and surprised.

Does he know I am Jewish? I wondered. *Should I tell him immediately to avoid a wrong slip of the tongue or embarrassment?* I decided not to say anything. I would just wait and see what the evening had in store.

Julio told me to get on the bicycle behind him, and he took me to his house. It was a hard and bumpy ride on a dirt road. I must say that my behind was pretty bruised by the time I reached Julio's home.

The Molnar's lively and beautiful five-year-old daughter greeted us in front of the house. She ran to Julio and gave him the longest hug I have ever witnessed. He showered her with kisses as he carried her inside the house without paying me any attention. I silently followed behind him. When I entered his home, Julio's 75-year-old mother said hello and welcomed me, but she didn't extend her hand for me to shake. Instead, she motioned me into the kitchen.

At the kitchen table, I found Mr. Molnar, her husband, who seemed to be older, about 80-years old. His skin was very wrinkled and white, as if it hadn't seen the sun for years. He sat smiling, his hands shaking a bit, as his wife sat down beside him.

On the other side of him sat a young boy of three or four, who turned out to be Julio's shy, little son, who felt comfortable and secure beside his grandfather. On the opposite side of the table, Julio and I sat next to his daughter.

Julio's wife, a tall, healthy-looking woman was standing near the sink, washing her hands. She dried them quickly on a dishtowel and came over to me. She extended her right hand for me to shake and said, "I am Rosalinda, Julio's wife. Welcome to our modest home."

I stood up, my hand clenching hers very softly. "My name is Sal. Thank you for inviting me. I am alone in your country, so I really appreciate your hospitality," I said softly.

Fish, fish, and more fish...Thank you, Jesus!

The table was set beautifully, though modestly. Rosalinda served the food one dish at a time, filling each plate from a stack on the counter. I was silently praying that I could eat the food she served and not cause any embarrassment. They would surely interpret it as rude and ungrateful. But, as luck would have it, she served several different dishes—all of them a different kind of fish. It was Friday, and fish was commonly eaten on Fridays. I still couldn't abide eating fish since the time my father had brought home the giant fish when we lived in Iraq when I was three years old. I had never eaten fish since.

On this night, I could hardly bear the smell of the food, much less eat it. I was beginning to look sick. Everyone was staring at me, but Julio's mother drew their attention as she bowed her head and said, "Let us give thanks to our Lord."

Everyone extended their arms and took the hand of the person sitting on either side as we bowed our heads. I was petrified. *Is it proper for me, a Jew, to participate in this prayer? Will they be angry with me when they find out? What shall I do?* I decided to do what they did and extended my arms and touched hands. I lowered my head and closed my eyes and hoped I was doing the right thing.

"Thank you, our Lord Jesus Christ, for our bounty," prayed Julio's mother. "And thank you for welcoming our dear friend Sal to our humble house. Please confer your blessings on him and his entire family."

"Amen" everyone responded and so did I.

As soon as the prayer ended, everyone began taking bread and eating from their plates. I made a fake attempt to taste the food but was afraid that Rosalinda would think that I just didn't like her cooking. I didn't think anyone would believe me that I couldn't eat fish. I reached for a slice of bread and took a bite. Julio's son stopped eating and looked at me. Then Julio's daughter turned her head at me in question. Finally, Julio's mother put down her bread and stared at me frankly, wondering why I wasn't eating from my plate.

Julio's wife walked over to me, but seemed to understand that I might find her cooking foreign. "You don't like my food," she said quietly. "It's alright. You can tell me. Why don't you try something else." She took my plate away and brought another one with a different entrée on it and placed it in front of me. "Please try this one. It's a special Hungarian dish, which I learned to cook for our Jewish friends when I worked as maid."

Now, I knew that they knew I was Jewish, and they didn't mind. They still welcomed me to their home. I was so relieved.

However, the second dish was also fish and smelled even worse than the first one. *What should I do?* I decided I must be truthful with my wonderful hosts so I told my story. "I am very sorry, friends. I do not like fish. I never eat fish, even when my mother cooks it," I told them. "It's a long story going back to when I was very young. Don't mind my eccentricity. Please go ahead and enjoy your supper."

They gazed at each other in total bewilderment. "A man who doesn't like fish?" they seemed to be thinking, "How can that be? It's Kosher!" The children seem to take delight in this predicament. I wondered whether they thought that having an adult refuse food validated their own food rejections. They began to giggle and cover their faces.

Rosalinda was not to be deterred. She was going to be a good hostess, no matter what. She came and took the second plate away, saying, "I understand, and don't you worry. No harm has been done. Now, what can I make you? You must eat something with us. It's Friday night, Sabbath night. We must celebrate the Sabbath together," she added, with a smile.

I was flabbergasted. *They celebrate the Sabbath? Are they Jewish? It can't be. They just prayed to Jesus.* I was confused.

Rosalinda was waiting for my answer for what she could feed me. Finally, I said, "Please, just give me some jam and butter. I love this bread. This will satisfy me tonight as we celebrate together." I took another piece of bread.

Julio's wife made a surprised gesture at my request. She must have expected me to ask her to make an elaborate dish. But it wouldn't have been polite to even ask after their hospitality. Besides, if it were customary to eat fish on Fridays, I supposed they would not want to bring another meat to the table. And, the bread was indeed very good.

Julio's mother looked at me wryly and said, "I can see how much trouble you must have caused your mother. She spoiled you good, didn't she?"

I smiled then and nodded. "Yes, she did, I suppose," I admitted. "It's because of her that I never learned to eat fish. Father would punish me and send me to my room hungry to force me to eat fish with the rest of the family. But, Mother always felt sorry for me and sneaked me some other food at midnight. My father never knew."

"That's a mother's love," Julio's mother answered. "I am not surprised. We all love our children beyond reason or logic."

I began to really like this woman. She had wisdom and infinite kindness, it seemed to me.

Rosalinda then brought me two kinds of jam on a plate and a wide-mouth jar of butter. She put it all in front of me and pulled the breadbasket closer to the plate. "Here, please eat," she urged. "Don't be shy. You are one of us. You are family." Rosalind sat down beside Julio and added. "My husband told me a lot about you. He loves you like a brother, which he never had. Please, eat as much as you want."

I gobbled up two jam-and-butter sandwiches, drank some pineapple juice, and then lingered over coffee. After supper, I played with the children and promised them I would bring toys the next time I saw them. They were so delightful to play with. They were the happiest, giggling children I have ever seen and had no sense of materialism. I envied Julio and Rosalinda and their happy life. The Molnars were safe in their own country, content with their lot, and hopeful for the future.

That night, I left feeling as if I were the luckiest man on earth. Julio and I became even closer over the coming months. We confided in each other and shared intimate family stories. Julio even once disclosed to me that his eighty-year-old father was still sexually active. Rosalinda had often used his father's experience as an ideal for Julio to strive for when she wanted to induce Julio into more frequent activity himself.

Chapter Thirty-Nine

Seventh-Day Adventist Church

I was invited to Julio's home at least a dozen times while I worked at Nilotex. I grew to appreciate his wise parents and his lovely children. Julio told me that he and his family had been Catholics and had converted to the Seventh-day Adventist church, a Protestant religion that began in the United States during the mid-nineteenth century. I was not familiar with this religion and found myself very curious about it. I wanted to gain a deeper knowledge of it since it came closest to my own Jewish tradition. Seventh-day Adventists kept the Sabbath as Jews did, celebrated the same holidays, and were looking for the Messiah.

History of the Seventh-day Adventist church

The Seventh-day Adventist church began in the late 1830s and 1840s as a number of Protestant Christian ministers from different denominations began to search the scriptures and come to similar insights. Rev. William Miller, a Baptist minister, led a movement that preached on the second advent of the Messiah or the Second Coming of Jesus Christ. He joined others from Christian Connection churches whose membership ranked fifth among Christian denominations in the country at that time.

Christian Connection churches believed that the Bible was the literal word of God, and through study one could know God's will, not only for the Church but also for individuals. These churches also valued individual freedom to search the scriptures for divine truth and to interpret the meaning of what they found.

The Washington, New Hampshire Christian Connection church became a church that preached on the Second Coming and thus became known as an Adventist church. This church and other Christian Connection churches that emphasized freedom were active in the abolitionist movement that sought to abolish slavery. They also encouraged women to take active leadership roles within the church and licensed many women as ministers of the church. They also opposed formalized creeds that they felt hampered their religious freedom. These churches were also active in the temperance movement and in health reform because they felt that the body was "the temple of the Lord." Not only should nothing pollute the body, but also a healthy body produced a clear mind that could perceive spiritual truths. For these reasons, Christian Connection churches forbade the use of tobacco and alcohol.

As church members continued to search the scriptures, more truths were expected to be found. This process of continuous, prophetic revelation helped develop the strong doctrine of the church today. Rache Oakes, an Adventist Baptist during this early period, had searched the Bible and was convinced of the validity of keeping the Sabbath on the seventh day of the week. Her strong belief was echoed by Thomas Preble, a Freewill Baptist, and Frederick Wheeler, a Methodist who pastured the Washington, NH church. As this doctrine became accepted, churches that believed this started calling themselves Seventh-day Adventists as early as 1860.

By 1863, the denomination was officially organized with 125 churches worldwide and 3,500 members. There was considerable effort by the denomination to go into the world and preach the gospel. Though a Czech member took it upon himself to try to evangelize Europe in 1864, the first official missionary was sent abroad from the United States in 1874. By the twenty-first century, there are ten million Seventh-day Adventists in the world. Only a tenth of them live in the United States. They have built schools and medical facilities in 98 countries and provide recreational and social activities to adolescents and summer camps to children. A hallmark of Seventh-day Adventist congregations is their ethnic diversity.

Seventh-day Adventists also practice full immersion baptism and practice foot washing as an act of humility when they serve communion. Like many Christian churches, they believe in original sin and the fallen nature of humankind. They also believe that each believer has a special God-given gift to be used to benefit humankind and to further God's plan. Every believer is also required to proclaim the Second Coming and to try to evangelize others. Members are supposed to dress modestly and to behave chastely. Besides avoiding tobacco and alcohol, members do not eat pork. They are permitted to divorce but only if the spouse has committed adultery.

Sister White

While I was attending the Seventh-day Adventist church in Sao Paolo, there was much talk about Sister White, an American, and her contribution to the denomination. Like many of her fellow believers, she studied the scriptures, searching for divine truth not only for her own growth in the faith but also for the wider church. Her writings and talks came at a time when the Seventh-day Adventist church was steeped in doctrinal controversy.

As the church formed, Seventh-day Adventists began to focus on following the letter of the law as laid out in the Ten Commandments and in certain books of the Old Testament, such as Leviticus and Numbers, which details how moral believers are to behave. By 1888, two clear camps developed. Uriah Smith and George Butler were staunch believers in the law, whereas young preachers E. J. Waggoner and A. T. Jones brought a new doctrine of salvation by faith. Smith and Butler feared that the faithful would be led down a path to antinomianism, which is the doctrine that says that once a person becomes a Christian that person is not bound to uphold any scriptural, civil, or moral law and that salvation comes through faith, even if the person behaves immorally.

In the middle of this controversy, Sister Ellen Goul White spoke at the General Conference Session in Minneapolis in 1888. Here, she taught a doctrine that attempted to bring these two disparate views together. In this talk and in her subsequent writings and sermons, she upheld the belief in salvation through faith in Jesus, but added that through the working of the Holy Spirit each believer would be moved to live a moral life and do good.

Unfortunately, many people didn't understand Sister White's message and others clearly misunderstood her meaning. Some people thought Sister White wanted to open the doors of charismatic practice within the church. They thought that her insistence that the Holy Spirit would guide believers seemed evidence for this idea. Sister White's writings, however, warned of the dangers of what she called sentimentality or emotionalism in religion, referring to the emotional responses and ecstatic speech of charismatic churches. She did, however, stress the need to be filled with the Holy Spirit and to be guided by it. According to her, the proof of the power of the Holy Spirit moving within the church would be shown in increased unity among its believers and enthusiasm in doing the ordinary business of the church and within the community.

Interestingly, Sister White herself reported to have had two hundred visions, which she professed came from God. Some researchers think these visions may have been the result of temporal lope epilepsy brought on by a head injury as a child. They also think that this condition was one of the reasons she wrote 100,000 pages of religious writing. Hypergraphia, an abnormal condition where a person writes all of the time, may not apply here since much of this writing has now been proven to have been copied from other nineteenth century religious writers. Though people with Hypergraphia can copy out book after book, they usually don't write anything original. If they do, it is stream of consciousness writing with little meaning. Sister White's writings are understandable but a bit complex.

I am in love: But my honor is on the line

It was no surprise, then, that I grew so close to these good people, the Molnars. My curiosity about their religion led me to attending their church with them. I was received with open arms by the church members. They called me by my middle name, Silas. It was closer to my real name than being called Sal by everyone else. I also felt somehow that Silas connected me to the scriptures, though Saul was just as biblical (The first king of the Israelites).

On the first day I attended church with the Molnars, I caught a pretty, blond girl, about sixteen or seventeen, staring at me. She lowered her eyes quickly, but smiled, and turned back to the minister's sermon. Each time I came to church, I found the pretty girl smiling at me. I was flattered and wondered how I could meet her.

This Seventh-day Adventist church often organized nature outings on the weekends for its members. Brazil was a lovely setting in which to do that. I was asked to come along on these treks.

During one of these church-sponsored nature outings, I noticed that the pretty blond was among the group. I went over to her and introduced myself. She was interesting to talk to, very serious, but had a ready laugh. We took a short walk away from the others, but stayed within shouting distance. We met like this during several church outings.

One day as we were strolling along, talking among the tress, she told me she thought she was in love with me. She said that this was her personal secret. She hadn't told anyone else and none of her friends knew, and certainly not her parents. She asked me how I felt. Before I was able to answer, she asked if I were open-minded enough to fall in love with a non-Jew. I told her that I was. At that moment, we were called back to the group, and I wasn't able to tell her more.

We rejoined the others and indulged in the wonderful dishes each family brought to the picnic. The girl had two younger brothers—but no older ones, thank God! Still, I had a feeling that her tall, athletic father had noticed us walking together, and I feared the consequences.

The Molnars and the other members of the church were my long-lost pillars of strength. They gave so much of themselves. I had their unconditional friendship and the example of a dignified moral life. They had restored my faith and assurance in humanity. The blond girl and I continued to sneak out of church and during church picnics to see each other. I made every effort to remain a gentleman and not to betray the trust the Molnars and the church members had in me. We had done no more than hold hands, and sometimes, on rare occasion, hugged lightly.

The girl's mother still greeted me with a soft handshake and a smile. Her father, however, was more stern-faced and distant. I found it increasingly more difficult to meet with this blond teenage girl without feeling a measure of guilt. I knew that soon our secret would not remain a secret for very long.

During one of the church picnics, I was flabbergasted when the girl's mother came to my table and asked me in the most polite manner if she could have a word with me privately. I got up and followed her into the nearby woods. There, her husband stood behind a tree, waiting. I began to shake. *Am I trapped? Is it going to get ugly? Is he about to beat me up or threaten me?*

"Sit down, Silas, please," the girl's father said, pointing to the grass.

I took out my handkerchief and spread it on the ground, then sat on it. The girl's mother sat down on my left; her father on my right. I did indeed feel trapped and a bit threatened.

"Silas, we know you have been interested in our daughter," her mother said. "There is no casual dating allowed in our church. And there are no secrets between our daughter and us. She told us everything. She is young, and she is in love with you," she continued.

My face must have turned red. I felt sweat dripping slowly down the back of my neck. Nervously, I rubbed my forehead.

"We discussed this matter between us," her father continued. "We don't mind it very much. We want our daughter to be happy with a family of her own. Do you love her, too?" He asked me, with a faint smile.

I hesitated. *Is it a trap? Is he going to dig further? What exactly did she tell them? We really didn't do anything?* "Yes, I love her very much," I finally answered. "But I have been a gentleman all along. I respect your ways and your church. I wouldn't dream of hurting her," I assured them.

"We know, Silas. We appreciate your treatment of our daughter," her father said gently. "But now, we must make some serious decisions." I listened attentively as he continued. "This clandestine activity cannot continue. Church members are beginning to talk."

"Silas, we all like you," the girl's mother assured me. "We will not only welcome you to our family. We will adopt you as our son. But—" She hesitated, looking troubled. Finally, she continued, "You must convert to our church. There is no choice in the matter. Will you?"

I tried to smile. But this was a matter of the utmost importance. *What was I to say? Could I really convert and leave the faith of my fathers? Was this the right path for me?* While all of these thoughts ran through my mind, I remembered that my goal when I had met the Molnars was to reach the United States as soon as I could. I had been saving a portion of my wages at Nilotex for that very day. I wanted to go to school. I wanted to experience more of life and see still more of the world. And, in the end, I did not wish to dishonor my family's long traditions.

While I was still thinking, the girl's mother reached out and touched my arm. "It's ok, Silas," she said gently. "We know this must be the most important step in your life. We understand. It's too big a burden, we know."

The girl's father continued, "Take your time to think about this, Silas. In the meantime, you must stop seeing our daughter immediately. This is our way. There is no sidestepping our church beliefs. Will you do that? Would you respect our wishes?"

I was somewhat relieved but still hesitated to answer him. "This will cause our daughter grief," the girl's mother added. "She might even be angry with us. But it must be done. Silas, will you do as we ask?"

Finally, I spoke. "I am sorry if I caused you any anguish," I said with some tremor in my voice. "I am still young and full of ambition. I dream of going to America to complete my education. Marriage is the furthest thing from my mind right now. Yes, certainly I will abide by your wishes and suppress my feelings for your daughter. She is a wonderful girl… a young lady… You have raised her well. Thank you for understanding."

They looked at each other and smiled what seemed to be rather bittersweet smiles. On either side of me, they each touched one of my arms. We got up off the ground. Then we all shook hands and thanked each other again.

They walked back toward the picnic area. I walked in the opposite direction toward a more populated area where I found a busy street and hailed a taxi to take me home. I did not say good-bye to their daughter. I kept my word of honor to these sincere Christian parents. I never saw my little angel again. I didn't dare return to the church for fear that my resolve would melt once I saw her again. I also feared that my presence would cause her more heartbreak than my absence.

My friend Julio Molnar, taking a great risk, acted as a courier between us. He passed short love notes between the girl and me until my very last day in Brazil. She was the purest, most innocent light in my life. But I was not ready for such a love or for marriage and a family.

Forty years later, I still wonder what had become of her. *Did she marry and have children? Was she lucky in marriage and in health? Did she ever think of me and what might have been?* I fervently hope the answers to those questions are all a resounding "Yes."

With my "adopted family", the Molnars, and cousin
Yeg-Al, Sao Paolo, Brazil, 1960 (41)

With girlfriend in Sao Paolo, Brazil, 1959 (42)

Chapter Forty

Leaving My Beloved Brazil

Yearning to be with my family

I had been in Brazil far longer than I had ever intended. I had promised my family that I would be home in just a few months, just enough time to get this adventurous spirit out of my system. I thought that here in Brazil I would get a good job and make enough money quickly so that I could return home. I guess deep down I really had dreamed of getting rich in this land of opportunity and coming home not only a world-traveler but also a rich and important man. After my heartbreaking love affair with the girl from the Seventh-day Adventist church, all I wanted now was to be with someone from my family. If I couldn't be with my parents, then I wanted to be close once more to one of my siblings. My brothers or sisters would understand what I had been through here. They wouldn't chastise me for leaving the family behind in Israel. Surely, my sister Berta would empathize with my plight. After all, she had married an American and left to live in the United States before I had left Israel.

As I mulled over my situation and plotted to find a way to leave this country that I had schemed and worked to visit, I began to form a plan to go to the United States and see Berta because she was closer than trying to get back to Israel. I also realized here in Brazil that I needed more education if I were ever able to make it in the wider world. I saw that I could do both things—see Berta and get an education—if I applied for a student visa to the United States.

I'm denied the promised land

The United States required that each person who applied for a student visa needed a sponsor. The only person I knew who might be able to help me was my sister Berta who lived in New York. I wrote to Berta and asked her to do what she could on my behalf to obtain a student visa. And, then I waited.

The months dragged on with no response from the US and no positive answer from my sister. Finally, an answer came and I was flatly denied. I wrote Berta again and begged for her help. Even so, I began to resent the State Department's requirements. I also was very angry with Berta for not seeing the urgency in my plea to come to the US. One day, I wrote her in a long, emotional letter.

I told her that I felt like the prophet Moses who had led the Israelite out of bondage in Egypt and brought them the Torah and the Law (the Ten Commandments). After two years of journeying from Egypt, he led the nation of Israel to the borders of the Promised Land and then sent twelve men to scout out the land and bring back a report about how perfect it was for them, just as God had said. This act was to confirm God's promise to them.

The scouts brought back pomegranates and grapes to show the abundance in the land, saying, "We went into the land to which you sent us, and it does flow with milk and honey." (Deuteronomy 1: 20) These were two foods that didn't require toil by human beings, except in the gathering of them. So the land was indeed a land of plenty and ease.

"But the people who live there are powerful," the ten other scouts reported. (Deuteronomy 1:28) They only saw the stumbling blocks to their possessing the Promised Land and convinced the entire nation of Israel that they could not possibly overcome those obstacles and to turn back toward Egypt. God punished this fearfulness and lack of faith by causing the tribes of Israel to wander in the desert for thirty-eight years. By default, Moses and the two optimistic scouts (Joshua and Caleb) were also denied entering the Promised Land.

It was unfair then, and I felt it was unfair to me now as well. There were indeed obstacles facing me as they did the children of Israel. There were powerful people who were keeping me from my family and from my next goal in life. I feared that I would stay forty years in this foreign land, estranged from my family and never finding that easy life of milk and honey. I also worried that like Moses in his old age, I still would only see pictures of my promised land, the United States, but would not be permitted to go there.

Finding a way

As I continued to pursue this biblical line of thought, depressing as it was, my thoughts turned to faith and faithfulness. I remembered meeting a Bolivian Jew who had converted to Christianity at Salvacao de Israel, the Baptist church in Bon-Retiro where I had many long theological discussions. This man was learned and had considerable influence with important people, including the United States Embassy in Brazil. I knew where he lived and one day called on him, laying my plight at his feet.

The gentleman was very persuasive. Within a few months, I had a student visa that permitted me to attend Columbia University in New York City. I had the visa in my hands on February 5, 1960 and quickly made plans to leave Brazil and become an exchange student.

I called all of my friends in Brazil and told them of my good news. I visited those who did not have telephones. It was bittersweet having to say goodbye again to good friends. It was especially hard to say farewell to my dear friend Julio Molnar and his entire family. His children climbed on my shoulders for the last time, calling my name "Silas, Silas" over and over. Julio's parents hugged and kissed me and wished me success.

Julio's wife, Rosalinda, did the same but whispered a question in my ear, " Do you want to see ... and say good-bye to her?"

I pushed Rosalinda away slightly to look into her face. "No," I said quietly, "it would be too difficult. But I'll write her and explain everything. Thank you."

Julio next gave me a long hug and added a tearful, "Goodbye, my brother."
I, too, had tears in my eyes.

During the next few days, I packed and tied up lose ends. I did not have time to sell my furnishings and the possessions that I had accumulated in my apartment. I left everything as a gift to my dear, loving landlady, who had grown to be my second mother. She made me promise to write her faithfully.

On April 12, 1960, I boarded a Varig plane to New York. Once again, I was leaving one land for another, having fulfilled one dream to pursue one more. Though I was excited about the challenges and opportunities of the student exchange program at Columbia University, depression began to envelope me. I loved the Brazilian people, the hot-blooded exotic factory women, the chaste Christians at the Seventh-day Adventist church, the Molnars, and my dear angel that I had left with such heaviness. I loved the political and theological discussions I had had with strangers who became friends at Salvacao de Israel, the Syrian restaurant, the garage, the factory, the market, and on the train. I loved my dear landlady who took such loving care of me. I loved their country, and I deeply appreciated their wonderful hospitality. I believed they were the most generous, good-hearted people on the face of the earth. *Could I ever repay them for looking after a stranger?*

The plane's engines revved up and started down the runway. As it took flight into the air, I started writing letters to my family in Israel, telling them about the wonderful people who had become my surrogate family in this strange land. I wrote story after story of these people and how I had fared these last few months. With each tale, tears started streaming down my cheeks.

Ten very brief hours later, the plane was over New York City and preparing to land. The island city, one of the biggest cities in the world, was spread out before me like an architect's cardboard model. Skyscrapers, crowding together, reached up toward the sky. The sun glinted off the glass and stone of the buildings, making them shine like jewels.

We landed at the international airport in New York that became known as JFK a few years later after President John F. Kennedy's assassination. As I walked down the airplane's landing steps and across the short distance to the terminal, I caught sight of two very familiar faces. There rushing toward me were my uncle Salman and my sister Berta. They waved as I quickly made my way through customs. Soon, we were all hugging and kissing each other. Suddenly, I reconciled my feelings about having left Brazil.

I had been faithful and had finally made it to the Promised Land. I was once again home.

Section Four: I

My Life In The U.S.A.

1960 – 2005 (Present)

Chapter Forty-One

Arrival in New York: April 13, 1960

After living and working in Brazil for nearly two years, I arrived in New York in the afternoon. Of course, I had ideas about what it would be like, had heard stories from my relatives, had seen pictures, but nothing could have prepared me for the packed density and sheer height of the skyscrapers of Manhattan. Flying over the "Greater New York Metropolitan Area" is a lesson in itself, in urban planning and suburban sprawl: How could the Native Americans who sold the little island to the new pilgrim settlers less than 200 years ago ever have imagined that such a complex (and tall!) concrete city could grow to consume what must at one time have been a wonder of nature?

After waiting in the long lines with the hordes of immigrants drawn to America by its democratic philosophy and the flaming torch of Miss Liberty, I finally cleared Customs. My sister Berta and Uncle Salman (Shlomo) greeted me at the airport and we had a warm get-together after not seeing one another for nearly four years. We sat at a local cafeteria and talked.

Many questions and some answers circulated around the table.

My sister asked me, "How did you survive in Brazil anyway? Without family, friends, or money?"

As I pondered her question, I wondered myself how I did it. I took a few sips of hot, black American coffee and sighed.

"It wasn't easy. I was hungry at some points. But, you know, our harsh experiences as children taught us all how to stand on our own feet and succeed."

My uncle and sister both nodded at this ironic, true fact.

"What did you think of the Brazilian people?" Uncle Shlomo asked. "How did they treat you?"

This, I could answer without hesitation.

"The Brazilian people are the salt of the earth: The best people in the world. I loved them, everyone I met."

I looked around at all the strangers surrounding us, eating lunch and talking, and wondered if I would ever feel the same way about Americans.

My sister must have been thinking about her next question for a while, maybe because she wondered about her own reasons for being here.

"Why did you decide to come to the United States now, Saul, instead of going back to Israel? Don't you think you'd be better-off there?"

"I want to go to college. I want to improve my odds of succeeding in life, by coming to live in the greatest democracy in the world." She didn't seem satisfied with my answer.

We finished our coffee and apple pie with vanilla ice cream, then Uncle Shlomo asked Berta how she would feel if he took me out for the rest of the evening. It was already getting dark out.

"Of course, Salman, show Saul where he has come to live." I detected a tinge of sarcasm, mixed with enthusiasm. I embraced my sister and thanked her.

"It will be a pleasure living close to my favorite sister again," I said.

As I settled into my uncle's car, he asked, "Where would you like to go? Do you have a preference?"

I immediately suggested, "Can we go to the Empire State Building?"

Salman laughed. "How do you know about that?"

"Oh, I know a lot about New York and the United States. I read a lot," I answered. "For example, I know this skyscraper was built in the 1930s, and is considered to be a miraculous, elegant structure."

We drove through the Midtown Tunnel. Emerging from the long dark tube into the clogged city streets, I marveled at the American technology and their ingenious use of architecture.

Uncle Shlomo was thinking his own thoughts, conjured up by my presence here.

He asked me if I still remembered how we fled Baghdad together.

"Do you remember how we huddled together on the floor of the boat while bullets flew over heads? I was sure we were doomed."

I often thought about that night, and recalled many details of that famous journey now. Though I would have preferred not to go back over the worst parts, I chose to express my most haunting memory out loud to my uncle, to release us from the horror of forgetting.

"Uncle Shlomo, do you remember how that poor woman suffocated her infant to death, trying to silence him, so no one would find us out there on the water, and kill us all? That, I shall never forget"

He was concentrating on driving, but there were tears in his eyes when he looked over at me, face full of the shared awfulness of remembering that baby who had died in his mother's arms, even as she was trying to save him, another Jew silenced by the loud savage hatred of our oppressors.

"Me, neither, I will never forget that."

"It was a significant thing that happened to us all, a turning point, an experience one cannot forget. I intend to write a book about our journeys some day." I disclosed.

"You always had a knack for being literary. I still recall all those teary letters you wrote me from the kibbutz. If anyone can do it, it's you. Do it for all of us, Saul"

He maneuvered us through lanes of crisscrossing traffic, braking and accelerating, pausing briefly at red lights then positioning us in the swift flow of cars and pedestrians, amidst the blare of horns and pumping thumping car radios. I was surprised that it was actually possible to reach our destination in the throng of so much activity. But suddenly there we were, at the junction of Fifth Avenue and 34th street, where the wondrous Empire State Building towered majestically skyward. Uncle Shlomo parked in a public garage, and he rushed to grab us an elevator in the massive decorated lobby.

I stopped to look at the magnificent black-marbled interior, but my uncle pulled me into the closed confines of our elevator.

"Let's go up, you can look at this later."

We rode with a crowd, locals and tourists from all over the world, to the top floor. As the elevator floor dropped with a jolt, we all gasped, then smiled, and filed politely through the doors. I could see my own feelings mirrored in everyone's faces: We were all stunned to be here, in front of this grand perspective on the city that history's visionary architectural minds not only dreamed of, but created in reality. Eyes wide, jaws dropping, awed, we surveyed the intricate Manhattan skyline. Infinite numbers of stars sparkled in the sky, and millions of lights flickered from building windows.

Typically, my uncle had been living here for over two years, but had never come here before.

"You know, Saul, there are millions of New Yorkers, people who were born here, who have never seen the view from the top of the Empire State Building. Yet you did it on your first day in town. It's amazing."

I smiled, proud of my own ideas. It was beginning to feel right.

We walked the perimeter of the edifice, seeing the world as the circle it is, studying New York from 360 degrees of sight. The more we saw, the more we marveled. I fell in love with New York and America that day.

Eventually, we descended back to ground level, then stopped at a popular steak house "Todd's" and ate dinner. Then Salman drove me to Berta's apartment on Riverside Drive, where her view of the George Washington Bridge over the Hudson River stole my heart.

Where have I landed? What am I doing here? What will become of me in this huge place?

I stood on my sister's tiny balcony overlooking the magnificent George Washington Bridge and stared as far as I could into the river and beyond, the same way I used to contemplate the sea from the boardwalk in Tel Aviv.

I had made the big move. Here I was. I knew my parents were happy that I had re-united with my sister Berta, rather than live alone in a vast country like Brazil. Now that I was here, I was anxious to get on with my life, go to school and complete my education. I knew America was the Land of Opportunity, a country founded on the admirable principles of freedom of race and religion; I wanted so much to participate in its future. For the first time I felt secure from enemy reach, and that I was living in a peaceful country, a place of limitless possibilities.

The longer I stood there, looking out at the view, the more I became melancholy for the past and worried about the future. In the present, I wiped away tears, took a deep breath, and went off to bed early.

There, I lay awake, thinking. Hopeful, yes, but also unsure of myself.

Did I do the right thing by coming here? Am I welcome here? Am I loved?

My body wanted to get some sleep. But my mind and thoughts were buzzing, and I was up all night.

Student at the Brooklyn Museum of Art: May 1960

Day by day I gathered myself together then implemented a plan. I registered at Columbia University for night classes, which were more affordable. I wanted to hone my English language skills and gain knowledge of my newly adopted country, the United States. I enrolled in "Public Speaking" and "American History."

Even with all my studies, which weren't so easy, I found myself with too much time on my hands, more than I was used to, growing up on a kibbutz and always working to help support our large family. Free time just caused me to pace and think, worry and wonder, so I also signed up for classes at the New School of Social Studies (to study writing and poetry) and at the Brooklyn Museum of Art (to practice painting and sculpture). If I kept busy, I figured, my head would be less filled with anxieties.

At the Brooklyn Museum, I attempted to learn to draw, paint, and sculpt. I wasn't very good at it, but I did enjoy the female models, who, in the classic art school tradition of learning to draw the figure, posed totally nude. I was aware of myself as perhaps an imposter in their midst, not a true artist, but just a lonely immigrant searching to connect to something that could ease my sense of anxious solitude and bitter yearning. Despite the loving presence of my sister and uncle and other relatives, despite the teeming masses of individuals I passed daily on the streets and crammed up against in the subways, I had never before felt myself so alone, so conscious of the edges of my body and the isolation of my innermost thoughts. I felt invisible in this crowded city, unappreciated, insignificant, unloved.

Regrets about coming here at all ate at me. I kept hearing the same question from my inside:

Did I do the right thing by coming here?

I met some interesting people at the New School, most of them twice my age, but that's what made them so interesting. I needed mentors and experienced elders in my life, more than I needed carousing, clueless peers (I had left enough of them back home).

I studied English literature, poetry, and writing with Mr. Broyard (I still remember his name). A writer-novelist himself, he was an excellent teacher, wise, and sympathetic to someone like me who had just arrived in the country. I made some quality friends in that class, but they were much more dedicated to the profession of writing than I was: They all thought of themselves as Writers, and wanted to make a career of the craft. Listening to them and all their plans of grandeur, I realized I was not as committed as they were. I didn't have what it would take to succeed in that world, not yet. At the time, I just needed to learn anything and everything, whatever might fill the void I felt in my heart, now that I had uprooted myself from all that was familiar and most dear to me, once more.

Money collection in the movie house: America's generosity

Not long after my arrival in New York, I was sitting alone in the dark inside a movie house one afternoon. This brought back scores of memories of nights spent in the dark in Israeli movie houses: with my old librarian Mrs. Newtoff, with my teenage girlfriends and my rowdy guy friends, with my brother Yeftah. It was mid-afternoon and I had ducked into a matinee to get out of the criticizing rays of sunlight that sent daggers of questions through my skin. I was feeling totally disgusted with my life, ashamed of my lack of progress towards achieving any of the goals I had arrived in New York to accomplish. I was simply running out of money, with no one to go to for help. For solace, the familiar embrace of the darkness, and to escape from my own problems, I often took myself to movies alone. The flickering dramas of others nursed my ego, soothed my anger, subdued my jangled New York nerves.

Before the movie began that day, I was flabbergasted to hear a plea from the management to please give a contribution to the ushers coming down the aisles. The lights came on and the fundraisers came along with boxes in hand, asking us to deposit donations to aid in research for treatments for cancer, polio, and other causes.

What caused me to reach into my thin pocket and contribute $2 from my very tight budget?

I thought, "So this is America? The great America that feeds the entire world? America that gives billions of dollars in foreign aid to poor countries, including my own country, Israel? Is this how it is done, dollar by dollar from the average Joe?" Like collecting pennies in churches to feed the downtrodden and hungry.

I was most impressed. America has a big heart, the biggest on earth. It felt good to be part of it.

Just look at history: It was America that liberated most of Europe and the Far East during World War II, sacrificing hundreds of thousands of American young men. Not only did it not hold on to these vast territories for itself, it spent billions to rebuild those enemy nations. Remember the Marshall Plan? This is but one example. I sat there wondering, what would have happened to the world if the Germans or the Japanese had won that war?

I must find a way to be part of this great country.

I resolved then and there to stop dwelling on the negative, start emphasizing the positive.

I must not give up.

I would find a way to play a meaningful part in this great democracy, the land of opportunity.

I must stay here. America must be my new, permanent home.

Picnic on Riverside Drive with Uncle Salman

I hadn't been in New York very long, but I was beginning to acclimate myself to the 24-hour noise, the fast pace, and the crowds.

One sunny day, I met with my Uncle Salman at Riverside Drive. He suggested we go to one of his favorite spots and we went and sat on the banks of the Hudson River. There, we studied the flowing water as it streamed by, oblivious to the crowds of needy, ambitious people and all our little problems.

We bought two containers of orange juice from a street vendor, along with two hot dogs and two hamburgers. We ate and we talked, for hours, reminiscing about our harrowing, yet ultimately lucky, escape from Baghdad.

"The journey to Israel was treacherous, too, don't forget that part," Shlomo reminded me.

"It wasn't that easy once we got there either."

"No, nothing was easy for us. We lost our innocence and our childhood."

"These days in the United States might turn out to be the best days of our lives, eh, Uncle?"

The afternoon air on the river was delightful, the boats floating by in such a leisurely manner, a breeze lifting women's skirts as they sauntered past us with their beautiful long legs and upright postures. But the conversation grew melancholy for both of us, too, as we remembered the hardships we encountered even once we got to Israel, and his parents left buried in a Baghdad cemetery, never to be visited again.

"Yes, Saul, it is good here," my uncle sighed. "But I will always long for my homeland. I hope you don't judge me for that"

Would America ever feel like my home? I wondered quietly. It would be a long time before I found the answer.

Chapter Forty-Two

Initial Immigration Troubles

Since I had arrived in New York at the beginning of April in 1960, I rapidly put my student visa to work. I registered at Columbia University for night classes, studying public speaking and American history in order to improve my English and learn about the United States. But my study load was not heavy there, and I had more time on my hands than I was used to. I had been accustomed to either studying or working long hours—or both. Idleness reminded me too much of the times I had been without work and starving in Brazil. Consequently, I also signed up for classes at the New School of Social Studies to study writing and poetry and at the Brooklyn Museum of Art to practice painting and sculpture.

Though these classes were affordable, they were quickly depleting my savings. What I had not anticipated was the work restriction on my student visa. As a student, I was not permitted to work, and I could not get a work permit because I was a student. *How was I supposed to support myself and continue my education if I couldn't work to pay for it?*

By the fall of 1960, I was depressed and feeling hopeless about my future. Like my dreams of finding success in Brazil had been frustrated, it was beginning to look as if the same situation was occurring here once more. I had nearly run out of money and there were no rich relatives to send me money as my friend Yeg-al's family had done for him in Brazil. I didn't want to return to Brazil and have to start over. Neither did I want to go back to Israel to live in fear of Arab reprisals or to return as a failure. Worrying, I spent my days in the movie theaters, trying to shake off my depression by escaping into the unreal world of film, and, in truth, hiding from the realities of life that awaited me just outside the cinema's doors.

The military option

I was desperate to find a solution to my immigration problem. I loved America, and I wanted to stay and become a legal citizen. I refused to break the law and work without a permit, as so many millions were doing. Instead, I began doing frantic research as I'd learned during similar crisis moments in the past. First, I went to the Fifth Avenue Library, New York's largest, and I began browsing the stacks. I was intent on making my selections for the day when I noticed a uniformed soldier, surrounded by a pile of books, at a long table about thirty feet away.

I don't know what made me approach him—maybe destiny. As I came closer, I saw he was studying patent laws. *Maybe he also knew about immigration laws*, I wondered. "Tell me, if you please, are you on active duty?" I asked.

He turned his eyes to the interruption. "Yes, I am in uniform, as you can see." He furrowed his brows, looked me up and down, and asked, "Can I help you?"

I hesitated, drawing up courage. I don't know what made me trust him or tell him my story, but it just came rushing out. "I am here in the U.S. on a student exchange visa, attending Columbia University. I can't continue to pay tuition unless I work and earn money. I can't get a work permit because I have a student visa. Do you have any advice for me?"

The soldier politely motioned for me to sit in the chair across from his. I could see him considering possible ways out of my dilemma. Finally, he said, "Well, that's the law of the land," he said.

Deflated, I thought, *okay, Israel, here I come.*

Then the soldier continued, "But you're young Why don't you join the Army?"

Here was a novel idea! I thought.

"You will be able to stay in the United States and continue your education in the service," he said. "In fact, the government will help you pay for it."

There I was, a desperate young man in the New York Public Library, handing the problems of my life over to a stranger. But, his suggestion made me tremble with excitement.

"You mean I, a foreign student, can join the U.S. Army? And the Army will pay for my education? Are you sure?"

He looked at me intently and smiled. "Go to a recruiting office. They will explain it all to you in detail. That's the only thing that I can think that could help you. Lots of kids do it."

I stood and thanked him, shaking his hand repeatedly. He couldn't have known how much he had helped me. Maybe to him it was only a casual suggestion, just to get me out of his way so he could get back to his work. Or, maybe there was more to this.

I didn't waste any time. I left the library immediately, bounding down the library steps, and got myself to Times Square, 42nd Street and Broadway, where I remembered once seeing a sign pointing to an Army/Air Force/Navy recruiting office. When I found the right place, the office was open, and I entered enthusiastically.

I approached the Army desk and told my story for the second time that day. The recruiter was an impressive figure in his uniform, with all kinds of medals pinned to his chest.

"You've come to the right place," he said. "Just fill out this form, sign here, and date it. "

I didn't think twice. I signed the paper right then. It was October 15, 1960.

"You'll be called within fifteen days to report for physical exams," he said. I must have looked worried. Then added with a knowing smile, "Don't sweat it. You'll pass. Everybody does," he said.

I was so excited I nearly saluted him!

At Fort Dix processing camp, U.S. Army,
prior to basic training, NJ, USA, 1960 (43)

Page 20—The Bayonet, Ft. Benning, Ga., Dec. 2, 1960

Ex-Israeli Airman

7th Cav Recruit Walked Desert to Flee Strife Riddled Nativeland

BY KEN WINSLETT

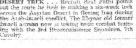

DESERT TREK . . . Recruit Saul Fathi points out the route he took in making a six-week trek across the Assyrian Desert in fleeing Iraq during the Arab-Israeli conflict. The 22-year old former Israeli airman now is taking basic combat training with the 3rd Reconnaissance Squadron, 7th Cavalry.

Clipping from The Bayonet,
Fort Benning, GA, USA, 1960 (44)

Chapter Forty-Three

You're in the Army Now

When I arrived at the recruiting office on Whitehall Street in Brooklyn, I saw that I was not the only one who had had this bright idea and had been called for their physicals. There was a whole gang of guys there; all kinds—tall, short, skinny, fat, black, yellow and white. I didn't imagine in that first encounter that there might be anyone in that sea of young faces I could ever call a friend or comrade. *Would I meet someone who could understand what my life had been like and all that I had been through to reach this significant moment where I was actually standing in line, preparing to become a solider in the United States Army?*

We had all been called together in this spacious room for our physicals. Most of us stood, but some lazy ones lounged on benches as if they were waiting for tickets to the movies. Thirty minutes later, a big black woman, weighing at least 200 lbs, wearing a white nurse apron, came out of a side door. In a raspy, commanding voice, she directed us to follow her to an adjacent room.

"Form a single line and face the wall," she said.

Facing the wall seemed odd. *Were we not supposed to see something in our first few minutes here? Was this some special treatment we were to receive? Or was it some kind of torture?*

My last thought was almost correct, but it certainly wasn't what I expected in the US Army. What the military nurse said next came totally out of the blue.

"Drop your pants, gentlemen," she said. "Everybody. And I mean **everybody**."

A few of us hesitated, including myself. Then, the nurse came right up behind me and spoke low into my ear. "Don't be bashful, son. I've seen 'em in all sizes, shapes, and colors."

I was beginning to warm up to her and was going to comply willingly.

Then, suddenly, she changed her tone and raised her voice, "Now, I said drop them pants!!!"

I dropped them all right. Everyone did. But, no one knew what to expect next.

I looked sideways and caught a glimpse of the big Army nurse's white apron. Suddenly, it conveyed no comfort at all. Beside her was another, more attractive, nurse putting on a rubber glove. I thought that perhaps she could be more comforting until I saw her stick her index finger into the rectum of the first guy in line. He grimaced and yelled as she twisted her finger deep inside his rear end. *Is this real or just another nightmare?* I wondered.

The attractive nurse removed her finger from the fist recruit, looked at it, and then discarded the glove into the wastebasket. "Okay," she said as she patted his rump, "you and move on to the next room for your shots." She put on a new glove and moved down the line, practicing the same procedure on each guy.

I chuckled to myself. *I wonder what is the exact title of her job?* As she approached me, I held my "cheeks" as tightly together as I could and closed my eyes in prayer, "God, let her skip me."

No such luck. She waited for me to relax my buttocks then winked at the other nurse before saying, "Son, open your legs or I'll call this here Wilma over to do it for you."

Wilma, the big, black nurse, was grinning from ear to ear. All she needed was a nod from the nurse.

That was a fate I wished to avoid at all costs. Reluctantly, I spread my legs and surrendered. "Go ahead, get it over with," I said.

It didn't last that long, but it was a painful and humiliating experience—a little torture. So, I had been right after all. I straightened up, pulled up my pants, and buckled my belt.

I ran to the second room where the young men formed another line, each holding his shirt in one hand and lifting up his t-shirt sleeve above the shoulder with the other hand. We were each given a combination of five vaccines and medications in a single "gun shot." An instrument, which I had never seen the likes of before, looked very much like a gun and was connected to a huge bottle of liquid by clear tubing. Each recruit was given a shot, then we dressed and went to wait in yet another room until everyone was done.

This was my first taste of the American Army life. I looked around at the faces of the men around me. We had just endured something traumatic together, and I was aware that this would be the first of many such stressful and bonding experiences. We had signed up for the unexpected, the dangerous, and the unknown. We would be trained and prepared to take on whatever presented itself. I wondered what their stories were, what brought them all to this place, this decision, at this point in their young lives. Somehow, I had a feeling that I was the only crazy volunteer among all these inductees.

A mere two hours later, we were escorted into a World War II bus and shipped out to Fort Dix, New Jersey, where we were processed and assigned to various basic training camps around the U.S. I now had several numbers attached to my name: U.S. 514-668-38 and Selective Service no. 50-56-38-754.

Basic training at Fort Benning, Georgia

After a few days in Fort Dix, we were flown to Fort Benning, Georgia. Within the camp, we were driven by bus to various barracks, and told to transfer all our belongings into the footlockers on the floor. We were issued uniforms, hats, underwear, socks, toiletries, shoe polish, and all the personal gear they thought would be necessary, no more, no less.

"All you Yankees, empty your pockets on this here table, including your switchblades," a tall sergeant shouted.

I guessed this was the New Yorker's reputation that we all carried switchblades and were members of gangs. I felt a little insulted, but this allegation didn't seem to bother anyone else as, within minutes, a great variety of items appeared on the table, a complete hardware store, including four switchblade knives.

What will the Army do with all these things? Is the sergeant going to keep them? I wondered, but I never found out. They were all confiscated.

A corporal and a sergeant took turns supervising us and ordering us around, from the first moments of our arrival. We were kept busy sixteen hours a day, training and getting acquainted with everything on the base. It was a humongous establishment, bigger than some whole cities. A few monuments, such as Custer's Last Stand, impressed me, more because I was astonished that the Indians were still considered the "bad guys," at least where we were, in the Deep South.

Our days began at 4:00 AM, when a trumpet sounded throughout the base via hundreds of strategically positioned loudspeakers. We frantically rushed to put on our fatigues (our working uniforms) and helmets, picked up our rifles, lined up at the pull-up bars, and ran to the mess hall. You never just walked in the Army; you did everything "on the double."

The meals were not as bad as I expected. I was introduced to cereal and cold milk, which up until then I had only seen in movies. After breakfast, we exercised and ran. The sergeant ran alongside of us, chanting Army songs, which were so familiar to the American-born, songs with lyrics like "You're in the Army Now" and "Left, Right, Left, Right, Left." We marched to the rhythm, left, right, left, until the sergeant hollered, "Your other left, Yankees!"

We were referred to as GIs (Government Issues) or recruits. First names were never used. I learned right away to end every sentence with "Sir," Yes, Sir," or "No, Sir." Most of our sergeants and officers were white southerners who appeared to love what they were doing. Only two were black, also from the South, judging from their accents, and it was apparent they had very little education.

Our sergeant, a slim 6 foot-plus, black man, Sergeant Perry, was very tough. But everything he asked us to do, he did with us. He was in great shape; we could hardly keep up with him.

"This here thing you call a gun is not a gun, you bastards, it's a rifle. You will guard and protect this Army issue with your life. You will carry it every-where, in the showers, in the mess hall, in bed between your legs, and in the latrine. It is your soul mate while you are in the Army, your only mate. Keep an eye on it, even when you sleep. Every day, you will undress it, take it apart, and clean it thoroughly, as you have been taught. Is that clear?"

We all shouted, "Yes, Sergeant."

He put his right palm on his ear. "I can't hear you."

This time we shouted louder. "Yes, Sergeant."

"You are in the Army now. It's your home for the next two to three years.

You might as well make the best of it. You might even learn to like it so much you will enlist for life, especially those of you who have no home life, back home."

We laughed, then put on a serious face right away. You aren't supposed to laugh in the Army, ever, especially when a superior officer is speaking. It's against the rules.

"Wipe that fucking smile off your ugly faces, recruits, and take five. Smoke it, if you want to. Keep the tobacco and the wrapper in your pockets."

We sat on the ground and began to smoke the cigarettes we had purchased from the canteen a few days earlier. I could tell some of the guys were smoking for the first time, like me. We inhaled and then coughed and spit on the ground. But we were "Men' now.

All the while, the sergeant looked at his watch. When five minutes were up, we were ordered to follow him in a single file wherever he went, running, jogging, never walking.

"Okay, now follow me on the double, single-file, rifle raised high above your heads, like so."

Sergeant Perry was a professional guy, trying to transform a bunch of city "softies" into iron soldiers, which was his job and his duty. However, he wasn't enlightened enough to treat all of us equally; he had his obvious favorites and those he disliked. He seemed to be a victim of his own deep-seated prejudices. In particular, he could not stand this one wise guy, a pampered city boy of Italian descent from Brooklyn, named Garagiolla, whose name Sergeant Perry could never pronounce correctly. No one knew the recruit's first name. His last name apparently annoyed the sergeant every time he had to address him.

Garagiolla knew this but didn't let it bother him. He was a real clown who joined the Army just so he could drop out of school an "have fun". Many punishments were inflicted on this unlucky Italian, as Sergeant Perry always found something to accuse him of, especially as he inspected his footlocker.

One day, as Garagiolla was participating in morning exercises, he dropped his rifle on the ground. He quickly bent to pick it up, but he had committed the ultimate Army sin.

The sergeant saw what had taken place, rushed to Garagiolla, and kicked him in the butt, whereupon Garagiolla fell on his face on top of his rifle.

This made Garagiolla mad. His Brooklyn blood was boiling. Garagiolla pointed the rifle at the sergeant and pulled the trigger. Of course, there were no bullets in the chamber, but still he had tried to fire on a superior officer.

The sergeant wrestled the rifle out of Garagiolla's hands and kicked him hard with his right knee between the legs. Garagiolla folded in pain. Sergeant Perry moved away from him, then challenged us. "Did anyone see me kick anybody?" he shouted at the top of his lungs.

"No, Sergeant," we all shouted back. We knew what he expected from us.

"I can't hear you," he bellowed. "Did anyone see me kick the shit out of this ugly motherfucker?"

We shouted back, louder than before. "No, Sergeant."

"I thought so… Good. Now this here boy dropped his rifle on the ground. He will stay here and run circles around this tree while we go do our thing and come back. While we are gone, Mr. Ga-ra-gi-ol-la here will hold his rifle above his head and say, loud and clear, "Sorry, baby, I won't drop you no moh—.""

Garagiolla picked up his rifle, hands high above his head, and started repeating the sergeant's mantra: "Sorry, baby, I won't drop you no morrrre."

The rest of us took off running as we had every day for the past three weeks, taking several five-minute breaks to smoke our cigarettes. When finished smoking, we unrolled the burnt cigarette, put the paper wrap in our pockets, and scattered the tobacco on the ground. All this was part of our daily rituals.

No one dared utter a word or mention our comrade's name, Garagiolla. We all started to envy him having been spared the agony of the infiltration course, the running, climbing, jogging, and crawling we endured for the next four hours.

But upon returning, we could see Garagiolla from a hundred yards' distance, still running around the tree trunk, rifle resting on top of his head, whispering, with tears streaming down his face, "Sorry, baby, I won't drop you no more."

We were amazed that he had continued to obey his orders. He must have thought the sergeant would be watching him the whole while or else he feared a court martial for trying to kill his sergeant.

Garagiolla never dropped his rifle again. He slept with it, showered with it, and kept it close to his heart for the rest of basic training.

They named me "Philosopher"

My old habit of reading books all the time didn't change just because I was "in the Army now." Some of the men found this to be a less than masculine thing to do, while others were seemingly in awe of the whole notion. Skip, a young black man from New Orleans, started calling me "Philosopher" because he must have thought being able to read conferred me with some kind of special powers, which of course it did since knowledge is power. I don't know where I would have been, how I would have gotten through any number of crises, without having access to the words and philosophy of history's great thinkers. They kept me sane. They taught me how to think about the world. They were my saving grace.

From the way he talked and expressed himself, I didn't think Skip knew how to read well. But, I never let him know that I could tell as I got to know Skip, I also learned that there are other kinds of smarts besides book learning, and I grew to admire Skip's kind of wisdom, too.

Another guy in my barracks, whose name I can't remember anymore, liked to call me Little Al, for Al Capone. It was his way of making himself seem bigger, by pocking fun at me, for being as short as Al Capone. I knew it wasn't a compliment.

At one point, I was administered a foreign language test, which I naturally passed with flying colors. When I was certified in four languages—Hebrew, Arabic, Portuguese, and Spanish—I thought, *oh no, I might end up in Army Intelligence!* This could have meant relief from the dangers of being a foot soldier on the one hand, or it could place me in much graver danger, as I knew from the sad story of Eli Cohen, Israel's master spy who was publicly hanged by the Syrians for his role as an intelligence agent for their enemy, Israel. I wondered how and where I would end up using my new skill as a member of the United States Army.

"Shooting the shit": The strange slang of the South

On a Sunday afternoon, while still in basic training in Georgia, some friends asked me to join them in an outing into the thick forests within the camp. This was where the statue of General Custer had been prominently erected as he was making his "last stand."

"Where are we going? It's cold out there," I said to my new buddies.

We were warm inside our barracks, sitting on our bunks. Our Army gear and firearms were stashed in the closet, under a combination lock, safe where they were supposed to be.

"We're going out to the picnic area, just to shoot the shit," answered Bobby.

Garagiolla had already made clear to us one of the first lessons we had been taught here: to guard our weapons with our lives and never drop or lose them under any circumstances. Some of us took this so seriously, we placed them under our mattresses when we went to sleep and took them along to the latrines and showers. So this outing was no exception. Everyone grabbed his M1 and other firearms and filed out into the courtyard.

From there we followed Skip, who seemed more familiar with the outdoors than those of us who were more used to city living. We were out twenty minutes when we found ourselves in the middle of the woods. The ground was covered with wet leaves, and we had trouble finding a dry spot to sit and talk.

I spotted an embankment covered with grass and ran to it. I sat down and began loading my M1 rifle. "Over here, everybody," I shouted in their direction, "here is an ideal little hill." I took a position on my belly and began looking for a target to shoot at.

"Hey, Philosopher, what the fuck are you doin'?" asked Skip.

I was puzzled. "Didn't you say we were going to shoot the shit?" I asked him, with a straight face.

They all burst into loud laughter, pointing accusing fingers at me. "You dummy, shooting the shit ain't shooting at anything. It just means 'talking' down here," explained Joe, one of the other recruits.

They continued to laugh at me, while I continued to puzzle over this stupid expression, 'shooting the shit." When I realized what a dumb foreigner I was, I began to laugh along with them.

I aimed my gun in the direction of the latrines. "Shooting the shit.... Let's all shoot the shit," I shouted jokingly.

I had never told them I didn't even know the meaning of the word *shit* until I heard my buddies refer to the bathroom as the Shit House.

Segregation at the movies

After eight weeks of basic training, we were allowed a two-day weekend pass, which for me was not long enough to fly home. My close friends who also lived far away and I decided to stay at the base and make the best of it.

On Saturday night, our friend Anthony showed up with some good news. He could get a jeep, and we could all go riding around town, even go to the movies if we wanted to, as long as he had the vehicle back before midnight. This was welcome news.

About mid-afternoon, we went to the mess hall and got a few snacks. Then, we came back to shower and change clothes. By 5:00 PM, we were on our way into town. It was winter, freezing cold, and we had no winter clothes to wear. There were five of us: Anthony from New Jersey, Bobby from Florida, Skip from New Orleans, Garagiolla and me from New York. As we drove out past the gates of the camp for the first time in four weeks, we felt like long-term prisoners, just released. We all felt such a great sense of freedom.

I marveled at Anthony's skillful driving, as I had not yet obtained a driver's license. When we approached a kiosk along the road, we decided to stop and have some "civilian food." It was only hot dogs and soda, but we enjoyed it very much.

"Okay, guys, we have the car till midnight," Anthony said. "Where would you like to go now?"

We looked at each other. None of us was familiar with the local towns.

"I hear there's an outdoor movie theatre somewhere not too far from here. Let's go see what's playing there," suggested Skip.

That brought a smile to all of our faces.

"Does anyone know where the fucking movie house is?" Anthony inquired in his typical vocabulary.

We had to shrug in ignorance. Bobby finally stopped a passerby and asked him where the theater was.

"Not too far, just a few turns in the road," we were told.

When traffic slowed almost to a crawl, we knew we must be close. We drove bumper-to-bumper for a while, then finally reached the entrance to the theatre. Hundreds of cars were parked in this huge, dirt parking lot, with speakers hanging on their rolled-down car windows.

I got really excited. I had never been to a drive-in movie before, but I had seen them in American movies.

Each of us pulled his wallet out.

"How much is it?" Bobby asked.

No one knew.

The man at the gate wore a uniform, but was neither a policeman nor a soldier. He was like a movie theater usher but outdoors. He came closer to the car, scanned everyone's face and pointed at Skip. "You can't go in, Buddy," he said. "I know you're a soldier and everything, but this is a segregated, for-whites-only theatre."

Skip stood up in the Jeep, enraged. "What the fuck are you talking about, man? You telling me I can't go in there and enjoy the movie like everybody else?"

He was mad. We were all mad. I, for one, thought that this kind of segregation had ended in World War II, when blacks demonstrated equal loyalty and bravery in the face of a shared enemy. Since joining the Army, I hadn't noticed any prejudice or segregation within our ranks, except insofar as everyone took kidding from everyone else, no matter what your race or ethnicity was. Guys liked to insult each other for any reason they could find. That's just the way they are. It's a way of showing affection just like we all would tease our younger brothers and sisters.

Anthony opened the door and stood close to the gate man, then quickly realized he was half the man's size. *They sure knew how to pick these guards,* I thought. Before Anthony could utter a word, the guard shoved him aside and pointed at me, Bobby, Garagiolla and Anthony.

"You, you, you and you can go in, no problem. But, not him!" he said, pointing at Skip again. Then, by way of apology, "Hey, I don't make the rules here." He threw his arms up in the air.

By now, cars were piling up behind us. Drivers were impatient and honking their horns.

But we weren't going to move our Jeep. We all stepped out of the car and made obscene gestures at the gate man.

"We're not movin'," asserted Anthony. "No way are we going in there without our buddy here. No way, man." He stomped his foot.

Skip noticed some drivers behind us had put their cars in Park and were walking toward us. He sensed grave danger.

"Come on, fellas, go ahead without me. I can wait outside. No sweat," Skip said.

We all shook our heads. "No way. Either we all go in, or none of us," I said. I grabbed the guys and advised them to avoid trouble and just get in the car.

As we got in, a group of bullies from another car gathered around us and stared at us with hatred in their eyes.

"What's the matter? Anyone looking for trouble here?" one giant, fat man asked.

The gate man replied, "No, go back to your cars. Everything is cool."

They reluctantly retreated one by one.

Anthony started the Jeep and moved it aside to let the other cars pass through the gate.

We sat for a few moments, cursing and trying to console our good friend, our buddy Skip. He was less angry than we were. I supposed he was used to it, if anyone can ever be. The rest of us had not encountered this kind of blatant racism since coming to the South.

What would have happened if we were armed? I wondered. *Would Skip have been able to control his anger?*

We drove back without stopping, totally silent the rest of the way. For the first time, I felt ashamed to be an American. But then I remembered I wasn't an American yet. I had volunteered to serve in her Army, and be killed if necessary, for the privilege of gaining American citizenship. *Things will change eventually*, I thought. *It must change.*

We never spoke of this racist incident at camp.

"In twenty words or less, who the hell are you?"

One day, I returned from an exhausting trip that began at 4:00AM. I had run five miles with full combat gear. My sergeant met me as I came back to my barracks and told me to report to Captain Cossgroff's office. I thought I might have committed some infraction, but I wasn't aware of any. I had always tried to be a model soldier, committed to excel in every endeavor because this was now my new home. *Why was I being called to the Captain's office? My mind raced.*

I went inside my barracks and washed my face and arms, changed my shirt, combed my hair, and made sure my hat was positioned on my head with just the right tilt as I was taught. I wiped the dust off my boots and walked briskly to Captain Cossgroff's office, some three hundred yards away.

I knocked gently on the flimsy door, which was covered with a mosquito net. No one answered. I knocked again, harder.

"Come in, come in," the captain finally called.

I entered and stood about eight feet away from his desk and saluted him, erect and proper. "Private Fathi reporting, sir." I waited for his permission to relax. I was shaking.

The captain took his time, leafing through a thick folder of papers in front of him. I remained at attention and saluting my commanding officer, who so far had not lifted his head to acknowledge my presence. By now, I was accustomed to these personal insults.

"At ease, soldier," he finally said, motioning me to come closer.

I moved nearer to his desk and stood "at ease" (legs two feet apart, standing firmly on the floor, hands clasped behind my back). I still wondered what I had done to warrant this attention.

The captain lifted his head, closed the file, and said, "Private Fathi, I have here your complete file. And, by golly, it's three times as thick as the other, normal files. And although you were cleared before getting here, I want to satisfy myself about it right now."

He snapped his lighter and lit up a cigarette. He did not offer me one, which I didn't expect.

I was taken aback when he said quietly, but ominously, "I have no time to fuck around, so don't fuck with me soldier. I will ask you one question and one question only. Do we understand each other?"

I snapped to attention again, without saluting. "Yes, sir, Captain. I understand, sir."

He looked at me suspiciously. "Private Fathi, in twenty words or less, who the fuck are you? Tell me everything, and don't fuck with me!"

I was startled. *In twenty words or less, how can I tell him my whole life's story? I am 22 years old; I have been to hell and back, several times. Was that what I tell him? What if I exceed the twenty words? Would I be punished or, worse, thrown out of the Army?*

I began counting words in my head. *How can I do this?* He was waiting for my answer. When I thought I had it, I saluted and began, "Sir, I was born in Baghdad, grew up in Israel, lived in Brazil and New York, and here I am, Captain."

There was a faint smile on his face.

Did I do all right? I wondered. I'm sure my face showed how worried I was about my simple answer.

Abruptly, he waved his hand in a half salute and said, "And I bet you don't know where you're going."

He had me there. I had no idea what the Army's plans were for me. And I was sure I wasn't going to find out from Captain Cossgroff.

"That's all, soldier. Dismissed."

I made a 180-degree turn, left his office, and rushed to get back to my bunk to write my answer down before I forgot. Once I had it down, I counted the words again and again. I felt proud of myself: I made it in twenty-one words.

Then, I felt an urgency to take a cold shower.

Saul (far right) at basic training in
Fort Benning, GA (USA), 1960 (45)

Chapter Forty-Four

Choosing Korea

"Soldier, you have a choice: Germany or Korea"

At the conclusion of basic training, the Army staged marching ceremonies and showed off its military bands. General Gibbs gave a rousing speech, congratulating us on successfully completing the "course" and qualifying to be fighting soldiers. Among other things, he mentioned Castro and Cuba, and said, "You may be privileged to kick some ass soon."

We all wondered if President Kennedy was about to start a war of liberation against Cuba. We doubted we were really ready to kick anybody's ass.

All of us were separated, with orders to ship out to different places. I was sent to Fort Eustis, Virginia. I assumed I would be serving my two-year hitch in the United States, doing some sort of job that the Army would train me for. Though I didn't want to be part of Army Intelligence, I thought the military might let me be a translator. Or, maybe they would use my electrical training to work on base electrical systems. While I waited for notification of my final deployment destination, I enrolled in evening classes at the University of Virginia.

Shortly after I arrived at Fort Eustis, an Army officer handed me my written orders, asking me to choose service in Germany or in Korea. I was stunned. I had joined the Army because I was promised a college education, for which the Army would pay two-thirds and I would pay the remaining third. My Army pay would more than cover my share of tuition and my living expenses. I thought that I only had to become a soldier and the US government would help me.

"What about the college education I was promised?" I asked the officer.

"Don't worry,' he said. "What the Army promises, the Army delivers. You'll be taking courses by correspondence, either from the University of Maryland or the University of Virginia. At the end of your tour of duty, you can take your exams."

I was skeptical. I had no choice in the matter. I must obey all orders.

"So, what will it be, soldier? What's your choice of destination: Germany or Korea?" he asked me again.

I thought for a while. The Holocaust was still fresh in my mind. The Germans had killed six million of my people, and caused the death of forty million innocents in all. I was not going to go there now, to defend the Germans from the threat of Communism. Besides, the Orient had always intrigued me. It was natural, then, that I chose Korea.

I was granted a brief leave to visit my family in New York, but I had to report to Oakland, California within thirty days, where I would board a ship to Korea, with stopovers in Honolulu, Hawaii and Yokohama, Japan. The Army arranged for train tickets both to New York and to California, as well as pocket money.

I said goodbye to my Army buddies at Fort Eustis and wished everyone good luck. I really hoped to meet them again some day. There were no hugs and no tears (except my new best friend Joe Stacy), though we were all family it seemed. But, we were men now. We gave each other hearty handshakes.

I took the train to New York. The reception from my sister Berta and brother-in-law Isaac was lukewarm. They thought I had chosen another adventure to add to my long list of exotic schemes. All the family nostalgia and my longing to see them evaporated within minutes. I decided not to wait out the thirty days in New York, but to utilize the unlimited train ticket and embark on a trip across the United States. If Berta and Isaac felt I was being cavalier with my life and just looking for adventure, I'd certainly put the truth to that speculation.

I took the Amtrak train at Penn Station and began an epic journey. The train headed down through the South, along the Atlantic Coast states, turned West and barreled through the Deep South, passing through my buddy Skip's home state of Louisiana, and sped through the Southwest, coming up all the way to Los Angeles. The train naturally made several stops each day, sometimes staying only a few minutes. At other times, especially when we had to change trains, we often had to lay over and sleep in a local hotel. The weather was good, and the whole train experience seemed luxurious and fun. It became one of the most memorable adventures I ever experienced.

As I looked out the train window, I kept thinking how blessed this America was and how deserving her industrious, generous people were. The more I saw, the deeper my love grew for the vastness and diversity within this country.

Jay-walking Yankee from New York

I continued north to Oakland, California where I hauled my full duffle bag out of the station and planned to hail a taxi to take me to the docks. I had to cross to the other side of the street in order to get a taxi going in the direction I needed to go. As I walked between traffic to get to the other sidewalk, a local policeman stopped me on the other side.

"Hey, you!" he yelled. "You're not supposed to cross the street from over here. You should have gone up to the traffic light." He pointed his hand to a crossing path at the traffic light and took out his citation book, ready to write me a ticket.

Out of habit, I saluted him for his official correction and said, "Sir, I am a soldier on my way to the Far East. I'm sorry. I don't know the rules." I didn't feel any confidence that he would have any sympathy for my story.

"You must be a Yank, soldier," he said. "No one jay-walks like you guys from New York!"

I began to worry. *New Yorkers have a bad reputation in California, too?* I thought. "Sir, please forgive me this time. I must get to my embarkation point. It won't happen again now that I know the rules," I pleaded.

The policeman appeared to believe me. He put his citation book back into his rear pocket.

"All right then. You're off the hook this time," he answered and gazed at me a moment, then smiled slowly. "And what's more, I will take you there myself. Hop in."

He motioned me to his parked police car. I smiled and thanked him, but I was suspicious. *Was this a ruse to take me down to the police station?*

I got into the police car warily, but the kind policeman drove me right up to the docks. I saw a long line of soldiers who were reporting for duty as I was. I got out of the car and thanked the policeman. I quickly ran to fall in, taking my place among all of the young soldiers shipping out to the Far East.

Aboard ship to Honolulu

Life on board a military ship crossing the Pacific Ocean consisted of plenty of work details, but there was also down time. I used my time to read up on the history of the places we were about to visit. I found out that Hawaii had a long history but didn't become the fiftieth state in the Union until 1959.

The first settlers were Polynesians who came long distances by outrigger canoe, using the stars as navigational guides. The first Europeans didn't reach their shores until the English explorer James Cook arrived in 1778 and found an open, generous people.

King Kamehameha I unified the islands under one sovereign rule in 1810. He brought a peace that encouraged agriculture and trade with other countries, especially merchants from America, China, and French Canada.

Hawaiian salt was in high demand by the American fur trade during this time because it was the best salt to use to tan hides. The French Canadians also employed Hawaiian workers to help built Fort Vancouver. They came as laborers, not as slaves, with some staying in the bush, becoming fur trappers. When Lewis and Clark made their way to the Pacific in 1805, they were greeted by what they called "black Indians," or Hawaiian mountain men.

Though contact with other cultures and peoples were making their way into the islands, King Kamehameha I re-instituted the hula as the national dance of the islands and encouraged the preservation of the Hawaiian culture. In addition, he traveled throughout Europe, collecting works of art and finely crafted furniture for his palaces.

With Western contact, infectious disease and acculturation usually followed. Hawaii was no exception. The native people learned to use guns, trade for profit, and drink alcohol. This, combined with missionary conversion that started in 1820, led to the decline of the traditional Hawaiian culture and religion.

Foreign investors began pouring into the islands, buying land and setting up sugar plantations as early as 1830. The abolition of the feudal land system in 1848 opened even more land to foreign investment and new industries were established. These foreign investors exerted powerful influence over the Hawaiian Islands, wanting more control of the Hawaiian government and economy. They also wanted to establish a naval base there. This influence was so strong that it overthrew Queen Liliuokalani, the last reigning monarch in Hawaii, in 1891, making Hawaii a U.S. Protectorate. President McKinley annexed Hawaii to the United States seven years later. The Hawaiian Islands became a U.S. territory in 1900.

All of this political maneuvering was instigated by greedy American financiers. Governor Sanford B. Dole's policies in Hawaii show this clearly. An American appointee to Hawaii, Dole eagerly expanded his fledgling pineapple plantation in Hawaii, marketing to ready customers in the United States. Putting Hawaii under American mandate allowed more American ownership of business and control of trade.

A naval base was established at Pearl Harbor to protect these commercial interests. US military personnel soon were flocking to Hawaii, not only to serve there but also to take their R & R. By 1941, there was a large US force in Hawaii and suffered the brunt of a surprise attack by the Japanese on December 7, 1941. During World War II, Hawaii became the base of operations for the Pacific, and the United States put the islands under martial law until March 1943.

Arrival in the Islands

Five days after leaving Oakland, our ship docked in Honolulu. We soldiers were driven to a nearby Army camp, where we were served drinks and sand-wiches, then lectured on the proper behavior of a soldier in Hawaii.

We were cautioned strongly against going to local prostitutes. They defi-nitely scared the devil out of us by describing, in detail, the symptoms of all the venereal diseases we could catch. Disgusting photos were shown and passed around for every soldier to see. I knew from my reading of Hawaiian history that it was Spaniards and American sailors who had brought these diseases to Hawaii in the first place, but that was not mentioned.

With those precautions ever present in our minds, we were all issued twenty-four hour passes. We could see and do whatever we wished before we continued with the remainder of the trip to the Far East.

Several new friends that I had made went with me into the downtown area. We consumed lots of hot-cooked food and plenty of fresh fruit. Ultimately, we all ended up in a topless saloon. We all had a lot to drink, and money seemed to jump out of our pockets. The waitresses were all over us, asking if we could buy them drinks. Of course, we all said that we would, just to show them that we were mature and macho and rich.

Virgin farm boys

Each time we were invited to "go upstairs and have a good time," one of the soldiers reminded the rest of us of the warnings we had received at camp that morning. Still, it was a very seductive situation, and we all desired to taste the local "pastries." The bronze-skinned girls with their long, silky hair and oriental eyes appealed to all of our senses. They were beautiful and exotic. We were healthy, young men with strong appetites—and we'd been out to sea for a while. For some of the innocent virgin guys from rural America, this was their first encounter with any girl in a sexual way, much less with experienced prostitutes.

We left the first saloon and went from bar to bar, only to repeat the same scenario. One guy got really drunk and agreed to let the girls take him "upstairs, to lie down, and rest." He was practically carried by the girls up the stairs.

We all kept watch for him, eyes on the stairs, until finally he came down with the biggest smirking grin on his face. His knees seemed shaky. Now, however, he was eager to leave, because he feared he might be tempted again, and he no more money to indulge himself.

On the way back to camp, he told us every detail. He told us the girls had dropped him on a bed, undressed him, and thrown him into a cold shower, as they waited patiently outside the door. When he had finished washing and felt able to stand on his feet, they escorted him to a bed and gathered around him to dry him off with soft towels and kisses all over his body. They began teasing him and touching him in ways he could not resist. Somehow, they knew he was a virgin farm boy. He could not resist. He had sex with all three, paid them all, and left the room with $1 in his wallet but infinitely richer in experience.

As he told us this story, he kept reassuring us (and himself, if truth be told) that he had not caught any disease from those girls. "they were all smooth-skinned and healthy".

When we got to the barracks, I noticed that he rushed to undress and run to the shower. He was in there a long time, apparently soaping and cleansing every part of his body.

Ocean swim drill

For the next ten days, we saw nothing but the vast ocean, with occasional ships and dolphins sighted. Several times a day, we drilled for all kinds of emergencies, including simulations of fire on board. Some of us were ordered to jump into the water.

I promptly notified the duty officer that I could not swim well, that I had nearly drowned twice in my life. He didn't buy it. He said he had heard that before.

He said, "Soldier, put on the life jacket and jump in."

I refused, swearing that I was telling the truth.

He physically put the life jacket on me and ordered me to jump. He was about to push me overboard.

I looked down over the side of the ship. It seemed a long way down. *Even if I could swim enough to keep my head above water, how in the world would they ever get me back into the ship?* I was petrified. I began to shake uncontrollably.

About fifteen men were already in the water by now, having a great time it seemed. They were shouting encouragements to me to jump.

"The water is warm and clear," one said.

"If anything happens, we'll look after you," said another.

Then, they all began to chant in unison. "Jump! Fathi, Jump!"

I gave the officer a dirty, hateful look and attempted to jump. But I just couldn't. I simply had no faith in the stupid little life jacket to keep me afloat.

I was ordered to go back to my quarters and wait there till the drill was over. I expected the worse. I didn't want to be labeled a coward so soon into my US military career.

When the drill was over, I waited to be called on the speaker system to appear before the captain and explain myself. I expected more than a reprimand. Surprisingly, that order never came. I stayed on my bunk, reading a history book about Japan, and missed dinner that night.

I had learned a lot about Japan from my pen pal Nagako Obata when we had corresponded so long ago it seemed. I missed her letters while I was in Brazil but I just could not think about trying to re-establish contact with her there since I had spend so much of my time trying to stay alive. Though I had finally gotten a steady job, I was by no means truly successful.

So, I read again of those exotic places that Nagako had first told me about. This had been the land of the Shoguns, territorial warlords who ruled Japan for 250 years. They were governors and soldiers trained in a code of behavior that put honor above all things, sometimes above the welfare of their people. The Shoguns offered internal stability but prohibited trade with other countries and suppressed the spread of Christianity. Because merchants as well as peasants were oppressed, uprisings occurred, and economic power began to shift away from the Shoguns.

When Commodore Matthew Perry, an American, forced Japan to open trade to the West in 1854, the Shogunate system fell. Instead of resisting foreign influence, the Japanese began to embrace Western culture, establishing a modern army and navy.

By 1941, Japan had become a world military power. Allied with Germany and Italy, Japan was determined to remove the US presence in the Pacific. On December 7, 1941, Japan bombed not only Pearl Harbor, but also Singapore and other US Pacific possessions. During the next year, Japan had extended its influence as far as India to the West and the coastal waters of Alaska to the East. After the Battle of Midway, however, the war turned in favor of the United States and the Allies. Ultimately, it took the catastrophic bombing of Hiroshima and Nagasaki to cause Japan to surrender in 1945.

When I finished reading these histories, I came out on deck and looked out over the ocean. I pondered the great history that had been played out on these waters. I felt small, not only to be in the middle of such a large ocean, but also to be part of a long American military history. *How had I come to be a representative of the mighty United States Army?* I knew how, but I still couldn't quite believe it, even as the huge transport ship carried me across these seas to the islands of Japan and the military bases there and in Korea.

Free time on board

There was plenty of free time on board ship. The other soldiers played poker, billiards, slot machines, and shuffleboard. I, of course, did a lot of reading. The library was stocked with war stories, history, poetry, and all the usual wonders of libraries.

All of us soldiers wrote letters home and mailed them from the each port. My reading about Japan had brought my thoughts back to Nagako. I began to wonder how she was and what she was doing. The closer that the ship came to Yokohama, I wanted to finally meet her, to talk about these ideas and histories I had read about her country. That was when I decided to send her a telegram, ship to shore, to ask if we could meet. Her response was swift and she agreed. We were finally going to meet!

Ten days after leaving Honolulu, we docked in Yokohama and I used my 24-hour pass to meet Nagako.

Chapter Forty-Five

Arrival in Pusan, South Korea

The Commanding Officer's welcome

Our ship docked in Pusan, South Korea, and some 1200 soldiers disembarked. We were gathered together to hear the commanding officer's welcoming speech. It was intended to be sort of a military pep talk, but I'm not quite sure it did what it was supposed to do.

"Welcome to South Korea," the commanding officer said. "Each one of you will be serving here for at least twelve months. You are expected to obey orders and do your duty for your country.

"Danger is always lurking around the corner. Some of you will be stationed on the border with North Korea, guarding the DMZ (the 38th parallel Demilitarized Zone). During the Korean War a decade ago, the US lost over 50,000 solders defending freedom and stopping Communist expansionism here. The North Koreans were and still are the enemy, and a formidable one at that, I may add. But we are here by UN mandate, as part of the United Nation's multinational peace force. And we intend to stay here until South Korean forces can protect their borders on their own." He puffed on his long cigar.

"This land is covered with this much shit." He held up two fingers about two inch apart. " Yes, you heard me right, Shit. Human shit." He smiled wryly. "Be careful eating out in restaurants and in the villages. The Korean use human waste for fertilizer. This can cause Hepatitis."

"Oh, yes, and try to conserve your energy. Don't waste it all on the girls and their Mamma-san. You will get the Clap, and God knows what else from these girls. Use your army issued condoms. They are free, and wash yourselves with soap and hot water as soon as you have had sex with these girls. And don't be surprised if you end up getting circumcised." Everyone laughed. "Yes, sometimes we have to cut off a piece of it, to save the rest of it." More laughter.

"The sergeants here will assign you a destination. You will be boarding the appropriate bus, which will take you to your compound. There, you will be issued some additional gear and clothes, particularly winter clothes. It gets colder than hell here. It dips to forty degrees below zero. Don't get frostbite. It's a nasty thing that can result in amputation. Whatever you do, keep dry and warm."

With all of this information, all of the soldiers including myself were beginning to look discouraged and depressed. I guess we all must have been wondering how we had gotten into this. Korea certainly wasn't Hawaii nor was it Virginia or Georgia. The commanding officer had just said forty below zero!

"Don't look so gloomy, now" the commanding officer said. "There're some pleasant things you can do and experience in Korea: The Officers' Clubs, Non-Com (Non-Commissioned) Clubs, the many orphanages we need you to volunteer for, movies and other entertainments, the lovely American Doughnut Dollies from back home. You might as well make the best of it." He paused and looked us all over, then said. "Soldiers, Good Luck!"

Strategic Air Command (SAC)

Some of my buddies were assigned to the Strategic Air Command (SAC) headquarters in Seoul. Everyone here was on alert 24/7. The pilots and their crews were always flying missions with B-52's, loaded with nuclear bombs, to keep them prepared and ready to strike any target on the face of the globe. The lucky crew would survive, high up in the air, dropping their bombs on command as the United States and the Soviets engaged in a nuclear pissing contest. If that ever happened, I wondered where those bombers could land safely. It was scary shit to think about.

I came to know this base intimately, as the Army field hospital was situated there and I flew with the helicopter crews. Regularly, we went up in helicopters to several thousand feet in order to survey what was happening on the other side of the DMZ, a technique called triangulation. North Korean soldiers had been entrenched behind the hills, on their side of the DMZ since the Korean War. Sometimes, the North Koreans directed some bullets in our directions, even though, technically, we were in South Korean air space. These incidents never made the newspapers, on either side of this conflict.

Saul as soldier with 1st Cavalry Division,
Korea, 1961 (46)

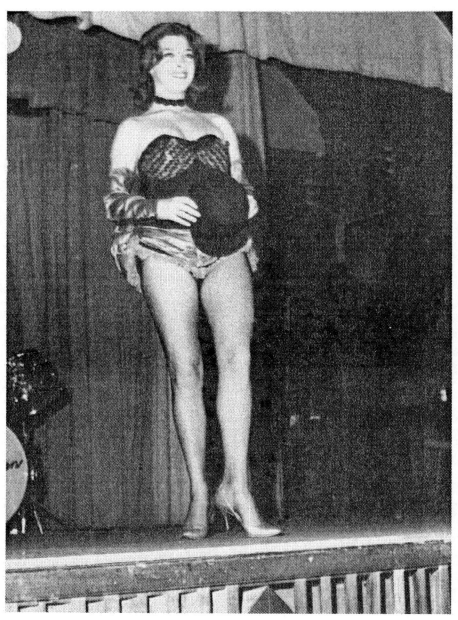

American "Doughnut Dolly" entertaining
the troops in Korea, 1962 (47)

Saul with 15th Aviation Company (1st Cavalry),
Korea, 1962 (48)

Saul, battle ready, 38th parallel,
Korea, 1962 (49)

Saul's military compound near the
38th parallel, Korea, 1962 (50)

"Steady" girlfriend, Korea, 1962 (51)

Saul, preparing aircraft for flight,
Korea, 1961 (52)

Saul, Korea, 1961 (53)

Saul with "Connie", Korean girlfriend,
Korea, 1961 (54)

One of many fixed wings crafts at the
15th Aviation Co., Korea, 1961 (55)

Korea: Saul invented an automatic tester
for aircraft control panels, 1961 (56)

Saul with 1st Cavalry, 15th Aviation Company,
Korea, 1961 (57)

Saul in full combat gear, Korea, 1962 (58)

Chapter Forty-Six

Life in Korea

Kimchee on the public bus

Sometimes, after work or on weekends, I took a public bus to go to Seoul. I was always nauseated at the smell of Kimchee that some of the passengers ate on the bus. Kimchee, a Korean specialty, is much like a salsa in the US. It is a relish-like dish, made of fermented cabbage and other vegetables, and heavily spiced with lots of garlic. Some of the US soldiers adopted a taste for it and even enjoyed it as much as the local people. But, I couldn't get past the smell and never could eat it. In fact, the smell set my stomach roiling whenever I was near the stuff, and bus travel was particularly unpleasant for me.

What made these bus trips bearable was the presence of many young mothers who chose to nurse their babies on the bus. It reminded me of the Middle East, among the Arabs, who did the same thing. Most Korean women had small breasts. Occasionally, a woman was found to have quite exquisite ones. The other soldiers and I often feasted our eyes on the smooth, plump breasts being sucked by happy infants, wishing we could be so lucky.

Communal baths

One of the most pleasurable indulgences in Korea was the public baths. They were strewn all over the cities and villages in the countryside. It reminded me of my childhood in Baghdad, when I was taken along to the public baths with my mother and sisters. My father thought it was safer for a little boy to be in the women's section of the baths than the men's.

In the public baths of Korea, we entered dark, steamy quarters with small individual rooms, each with a professional masseuse. The masseuse was always young and dressed in a sexy manner. She bore a clean towel on her shoulder, which she had obtained from a stack of towels on a convenient shelf. Inside, were benches made of wood and covered with vinyl cushions. Like all of her clients, the masseuse always greeted me with a wide smile and helped me undress. There was no shyness here. Inhibitions went out the window within minutes. Once nude, I then lay down on the bench, face down, and the masseuse covered me with a hot, steamy towel.

Slowly, the masseuse started the massage, beginning with my neck, slowly working her way down to my feet. I couldn't help but moan in sheer pleasure as the masseuse manipulated every muscle in my body. She then cracked each knuckle of my fingers and toes. Then she had me turn over. There I lay in my cubicle, still stark naked and facing the ceiling. The masseuse's hands began walking over my flesh again, top to bottom, very slowly and very thoroughly. If any of the clients, like myself, happened to get aroused by her ministrations, she took care of that by helping us release all of the tension in our minds and bodies by using either her hands or her mouth. Most curiously, if you ejaculated in her mouth, she did not run to the sink to spit your stuff out, as was customary with other ladies of the night. That led to a curious appreciation of the masseuses of the bath by us soldiers.

When this was done, I was asked to turn onto my face again. The masseuse then slipped out of her rubber sandals and climbed onto my back. She began walking up and down my back, squeezing her toes into the muscles, making all of the remaining tension disappear. These masseuses were usually small women, weighing very little. They were also very graceful as they strolled, perfectly balanced, not holding onto anything, over our necks, our backs, and even over the backs of our legs, right down to our heels. This signaled the end of the massage. The masseuse then returned to the floor of the bath and wiped down my body with another steamy towel. Then, she politely motioned me toward the hot shower.

After showering, the masseuse led me to a communal pool where I unabashedly joined other men, some wealthy Koreans but mostly Westerners, who were also sharing the delights of the Korean baths. I sat there in bubbling, hot water up to my neck, for as long as I wanted. When I'd had enough, my masseuse led me back to my private room where I had left my clothes. She helped me get dressed like a female valet, and even aided me in brushing my hair and teeth. Then, she escorted me to the exit and then to a massive, dark bar. There, we customers could sit on comfortable, cushioned sofas and have a drink while we continued our rest and relaxation, cooling off, before we hit the street.

Even though we soldiers were considered wealthy by Korean standards, the cost of these services was still very expensive. We were able to afford this delightful practice only once a month. The pleasure of the experience, however, stayed with us for many days.

Swamps and crocodiles

While serving in Korea, now and then some salesmen arrived from the States to sell the cash-laden American soldiers something. Most of these salesmen sold life insurance to protect the soldiers' loved ones in case war broke out here on this very volatile outpost. Most of the salesmen returned to the US with a briefcase full of signed insurance polices. The worry about war and death was with us every day. We were ideal customers for the insurance business.

One day, a salesman came to our compound to sell us something different and very unique. He was offering land in the state of Florida. He had maps of various counties and parceled land in all shapes and sizes. I was very tempted. *Could I really own a piece of the land in America before I am even a citizen? Will this help me in my struggle with the immigration authorities?* I was excited.

A bunch of us congregated at the Officers Club and sat around several tables, drinking beer and smoking cigarettes as we listened to the salesman's pitch. He pointed to some of the land parcels and stated that this acreage even had live citrus fruit trees on the property.

"You have heard of Florida orange juice, haven't you?" he asked, knowing that we certainly had heard about Florida oranges. "Well, that's what it is, man. It's all here in the great Sunshine State—all the orange juice you can drink and sell."

I was becoming more convinced by the minute. Unlike the men around me, I was a foreigner, nearly alone in America, and never having owned any land or property of my own before. *Why not invest in the future and spend less here in Korea,* I thought. It sounded logical to me. I approached the salesman and asked to see the purchase agreement in order to examine the legal wording of the sale. When he showed it to me, it appeared to be legitimate.

I took the salesman's grease pen and circled a parcel of land on the clear plastic, covering the map of Florida. "I am interested in this piece of land. Here's what I want," I said, grinning from ear to ear.

The salesman appeared very happy. "Here we go. Mr. Fathi here chose this piece of property. Who would like to be his neighbor and buy the parcel next door?" he asked.

I waited impatiently for someone to come forward and buy land next to where I had circled. One or two of my fellow soldiers could be more than Army buddies; they could be neighbors.

While the other men were hesitating, the salesman began filling out my purchase agreement. "Whom do you designate as beneficiary?" he asked me.

I was puzzled. *What is a beneficiary?* I wondered. I had never heard this word before.

"In case you die or something," the salesman explained. "Who do you want to end up inheriting your land?"

I hesitated. "No one," I said. I had no wife or children. "I have no one to leave it to in the States. Can I leave it to my parents in Israel?"

He laughed loudly. This was new to him. "Yes, of course you can leave it to your parents in Israel," he assured me. "The God-damned government doesn't care who the fuck inherits your land. Sure you can."

When he had finished filling out my purchase agreement, the salesman called me over to sign it. Then, he told me that I had to give him a down payment of ten percent, or $450 for a 100-acre parcel. He was all smiles. I was excited.

As I pulled my wallet out of my pocket, my friend Roger, who had been sitting all this time in total silence, grabbed me by the shoulder and pulled me down toward him so he could whisper in my ear. "Saul, aren't you rushing a bit?" he asked me.

I thought he was just jealous. I straightened up and moved out of his way. "I know what I'm doing. Leave me be," I retorted.

Jake, another trusted and close friend, shouted across the room at me. Though he hadn't heard what Roger had said, anyone could have inferred his intention. "Saul, listen to Roger, man," he said. "You know nothin' about no land in the Sunshine State. And forget about all the orange juice you can drink and the citrus you can sell." He started laughing, and soon everyone in the room burst out laughing, too.

Another soldier shouted in my direction, "And you can bet it's all under water, full of crocodiles." Again, everyone roared.

I looked over the crowd to get a good look at their faces as they drank their beer and laughed at me. *What was the matter with these guys?* I wondered. *Do they mean what they were saying? Should I believe this salesman?*

Roger then put his arms around across my shoulders and guided me to the back of the room. "Saul, please don't do this. Don't be the first to buy," he said. "There's got to be a catch. Jake is right. I'm right. Listen to us. We're your buddies."

He was convincing. But I still needed proof to decide for myself. The salesman was calling my name over and over, trying to get me to sign the contract. I walked back to him and asked in a straight face, "Will you put it in writing? Will you write in the land that the land is covered with citrus trees, not submerged under water, and no crocodiles?" I asked. Everyone burst into wild laughter again. I was getting mad at their ridicule.

The salesman was also getting mad and becoming very agitated. "What the fuck are you talking about? I can't do that. The bill-of-sale won't let me do that, and I can't modify it. It's legitimate, I tell you. Don't listen to your ignorant buddies. Now, sign it right down here. I already done all the fuckin' work on it."

Now everyone was shouting, "Bullshit, don't fall for it. Ask him to put it on paper."

I looked at the salesman. Even though I had agreed verbally, I felt I could change my mind. Boldly, I looked him in the eye and challenged, "Sorry. You put it in writing, or I won't sign." I waited a minute to see what the salesman would do. When nothing happened, I took the unsigned copy and walked out of the room.

Roger and Jake followed me, drawing up on either side. Jake said, "You did right, man. You would have been taken. The land is definitely under water and infested with crocodiles. For that price, It has to be."

Roger added, "We saved your ass, man. You'll thank us someday when you get back to the States and check things out."

That was the end of my dream of owning a piece of land in the States, at least for a decade or two. Ironically, twenty years later, I told this story to my wife and daughter Suzanne, and they were suddenly curious about the land I almost bought. They looked up the location of the parcel I had indicated that I had wanted, and pointed out to me that I had made another blunder with my investments. It seems that my parcel of land was in Orlando, Florida. It was indeed a crocodile swamp in the early 1960s, but it later became the part of the allocation of land that Walt Disney bought to develop Disney World in Florida. That original $5,000, 100-acre piece of land would have had a value of at least

$1,000,000 not long after I bought it—crocodile swamps notwithstanding.

Imagine owning a hundred acres in Orlando today! I would have been on my way to becoming a millionaire! But I guess it just wasn't meant to be.

Chapter Forty-Seven

The Night Girls and Mamma-Sans

One of the first things you learned in Korea is the abundance of available, easy girls, always ready to satisfy every fantasy you may have. Although the young and hardly-experienced American soldiers held out for a time, they eventually all succumbed to temptations of the flesh. Even my good friend Roger, who had studied to be a Christian minister back in the US, could not resist sneaking out to the village and surrendered to his carnal desires.

The higher-ranking officers had a trick up their sleeves. In order to minimize the possibility of catching a venereal disease (VD), they would "go steady." That is, they would see one young prostitute exclusively, hoping to reserve her for themselves like a choice mistress. Of course, occasionally, these very girls drifted to other soldiers at the requests of their mamma-sans.

The culture of mamma-san goes back thousands of years, crossing borders all over the world. She is a woman who, most likely, began her career as a prostitute, and grew too old to satisfy the male appetite, so she went into management, becoming a Madam in charge of a stable of young ladies of the evening. She typically offered these young, poor village girls, shelter, nice clothing, protection from abusive men, food, and some money (left over after paying back the mamma-San for her services). The money their girls made went to her family for the sustenance of their parents, brothers and sisters, and grand parents.

Sometimes, a mamma-san acquired a young, virgin girl. "She young, very pretty, virgin-virgin," the mamma-san would say to lure soldiers to her business. "You like? You gib (Give) two hunded dallas, you get pretty virgin-virgin."

The mamma-san usually spun the girl around to show all of her young features, sometimes pointing to her milk-white complexion, her unblemished skin, or that fact that her young body was devoid of any hair. There were always takers. I never understood how the taker could prove her claims, and why a virgin was this so prized.

Otherwise, you paid an average of ten to twenty dollars for a quickie in the hut or *Hootch* as the Koreans called it. The young girls always seemed to speak better English than their mamma-sans. That was puzzling to me since neither had much opportunity for education and since the mamma-sans were out communicating with soldiers every evening, trying to get them to come in to their establishments.

The mamma-san took about seventy-five percent of the proceeds and changed girls when they reached the old age of twenty-five. These retirees either returned to their families or became streetwalkers and bartenders. If they were lucky enough to have some money saved, they became mamma-sans themselves.

Sometimes, instead of going to the nearest village and paying a mamma-san, a soldier picked up a "dancing girl" at the local bar or the Officers Club. There were cases where a bunch of soldiers took their turn with the same girl, all night long, sending her home with more money than she could earn in a year's work. These young soldiers, most of whom arrived in Korea virgins, had no inhibitions whatsoever about having sex with strangers. Some of them even married these girls and brought them back to the US.

Having been sexually mature since I was thirteen and gaining extensive experience with the beauties of Brazil, I was a bit more selective. After a few months of abstinence, I found a beautiful teenage girl, Kim. I made arrangement with her mamma-san that when I came over, Kim and I would take a sponge bath and spend the night in her *hooch*. Soon, Kim became a sort of semi-exclusive girlfriend. The mamma-san knocked on my straw-door to wake me up at 5:30 A.M. and made sure I was fed and shaved, my uniform pressed, and ready to report to my duties in the compound just a few minutes Jeep-driving distance away.

In time, I grew fond of Kim. This was the closest thing to the officer's concept of "going steady." I often picked her up in my Jeep on weekends, and we would climb the hills, or I would take her with me to the children's orphanages I sponsored. Naturally, I had to pay mamma-san for every hour Kim was with me, instead of working, but I was glad for her company.

Sometimes, when I felt that Kim's affections were genuine, I showered her with food and gifts, which she sent to her family, without the mamma-san finding out. She told me repeatedly that her parents did not know the nature of her work. They were told she worked in the kitchen of an Army base.

One night, on a Friday, I showered and put on fresh underwear and a uniform, and drove over to the village to see Kim and to stay overnight. After we bathed together, being scrubbed and sponged by her mamma-san, we had some soup and tea, sitting on the floor, which was heated by burning wood under it. We retired to our room where we eagerly began caressing and engaging in wild sex.

Afterwards, for some unknown reason, I could not sleep. Kim never went to sleep before she made sure I was asleep first. That night, we made love six times. My energy seemed endless, inexhaustible. Kim was surprised, but most accommodating. In the morning, after I had only a couple of hours of sleep, mamma-san knocked on my door. I jumped out of bed, put on my Jockey shorts, and rushed to the bathroom. There, I discovered bloodstains on my shorts. I was flabbergasted! *Had I been fooled by Kim? Had she been seeing a lot of other soldiers besides me? Had she contracted VD and had failed to tell me? Did she have her period while having sex with me?*

I rushed to wash and have a bite to eat and some tea. I left the hut and went straight to my compound. I rushed in to see the medic, who was everybody's friend.

After I told him what happened, he examined me and inserted a round wooden rod into my penis. "That's nothing, Mr. Fathi. You just over exerted yourself last night."

I was relieved, but mistrusted his findings. "Are you sure that's all it is?"

He looked at me with a wide smile. "Yes, that's all it is," he reassured me. "It's your own blood. It dripped out of your penis. You worked too hard, that's all." He was twice my age, a career soldier. I stood up to shake his hand and thanked him profoundly. He was still smiling as I left the infirmary. I heard him say, "Six times, ha? You devil, you!"

With orphanage kids (I sponsored),
Korea, 1962 (59)

Chapter Forty-Eight

Serving at the War Orphanages

We had finally settled down to our assigned chores in the US Army compound in South Korea. I was assigned to the First Cavalry Division, the 15th Aviation Company, situated a stone's throw from the DMZ, on the 38th parallel.

My personal duty was that of chief technician, maintaining, testing, and repairing all electrical systems in our helicopters and small fixed-wing airplanes. I had to read many technical manuals and certify (sign-off) the flight logbooks before a pilot could take off. It was a responsible, respectable job, with plenty of free time. This allowed me the luxury of reading and designing test apparatus and pursue inventions and patents for the US Army. A reporter from the Stars & Stripes, the Army's major publication, interviewed me and wrote a nice article with my picture in it.

But, the most enjoyable work I had was something I volunteered for. Called sponsoring, many of us shared the task of taking care of Korean children in orphanages. Many children had lost their parents during the Korean War, (some fathered by American soldiers). Several orphanages had been set up to care for these waifs. On weekends, and sometimes on weekdays after work, I put on a clean, neat uniform, grabbed my camera, and stopped at the Canteen to buy chocolate bars and other goodies. Then, I'd hurry to one of the orphanages I sponsored.

As I arrived there in my assigned Jeep, the children always greeted me at the shabby gate, shouting their welcome to me, some in English, some in Korean. Their eyes were wide and eager, as they smiled and extended their little hands. They often ran behind my Jeep and tried to hitch a ride before it came to a full halt. I always chuckled, remembering my own wild rides behind the horse carriages in Iraq when I was their age. This enthusiastic greeting by the children always made me forget my own troubles and any sad longing for my family that I might have had that day.

The teacher at the orphanage came out to greet me, too. She wore her special, colorful kimono, with a "pillow" on her back, and at least one child hitching a ride on her shoulders. "Ah, Mr. Fathi," she always said politely. "Welcome, welcome. Please come, come. I have hot tea on stove. You like, yes?"

By then, the children usually overran my Jeep, touching the instruments and the steering wheel, pretending to drive, and refusing to get out. I asked them to follow me inside, holding up the bag of treats I had in my hand like a small Santa's sack. They tumbled out of the Jeep and bolted after me, hanging onto my arms and tugging at my uniform, shouting with glee.

Inside the straw *Hootch* that was the orphanage, we sat on pillows on the floor around a low, lacquered, wooden table. Our feet touched under the table, as we sipped delicious tea and basked in the joy of each other's company. The teacher then took the bag from my hand and spilled its contents onto the table, admonishing the greedy ones, in Korean, to behave and to take only one of each kind of candy. Some of the children listened obediently to the teacher. Others did as they pleased and grabbed as many things as their little hands could grasp.

A little later, we usually went out to the backyard and played. Some kids climbed into the swings, built there by other soldiers, and begged me unceasingly to push them on the swings as they stuffed their mouths with candy. Other children were a bit more withdrawn and shy, waiting patiently for my attention. These ones were the most affectionate. They often grabbed me around the legs, burying their faces between my knees. Some posed and begged me to take a photo of them, which I was obligated to bring back on my next visit. They never forgot when I took pictures to ask about the photos the very next time I visited. When I did, they often looked at their pictures and giggled, pointing their little fingers at some detail, and laughed for a long time.

Then when I was ready to leave, I always felt sad because I felt I had taken more away with me than I had given to these children. What could a few chocolate bars be compared to their joy and delight! Before I left, I always went back into the *Hootch* and gave a few dollars to the teacher for help with the children. She always thanked me profusely, bowing her head several times, saying, "*Taksan Hammidah*" ("Thanks very much.")

The children always ran after my Jeep, yelling and waving goodbye. Though these sweet children made my life in Korea bearable, I can never forget their blazing, accusing eyes. They would not have been in the orphanage if it hadn't been because of soldiers like me. Those blazing eyes still haunt me even forty-five years later.

Chapter Forty-Nine

Talent on the Mountain: The Korean Boy Painter

While in Korea, I loved to use my free time to go wandering among the many hills and mountains of that country. There, I met some fascinating village characters who had various stages of command of the English language. I especially loved the young children who came to greet me as they spotted me climbing their hill.

One day, one of these cute children pulled me by the hand and brought me into the backyard of a shanty resident of the village. At first, I thought the child was bringing me to a prostitute mother or sister, as they often did, but not this time. The child pointed to a straw-sandaled youngster, sitting outdoors before a small easel. He was painting a portrait from a wallet-size picture, slightly larger than a passport photo. It was magnificent. Upon inquiring, I learned it was the portrait of the bearded village elder, a highly respected figure in Korean society.

The young artist stood up and shook my hand, smiling. "You like picture?" he asked in broken English, pointing with pride at his painting.

"Yes, it's beautiful. It's real good," I responded enthusiastically. "Go on, please. Don't let me interrupt you."

The boy sat down on his straw chair and applied a few strokes to the painting. I was amazed at his talent. *Where did he learn to paint this well?* I wondered. I wanted to encourage him.

I pulled out my over-stuffed wallet and proceeded to look for a photo he could paint. He thought I was going to offer him money for the painting of the village elder. He got up and waved his hands to tell me that this painting was not for sale: It was for the local temple. I apologized and presented him with a small photo of Winston Churchill, one of most admired statesmen of the 20th century. I had carried this photo in my wallet for over ten years, next to my parents' photo.

The boy's eyes lit up. "You want I make picture?" he asked.

"Yes, please make a picture for me this big," I answered and gestured with my hands, showing him that I wanted the painting to be approximately 11" x 14."

The young painter grinned. From among his wares, he took out a roll of silk canvas and a pair of scissors. Then, he showed me where he was going to cut, to see if it was the appropriate size. I nodded my approval. The boy cut a piece slightly larger than the size I had asked for and stretched the silk on a bamboo frame. He propped the canvas against the easel and thumb tacked Churchill's photo onto one of the wooden easel supports.

By the time he was ready to paint, about seven little children had gathered around us, laughing and chattering in Korean. Some of them stuck their chubby little hands into my pockets, expecting to find some goodies or small change. I laughed and politely pulled their hands out of pockets. Still, their hands came away, clutching some of the chocolate bars I had brought with me. They eagerly unwrapped the candy and took their first bites. Their smiles melted my heart. We were communicating, without the benefit of language.

The young artist first sketched Churchill's image with a pencil. Then, he started using paint, squeezing the tubes as if they contained melted gold, just a little at a time, mixing colors in small but exact amounts. After about an hour, the painting began to come alive, taking on Churchill's most distinguishing features.

I told the boy to take a break because I thought these things needed time to come to artistic completion. He laughed and waved his hands, telling me he didn't need a break. He sat at his easel and worked for nearly three hours.

While he worked, I played with the children, twirling them by the arms and pulling them up to my shoulders. Some of their mothers came out of their straw huts and scolded them for bothering me. One of the children kept tugging my hand until she got me to follow her to her hut. I took off my hat and shoes at the door, as was the custom. The little girl motioned for me to sit on the floor on a mattress before a lacquered table. I sat down, slipping my legs under the low table, which was only about 15" high.

The child moved closer to an old woman who began serving me boiling hot tea. It was social courtesy, and I felt quite honored.

As I drank my tea, the village children crowded around the door and began to filter in, sitting around the table with me. The old lady smiled at the children and then emptied a bag of Korean candies onto the table. The children politely took two or three candies each and began unwrapping them. It was so much fun to watch them.

When I finished drinking my tea, I stood up and bowed to the lady and thanked her for her hospitality. "Taksan-hammida," (Thanks very much.) I said. I pulled out my wallet and gave her a five-dollar bill.

The woman waved her hand in refusal. She had offered me her hospitality and did not require payment.

I insisted. Her courtesy honored me, and I could see that she could use the money. In Korea, this was more than the wages of two weeks' work. The woman took it, bowed, and kept thanking me.

I put on my shoes and walked out to check on the progress of the young painter. I was flabbergasted at what I saw. The boy was even able to articulate Churchill's wrinkled face, with the blood vessels bulging through the skin.

The young artist pointed to the painting with pride. "You like? Ok?"

I shook his hand vigorously. "Yes, I like it very much. Thank you," I said. "How much do I owe you?"

He understood but his hands told me he was unable to determine a price. As he pointed to me, I realized that he was relying on me to set the price. I pulled out my wallet again, and looked for a ten-dollar bill. I hesitated. *Is this enough?* I wondered. I figured it was equivalent to a month's salary in Korea and thought that a month's salary anywhere would be appropriate. I offered him the money.

The boy hesitated, then slowly extended his arm, finally taking the bill with a great grin. "Tank you berry much," he said. "I happy. You happy?"

"Yes, I am very happy," I answered. "You have great talent. I want you to sign the painting on the back." I flipped the painting upside down.

The boy understood. He picked up the finest brush he had and signed it carefully, almost not believing the honor I bestowed on him. Apparently, no one had ever asked him to sign his work.

I bid everyone in the village goodbye, and, painting in hand, I left on foot back to my dreary, Army barracks. I quickly wrapped the painting with a towel and tucked it deep inside my footlocker. It had been a very pleasurable day in Korea that day. The silk painting would be a memorable souvenir I would always treasure.

Now, forty-five years later, that beautiful painting of Churchill is hanging on the wall of my basement office, right behind my computer. Sometimes, I feel that Churchill is staring at me, asserting the presence of a great man.

I have often wondered what fate had befallen that young painter. That young boy would be in his fifties now. *Did he continue painting? Did he become one of Korea's famous artists? Or did the cruel poverty force him to give it up and seek out a regular job to earn sustenance for his family?*

Chapter Fifty

Crying on Guard Duty

Having lived in the Middle East and in a tropical country like Brazil, the winters of Korea were almost unbearable. The temperatures often dipped well below thirty degrees below zero.

During one night when I was assigned guard duty of our compound, I was dressed in winter gear, head to toe, with fur mittens that covered my entire arms, but no fingers. I kept wondering, *how the hell are you supposed to shoot the enemy under these conditions?* In my mind, I imagined the tens of thousands of North Korean soldiers in the war here, descending the neighboring hills in mid-winter, wearing ragged wool coats and no hats or fur mittens, without even shoes. And, here I was, standing on duty with all of these warm clothes on, and I still was freezing.

I wondered how I would ever stop anyone who tried to breach the security of our compound, much less a horde of Communist soldiers swarming over the hills toward me. I couldn't even put a finger in the trigger of my M-16 to pull off a round because of these big mittens. The only way I could defend myself and my station would be to remove my mittens, and put my fingers against that cold metal, hoping to get off a few rounds before my fingers froze to my gun.

If I came face-to-face with a North Korean soldier, I wondered if I would be able to kill him, realizing by his poor tatters that he had a miserable life back home and probably had a wife and children. I struggled with the alternative. If I didn't kill him, would he kill me without hesitation? I was beginning to question the morality of war. To kill one poor soul or to be killed by one—that was the choice I would face every day here in Korea. I could not find any morality in any war, no matter what the causes or motives were.

Previously, I had been shown photos of solders whose ears had cracked and fell off from the freezing cold. It seemed like a joke. It was supposed to be hilarious. But I certainly was not laughing now as I experienced this cold first hand.

The only reason American soldiers were still here on the border between North and South Korea eight years after the armistice was signed was because the North Korean army hadn't been given new orders to march south or retreat farther north. If they ever crossed the demilitarized zone into South Korea, the American military would most certainly have to use the ultimate weapon again—nuclear bombs. President Truman had not allowed General Macarthur to use them to win the Korean War. No one won that war, and the United States still refuses to admit that perhaps we may have truly lost the Korean War. The crisis continues here because we never put an end to the threat from the north. Would a future president ever authorize the use of our humongous nuclear arsenal, killing millions of innocent enemy citizens in order to finally end the conflict here?

While I was contemplating my fate in the event of another war with North Korea, I heard a baby cry in the village across from the fence around our compound. His mother was trying to quite the baby down. I could hear the pleading in her voice, but it did no good. The baby kept wailing. *What was hurting him?* I wondered. *Is he hungry? Does the mother have enough milk in her breasts? Is he sick?*

The child certainly sounded like any other baby crying. *Is he really the enemy from the day he was born?* I wondered. *Does an accident of birth make him my enemy?* Oh, the futility of war!

I remembered a scene from the life of Napoleon I had once read. Upon becoming the emperor for life, a political challenger criticized Napoleon's wars and conquests by asking him to define morality. Napoleon answered, "I cannot define morality, but I know it is on the side of the heavier artillery." What arrogance! I wondered how many world leaders still held to that same opinion, to this very day.

As the baby continued to cry, I became melancholy. I pictured in my mind the little boys and girls that I sponsored in the local orphanage. They had bulging stomachs, penetrating, dreamy eyes, and an absolute hunger for love and affection. A simple hug was more nourishing than bread to them. My entire (and very brief) childhood flashed before my eyes. My near-idyllic childhood had been lost forever, as I had been forced to grow up at ten years old and look after my younger brother Yeftah when we had escaped from Baghdad and fled first to Iran and then to Israel.

I began to cry as I stood on sentry duty. I wished I had had a piece of paper to write on, to write out all of these feelings, to fill the page with prose and sing the tragic, universal hymn of humanity. As a soldier in the mighty Unites States Army, was I supposed to be ashamed of crying? Perhaps, among some of these men. But, to me, the truth was all so real. We were all one people. We were all members of the same human race, the same ancient family. Our original source is one source, and our final destination is surely the same. *Why, then,* I questioned, *are we killing each other? Why haven't we learned, after 10,000 years of civilization to love and respect one another? How many millions of us have died in the name of a religion, a flag, a country?* Imagine what the world would be like today if all nations embraced in a single purpose: the betterment of the human race. What wonders we could create and what community! *Is there intelligent life on this earth?*

As I kept walking sentry duty, I carried my rifle on my left shoulder. I moved back and forth along the entire path behind our fence. It was my duty, but I did it also to keep warm. My face had begun to freeze in the cold. I found it hard to catch my breath through my wool-knit hood. I looked up at the night sky. It was crystal clear, with millions of stars beckoning from the distance. I remembered looking up at the night sky during my night shifts at the Nilotex factory. I felt homesick for my good friends in Brazil, for my family back in Israel, even for my sister in New York who had not understood me. I asked myself yet again as I had so many times in my long, winding journey of life:

What am I doing here?

I remembered the insignia sewed on the back of our flight jackets. I didn't think much about it when I was issued my own jacket. The insignia read: "**I am sure to go to heaven, for I have spent my time in hell: Korea, the land that God forgot.**" How very appropriate! For a brief moment, I wondered if God had forgotten me, too.

Forty-five years later, my flight jacket has long since disintegrated, but I still have the insignia hanging on the wall of my basement. It's a perpetual reminder of my bewilderment as a soldier. I look at it every day and ask myself, *was the death of 50,000 American boys justified? What was gained in return for their young bodies? Will future politicians subject us to similar futile sacrifices? When will the United Nations assume the role of world leadership as it was intended to be by the founders of that body? Is anyone listening???*

Chapter Fifty-One

Bigotry & Betrayal

If the US declares war on Israel, will you shoot a Jew?"

While en route to Korea on board a military transport ship, I made a few new friends. I found we had a few traits in common: a love of reading, laughing, and exploring. In order to avoid embarrassing faux pas on their part, I always made everyone aware of my background and religious affiliation.

One evening while lounging in the ship library, one of the crewmen asked, "Can I ask you a hypothetical question? I'm just curious. If the U.S. declared war on Israel, would you be willing to fight against the Jews? Would you be willing to shoot at them?"

I was startled and caught off-guard, but found a truthful answer. "Didn't the Americans of German, Italian, and Japanese descent fight with distinction for America in World War II? My answer is, 'Yes!' If it ever comes to that unfortunate situation, I will prove my loyalty to my new country, America," I replied.

The crewman and some of the others around us smiled, slightly embarrassed. He got up and touched my shoulder. "I knew you would. I had no doubt, Fathi," he said and left the room.

I thought that there had been more to this simple question. There was bigotry lurking just bellow the surface. For the rest of the trip, we didn't speak to each other.

Did you ever meet an honest, hard-working Jew?"

One of my best friends in Korea was a Midwesterner whom I will call Roger. We bunked about thirty feet apart in the same barracks, separated by four other beds. He was a religious young man, who attended church every Sunday, always carrying his own personal Bible with him. Unlike me, Roger never visited the village girls and the Mamma-sans, at least at first. He was an avid reader so we always had much to discuss. We had long conversations on philosophy, literature, poetry, and history. I really cherished his friendship.

Roger was inducted into the Army a few weeks after he had become engaged to be married. He showed me pictures of his wife-to-be with great pride. He often sat by the table lamp late at night, writing letters to his fiancée. He always expected a letter from her every week, and always got one. I admired them both. I hoped that someday after our tours of duty, Roger and I would get together with our wives and children.

Besides my regular Army job in the Electric Department, Roger knew that I was an Army-certified linguist, fluent in five languages, a trait that he respected very much and seemed amazed by. Occasionally, he scribbled down a few words and expressions in English and would ask me to translate them into Arabic, Hebrew, or Portuguese. I readily obliged him, and he tucked the paper neatly into his pocket. I never knew what he did with them.

Roger and I had another obsession. We both loved to volunteer our services to the local orphanages. We loved the big-eyed children who always expected us on Saturday evenings and Sunday mornings. We each had our favorite kids, whom we showered with gifts and candy and had photographed on many occasions. We developed the film by ourselves and printed scores of memorable photos.

One day, as we did every morning, we stood in the bathroom shaving, towels wrapped around our waists and shaving cream smeared on our faces. He asked, "Did you ever meet an honest, hard-working Jew?"

I was flabbergasted. Where did this come from so suddenly? I stopped shaving and looked at him puzzled. I was so shocked; I could not utter a word.

"Come on, Saul. What's the matter? Can't we be honest after all these months of close friendship?" he asked with a smirk on his face. "Have you ever, in all your travels, met an honest, hard-working Jew?" he repeated. "It's a simple question."

Finally, I found my voice. "Yes, Roger," I answered, "I meet him every morning when I stand here and shave. He appears mysteriously in the mirror."

Roger's face wrinkled as he tried to figure out what I said. Then, the answer sank in, and he looked embarrassed. He evidently must have thought that I was an Arab, a Muslim, because of my name and command of Arabic. Roger cleaned the shaving cream from his face with a towel even though he had not finished shaving. He walked over to me and put his hand on my shoulder. "I am very, very sorry, Saul. I thought you were an Arab," he admitted. "I apologize. I was out of line. Will you forgive me?"

Although I was appalled by his bigoted question, I felt convinced he was sincerely sorry. I nodded acceptance of his apology and became determined to educate him about myself and Jews in general. "For your information," I told him, "I was born in Baghdad, Iraq. As such, yes, I am Arab by nationality, but I am Jewish by religion and heritage."

Roger looked even more confused. "But you don't look like a Jew," he exclaimed.

I tried to manage a tolerant smile because he obviously was ignorant of much of the world except for his small part of the Midwest. "I may not look like the Jews you are familiar with in the States," I explained, "but neither would Jesus, if he were to suddenly appear before us right now."

Roger looked intrigued. "What do you mean, Saul?" he asked in subdued voice. "Explain it to me."

I wiped my face clean. As I began to get dressed, I explained, "Jesus was a Jew, born in Bethlehem, where Israel is now. He was not a blue-eyed blond like yourself. He was brown-skinned and black-haired like many in the Middle East, like me. He looked more like me than like you." Then I smiled. "Skin color is only an external pigmentation; my friend. We all have the same blood flowing in our veins. We all sprung from a common source, making us brothers, members of the one human race. We should love one another."

"Of course, Saul, of course, I agree," Roger said reassuringly. He thanked me for clarifying things, but I could tell he was still uneasy because of his insensitive question. It would take months of effort on my part to restore our friendship to where it once was. From then on, I knew that whenever friendship sprouted between Gentile (a non-Jew) and myself, I would introduce my religion as soon as possible to avoid the embarrassment and misunderstanding that Roger experienced.

After breakfast that day, Roger followed me to my office at the Electric Department. "Tell me more, Saul. I want to learn about your people. I thought I knew all about Jews, but I feel real ignorant."

I hesitated. Then I decided to give him a comprehensive history of my people. I also pointed out the subtle prejudices that had always seemed to lurk under the surface.

"Roger, my people are 5,000 years old," I said. "They were one of the first people to advance the revolutionary idea of Monotheism, the belief in one God. It is these people who gave the world the Bible (the Old Testament) and the Ten Command-ments. You must have learned this in your own church, didn't you?"

"Yes, of course, I did, but not the way you put it," he admitted. "Go on, please. I want to know more."

"As to the subject of hard work, do you know that nearly thirty percent of all Nobel Prize winners were Jews? Do you think this is achieved by being a lazy, unproductive part of society?"

Roger was looking at me intently. He didn't need to answer my question since it was really rhetorical.

"The Jews comprise less than one-tenth of one percent of the world's population and less than three percent of the U.S. population, yet look at our contributions to science, engineering, chemistry, medicine, literature, etc. Are these accomplishments not the products of hard work? Being innovative, industrious, energetic?"

Roger nodded, "Go on, please."

"And since you and I are in the military, do you agree that the atomic bombs we dropped on Japan helped end the Great War and saved millions of lives? Did you know that the Manhattan Project was organized and directed by Jewish scientists, such as Robert Oppenheimer, Leo Szilard, Edward Teller (principle developers of the Hydrogen bomb)? Not to mention Einstein's contribution to the world." I was on a roll, and I had Roger's full attention.

"But then there is the other side. There were countless pogroms (brutal ethnic raids) in Eastern Europe, the Spanish Inquisition, and the expulsion of the Jews from Spain, not to mention the horrors of the last war's Holocaust, when six million of our people were annihilated by the Nazis, just for being born Jewish.

There were over a million children under the age of ten who died by Nazi hands."
By now I was getting angry at the injustices my people had suffered. I didn't
want to go down this road so I turned the discussion to more positive points.

"If you ever are fortunate enough to visit the Holy Land—Israel—one of the
youngest countries in the world, you will be amazed by its achievements and the
total emulation of U.S. Democracy. It's the only democracy in the Middle East. It
is one of the most ardent supporters of the United States and its ideals, a true and
loyal ally. There is only one race, Roger,—the Human Race—and we must live
by only one universal rule: brotherly love." At that point, my voice quivered with
emotion. "We must eradicate all hatred and prejudice, Roger."

I stopped talking and turned back to my work. I began reading the flight
logbooks, getting ready for the day's many duties.

Roger sensed that I said all that I wanted to say on the subject for the
moment. "Thanks very much, Saul," he said. "Let's pick up where we left off
some other time. Again, I apologize. Forgive me. Let's stay best friends."

Roger and I tried hard to restore our trust and mutual respect. Regretfully, we
both failed. I had forgiven him completely, but he hadn't forgiven himself. Yet
strangely, I felt guilty for his pain.

It reminded me of a story my father told me years ago. It takes place in India.
During an annual harvest procession led by a king riding a huge elephant, a
multitude of villagers lined up along the road, shouting praise and prayers and
tossing flowers. This went on for several hours.

Toward the end of the festivity, an aristocrat noticed that he had been
standing on the foot of a local Buddhist monk as he had jockeyed to get the best
view of the festivities. "Forgive me please," he told the priest. "Have I stood on
your foot all this time? I am terribly and genuinely sorry. Please pardon me."

The monk raised his head and clasped his hands together as if in prayer. "No,
Sahib, I beg your forgiveness for causing you the pain of guilt. Please bestow
your kindness on my poor soul."

I felt exactly like the Buddhist monk.

Twelve months later, we were discharged from the Army, Roger and I
eventually got married and started our families. I often thought of Roger and
wished to God I could find him and get our families together. Will fate reunite
us? I am still searching for the universal brotherly love.

Roger, my dear friend, (you know who you are) if you are reading these
lines, then get in touch with me. Yes, let's pick-up where we left off forty-five
years ago, as you had suggested back then in Korea.

Chapter Fifty-Two

Local Korean Relations

UN Security Forces and the Korean economy

During my service with the US Army in Korea, I learned first hand about the great disparity between life in the United States and life in less developed countries. Like the State of Israel, South Korea needed to maintain a strong army to defend its borders, thus dedicating a great portion of their GNP to defense. The Korean people by and large were poor, with few social and government services. If you were born into poverty, it was a certainty that you, your children, and grandchildren would die poor and destitute.

Add to that the unfortunate constant comparison between Korean citizens and us, members of the U.N. security force, who were guarding the South Korean border. To them, we were lavished with high pay and great food, and supplemented by hazardous duty benefits. The result was that an average US Army soldier's salary exceeded that of an elected Korean official. There was much envy on the part of the Korean citizens, notwithstanding the fact that we were there to protect them. To them, we were actually protecting our turf by keeping the enemy far from US shores.

We were periodically lectured by our superiors to be sensitive to these feelings and to avoid entanglement with the general populace. Even visiting the young prostitutes and Mamma-sans in the villages was considered offensive to some of the Korean people. Some soldiers ended up in the stockade for mistreating Korean prostitutes or cheating them out of their earnings.

Though it might be misconstrued as a display of our financial superiority, soldiers were encouraged to help the local Koreans by spending their pay for necessary services. The laundering and pressing of our clothes, even the shoe-shine services, were provided by South Korean natives. Their restaurants and bars could not possibly exist without the soldiers spending their entire salaries. At the time, some seven years after the armistice was signed, there were upwards of 50,000 US soldiers in South Korea. This had a profound effect on the country's economy and their emergence from poverty. It was absurd to think that any of our leaders ever expected the South Koreans to reach a position of not needing us there. It was a classic conflict of interest.

Some of the US military compounds were situated directly next door to the old villages. Not only could you observe Koreans working in the rice fields, walking to school, or doing their laundry, you could actually hear them talking and playing their music. At the end of each day, our KP's would bring out the kitchen leftovers and dump them in huge metal dumpsters, to be taken the following day to the top of the hill, set on fire, and reduced to ashes.

During the night, the neighboring villagers usually sneaked into the dumpsters, rummaged through the leftovers, and took out what they could eat and use to sustain their families. The US military powers-that-be didn't like that. Signs were posted, in Korean and in English, prohibiting any garbage looting. Sometimes, an overnight guard was even posted to prevent this looting by the locals.

There was no sensitivity in this instance to fostering goodwill between the Koreans and us, the rich, foreign guests in their country. The kitchen scraps and leftovers could have been distributed to the poor. Today, forty-five years later, restaurants in New York City near my home and in other cities across the country gather their leftovers and send them to local missions and soup kitchens that serve the poor and the homeless. The US military could have done the same in Korea, but they lacked imagination.

Revenge of the Turks

Not too far from my compound in South Korea, there was another base manned by soldiers from several countries, including Turkey. The soldiers there resented having to enforce these stupid rules against garbage looting by standing guard all night. An enterprising group of them decided to "teach these fucking Koreans" a lesson that would make them stop coming to steal food from the garbage cans.

One night, they caught a Korean teenager rummaging through the garbage and sorting out bread, fruit, and vegetables that he though he and his family could eat. The soldiers brought him into one of the barracks, held him against a boiling potbelly stove that heated the barracks. The stove was red-hot and scorched the back and the stomach of the youth. As the soldiers took turns torturing the boy, they watched and drank ice-cold beer. The youth screamed as his skin became severely blistered. Not yet satisfied, one of the soldiers tried to hang the boy by inserting a rifle-cleaning rod through his ears. As blood gushed through his ears and mouth, the boy nearly passed out.

Finally, one of the soldiers decided that the boy had learned his lesson. They took him outside the gates of the camp and threw him on the cold ground. They left him there to die in the freezing cold.

When the teenager was late returning home, his brother was sent to check up on him. The brother discovered the boy moaning, curled into fetal position on the ground in a pool of blood. The brother managed to gather him up and take him home. His horrified family immediately went to their village elder to complain. The elder summoned the police. Within hours, all hell broke loose. Hundreds of villagers converged on the U.N. compound, escorted by dozens of police, clubs in hands, ready to storm the compound and set it on fire.

The commotion roused the military police within the compound. They wanted to avoid any indiscriminate retaliation from taking place on either side of the incident. Since the boy had stayed in his hut, attended to by medics from the police, there was no one at the compound to identify his attackers. Justice couldn't be served, according to the military police's point of view. The crowd was outraged. The noise and the screaming of the crowd continued into the morning.

For the next two days, every newspaper in the country carried photos of the injured boy. A great uprising of the population spread throughout the country. There were even riots in the capital of Seoul.

The generals of both UN and South Korean forces were alarmed, to say the least. They conferred continuously for days to try to calm the Korean people, making public apologies and conducting newspaper interviews, trying to assure the people that something was being done. But the Korean people wanted revenge. They demanded the surrender of the guilty soldiers so that local Koreans could administer their kind of justice to them. However, the Turkish soldiers who had perpetrated this heinous act were hastily flown out of Korea, back to their native country.

All of us UN soldiers were lumped into the category of Ugly Imperialists. Life was never the same in South Korea after that incident.

The Stars and Stripes, the military newspaper, hardly covered the unfortunate incident. I doubt it ever reached any American newspaper or magazine, and it definitely didn't make a radio or television story. President Kennedy and the military brass certainly knew something about public relations.

Military ship approaching Pusan Harbor,
Korea, 1961 (60)

Aboard military ship to
Yokohama, Japan, 1961 (61)

Aboard military ship, Yokohama,
Japan, 1962 (62)

Saul with Nagako (Japanese pen pal) in
Nagoya, Japan, 1962 (63)

Saul visited Nagako on Army leave (R&R),
Japan, 1962 (64)

Pen pal Nagako in Tokyo, Japan, 1962 (65)

Nagako Obata, Japan, 1961 (66)

Nagako Obata in traditional Kimono, Japanese pen pal,
Hiroshima, Japan, 1963 (67)

Chapter Fifty-Three

R & R with Nagako in Japan

In August of 1962, I had thirty days leave coming to me. We soldiers could take our R & R in a number of locations. Most of the guys from my unit flew over to Japan because there was more to see and do there. They were especially interested in the prostitutes referred to as *geishas*. The original *geishas*, who were trained from birth, had been part of the social dynamics of Japan for centuries. They never sold sexual favors, but were intelligent companions who offered men company, wit, and diversion, and who knew how to pamper men. Many were entertainers, skilled musicians, singers, and dancers.

After World War II, many prostitutes co-opted the name *geisha* because it was identifiable to soldiers as men's companions. Almost none of these new *geishas* had any training, much less education. They did, however, know how to please men sexually. Tokyo's Ginza district in the 1960s was home to the traditional *geisha*. Many of these *geishas* were well educated. They were great conversationalists, and some even spoke several languages. Almost all of them spoke fluent English.

I decided to spend my leave in Japan as well. But instead of pursuing either of these types of female pleasures, I wanted to spend my R&R with my pen pal, Nagako Obata.

Nagako's correspondence

We had written to each other since we were teenagers; I had been seventeen, and she had been sixteen. We wrote of our countries and cultures as well as our families and friends. Through her letters, I learned a great deal about the history of her country.

Like many Israelis, I had been fascinated by Japan, a country shrouded in politeness and mystery. Japan was one of the countries Marco Polo wrote of in his book, *The Description of the World*, in the 13th century. Because of his facility with languages, Polo became one of the ambassadors of the court of Kublai Khan, the Emperor of China, and visited India, Ethiopia, Madagascar, Ceylon, Siam, Java, and Burma. He was the first European to visit the string of islands that came to be known as the Japans.

Though Marco Polo had introduced the world to this country, it wasn't until 1854 that a treaty brokered by US Commodore Matthew Perry opened up this region for trade. The treaty also insured help for American ships that often were stranded off the Japanese coast because of foul weather. These islands became vital stops for American ships to take on water, coal, and supplies as they traveled the Pacific.

Japan's location and growing power made it a formidable force in the

Pacific. The Sino-Japanese Wars expanded Japan's control not only of its own large island chain but also parts of costal China. During the first Sino-Japanese War (1894-5), Japan and China fought over control of Korea. Japan supported Korea's bid for independence and pushed troops far into China. When the war ended, China not only had to pay high war reparations but also had to cede Korea, Taiwan, and the Pescadores to Japan. Korea, though granted independence, was in truth a Japanese protectorate. China also had to grant Japanese nationals the right to open its own factories and engage in trade in Chinese ports. Under the most-favored-nation clause, this right was extended to Western maritime powers, including the United States.

In 1904, Russia wanted Japan to give up Korea and Manchuria. Thinking it would be an easy victory, Russia actively retaliated when Japan attacked Port Arthur, bottling the Russian fleet. But Russia was mistaken. Japan won battle after battle. The Treaty of Portsmouth, negotiated by US President Theodore Roosevelt in 1905, returned Korea's control to Japan, offered the Liaodong Peninsula, which contained Port Arthur, and continued Japan's management of Manchurian interests. Though the territories ceded to Japan were small, they were important tokens of the acknowledgement of Japan as a pre-eminent power in the Far East. The Russo-Japan War led not only to Russia's abandoning its desire for expansion but also was a direct cause of the Russian Revolution.

Meanwhile, resentment festered in China, but the government was unable to do anything about Japanese control because it lacked a unified infrastructure and an organized military. Japan, on the other hand, grew in strength and wanted even more control of Chinese resources and commerce. By 1937, Japan took China's coastal cities in the second Sino-Japanese War and began pushing further inland until it had taken the capital Nanjing. Nevertheless, fighting continued until 1941. The Chinese could never successfully push back the Japanese because they were too busy fighting among themselves. A new leader, Mao Tsetung, and a new form of government, Communism, began to emerge.

As Japan grew in power, it believed it could take on a major world power like the United States, prompting its attack on Pearl Harbor in 1941. Japan's military tactics included the use of suicide aircraft pilots known by the rest of the world as *Kamikaze*. Among the Japanese, *Kamikaze* referred to a typhoon that saved the country from a Mongol invasion by Kublai Kahn in 1281, so it was an apt appellation by the rest of the world. Often carrying bombs or tanks of fuel, over 2,500 *Kamikaze* planes crashed into Allied ships, sinking 34 ships and damaging 288.

The *Kamikaze* were not experienced pilots, but were young university students with bright promise. They volunteered by the thousands as an act of loyalty to Emperor Hirohito and Japan or as a way to bring honor to their families and their ancestors. Some may have volunteered to prove their manhood. After all, *hari Kari*, ritual suicide, was an honorable way out of many embarrassing situations in order to save face.

It may have been this deep sense of saving face, and not necessarily the casualties, that prompted Emperor Hirohito to finally agree to surrender after the bombing of Hiroshima and Nagasaki.

The peace that was negotiated by General Macarthur, the Allied supreme commander in the Pacific, created a new Japan that prevented its becoming a major military force again and also sowed the seeds for Japan's future economic success. Macarthur's staff drafted a new Japanese constitution that held the framework for a free society. Drawing heavily from the US Bill of Rights and the Constitution, Macarthur's team included universal adult suffrage, marriage and property rights for women, the right of the labor force to organize, and the abolition of the feudal land system. The most important provision in the new constitution was Article 9, which forbade Japan from creating a military and denied them the right to wage war.

By focusing away from weaponry and building a military machine, Japanese creativity and energy was diverted to rebuilding, developing new industry, and creating commercial networks around the world. Business and manufacturing advisors from the US came to Japan and used the Japanese team work ethic to its best advantage. The automotive industry and electronics soon flourished.

General Macarthur's only regret about administrating the Japanese occupation was his failure to convert the Japanese to Christianity. He felt that no true democracy could exits without a Christian spiritual foundation. Notwithstanding, the ancestor and meditative religions of Japan, Shintoism and Buddhism, were already in place and provided the spiritual grounding for the country's democracy to flourish.

As Nagako and I continued to write each other over the years, we began to confide in each other, realizing that this other person so far away was really the only one who understood our own hearts. We wrote regularly, except when I made my ocean voyage to Brazil. While in South America, I became preoccupied with trying to find work and my next meal. Through my darkest days in Brazil, I didn't write Nagako. I was reluctant to reveal that pain to anyone. Later, I also became emotionally involved with another young woman, and I was distracted by this new joy in my life. When that relationship did not work out, I made plans to go to America.

My military service eventually took me ever closer to Nagako's home and spurred me to renew our friendship. On board ship on my way to Korea, I had wired Nagako, asking to meet her in Okinawa. She agreed, and we had a pleasant dinner together. Unfortunately, I had been disillusioned by that first meeting. I had hoped that she would have been more fluent in English and a bit more poised. She was shy and awkward and we resorted to writing notes to each other, because that was the best way to communicate clearly.

Whirlwind sightseeing tour

That summer, I flew over to Tokyo and met Nagako at the airport. She had agreed to be my guide and show me some of her favorite places. We traveled mostly by train. They were clean and fast, with white cloths covering the headrests. Food vendors pushed carts down the middle of each train car, allowing us to select from what was available. It was convenient. We didn't have to leave our seats to find space in a dining car. We could just buy something and continue our conversation. I particularly enjoyed the experience because it was the first time I had sampled, authentic Japanese food.

Nagako and I continued to communicate by writing notes to each other. Though her spoken English was rough, she could read and write it very well. As we wrote notes to each other, the passengers on the train looked at us with sympathy, thinking that we were deaf and dumb.

The first stop on Nagako's itinerary was a visit to her elderly uncle in Hiroshima, where she made her home. After nearly fifteen years, the destruction brought by the first atomic bomb was not that visible, except for several sad memorials. Trees and grass were growing everywhere, proving the scientists wrong who had predicted nothing would be able to grow there for a hundred years. Nagako lived with her uncle and taught in a local primary school. I was warmly welcomed by her uncle who immediately offered me a dip in the family communal bath.

After a few days with her uncle, Nagako and I boarded another train and started off on a lengthy sightseeing tour. The first place we explored was Tokyo. Known as Edo before 1868, Tokyo was a castle town in the 16th century, growing in power to a political center by 1603. After the Meiji Restoration, the emperor moved the capital to Edo and changed its name to Tokyo, which means "Eastern Capital." Much of Tokyo was destroyed by the Great Kanto Earthquake in 1923 and the Allied air bombing during 1945.

Nagako wanted to take me to the historic Uogashi or riverside fish market, which had been in continuous existence since the 1500s. I knew I could never abide the smell. Nagako said quietly that there were more things for sale there than just fish, but I wouldn't agree to go. I hoped that this disagreement wouldn't set a tone for the rest of our trip. Nagako, however, was the epitome of politeness and quickly suggested a tour of historic buildings in downtown Tokyo. We also walked through the Ginza district where the teahouses were and the *geishas* lived.

Nara was our next stop. Here, rice was first cultivated in the third century BCE as immigrants from China and other Asian countries settled there and brought rice cultivation techniques with them. Nara is famous for its high rice yields and its Yamato watermelon. This area also has native forests that became a source of lumber for rebuilding after World War II. In addition, textiles and pharmaceuticals are manufactured there. But what drew us were the historic temples and Buddhist images that have been restored in the region.

We were given a special treat when we went to Kyoto. The site of Japan's capital from 794 to 1868, Kyoto also held the emperor's residence. Kyoto Gosho or the Kyoto Imperial Palace burned down and was moved to several different locations throughout the city. The one that Nagako and I saw had been built in

1855. (The current emperor resides in the Tokyo Imperial Palace.)

Also in Kyoto is Nijo Castle, another palace, but this one was built by Tokugawa Leyasu, the founder of the Edo Shogunate, in the early 1600s. We were told that Ninomaru or "secondary castle," a beautifully appointed building with delicate gingerbread carvings on its roof peaks, had wooden floors that squeaked like nightingales when walked upon. It was an old-fashioned security system to prevent intruders.

Osaka, Japan's first capital in the 7th century has become a tourist Mecca. Known as the water capital, Osaka had many beautifully designed bridges, and offered cruises along its landscaped riverbanks. We also visited the Floating Gardens, a contemplative place within the heart of Osaka. Nagako told me that Osaka was where Kabuki Theater, the tea ceremony, and flower arranging had been developed into high art forms. We saw examples of some of these arts and also sampled the world-renown food Osaka had to offer because of its location as a port city. As we strolled along Midosuji Street, I marveled at all of the Gingko trees with their fan-shaped leaves that lined the avenue.

At one point near the end of our long sightseeing trip, we checked into a quaint, little inn and were offered one room with one very low bed, built almost on the floor. Since it was the only bed available, we both climbed into it. Having Nagako only a few inches away from me kept me awake. I knew I had to be a gentleman, but here was someone I was growing fond of, and she was so unattainable. Unsure whether she was asleep either, I decided to get up and take a walk to clear my thoughts and cool my desire.

As I rose with all of these thoughts in my head, I slipped and fell against the rice-paper divider, putting my limbs through the delicate panels. I was petrified and ashamed as I struggled to my feet. I stared at the destruction, not knowing what to do.

Nagako got up from the bed and came to me. Standing behind me, she put her arms around me, repeating softly, "It's OK. It's OK. Don't worry."

Her innocent comfort gave me strength. I had to do the honorable thing. With Nagako by my side, we walked to the front desk and awakened the sleeping lady clerk. Nagako translated for me, telling her what had happened and that I would pay for the damage.

The lady clerk bowed, clasping her hands apologetically, as if it was her fault that I had caused the damage I did. She kept shaking her head, refusing to accept any money. I took out a one hundred dollar bill and practically threw it on the counter as she continued to protest.

Nagako and I quickly left the lobby. She directed me to the path that led to the garden in behind the inn. Nagako guided me to a bench, and we sat quietly, holding hands. As looked at the garden, I couldn't help marveling at the workmanship, the industriousness, and the love of nature the Japanese possessed. Seeing this great beauty calmed my spirit.

Then, Nagako said softly, with a shy smile, "She thinks we are husband and wife. At least, lovers."

I was surprised Nagako could be so articulate in these matters. I realized also that anything that I said might have me regret it sooner or later. I chose to remain silent. I just smiled.

We got up a bit later and walked over to a small, red, wooden bridge that arched over a shallow ravine. There, we found another bench and sat once more, speaking very little.

We spent the entire night alternately walking and sitting in the garden, like ghosts floating among the beautiful plantings. Nagako was a perfect companion. I was determined to remain an honorable gentleman, remembering that in Japan a non-virgin woman could not marry and would most likely be condemned to a life of prostitution. I was not going to condemn her to a life of disgrace. So, we walked and sat, holding hands. I felt heat and love flowing between us, and I resisted escalating this to any higher level. At one point during that long night, we shared the merest kiss, just brushing our lips together and quickly pulling ourselves apart, not risking further contact. Very few words were spoken that night.

Mt. Aso

In the morning, we ate breakfast in a hurry and called a cab to take us to the train station. We headed for our next stop on our tour—Mt. Aso.

Many Japanese people believe that mountains contain spirits, either friendly or evil. That is why they consider many mountains sacred, including Mt Aso and Mt. Fuji. Mt. Aso is a popular sightseeing spot.

Though taking photographs of Mt. Fuji in Tokyo is forbidden by locals, photographing Mt. Aso is permitted. In fact, during the Japanese occupation, US soldiers often sneaked photos of Mt. Fuji and labeled them "Mt. Aso" so that they wouldn't offend the Japanese.

Japan has approximately eighty volcanoes. Mt. Aso is composed of five volcanoes: Mt. Taka, Mt. Naka, Mt. Neko, Mt. Eboshi, and Mt. Kishima. Collectively, they are known as Mt.Aso-Kujyu National Park. Mt. Aso boasts having the largest caldera, or volcanic crater, in the world, measuring 11 miles east to west and 15 miles north to south. Cows and horses graze on the lush grass growing there, and 50,000 people live in towns and villages inside the caldera.

Nagako and I hiked through part of the caldera and climbed up on one of the active domes. We stood at the rim, looking down at the lava bubbling inside as smoke spewed nearby. It was an awesome sight and a little bit frightening to see Nature raw and unpredictable, raging in front of us.

It was then that Nagako told me that this mountain was sacred because it was a favored place for suicides, mostly teenagers in love. I wondered why she wanted to bring me to this place and to tell me that fact. *Did she intend to end her life? Or, horror of horrors, did she expect me to take her hand and leap with her?* I faced the threat of death every time I did guard duty in Korea, and I had come near death so many times in my life, from escaping from Baghdad to electrocuting myself—twice!—to nearly drowning—twice! I certainly had no thought that life meant that little. No, I had no intention of taking my life here with Nagako.

The moment passed, though I could see that there were tears in her eyes. We were both entranced by the beauty and tragedy of it all. We finished our hike and made our way back to town where we got on another train. This time, it was heading back to Tokyo.

Parting from Nagako

At the airport, Nagako and I promised each other that we would continue to write. She had been crying on and off for two days. *Was she terribly disappointed in me? Had she expected me to propose marriage to her?* I had no answers but was sure Nagako would give me no clues as to her expectations.

All I could think of as I left Nagako was getting back to my Army unit and returning to the United States in a few months to complete my education. On the flight back, I wrote a nice, lengthy letter to Nagako, thanking her for her wonderful hospitality and the hospitality of her lovely family. I wished her a happy future. I hoped that I did not hurt her.

Chapter Fifty-Four

Interviews by the Military Newspapers

My story intrigued reporters from military publications. Three stories appeared in two newspapers, *The Bayonet* and *Stars and Stripes.*

The Bayonet article

The first story appeared on December 2, 1960 in *The Bayonet*. *"Ex-Israeli Airman: 7ᵗʰ Cav Recruit Walked Desert to Flee Strife Riddled Nativeland"* by Ken Winslett

"A 22-year old youth who served in the Israeli Air Force at the age of 14 presently is undergoing basic combat training in the 2ⁿᵈ Infantry Division.

Arriving in this country via Brazil in April, Saul Fathi elected to join the U.S. Army rather than face his impeding return to the Middle East. Now, he says he plans to make the Army his career, and professes aspirations of becoming associated with Army aviation.

Flees to Persia

With 18 other youths, Fathi traveled for six weeks, wearing bundlesome clothing for protection against the bitter cold and often going for days without food and drink.

Reaching neutralist Persia, Fathi and his brother stayed in a Teheran youth camp before being evacuated by an Israeli government-furnished plane. Two years later—at the age of 14—he enlisted in the Israeli Air Force, where he remained for four years until his father's ill health forced his return to civilian status.

Taking a job at an Army camp, Fathi continued his schooling through a British correspondence course. Then, on September 19, 1958, Fathi boarded an Israeli boat with the ultimate goal of reaching the United States.

He went to France, where he caught another boat to Brazil. In Brazil, he worked at his own electrical and hydraulic business and in an American nylon factory until his visitor's visa to the United States was approved in March 1960.

Arriving in New York City, he lived with his sister, the wife of an American soldier, and was soon granted a student's visa. He enrolled at the Brooklyn Museum of Art, but diminishing funds forced him to quit in October.

With his student's visa no longer effective, Fathi turned to his only means of staying in this country—he visited an Army recruiter.

After his acceptance, Recruit Fathi was forwarded to Fort Benning for basic combat training with the 3ʳᵈ Reconnaissance Squadron, 7ᵗʰ Cavalry.

In reaching the halfway mark in training, Recruit Fathi says he has decided

to remain in the Army. The ambitious youth now has a new goal: to be an Army pilot."

First *Stars and Stripes* article

Stars and Stripes, Sunday, August 5, 1962
"1ˢᵗ Cav. Electrician: Israeli Veteran Serves in ROK
HQ, U.S. 1ˢᵗ CAV. DIV. Korea
   An Israeli Air Force veteran with a skill in electronics is now serving with the1st Cav. Div. in Korea in hopes of becoming as American citizen.
   PFC Saul S. Fathi, 24, company electrician for the 15ᵗʰ Aviation Co. and the 15ᵗʰ Transportation Detachment worked his way through six countries before reaching the United States. He found the early going difficult, but was helped by his ability to speak five languages—English, Arabic, Hebrew, Spanish, and Portuguese.
   A native of Baghdad, Iraq, Fathi fled to Israel in 1949 during the Arab conflict. He became a citizen of Israel and entered Israel's air force in 1952 as a specialist in electronic work. Discharged in 1956, he worked for an electrical company while attending Hebrew University in Tel Aviv. Meanwhile, he was able to save a little money for his trip to America.
   Because Israel had a small quota for persons entering the U.S., he decided to apply for admission on Brazil's quota. He worked his way through Italy, France, Spain and West Africa to Brazil, where he set up and operated his own electric and hydraulic shop for two years. After obtaining a student visa to enter the U.S., he enrolled at the Brooklyn Museum of Arts in New York.
   In 1960, he joined the U.S. Army where his skill in electronics is paying off. At the 15ᵗʰ Aviation Co., he has designed and built several pieces of electronic equipment, including a multiple test board used in checking electric components from aircraft. He has also designed an aircraft range and speed estimator on which he has a military patent.
   Due for discharge in October, he said he hopes to remain in the United States, continue studying electronics and eventually realize his desire to become an American citizen."

Second *Stars and Stripes* article

Stars and Stripes, August 10, 1962
"15th Aviation. PFC Speaks 5 Languages: Israeli AF Veteran Seeks U.S. Citizenship Via Army 15ᵗʰ AVN. CO
   An Israeli Air Force veteran who speaks fluent English, Arabic, Hebrew, Spanish and Portuguese, and who traveled through six countries to reach the United States and try to become an American citizen, is now serving with the1st Cavalry Div. in Korea.
   PFC Saul S. Fathi, company electrician for the 15ᵗʰ Aviation Co. and the 15ᵗʰ

Transportation Detachment. (Aircraft Maintenance.), was born in Baghdad, Iraq.

In 1949, during the Arab-Israeli conflict, he fled through the underground, entered Israel and became a citizen.

Fathi, 24, entered the Israeli Air Force in 1952, specializing in electronics. He was a member of a flight crew, checking instruments on aircraft while in flight.

Upon his discharge in 1956, he went to work for the Israel Electric Co., attending Hebrew University, Tel Aviv, at night to study political economics.

While working for the electric company and going to school, he was saving money so he could go the U.S. and become a citizen.

The Israel quota for persons entering the U.S. was so small that he decided to try to enter the country through other legal means.

He decided to enter the U.S. through the Brazil quota. Working his way through Italy, France, Spain and West Africa, he arrived in Brazil, where he ran his own electric and hydraulic shop for two years.

Finding out it would take him another four years before he would be able to enter the U.S. through the quota, he decided to enter on a student visa and study at New York University, New York City.

Unable to afford NYU, he enrolled at Brooklyn Museum of Arts, New York City, where he found that under immigration laws he wasn't allowed to work while going to school.

He entered the Army in November 1960, in hopes that it would give him a better chance of becoming an American citizen.

He joined his present unit in July 1961, where he has designed and built a number of electronic pieces, including a multiple test board, used in checking electric components from aircraft.

He has also designed an aircraft range and speed estimator and has been granted a military patent on it.

Fathi is due to be discharged in October and is a little uncertain of his future. If he is able to remain in the U.S., he wants to study at the RCA Victor Electronic Institute in New York and get his engineering degree.

"I want to become a citizen of the United States," said Fathi. "I am willing to do anything for the privilege of becoming an American."

It is amazing to me that each of these articles tells the same story, but none of them have quite gotten the details right. Nevertheless, I was very grateful that these stories were published. They helped put my plight into the public eye—at least, the military eye. I wish I could say that they got the attention of the Immigration Office, but they didn't. It was still some years later that I finally received my green card and became a naturalized US citizen.

Chapter Fifty-Five

Honorable Discharge

On my return from the Far East on October 23, 1962, I was processed out of the Army and given a certificate of Honorable Discharge. I was also given an airplane voucher to get me back to New York, which I promptly traded it in for a Greyhound bus ticket so that I could not only see more of the United States but so that I could have the difference in the fares for spending money. I had an even deeper appreciation of what I hoped would be my new country since my tour in Korea.

As I sat in the back by a window on the bus to New York, I looked out and drew in all the wonderful scenery along the way. At one of the bus stops, a young lady got on and came to sit next to me, putting her pocketbook on the seat between us. It was strange, as there were many empty seats all around me.

She encouraged conversation by telling me that she was the wife of a career sergeant serving in the Navy in the Pacific. She asked me if I was a returning soldier. I was amazed that she could so readily guess that, as I was out of uniform. Later, I found out that she had noticed my Army duffle bag on the rack above me. She was observant but no psychic or Sherlock Holmes. As we continued to talk, I understood that she had not seen her husband for the past five months, that she had a three-year-old son, and that her husband had been called into service less than a week after their marriage. I felt comfortable with this gregarious, young woman and sensed a friendship being forged. I introduced myself and began telling her about myself and all of my travels and escapades. She was fascinated.

At some point, she put her right hand on my knee and moved it up and down my thigh. I was flushed, as people were sitting all around us, although the bus was not full. I began hoping for a bus stop so we could disembark, check into a motel, and spend a few days together. We could always catch another bus to continue our journey.

As I was fantasizing, she became even more aggressive. "My name is Bea. I live in South Carolina with my boy and my mother," she said. "I like you; you're interesting. My life is a bore compare to yours." She smiled at me so enticingly.

"Every life is an interesting story. I am intrigued with yours, too," I said.

I was beginning to be aroused and decided to separate myself from her by going to the bathroom, tucked nearby at the back of the bus. She got up to let me out. I went inside, closed the door, and started splashing cold water on my face. A few second later, Bea pushed the bathroom door open and saw me washing face in the sink. She closed the door behind her and then reached around me, unzipping my pants and squeezing my genitals. I was petrified at her daring. There was hardly room for both of us to stand inside. She put the toilet seat down and sat on it, then began to perform oral sex on me.

"Bea, please," I protested. "The other passengers may have seen us go in here. Bea, let go of me. "We'll get off at the next stop and pickup where we left off, I promise"

But there was no stopping Bea. She opened her blouse, baring her breasts by pulling down her bra and grabbed my hands to caress their firmness. It was awkward. She was breathing heavily by then. I urged her again to stop and threatened to open the door and let everyone see what she was doing.

Finally she relented. "I'm sorry, sweetheart," she said, her eyes fixed on the floor. "It's been a long time. I'm so lonely." As she began buttoning her blouse, I got out of the bathroom and rushed back to my seat, and sat there looking out the window. I was very embarrassed and couldn't tell if anyone had noticed what had just taken place in the back of a Greyhound bus. A few minutes later, Bea emerged and sat across from me, two seats away. We didn't speak for hours.

At the next stop, we both took down our belongings and got off the bus. We bought cold sodas from a kiosk and sat down together on a nearby bench, trying to decide what to do. The bus driver then called out, "All board," just like on a train. But, we just sat there and stared at each other. After the bus had pulled out and went on its way toward New York, we stood up and finally hugged.

"Let's have a snack," I suggested. "Are you hungry?"

She nodded, with a sneaky smile. "You boys always feel hungry after you have had your fun," she said. I had a feeling that she knew that was true all too well. I was certain that this hadn't been her first time seducing another soldier.

We spent two days together, staying in our room all day and going out only at night. We finally boarded another bus and continued on toward New York. We exchanged addresses, and we promised each other to write since neither of us had a telephone.

We went our separate ways. I arrived in New York. Days turned into months and months into years. Neither one of us ever wrote the other, and that was probably just as well. I never knew just how big her sergeant husband was.

Section Four: II

(Back to the U.S.A.)

My Life In The U.S.A.

1960 – 2005 (Present)

Chapter Fifty-Six

McDougal Street, Greenwich Village: My personal hideaway

Greenwich Village, New York, 1963. More precisely McDougal Street. To be exact, the Candlelight Café: Peter, Paul & Mary, Joan Baez, and so many young, lesser known folk singers, poets, drunks, haranguers, and beatniks. The air was full of smoke and smelled of beer, alcohol, and who knows what else? Any night of the week, you could show up and there'd be someone standing in front of a mike, playing a guitar, singing a song, reading their lines and rants of poetry for all the world like it meant something, real bohemian style. I hadn't felt this excited by a "scene" since my years as a James Dean fan, trying myself out as an actor, living the life of a future movie star. Years had passed since then, I'd been in the Army, crossed the ocean and back, but here I was living in New York at the start of the huge transformative decade that is now called "The Sixties." At the time, all we knew was that we were young, healthy, idealistic, and in love with the world and its most romantic possibilities. I loved it. For awhile, I believed I had found my spiritual home.

Woody Guthrie had written "This Land Is Your Land" many years before I heard the next generation's voice of the people, Bob Dylan, sing it on McDougal Street at The Bitter End. He was a scrawny Jewish kid with the most unlikable, unlikely voice, yet I knew that I was witnessing something important the night I heard him wheeze out every verse and chorus of Guthrie's tribute to America and the different shades of people who lived here, all across its wide vast map: "from California to the New York Islands/This land was made for you and me."

I heard Dylan sing "Blowin in the Wind":

How many roads must a man walk down
Before you can call him a man?

When those lyrics came through loud and clear to my smoke-filled, alcohol-hazed, dreamy mind, I snapped alert, wondering if I had yet walked down enough roads to finally be called a man. Though I had lived in many countries, and traveled many seas, there was a part of me that knew manhood would ask still more of me before I could call myself "a man."

Mama Kass (Elliott) was big and fat and not the most attractive woman I had ever seen, but when she opened her mouth to sing, she transformed into an angel, with a voice like silk and satin. I was enthralled with the heart and emotion her songs gave out, and I was really surprised when she brought me to tears singing "Jet Plane," as it called forth all the times I had left, and caused me to remember what "lonesome" really felt like. I knew the feeling well.

All my bags are packed
I'm ready to go
I'm standing here outside your door
Hate to wake you up to say goodbye
But the dawn is breaking
It's early morn
Taxi's waiting
He's blowing his horn
Already I'm so lonesome
I could cry
So kiss me and smile for me
Tell me that you'll wait for me
Hold me like you'll never let me go
I'm leaving on a jet plane
Don't know when I'll be back again
Oh babe, I hate to go....

I tried hard to make myself a meaningful life during the days of my soul-searching in that sweet era in Greenwich Village. I suppose everything I did to improve my life along the way has added up to make me feel like a lucky and prosperous man, but it was at night when my heart came to life that year, when I sat smoking Kents in those ill-lit clubs listening to the poets speak in rhyme and the saxophones wail. The night Bob Dylan played harmonica and sang "The Times They're a-Changin'" I and everyone else in the room had a deep feeling he was on the big pulse of something, and that not everything about the changin' would be easy. Outside people were shouting and marching in the streets: Stop the War in Vietnam, Civil Rights, Women's Liberation, Abortion Rights, Power to the People, Make Love Not War. Across the street: America, Love It or Leave It. The songs, the poetry reflected these calls to action, responses to government policies, amassing the will of the people to fight for change, overthrow the establishment. America was founded in 1776 by rebellious, restless pioneers. "Live Free or Die" was their motto. Ten years before America's Bicentennial, this remained the mantra, as Dylan rallied forces through song.

Come gather round people, wherever you roam
And admit that the waters around you have grown
And accept it that soon you'll be drenched to the bone
If your time to you is worth saving
So you better start swimming, or you'll sink like a stone
For the times, they are a-changin'

I had never been a good swimmer, I had almost drowned more than once in my life; still, I wanted to be part of the changing tide. I wasn't sure how, at that point, but I trusted the poets to lead me on.

Song writing experiment

I had returned from service in the Far East a changed man, a grownup, an American soldier. I loved the Village and its energetic voices crooning soulfully in every dive and doorway. I felt I needed to nurture my soul, be a part of all that, so I tried my hand at writing down some of the songs that I used to hear running through my thoughts as I was falling off to sleep onboard some big military ship, or in the middle of doing some especially unpleasant Army chore, like cleaning latrines or standing guard. I searched on New York City's Broadway, that wide boulevard of hopes and dreams, for a studio where I could "cut" a record. I found a small place on the fourth floor of a building in Times Square. Most of the people I met there were amateur musicians trying to eke out a living. They met me at the door and embraced me as a newcomer.

The head of the company asked me to follow him to his office. His tiny office was piled high with music sheets, one desk, one chair, and a small piano in the corner.

"So you want to cut a record, ha?" he beamed. "Lots of dreams are made here. Who knows? You might have a hit on your hands!"

I smiled, feeling confidence and a welcoming atmosphere.

Next door, I could hear a trumpet. I began fantasizing.

"Yeah, I want to try this star-maker route, before I have to settle down to some serious job and earn a decent living."

He smiled. "Like I said, this is where dreams are made. You've come to the right place. Now, do you know anything about this business? It's not cheap, you know!"

I hesitated.

"No, not really. But I'm here to learn. Tell me more."

"You will need to hire at least four musicians, maybe five: a piano, a clarinet, a drum, and two guitars. That's the minimum. It might take an hour, it might take longer, it all depends. There are different charges for each instrument. Altogether it will cost you about $350 an hour. When we finish recording your song on tape, then we cut your records. They cost $50 each, as many as you want."

He leaned back in his chair, and waited for my reaction.

"Wow, $350 an hour?" I tried not to sound as disappointed as I felt. I always went into things with the highest hopes, without thinking through the reality, like what it might cost me.

"You will also want to hire a singer, unless you plan to sing your own songs." He paused to light a cigar. "I don't recommend you trying to sing your own songs." He stretched his legs over his desk. He was pretending to be a big shot with his big cigar, to appear successful and prosperous (somehow I had a feeling he wasn't all that successful but I ignored that).

I thought it over and surprised myself by saying, "Okay, when can we start? I am ready to try one hour."

He blew smoke into the air.

"One hour? I can't assemble musicians for just one hour. These are professional, proud people, you know. But, let me see what I can do."

He wrote up an invoice in his bound book. When he handed me the piece of paper, I noticed he did not write a total. Only $350 per hour, plus the cost of a singer.

I folded the paper and tucked it in my pocket, saying nothing more.

"No, no, my friend. You sign this contract and give me half the cost now and half when I hand you the record."

I studied the paper then surrendered to my own wild plan, signed it, and scrambled to find that much money in my wallet.

"Here's $250 for now. Can you trust me?"

He laughed, "Yeah, I trust you. My instinct tells me you're a straight shooter. Besides, if you screw around with me you'll be blacklisted in the music industry, and you'll never set foot in any studio, anywhere. I'll call you in a few days when I have a crew ready."

In a few days I was called as promised. I showed up with my handwritten song lyrics and musical notes all lined up on crisp white sheets. We played music for two and a half hours, and it was a lot of fun—until I was handed the bill for a total of $1,150. Including the singer and two accompanists. (by the way, the records and the lyrics were destroyed in a basement flood in Huntington, some thirty years later).

What did I have to show for what was over 12-months rent on my apartment? I got two 45rpm records of scratchy sound quality and not the world's greatest musical artists, to tell the truth.

I never set foot in that (or any other) studio again, nor did I try to promote the record. I was disappointed; felt cheated.

I came upon these early attempts at expressing my soul one day when I was clearing out some old drawers in a bureau I hadn't looked into in years. At least I was able to show my daughters, all these years later, their father's "sensitive poet" side, with some pride. It didn't sound so bad. Maybe I should have done more to promote it!

Some lyrics from some of my songs:

Your gentle hug I feel
Your sweet skin I smell
My wounds did not yet heal
In my eyes the tears well
My little girl, only days or a few hours
Since I saw you last, a little girl like a flower.
How many years have passed?

And if this place I leave
and mountains I'll climb—

Is this enough to achieve?
Will my life be worth a dime?

Why does my heart ache?
Why do my eyes cry?
Soon these chains will break
and back to you I'll fly.

"Poetry is the shorthand of wisdom,"

I had written in the margins of one of my "songbooks." Ah, the wise and emotional outpourings of youth.

The Miracle of America: "This I believe"

I still have this book. I have treasured it all these years. It was compiled by the renowned journalist Edward R. Morrow, attesting to the greatness of America and its great people.

Quotes:

"... Life is a continuous series of adjustment to reality..." (Robert G. Allman)

"... Cast your bread upon the water and it will come back to you in abundance... Spirituality is the needed seasoning to America's materialism..." (Dr. Samuel M. Best)

"... I try to suit my aspirations to goals within my probable capacity to attain... Death teaches us the things of deathlessness...(Carroll Binder)

"... Money is a wonderful thing, but it is possible to pay too high a price for it..." (Alexander Bloch)

"... Hatred cannot last unless it is continuously nourished and stimulated..." (Dr. Edmund A. Brasset)

"... War is only a cowardly escape from the problems of peace..." (Thomas Mann)

"... Nothing that can happen to you is half so important as the way in which you meet it..." (Unknown)

"... I enjoy life because I am endlessly interested in people and their growth... The human heart is born good...It is a contest between ignorance and death, or wisdom and life. My faith in humanity stands firm..." (Pearl S. Buck)

"... Freedom is a child of truth and confidence..." (James B. Carey)

"... No man is an island... The dishonesty of any one man subverts all honesty..." (Carroll)

"... The unexamined life is not worth living..." (Socrates)

"... The most important thing in the world is the freedom of the mind. All progress and all other freedoms spring from that..." (Elmer Davis)

"... I discredit credulity, or blind faith. The progress of man is based on disbelief of the commonly accepted…Not all hard truths are beautiful, but beauty is truth…" (J. Frank Dobie)

"… It is better to love the good than hate the bad…" (Unknown)

"… Half the battle is won if I can face trouble with courage, disappointment with spirit, and triumph with humility…Defeat may be the forerunner of final victory…The opportunity for happiness and the happiness of attainment are all too often lost in the chase itself…" (Nelson Glueck)

"… We shall have overcome one of the largest obstacles to a solution of man's favorable relationship with man when we know and acknowledge how little we know about ourselves…" (Lewis B. Hershey)

"… The years teach much which the days never know…" (Emerson)

"… There is a destiny that makes us brothers, none goes his way alone. All that we send into the lives of others, come back into our own…" (Edwin Markham)

"… Ye shall know the truth, and the truth shall make you free…Man is basically good in heart, spiritually indestructible, and his place in the sun is assured…" (H. Lloyd Jordan)

"… A satisfactory life must be measured by its usefulness to others… There are no visible limits to the heights to which mankind can rise…" (Mrs. John G. Lee)

"… We get out of life is in direct proportion to what we put into it… I owe life as much as it owes me…Respect begets respect. Suspicion begets suspicion. Hate begets hate… The only way to have a friend is to be one…" (Herbert H. Lehman)

"… Faith is the thing at the core of you., the sediment that's left when hopes and illusions are drained away… Men need a religious belief to make sense out of life…" (C. Day Lewis)

"… Anger is a waste, it hurts nobody but me…The great tragedy of life is not to be needed…Your mind will die if you lose your curiosity…" (Lillian B. Mc Cue)

"…No one ever finds life worth living, one always has to make it worth living…" (Richard H. Mc Feely)

"… I was never given more to bear than I could endure…I came to realize that suffering is universal, it's part of one's essential learning process…" (Mrs. Marty Mann)

"… Life is possessed by tremendous tenacity… With the aid of time, man becomes capable of wresting the immortal from the mortal…" (Thomas Mann)

"… Once an individual has a fair start he or she can rise to great heights, regardless of circumstances of birth or racial origin…It is for those who are strong to help the weak…" (Newbold Morris)

"…If I am foolish enough to think that I see all there is to be seen in front of my eyes, I simply miss the glory… We walk humbly before the great unknown…" (Harry A. Overstreet)

"... Laugh and the world laughs with you, weep and you weep alone..."
(Unknown)

"...I am pretty much of a fatalist. You have to accept whatever comes and the only important thing is that you meet it with courage and with the best that you have to give..." (Eleanor Roosevelt)

"...My happiness must come from within myself. I can't get back anything I don't give out...Laughter is a great soul cleanser..." (Virginia Sale)

"... I believe in the innate dignity of the individual... People are as we choose to find them. Reason can overcome prejudice, knowledge can overcome ignorance, love can overcome hate, and goodness can conquer evil..." (Dore schary)

"... If we are to transform the world, we must begin first by transforming ourselves..." (Francis Bacon)

"... Everything potent, from human love to atomic energy, is dangerous; it produces ill about as readily as good...No right comes without responsibility..." (Wallace Stegner)

"... War is evil, social injustice unendurable. Religion is incomplete without service...Sorrow and suffering give opportunities for growth..." (Elizabeth Gray)

"... We must understand in order to live richly within ourselves, and usefully to others. Misunderstanding and suspicions come from ignorance...Happiness is the by-product of service...We can never build happiness on the misery of other people...Growing old should be a rich summation of experience, not a decay..." (Constance Warren)

"... One should never expect any other reward from charity than the satisfaction it gives..." (Darryl F. Zanuck)

"... A thread of permanence runs through everything from the beginning of time, and the most valuable residue will survive..." (William Zorach)

Hot soup and chili at Horn & Hardart

Horn & Hardart was an old-fashioned coffee shop that became world-famous for its coin-operated "automats," a vending machine style of serving pre-made food such as sandwiches, thus becoming the first "fast-food restaurant in the U.S. Founded in 1888 in Philadelphia by Joseph Horn and Frank Hardart, they served "fresh-brewed coffee," freshly roasted, fresh-ground beans brewed using the drip method, a radical idea in a time when coffee was more typically thin, overboiled, tasteless dreck. When the partners expanded their operations to New York, they became the first restaurant "chain" in America. I liked to stop there in the mornings, as an American way to start my day as an American, and watch the commuters as they hurried off to do business, properly caffeinated, wiping donut sugar from their lips as they passed through the revolving doors. A sign inside the door informed me that, "Horn & Hardart feeds upwards of 800,000 daily in the Tri-State Area." At its height, there were over 180 Horn & Hardart throughout New York and Philadelphia.

After my morning coffee, in that period of life when I was still in search of myself (in other words, unemployed and a little bit lost in the world), I lived in New York as a tourist in my own town. I went back to the top of the Empire State Building often, to pay homage to my first day in the United States, to orient myself, to think. The Statue of Liberty held a similar allure for me, as a place to locate myself in space and time, compare my own story to the stories of the millions who had passed through Ellis Island's shores, letting the torch of liberty shine the way to a new home.

From 1892 to 1954, over 12 million immigrants entered the U.S. through Ellis Island, a small island in New York Harbor in the upper bay just off the New Jersey coast, in the shadow of the Statue of Liberty. Standing in the same location where so many others had come here full of the same hopes and dreams as I had, moved me to tears, and I read that this place was once called "The Island of Tears."

Despite the island's reputation as an "Island of Tears" the vast majority of immigrants were treated courteously and respectfully, and were free to begin their new lives in America after only a few short hours on Ellis Island. Only 2 percent of arriving immigrants were excluded from entry.

I read that they could be excluded if they were thought to have a contagious disease, or if they were likely to end up as a "public charge or illegal contract laborer." When I saw that, I wondered: if things didn't start looking up, was it possible that I could fall into one of those categories!

So, at Horn & Hardart, I drank coffee and watched the commuters. At Ellis Island I considered my work life and how I might eventually come to contribute something to my new country; at night I ate dinner at Bilbainia Restaurant, then danced at Roseland or Fred Astair studios, or at the nightclub Port Said. I remember an especially high night at Port Said with my best friend Fuad (Adam) Manzur and two Cuban girls wearing the sexiest red dresses and the highest heels I'd ever seen. But those girls knew how to move on those heels, and it was hard to tell at times that night who was leading whom. Not that it mattered!

The Roseland Ballroom was another place I went to a lot. Roseland had first opened on New Year's Eve in 1919 and it's still there on West 52nd Street, between Broadway and Eighth Avenue, along with the ghosts of Duke Ellington, Benny Goodman, the Dorsey Brothers, and Saul Fathi, who danced there in his more spry and younger days.

Living in the Bronx: Broke and depressed

For a short, desperate time, I lived in the Bronx, on Grand Concourse Avenue. I was attending Fordham University at night, studying literature and religion, and living in a modest apartment with three bedrooms, a kitchen, a bath, and a living room. I rented one room to a young guy my age named Bill Bohmar, who was an aspiring writer, and the other room to a young woman with a five-year-old son. She was nice looking and very attentive to her son and his needs. I knew nothing about her occupation or how she managed her living, but I began to suspect she was a streetwalker, a lady of the night, because she stayed at home most of the day, but then she'd dress up and apply makeup in the evening, tuck her son into bed, and kiss him goodbye. She wouldn't return till the early morning. Sometimes I would still be up reading in the common living room and see her come in. She immediately jumped into the shower, put on one of her sexy nightgowns, and joined me in the living room to drink a cup of coffee.

We never discussed where she had been or what she was doing to "make ends meet," we discussed other things, like Joan Baez or the Beatles. We never mentioned her profession once, not even after she followed me into my bedroom to lie down beside me and we became intimate.

Her excuse the first time was, "My son is sleeping, I don't want to disturb him. Do you mind if I sleep with you tonight?"

I didn't mind, it had been too long since I had done more than dance with a woman, as pretty as she was.

Our roommate, Bill, was aware of this relationship, and never made a move toward her. He had had a sad and painful rejection from a girl he loved, and it seemed he was trying to find himself again, by burying his emotions in his writing. He showed me several unfinished novels about love lost and dark nights of the soul.

Meanwhile, I was enjoying this newfound pleasure of the flesh, at home in my own apartment. At first it felt like harmless free sex, in the spirit of the times, but then our lovely roommate stopped paying rent and I understood that she expected me to cover it, in the spirit of exchange for services rendered. I didn't like thinking of myself as a man who paid women for sex, and I broke it off. She was tenacious though, and eventually it was me who had to move out, to get away from her.

I moved out of the Bronx the day after I met Rachelle, who was to become my wife, a fact I think I probably knew from the moment of our very first meeting. I lost contact with Bill Bohmar and the single mother I slept with, whose name I no longer recall, perhaps with good reason. I was glad to get out of the Bronx, and away from suicidal, moping Bill, and the nameless whore mother. From time to time, I have wondered about them, what became of them and whether they are still alive.

Nagging thoughts of suicide

I had read enough Shakespeare *(Hamlet)*, Sartre *(Nausea)*, and knew well enough the fate of Virginia Woolf, Hemingway and countless other famous suicides, that it would have been remiss of me not to have pondered the possibility of taking my own life during those days of depression and cigarettes.

To be or not to be, that is the question
Whether tis nobler in the mind

To suffer the slings and arrows
Of outrageous fortune
Or, by opposing, end them

My Bronx roommate Bill Bohmar was, at this time of mourning in his life, often inspired to read to me from those famous despairing scribes, because he could identify so well with the brooding sentiment. Lost in the beauty of the poet's call to self-destruct, I listened to Bill recite the clarion words. We sat up talking about the meaning of life and the desire for death long into the nights (while our lady roommate was out on her "dates," her son safely sleeping in the room next door).

We called it our "appointment with destiny" and set a deadline when we would jump out of a top floor of the Summit Hotel on Lexington Avenue. This was our joint fantasy, and we discussed it many times. (Thirty years later I began treatment for depression at the VA hospital in Northport, Long Island, which lasted 5 years, before I was able to extricate myself from the dark forces of thoughts of suicide).

Our roommate probably felt equally as desperate as we did at times, the woman with a child who crashed at our place for free, in return for sex. But we didn't include her in those conversations. We planned our suicides as men, with cold logic and self-centered justifications, in much the same way generals planned equally unjustified wars, I suppose.

I didn't jump that year I lived in the Bronx with Bill Bohmar, the novelist. But there was a time, after I married Rachelle and was a father to two lovely daughters, several business failures later, when I felt a new desire to end it all, a feeling that wasn't so glamorous or poetic as the suicidal longings of youth; something more dark and untenable was seizing my heart.

I felt trapped in my own life, like there was no way out, just like in the movies.

Drive off a bridge?
Crash into a tree?
What if I am crippled instead of dead?

I thought again about jumping from a high window, and remembered my plan with Bill Bohmar, to leap from the Summit Hotel on Lexington Avenue. (I don't know why that was the place we fantasized about.)

I didn't jump then either. I thought the whole thing through, and decided against it. There was my fear of stigmatizing my own children. How would my family collect insurance or support themselves without me? How could I end my own life, when I was a man who loved life?

I am one who lives in the past, and the past was quite colorful. But I was also interested in what the future might hold. Success in business was illusive.

Chapter Fifty-Seven

Upon Returning from Duty in Korea:

My struggle with immigration authorities

I had joined the U.S. Army on the promise that I would be able to finish my college education and remain in the United States as a permanent resident, eligible to work here and live in peace. After I was in Korea for nearly a year when one day I opened a formal typed letter from U.S. Immigration. It stated that I should not be in the military, my recruitment was an unfortunate mistake, and that any law which permitted such action was abolished at the end of the Korean War, in 1953.

Here I was in my uniform, serving my time as a good solider in the U.S. Army, a mere few yards from the dangerous demilitarized zone with North Korea, and subject to annihilation at any moment. Hell, I was even being paid extra for hazardous duty! Yet these so-called authorities wanted to toss me out of the country upon completion of my service duty.

Thanks for your service and sacrifices, goodbye, go back to Brazil.

This was an outrageous insult. Unfair by any standard. Even the prostitutes who wed GIs were allowed to go and live in the States. While Saul Fathi, a good man who was recognized with distinction and written up in the *Stars & Stripes* for devoted service and ingenious inventions put to use by the military, Saul Fathi was being ejected.

I remember I spoke to my direct Officer, Lt. Ronald Nelson, and now as I think back on his kindness to me, I wonder what became of him: *Is he still alive? Did he survive Vietnam? He was a superb helicopter pilot.* He showed great sympathy toward me and expressed his indignation at the Immigration Department. Officer Nelson talked to his superior, Capt. Donahugh, and they both assured me something would be done to help me out.

"You will not be deported, no way, no how," they told me.

The men had an idea: Print out a "brochure" detailing my story and circulate a petition on my behalf, attesting to my positive character and contribution to the army, to be signed by Officers as well as enlisted men serving in Korea, especially within my Division, the First Cavalry. Within two months, we had gathered nearly 1,000 signatures. We made copies and sent the documents back to my New York Senator, Jacob Javits, who was a Republican Senator for 24 years, 1957-81, and Representative in Congress from New York's 21st District, 1947-55. He served in the U.S. Army in World War II, so he was someone who knew what it meant to lay your life on the line in the name of patriotism and duty.

Lt. Nelson sent a copy and letter to his senator in the state of Washington. I was so grateful for their support and willingness to put their names behind it, I wished to kiss their hands and thank them for restoring my faith in America and its great sense of morality and fairness.

After many exchanges with Senator Javits, I received a letter from the White House (this was during the Kennedy administration), assuring me fair treatment upon my discharge from the service. The president personal secretary implored me to be patent and hopeful.

Upon my discharge from service, I was allowed to return from Korea to the States, but my status remained unclear. This made my homecoming feel less than victorious, and at times I felt like such a fool for believing the lies of a government that had merely exploited my best intentions.

I continued to update my Army superiors of my progress, and lack of progress, which culminated in a "Stay of Order of Deportation" pending a court resolution.

The matter dragged on for years. I was allowed to remain in the U.S. and work legally, and it was during this period of "limbo" that I met and married my wife. Rachelle already had a "Green Card" which granted her permanent status. Against my sense of rightness and "what they owed me," I decided to re-petition the Immigration Department on the basis of my marriage to Rachelle, instead of on the basis of my service in the Armed Forces. After a few more years of frustration and disrespect, I was finally granted the cherished, long-sought-after, hard-won Green Card.

If you're so smart, how come you're not rich?

For a while after I returned from the Army, I worked as an electrician for a small New York-based company, managed and owned by an Italian immigrant named Mr. Bataglia. As ever, I was always trying to improve work procedures and reduce project costs. On one of these occasions, after proposing a set of recommendations, Mr. Bataglia sprung up from his seat and lashed at me, with a heavy Italian accent.

"Well, if you're so smart, how come you're not rich? How come you work for me?"

I was taken aback. I looked at him and I noticed the gigantic gold cross on his necklace. I came back with what I thought was a clever reply. "How rich was Jesus? I am sure he was smarter than you and me both."

Mr. Bataglia stared at me with fierce eyes and then apologized.

I thought that was the end of it, but a week later I was fired.

"It is slow now, sorry, I have no more work," he justified.

I nodded, saying nothing, as I had learned to do in the face of bigotry and ignorance.

Saul's cousin/friend Tammy, USA, 1965 (70)

Chapter Fifty-Eight

Sex Before Marriage

Five couples rent a lodge in the Catskills Mountains: Living life to the fullest.

During the first three years after my discharge from the Army, I was a service manager for a NYC company, Alpha Business Machines. I was making a good living for the times, and tended to live life to the fullest. I cultivated a few good friends who also worked in Manhattan but lived all over the outskirts of the city.

Every winter, from mid-November to mid-February, we all chipped in to rent a huge family house in the Catskills. We were five close couples in various stages of courtship and commitment. On Fridays, we drove our cars into Manhattan, parked them in public garages, and took off after work for the three-hour drive to the mountains. We usually met up at the lodge by 8:30.

The first couple to arrive cooked supper and made grand salads and coffee for those who arrived later. It wasn't the same house every year, but we tried to find a place with five to seven bedrooms, a big living room, kitchen, and at least two toilets and showers. The rooms weren't assigned: It was first come, first served.

Once we were all there we enjoyed a rowdy dinner, sipped wine or beer, then retired to the common room to watch TV, play games, and "shoot the shit." At that point in the festivities, we'd share some coffee or tea, and cake or ice cream, usually served by the women.

Sexual escapades with Marsha the Nymph

The games were checkers or backgammon, charades, or cards. Many nights, while the group was engaged in these diversions, amorous couples excused themselves to retire to their rooms to (we all fantasized) engage in intimate activity. We each knew our place in the group and, for the most part, respected the relationships of couples. However, there was one exception: Marsha. She was a real knockout, very funny and sexy in every aspect. Her goal seemed to be to sleep with every man in the group, which made some of the partners uncomfortable and jealous. The puzzling part was that her boyfriend didn't appear to mind it; he rather admired her prowess.

To keep the tension low, cheating boys made love to Marsha outside the house. One year we had a big tool shed in the backyard, and Marsha coupled there from time to time with the designated guy of the evening, in the near-freezing temperatures of New York winter. When my turn came, I thought I could distinguish myself by showing off my brand new car, a red Rambler. I loved that car. To me, it represented my success as an American, my success in the world. I suggested to Marsha that we go for a ride, and to my pleasure she readily agreed.

We drove out on a long winding dirt road covered with snow, laughing and drinking, and when my eagerness to handle her willing body overtook my better judgment, I pulled the Rambler into the parking lot of my favorite Catskills deli, which of course was closed by that late hour of the night. We made wild sex in the front seat of my little car, somehow managing the gyrations of stripping our lower halves of our clothes and mating like animals in the most ancient of earthly rituals. I knew it was Marsha and I caressed her accordingly, yet as my body was performing my mind was drifting to my days as a soldier in Korea, and memories of very young, beautiful, and seductive girls in the villages there.

The most expensive sex of my life

After the exciting embracing and thrusting of sex in a car, we re-arranged ourselves and our clothing and sat in the steamy car in the cold winter night, smoking cigarettes and sipping wine directly from the bottle. After awhile we agreed it was probably time to get back, except she wanted to drive. I don't know what made me think it was a good idea to let her, but we switched places and I let Marsha assume the role of driver.

We were still aglow and happy in the snowy night until the car was suddenly skidding from one side of the road to the other, zigzagging in an uncontrolled dance. All of a sudden a small truck passed us. In her muddled, drunken, post-coital mindstate, Marsha thought, to avoid collision with the truck, she had to veer sharply to the right but we continued to skid off the road and up onto the embankment. There we hit a tree and stopped hard.

Suddenly sober, I went outside to assess the damage. The entire front of my beautiful Rambler was caved in. The tires dug deep into the snowy earth. The situation was bleak. Marsha joined me in the darkness, apologizing for her driving, and blaming it on the wine.

"What should we do?" I asked her.

Here we were, in the middle of nowhere, in the dark and freezing cold.

We had chosen to reject the tool shed in order to conceal the nature of our escapade, but of course by now it would be obvious to everyone back in the house what we'd been up to, and there were more serious consequences besides their censure.

We studied the angle of the car and the possibilities. We couldn't very well lift the car ourselves and extricate it from where it was stuck; even if we could, the fenders were crumbled on top of the tires. The car was totaled. We had no choice but to go back on foot.

We walked unglamorously back as wet droopy snow fell upon us and we pondered our fate and our reception. Upon arrival at the house, to our dismay, we found everyone still up, sitting around the living room playing checkers and backgammon. They were all wide-awake and looked at us knowingly as we walked through the door. Everyone had smirks on their faces.

The secret was out, and no one seemed to care!

"Come on in, sit down, have some fresh coffee," Marsha's boyfriend offered.

I felt humiliated, guilty. My girlfriend for the weekend was already in our room and I wondered what she thought about where I was.

"We went for a ride, to discover the countryside," I said, practicing what I would tell my girl.

The boyfriend shook his head, smiling. He knew his Marsha.

I went on to spill the truth. "We had an accident. We just left the car there and walked back. I have no Rambler to get back to the city."

They tried to show sympathy, but it was hard for them to absorb the seriousness of the situation. They had been here, warm and cozy all along, while Marsha and I were out on our wild ride.

Her boyfriend served us coffee and brought towels from the bathroom and began to dry her wet hair and neck. Then he stuffed the towel in her sweater, noticing she wasn't wearing her bra.

The others gradually retired to sleep, including Marsha. Then it was just me and her man. He came to sit beside me and patted my knee, saying, "Saul, it's okay to look at me. Don't worry, I know what you've been up to. I know Marsha very well. I can't satisfy her, she's a nymphomaniac, I swear. I live with it and let her get it anywhere she can, it's the only way I can keep her. I love her, you understand?" I nodded my head and said nothing. I couldn't look at him.

A minute later, he continued, "Don't worry about your car, we'll go out there in the morning. I'm sure we'll be able to figure something out."

I thanked him for his kindness and looked him in the eye then, two mature men who understood the complexities of mating and vehicles.

In the morning we had a hearty breakfast, the night before nearly forgotten as Marsha hung her body around her guy and he responded happily to her attentions. My girl had asked no questions, she was already asleep by the time I joined her in bed, and by morning the day was new again and there was no need for questions.

Though of course I had to tell her about the car. I blamed it on the snow. We drove in two cars to the site of the crash. When we assessed the extensive damage by daylight, the others were surprised we came out alive, with hardly any bruises. Two of us stayed with the car, while the others drove into town to find help.

Two hours later they returned, disappointed: It was Sunday. Everything was closed. Not one mechanic or towing service could be found. They suggested I leave the car where it was, then write a note to the local garage mechanic and pin it on their door. When they came to work Monday morning they would hopefully see the note and attend to my poor car. And so that's we did.

I wrote a short note for the garage owner, giving him my daytime telephone number in the city. I rode back with my friends to Manhattan, and took a taxi to my apartment. On Monday, I anxiously waited to hear from the garage owner, but I didn't. I finally called and he confirmed seeing the note, but upon first inspection of the car, he felt the damage was extensive. He intended to go back later with a flatbed to pick up the car. He promised to call back with an estimate.

At about 2:30, he called with a long list of items needing repair or replacement and what it would cost: $2,350, plus the expense of transferring the car down to Manhattan.

I flipped out. But had no choice but to accept whatever he said. I gave him my American Express card number. He promised to have the car back to me within 10 days.

I marked that down as the most expensive sex I ever had.

Tammy and I under the George Washington Bridge: May 1964

Tammy is a distant cousin who came to visit her American relatives from Israel. She was a beautiful, slim, immaculately dressed woman in her early twenties when I was just a few years older than her. My reputation in Israel, I was later told, was that of an international playboy and eligible bachelor, tired of the lifestyle and ripe for marriage. Her mother, my dear aunt with a perpetual smile, had convinced Tammy to come to New York and relieve me of my wayward ways.

Another cousin who lived in Queens met Tammy at the airport. I was working and living in Manhattan at the time. When Tammy called and expressed an interest in our meeting, I suggested she take the train from Queens and meet me in Manhattan.

We met at Penn Station after I got off from work. I was immediately taken by her polite manners and positive demeanor.

"Where would you like to go? Any particular place?" I asked her, as she entered my car, my Rambler, a little worn and still showing scrapes but repaired and back on the road.

"No, no special place, let's just ride around. I want to see all of New York!"

I decided to show her the Hudson River, a spot I loved, where I had picnicked many times. We drove toward the George Washington Bridge, and stopped a short distance away to look at it and marvel at its graceful construction.

"How old is that bridge? When was it built?" Tammy asked me. "It was built in the 1930s, when America could do anything it wanted to. Most of the great bridges and tunnels in America were built during that time, between the two World Wars."

"Where does it go? What's on the other side of the bridge?" she asked.

It felt good to be the local, the American, and I regaled her with a little of my knowledge of America and its geography and history.

"The bridge connects between New York's Manhattan and Fort Lee, New Jersey. There are many equally great bridges connecting Manhattan to its surrounding places. Manhattan is an island, you know."

We got back in the car and continued north toward the bridge. As we approached, as usual, the traffic got heavier, and I wanted to avoid getting on the bridge and ending up in New Jersey. I pulled to the right lane and continued upriver, toward West Point, the U.S. Army Academy.

"Are you hungry?" I asked.

"Not so I can wait a bit. I don't want to miss out on this great view."

I continued to drive for a while and we both enjoyed looking out the car windows at the beautiful tree-lined river.

"I know what we can do: Let's pick up some sandwiches and cold drinks and come back here and picnic. Would you like that?" I suggested.

Tammy's eyes sparkled. "Oh, yes, I would love it."

We got off at the next exit, purchased a few items at a deli, and rushed back to the Hudson River. I soon found us a desirable, perfectly manicured lawn on the bank of the Hudson, peppered with a few trees, and, most importantly, overlooking the George Washington Bridge.

We sat under a tree on the grassy lawn. I took off my jacket and put it on the ground, motioning Tammy to sit on it, so as not to stain her dress.

"What a gentleman, I'm impressed, thank you," she uttered with a smile and sat down.

She immediately took off her shoes, and her shapely feet and polished toenails caught my eye. That may have been the moment when I stopped thinking of her as a little cousin, and recognized her as a lovely woman.

After a sandwich and cold drink, the sun went down, and it grew dark. Millions of lights glistened in the distance, on the other side of the Hudson, and the night was quiet and romantic. I shifted my position to a spot in back of Tammy, so I could lean up against her back. We sat back-to-back, pressing against each other. We were silent, contemplating the starry universe.

Tammy marveled at the gorgeous scenery and thanked me for bringing her to such a magical place. Impulsively, I turned and kissed her on the neck, wondering how she would react. I didn't have to wait long, as she turned to me swiftly, grabbed my face in her hands, and kissed me soundly on the lips.

I thought to myself, "Maybe my luck will be good tonight."

I must have looked surprised by her kiss because she said, "What's the matter? Are you shy? Didn't all those Oriental girls teach you anything in the Army?"

"Oh, and what do you know about my life in the Army, young lady?"

"You are famous where I come from," Tammy said.

Now I moved away from her a bit, wondering what she'd heard about me. I lay back, thinking about what to say next.

I decided to retaliate and put her on the defensive. I knew she had served in the Israeli Army.

"What about you? Didn't you learn a few things in the Army?"

She didn't hesitate. "Of course I did. Would you like to know what?"

She was smiling big, but I was puzzled by the spontaneity of her answer.

I said nothing.

Then she sat on my stomach and began loosening my tie, and threw it on the ground.

"We don't need that ..."

I didn't say a word. I grabbed her hands and placed them on my bulging privates. She squeezed tight.

"Oh, you're not so shy, are you?" she said.

I began unbuttoning her blouse and removing her bra.

"Saul, is this okay? Is it safe here?" she paused to ask, not really concerned.

I stuttered, "Yes, it's okay, don't worry."

A few minutes of foreplay and we were making passionate love.

Minutes later, she asked if I had a handkerchief. I reached to my pants and pulled it from my pocket and threw it at her impolitely, without saying a word. We rushed to dress, but continued to lie down, facing the sky.

"Hey, Saul, where are the stars? Don't you have stars in the sky in America?" she asked me in bewilderment.

I laughed. "No, we don't have stars in America. You people of the Middle East stole them all," I said, and we both laughed.

We stood and walked hand-in-hand along the bank of the river. She threw the soiled handkerchief into a trashcan.

"It's getting late, Saul. Can you take me home to Queens?" she asked.

"Of course I will," I said, picked her up in my arms, and kissed her on her breast, one last time. I carried her to the car.

"I had a good time, did you?" she asked me as we drove up to her cousin's apartment in Queens.

"Yes, I had a great time, I'll never forget it," I replied and immediately regretted what I said, worrying. *Will I be shackled now? I am only 26!*

"We'll see," she said with a smile and a degree of skepticism, perhaps because she too was worrying about the same thing.

She squeezed my hand as she left the car, and walked up to her door, without looking back.

Rachelle and I near the Bronx Botanical Garden: August 14, 1965

While I was dating Rachelle, my future wife, she lived with her parents in the Bronx, and I lived in Lefrak City, Queens. Once or more weekly, I would drive the long highway leading to the White Stone Bridge, cross the Harlem River into the Bronx, and go meet with her. I always picked her up at her home, where I was greeted warmly by her father Joseph and her mother Hannah Gertel. Somehow, I knew in my heart that these people would be in my life for a very long time. I felt like a member of the family around them, and this made the relationship with Rachelle feel different than what I'd experienced with other girls before her. Besides the fact that she was beautiful and smart and fun to be around.

There was always candy on the living room table, which her mother supplemented with at least three kinds of cookies and hot tea as soon as I walked in. However, her parents seemed puzzled when within minutes Rachelle and I excused ourselves and promised to come back later. Of course, now I know that it was obvious what was on our minds all along, and that her parents weren't stupid people.

On one occasion, we drove away and I had this great idea to park just outside the renowned Bronx Botanical Garden, thinking it was "safe" and we could have a little privacy, nestled between other cars and trees. Looking around, we appeared to be alone so we eagerly climbed into the back seat and engaged in some of our best, most passionate necking and French kissing since we'd started dating.

About 30 minutes later (long enough for things to be pretty steamy), we were startled to hear a knocking on the car window with a stick.

It was a uniformed policeman, and he did not look pleased.

I lowered the window and tried to soften him up with a smile.

"Hello, Sir, what's wrong?" I asked.

The policeman said in a serious voice, "What are you doing in there? This is not allowed here!"

I had never been addressed that way by a policeman and started to worry that this could cost me money, if not something more drastic, like my girlfriend.

Rachelle was combing her hair and buttoning up.

"Officer, we weren't doing anything. We were reading a magazine," I said in my quivering voice.

The policeman stuck his head inside the car.

"What magazine? I don't see any magazine."

I didn't say anything because, true enough, of all days, there was not a single magazine in my car. I couldn't believe it.

He suddenly pulled out a notebook and began writing. Rachelle almost fainted. I was about to have a heart attack.

"Officer, what are you writing? I told you the truth. We weren't doing anything."

"What is your name? I want you to give me your name, address, and telephone number. Here, write it down yourself."

He handed me his notebook and pen.

I was shaking as I scribbled down the information, then handed him back the pad and pen.

Rachelle was looking out the opposite window, into the Botanical Gardens, trying to be invisible and praying that he didn't ask her for the same details.

"And you, young lady, what's your name? Just give me your name," he demanded.

Rachelle's face turned red as a ripe tomato, and she couldn't answer.

I said, "Her name is Rae, R-A-E."

"Rae, what kind of name is that?"

"It's short for Rachelle."

The policeman looked at me suspiciously. "R-A-E? Okay, let's assume this is her name. I am going to keep this to myself, not file a report. But during the next six months, if my precinct gets a complaint about a girl being knocked up, I will be all over you, and I will know where to find you. You get my drift?"

I stuttered, "Yes Officer, I heard you. Please, can we go now? Her parents are waiting for me to bring her home."

The policeman stepped aside and put the notebook in his back pocket.

"Yes, you may go now, but remember what I told you. I will be on the lookout for you."

I rolled up the car window and we both slowly moved up to the front seat. I started the car and drove away. Minutes later, we were at Rachelle's parents' door.

She looked upset and I could tell she felt humiliated.

"Do you mind if I don't come up?" I asked her, cupping her face with my hands.

She shook her head with understanding.

"Make up some excuse for me. I will see you soon."

She just nodded. There was no goodnight kiss.

She climbed the front stairs to her building. I took off without even a wave.

I wondered, will this be the end of our relationship?

Saul and Rachelle's wedding, USA, 1965 (71)

First daughter Suzanne and her proud
grandparents, USA, 1967 (72)

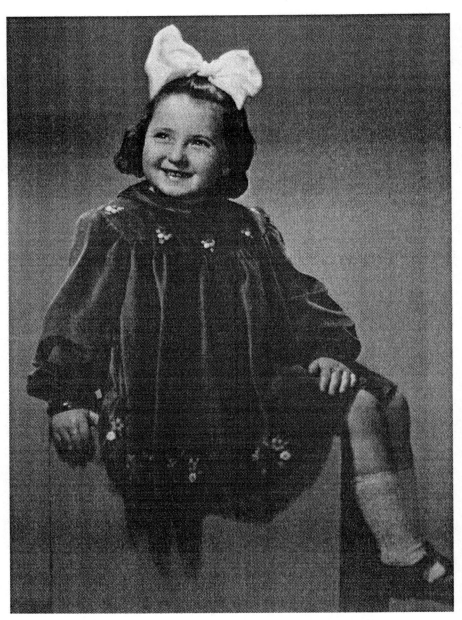

Saul's wife Rachelle in Lodz, Poland, 1952 (73)

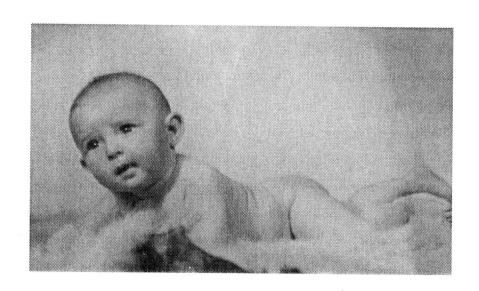

Saul's wife Rachelle as a baby, Poland, 1947 (74)

Chapter Fifty-Nine

Marriage and Children

Manuel First, the man who introduced us: March 5, 1965

When I was working for Alpha Business Machines as a service manager, my job was to train and dispatch about fifteen men throughout the Metropolitan area. I was earning a good salary; I had enough to cover all my expenses, have fun, plus save some money.

One of the typewriter mechanics at Alpha was a concentration camp survivor by the name of Mr. Manuel First. He was a devout Jew and always wore a *Kippa* (like the Pope). He knew I was an Israeli Jew and was eager to lecture me on Jewish traditions, particularly on observing the *Sabbath*. Occasionally he would wander from his cubicle and come into my office to chat. I kept a very busy schedule, but I felt horror for what he had gone through in the Ghetto and treated him with respect. I always offered him a chair and a cup of coffee.

One day he started asking me about my personal life.

"Saul, do you live alone? Where is your family?" I was patient and answered each question in turn.

"Yes, I live alone. I just recently moved to the Bronx. My parents and my entire huge family is in Israel."

"Tell me about your life. Were you born in Israel?" he asked.

"Oh, Manuel, it's a long and sad story," I told him. "No, I was born in Baghdad, Iraq. I escaped at age ten to Israel, in 1948. I'm sorry, I can't go into details right now."

He sipped on his coffee. "I understand, believe me, I understand. Me too, I don't like to talk about the Holocaust and all that I went through. I lost my entire family in the gas chambers. What can I tell you? This is our destiny. We are the Chosen People. Chosen to suffer, that's for sure."

We were both growing melancholy.

"Come on, Manny, let's not get so serious now. We can always find a reason to laugh about something. We are alive, aren't we? Let's make the best of it. Let's live," I asserted.

He sipped some more on his coffee. I noticed teardrops rolling down his cheeks. It was the middle of the afternoon. Any moment, someone could come in and see us in this mood. I got up and helped him to his feet.

"Manny, I want to hear all about your life, but not now. We have work to do. Let's have dinner one of these days, on me."

He wiped his cheeks with his greasy sleeves.

"Okay, Saul, that's a good idea. Thank you for listening to me. I have no one to talk to, you understand, my family is gone. All of them. I am alone in the world."

I escorted him to the door and sat down. But I couldn't pretend all was fine and normal. I sat there and cried, locking my office door so I could weep in peace and privacy for all the hardships I had endured, for Manny's terrible losses, and the devastating stories of the millions of Jews I had never even met.

A couple of weeks later I passed Manuel First a little note, inviting him to meet me for dinner at the nearby Stage Deli. I knew he would savor this kosher food and feel significant among the Broadway personalities that frequented this famous deli.

We had a sumptuous meal: double-decker sandwiches on rye bread and chicken soup. We sat at a table in the middle of the room, surrounded by people so Manny couldn't talk about the miserable old days. I was glad. I told him a few jokes and he actually laughed, maybe for the first time in years. We ate slowly, and stayed there about two hours.

"Let's do this again, Saul. Next time it's on me," he said as he shook my hand.

"Yes, by all means, let's do this again. I hope we can regard each other as a friend. You can trust me with anything that comes to your mind."

Weeks passed and we met again for dinner. During that time, I was engaged in this partying thing, where five couples rented a cottage in the Catskills and spent the weekend eating great food and enjoying free sex. Manny, somehow, heard about it.

"Saul, are you dating someone right now?" he asked me as he took a second bite of his humongous sandwich.

"Actually, yes. But nothing serious, just having fun. Why do you ask?"

Manny smiled his rare smile.

"Oh, just asking. You know, I recently met a very good landsman of mine. Someone who was with me in the concentration camp. He, too, lost his entire family. But he got married after the war. He immigrated to Israel, but now he is here, and lives in the Bronx."

I looked at him, puzzled. "So, how does that relate to me?"

He hesitated.

"My friend has a nice young daughter, about nineteen years old. He wants her to meet a nice Jewish boy. Someone like you. He wants her to get married and bring him grandchildren. That's what we all prayed for in the Ghetto: To some day have grandchildren so we can tell them our story, what happened to us, and the six million Jews that perished."

"Manny, don't get sad on me again. Not here. Please. I am still young and ambitious; I want to accomplish so many things, I can't be tied down. I am not ready for marriage."

Manny looked down. Now he was concentrating on his matzo-ball soup.

"Saul, I'm sorry. You see, I promised my friend I would talk to you. How can I go to him now and say you're not interested? He will be so disappointed. What can you lose? Just meet her. Say hello, and that's it. If you don't like her, no harm is done. Just say hello, they are such nice people."

I couldn't get away from his persistent prodding. I promised to call her, if and when I got her number. Manny waited until we were outside the restaurant, then pulled a piece of folded paper from his deep pocket

"Here, I almost forgot to give it to you. Here is her telephone number. Just call her."

I smiled at his trickery and took the note.

It was her work number in Manhattan. I promised to call Miss Rachelle Gertel.

Meeting my future wife, Friday February 19, 1965

For the next two weeks, Mr. First kept sticking his head into my office and asking me "So, Saul, did you call her?" and when I said I hadn't, he came back with, "Just call her, what harm can it cause?" Each time I promised to call her that very same day, and waved the scrap of paper in his face to show him I had not thrown it away.

I was puzzled by how to handle this delicate matter. I was having a great time with my intimate friends. I was not ready for a commitment or permanence. I did not want to disappoint anyone or cause grief to any parents or nice young women. But Manny wouldn't let the matter drop.

I must find an honorable way out of this.

Every day I thought about my dilemma. One Wednesday I figured it out.

This Friday, instead of going to the mountain retreat, I'll meet Rachelle. I'll set the meeting for right after work in a local pub. If she's hideous, I'll make an excuse and leave. My car will be in the garage as usual and I'll still be able to salvage the night.

I mulled this strategy over. It sounded plausible.

From my office at Alpha I dialed Rachelle's work number. An operator answered.

"May I please speak to Miss Gertel?"

The voice answered snappily, "She's on the phone, who wants her?"

I hesitated. "It's a friend. I'll hold."

Moments later: "Rachelle speaking, may I help you?"

I hesitated some more.

"Look, I'm sorry, you don't know me. My name is Saul. I was asked to call you. Were you told to expect my call?"

Now she hesitated. "Ah, I think so. My mother told me something. But I really didn't expect to hear from you. My parents are old school, you know, trying to fix me up with someone of their choosing. I'm sorry if someone pressured you into calling me."

She sounds nice! Now I am intrigued.

I said, "Well, we're talking, aren't we? What's the harm in meeting just once? I owe this to Mr. First, and I guess you owe it to your parents."

She laughed.

"Let's say you're right. Where and when?"

I gave her the name of the pub and directions how to get there.

"How's Friday night, say, 6:30?"

She agreed and asked, "How will I recognize you?"

I wanted to say something funny to describe myself, and couldn't figure out how to paint some enticing picture for her.

"Well, I am brown-skin, 5 feet 4 inches, 150 pounds. I'll wear my blue suit and a red tie. Don't worry, I'll find you."

She'll be wearing a feminine dress and have a beautiful smile.

On Friday after work, I decided to wait in front of the pub.

That way, if she's late I won't be nursing my third drink already. I want to be alert and presentable.

Fifteen minutes later a cab pulled up and a young, pleasant-looking girl emerged and leaned in to pay the driver. I studied her appearance.

Can this possibly be Rachelle? She's actually very pretty. Her smile is lovely.

She approached the entrance and I leaped forward, thinking, *if it's not Rachelle, I should introduce myself anyway, maybe I can work something out with this one....*

"Are you Rachelle?"

She seemed pleasantly surprised. "Yes. Are you Saul?"

We both smiled.

Hmmm, thank you, Mr. First!

I held the revolving door open for her and she passed before me from the light of the street into the dark of the beer-smelling pub. She gave off a scent of lilacs and talcum powder, a smell that reminded me of my sisters and mother. A crowd stood around the bar drinking, the usual Friday-after-work gang, mostly men, talking loud, their ties already loosened. For now, I was keeping on my suit and tie. I suddenly felt self-conscious, like I needed to make a good impression. Rachelle ordered a 7 and 7, and I asked for Jack Daniel on the rocks, my favorite.

We tried small talk. It was a noisy place... I realized she was not very comfortable in this place.

"Would you like to get out of here?" I asked, and she nodded agreeably.

I dropped some money on the bar and we left the drinks half-full.

"I have my car here. Where do you live?"

She looked at me as if I should know where she lives.

"In the Bronx. It's pretty far, I'll just take the train, I do it all the time," she said in her polite manner. Maybe she was worrying that I didn't like her and wanted the date to be over. But I just couldn't think where to go. I was used to getting in the car on Friday evenings, and heading to the mountains. My body naturally gravitated towards the Rambler at this time of day.

I looked at her standing on the street with this stranger her father told her she should meet, now knowing what she was getting into or how she was supposed to behave. She seemed innocent, like she had never done something like this before, and it was all a big mistake.

But I was beginning to like her.

Is this possible? I should be careful.

"Let me take you to the Bronx because, actually, I live there, too."

She was pleased to know we lived in the same neighborhood, then I remembered: "But tomorrow I am moving to Queens." We laughed.

We walked toward the garage at Rockefeller Center, saying little on the way, feeling awkward, as much because we were attracted to each other, and surprised that this could be possible, while at the same time holding back, keeping our feelings in reserve, not knowing if the other could be thinking the same thing.

We settled into the small seats of my car, which felt pretty intimate after the crowds of the pub and the streets. Our cheeks were flushed and we couldn't look at each other as I paid for the day's parking and we left the dark cement structure and emerged into a colorful twilight, heading West and Uptown, taking my familiar Riverside Drive, where I had enjoyed many picnics and walks and slow commutes home.

Soon the George Washington Bridge glistened from a distance; a hypnotic view. We passed it, trying to describe its beauty to each other. I drove east and crossed the little bridge connecting Manhattan with the Bronx.

Rachelle gave me directions to her home. But I didn't want to go there and have to meet her parents; not yet, this was only our first meeting. On Alerton Avenue I noticed the familiar shape of a White Castle restaurant.

Fast food, could that ruin everything? No, she is so down to earth, she might not care.

"Would you like to stop and have a cold drink or coffee?" I asked, with a little fear in my voice.

Is this a tacky invitation? Should I be dazzling her with some fancy place?

"I live nearby," I told her. "I've driven by this place a hundred times, but I've never gone in."

She shrugged. "I'm open to try it."

I parked the car and held the door for her at White Castle as if we were at the Hilton. Neither one of us wanted to be seen there by anyone we knew and we looked over our shoulders and around the room. But it was a bunch of strangers. We ordered some hamburgers, French fries, soda for her, and coffee for me.

A total of $ 2.65. This is real cheap. I hope she doesn't get sick and vomit all over the place.

We barely spoke as we consumed the half-dollar size pile of burgers on buns, acting like Americans, eating food with our hands.

Outside, she told me her apartment was just a few blocks away and she could walk from there.

"You're moving away tomorrow? So soon? Is it me?"

She's pretty and she has a sense of humor! She chuckled.

"No, no, it has been in the planning since way before I met you. I don't like living here. I have been in the Bronx only six months. Originally I moved here in order to take classes at Fordham University."

I convinced her to let me drive her the rest of the way home and then finally, when we were at her doorstep, we started really talking to each other. We must have stood out there for half an hour, telling each other little pieces of the story of our lives. Then Rachelle started worrying where her parents were and what they must be thinking about all this chatter, why we didn't just come inside.

"I should probably go in," she said worriedly.

I admit I was relieved when she didn't invite me in, I wasn't ready to meet the girl's parents quite yet, but I surprised myself by saying, "Ill call you once I'm settled in my new apartment."

She reached to shake my hand and I surprised both of us by reaching out to cup her face and pull her toward me so I could kiss her lightly on the lips. I had to be in control.

"I'll call you," I shouted as she pulled away wiping her mouth, and ran up the stairs to her apartment.

As I drove home, a few miles away along Grand Concourse Avenue, I asked myself what had just happened.

Can I be smitten so soon? Am I getting weak?

My better self answered my playboy self: *She is a nice girl. You like her.*

Engagement and marriage: May, 1965

So I moved out of the Bronx to my new studio apartment in Lefrak City, Queens a day after I met Rachelle. Then found myself commuting the very same highway and bridge to get back to her. I couldn't get enough of her; she was more genuine and smart and funny than any of my Catskills lovers, and I enjoyed her bright company over that of just about anybody else in my life at the time. Our relationship flourished. I met her parents, Joseph and Channah, and felt immediately comfortable with them. Before I knew what hit me, we were engaged. My playboy self believed it was just so we could legitimize our desire to live together and avoid the long-distance dating across the Whitestone Bridge, when really what this was, was the beginning of a lifelong love.

Joseph and Channah were elated at our announcement. We invited around thirty friends and her parents invited five elder couples, close family friends who had known Rachelle since she was a baby, in Lodz, Poland. We conducted a homemade engagement ceremony in my studio. It was a very small space, so crammed that some of the guests actually stood in the bathroom and inside the bathtub to sip their drinks and eat the catered kosher food.

I presented my lovely Rachelle with a modest engagement ring and she accepted it graciously. (It was replaced in later, more prosperous years with a fine diamond.)

Our wedding day: November 6, 1965

Soon my fiancé was sleeping over in Lefrak City three and four nights a week, going to work in Manhattan by train. Weekends, we visited her parents in the Bronx to share meals and practice being members of the same family. The pace of things accelerated and everyone was planning our wedding with great anticipation.

Six months later we were married!

Most of Rachelle's family and friends lived in the Bronx, so we rented a magnificent wedding hall there, on Grand Concourse Boulevard, a place called "Concourse Paradise." I was 28-years old, Rachelle was 20.

I notified my parents in Israel and, after swallowing their shock that their free-wheeling son might actually settle down to marry, they promised to attend. Everyone at Alpha Business Machines was invited along with their spouses and significant others, including my boss, the owner, and Mr. Manuel First, that matchmaker. My Catskills friends were stunned by the speed with which I was "captured"; they'd felt sure that I would be the last one of our group to marry.

None of my sisters or brothers in Israel was able to make the long journey to the United States for the occasion, but our wedding was a memorable and happy evening, with great music and food. Hundreds of professional photos were taken of us looking young, healthy, and radiantly happy. One very important person did not show up: Mr. Manuel First. We were puzzled and wondered why. We needed to thank him for nagging me to meet Rachelle, never relenting until I surrendered and said yes just to shut him up.

Manny First dies of lung cancer

When we returned from our honeymoon in Virginia, I returned to my regular work schedule and sought Manny out. He seemed to be avoiding me and I couldn't figure out why.

I finally cornered him.

"Why weren't you at our wedding? You were sorely missed."

"I didn't feel good that night, " he said with such detachment, that I felt there was more to the story.

When I got home I discussed with Rachelle how weird he was acting.

"Why do you think he didn't show up?"

She said, with some embarrassment, "Maybe he expected a gift from us or from my parents, for introducing us. I don't really know".

I was ashamed of my own lack of sensitivity to his feelings and wrote a short letter to Mr. First, apologizing for not thanking him properly. "I hope we can always remain close friends and have lunch together soon."

But Manny kept avoiding me at work. I didn't know what to think, but I decided not to pursue it very hard. I was busy establishing our life as a young couple and pursuing my own selfish pleasures.

A few months later someone called Alpha Business Machines to report that Manny First would not be coming to work that day. Apparently, he had been suffering from lung cancer for months. He died in his sleep.

Manuel First was only one of millions of Jews wrecked by the Holocaust, who never learned to enjoy life after witnessing such horrors. Manny did not know fun. His childhood was lost in the concentration camps, together with his entire family. He had no joy in his life. He died alone. Rachelle and I cried for him, and carried a sense of guilt for years.

A painful decision: Abortion, October, 1968

We felt forgiven by Providence and by Manny when we were blessed with a healthy baby girl, our daughter Suzanne, on August 5, 1967. We were living in my Queens studio and though we were happy and in love and able to somehow make room for baby furniture and all the stuff that new babies require, life in Lefrak City was squeezing us pretty tight.

When Suzanne was just a year old, Rachelle discovered she was pregnant again. We were taken by surprise and wanted to feel grateful, but we were scared. We felt that we hadn't given the daughter we already had nearly enough love and attention, we couldn't possibly have another child now: Wherever would we fit another body in our tiny little apartment?

Rachelle confided in her closest friends. One of them seemed to have experience in these matters and suggested an abortion. This was still an illegal act in those years, and potentially dangerous. We considered it and worried about possible consequences. We talked it over every day as my Rachelle was vomiting with morning sickness and napping from fatigue in the evenings when I came home from work. Suzanne was just learning to walk and we were thrilled by her growth and charms, and by the depth of love we felt for this little girl. We felt selfish yet we needed to be practical, and do the right thing for the good of our family, the one that already existed. The idea of abortion went against our higher morals but reality sometimes asserts its own moral ground. Reality insisted that we heed simple truths about available space and the amount of energy we would have to give to a new baby so soon after giving birth to our first. Reality demanded that we seriously look at our finances and what it would cost to add another member to our family at this point in my career. As days passed and the fertilized egg took shape in Rachelle's womb we felt the urgency and pain of making such a profound decision. But finally, with much trepidation and a fair amount of shame, we decided to have an abortion.

I was worried to death about Rachelle's health and safety, and accompanied her to a recommended place in downtown Manhattan.

A lady met us at the apartment door with a man who looked to me just like a pimp or a bodyguard. The woman seemed nice enough, greeted Rachelle, and escorted her inside, while the "pimp" motioned me to stay in the hallway.

Why can't I go in? What goes on in there? What procedure are they following? Are they experienced in safe abortions?

It was such an "underground" act in that era before the laws changed, that you almost didn't dare ask questions, for fear that these people who were willing to break the law to provide a service they believed was necessary, would tell you to just go home if you didn't trust them.

As they closed the door to the private room, my wife looked back and stared at me, petrified, her eyes asking, "are you sure we are doing the right thing?" I didn't know and sat there sweating and praying, asking forgiveness from our Maker. I kept my ears to the door, but I couldn't hear a thing: they were deep in the apartment, inside a back room with the door closed tightly.

After a long time (which was probably less than an hour) my previously innocent and relatively carefree wife came out limping and holding her lower belly. I could see she was in pain. Her face was flushed, her eyes were teary. She couldn't look at me and didn't say a word as she passed me on her way to the exit.

Does she blame me for this? Is she right to blame me, if she does? I suffered terrible guilt for agreeing to subject her to this primitive act. *What were we thinking? This is horrible! We have committed a monstrous act.* I comforted myself that it was a mutually agreed-upon decision. *We did it for sound and righteous reasons. We wanted the time and the means to be able to love and pamper our firstborn.*

Rachelle was totally silent in the taxi back to Queens. (I splurged; I didn't think she should have to ride the train in her condition.)

I broke the silence with what was apparently a stupid question: "Was it a boy or a girl?" Like many men, I would have loved to have a son to call my own someday.

My heartbroken wife just stared at me with amazement that I could ask such a thing. Such questions made the situation more starkly real: No matter where you stand on the right-to-life issue, there was no getting around the fact that we had taken a potential life. That small product of the union of our bodies, made from love, might have been a boy or a girl someday.

Rachelle turned her face away from me to the taxi window and silently stared at the autumn landscape. Leaves were falling one at a time from the trees of the city, each one a tear for our lost child, each one a symbol of the death that would come to us all one day.

Nothing was ever said again about this matter, not between us or with anyone else. As Suzanne and her two sisters grew beyond their teenage years, I wondered if Rachelle ever divulged this shameful secret to them. But I never asked. This book may be the way that they and others find out. I hope that all who read this can understand that we made no decisions lightly, prayed for grace and forbearance from our God, and have tried since that day to live an honorable and moral life of gratitude for all blessings bestowed.

Chapter Sixty

Nagako Obata: My Japanese pen pal

As a gesture of peace after wartime, there was a moment in history when the youth of Japan were encouraged to correspond with the youth of Israel. I was a young, idealistic teenager in Israel who believed that this small individual outreach could actually serve to create the beginnings of understanding between entire countries, and that eventually the world could be a place where wars were a thing of the past. It was also true that, as an outlet for the poetic yearnings of a lost Jewish boy, having a sympathetic Japanese pen pal was great for my spirit.

I was lucky to be hooked up with a 16-year-old girl named Nagako Obata who lived in Nagoya. We wrote to each other all about our lives, our friends and families, our people and history. I wrote to her about the Holocaust in Europe and my escape from Iraq, and she wrote me about World War II, the dropping of atomic bombs in Hiroshima and Nagasaki, and the history and traditions of the old Samurai. We exchanged photos, and soon we were expressing the hope that we could meet one day and get to know each other. This seemed like a huge and unattainable dream for both of us. Our countries were very far apart geographially, and we both came from lower-middle-class families.

We wrote to each other for several years, until I left Israel "to see the world." Many years and countries later, I was on my way to Korea, via Japan, and on a whim sent a telegram from aboard the military ship to my old pen pal.

And so it was: I met Nagako near the Officers Club. She was a bespectacled, skinny woman wearing a nice, conservative suit, while I wore a United States Army uniform, with citations pinned on my chest, hat in hand. Soon I realized that, although Nagako could write decent English, she could not carry a conversation. She kept consulting her pocket dictionary for words to complete a sentence.

We spent the afternoon struggling to overcome our differences, took pictures of each other, then she walked me to the Yokohama port, and came as close as she was permitted to my ship. We said goodbye with a handshake and a brief hug. No kisses.

After I married Rachelle, she noticed the many photos of me with Nagako in Japan. She was curious who this young Japanese woman was. I told her the whole story and told her I would destroy them if she felt at all weird about having them.

To her credit (and this is just one of the reasons I married this wonderful woman), she said, "Why should you? It's part of your life story. It's history. It doesn't bother me."

Rachelle not only sent Nagako an invitation to our wedding, she began her own correspondence with her, while I stood "on the side."

Postcard from Nagako: December 26, 1966

"I wish you a Happy New Year. May this year bring deeper happiness to you and to your home. I am sorry for my silence, but remember that you are both always in my happy dreams and daily prayers. I am glad to inform you about my marriage which will come to us soon. I have been engaged to Mr. Tsutsumi since July. Wedding will be on 5th February 1967, at some church in Nagoya. Sincerely yours, Nagako."

Letter from Nagako Obata: February 1, 1967

To Mr. and Mrs. S. Fathi:
"I don't know how to express my thanks for your thoughtfulness which you showed in your present to me. I received it with surprise. I hope that we will be a wonderful couple as you are. I am proud of our friendship, which has been kept till now, and I believe this will never change, as far away as we live. In my present state, I am sorry I cannot decide yet, whether we should keep corresponding or not. But I am sure the more blessed time will come for us all to share more joy and happiness. The sweet news about your baby pleased me so much, for I had been waiting to hear about it. I hope all the things around you will go best. I wish I can write you again. Best wishes and many thanks.

Love, Nagako Obata"

Nagako informs us she's getting married: Saturday, February 7, 1970

My dear pen pal wrote a lovely letter to my wife requesting that we never correspond again, as this may offend her conservative-minded husband, who would not understand our strictly platonic relationship. We respected her wishes and never wrote her again.

Saul, Technology Consultant to world's largest
trading companies, Hong Kong, 1985 (75)

Chapter Sixty-One

A House on Long Island

Moving: The Biggest snowstorm of the year, February 22, 1969

We lived in Lefrak City, Queens, for a year and a half then moved to a three-bedroom apartment in Forest Hills, Queens, where we stayed until after Suzanne and Sandra were born. During those early years of our marriage, my career took me on dozens of trips to the Orient, a lifestyle I was used to and even thrived on, but now I felt guilty for being away from my wife and children so much.

The day of the biggest snowstorm of the year, on a Friday, February 22, 1969, we moved from Queens out to the suburbs, as all good, middle-class American families were expected to do. Our beautiful four-bedroom house in Huntington, Long Island, sat on a nice piece of property, half-acres land, at 73 Sherwood Court. The movers' truck had huge tires with thick tread and was able to plow right along on the Expressway as the snow accumulated in inches on the surrounding landscape. My Rambler was long gone and now I was driving a large GTO, but I still recall how we slid all over the road that day, the backseat stacked with my boxes of books so I couldn't see out the rear window. I couldn't see out the front window either, as the windshield wipers worked to no avail to keep the drifting snowflakes from obscuring my view. Somehow we made it. Slowly! That entire weekend we stayed inside the new house, sleeping on the floor carpet as our beds and mattresses were still in Queens. I kept a continuous fire going in the big living room fireplace and we imagined we were camping out in a winter snow in the days before furniture had even been invented. We made coffee and toast on the fireplace. It was both hardship and fun.

The house was near Cold Spring Harbor, and once that first winter passed we enjoyed discovering its fine restaurants, bars, nightclubs, and magnificent marinas. My in-laws were delighted at our financial progress and loved coming to stay with their two granddaughters so Rachelle and I could get out and enjoy a little nightlife. My father-in-law, Joseph Gertel was retired from work by now and loved getting his hands dirty on various projects around the house. We finished and paneled the basement, erected a big tool shed in the back yard, and built a spacious concrete patio. When weather permitted and summer was on its way, we laid down sod and planted trees all over my very own cache of American land.

House is flooded: Act of God

During our third winter in Huntington, torrential rains poured down upon us for four days in a row, significantly less than 40 days and 40 nights, but the house was no ark, the Long Island sewer system couldn't absorb all that water, and our entire neighborhood flooded. My car, parked in its usual spot outside in the driveway, could not be found in the morning.. I panicked when I looked out the window and called my wife to come down from the bedroom and look. We were surrounded by water; my car was buried at the bottom of this sea. She was flabbergasted.

"Did you check the basement?" she asked frantically.

"No, not yet," I answered and ran downstairs. But I could take only two steps before my feet were soaked. Our basement had over six feet of water in it!

I screamed. "My books are all underwater... What am I going to do?"

By then our children were awakened by all the shouting and came downstairs. They couldn't believe their eyes.

"How could this happen?" Suzanne wondered.

What do we do now? I wondered.

My wife called our friends who lived a few doors away.

"Is your house flooded, too?"

Yes, the entire neighborhood was flooded. Everyone was struggling to remove their possessions from the lower floors of their rain-soaked homes to the bedrooms upstairs. We did the same, but everything was drenched.

Rain continued to fall.

What will happen to us?

"Should we call the police?" Rachelle asked.

"Maybe the sanitation department?" I said.

At least it was a Saturday morning. We could stay home and deal with it. The entire neighborhood was outside in the downpour, staring in total disbelief at what a little rain could do. We were islands in the middle of a four-foot-deep lake and there was no way to stop the torrent from coming down. There was no place to drain the water; the system was full and overflowing. We did what we could, but mostly we prayed and cursed.

In the afternoon, we thought maybe our prayers had been heard, because the rain subsided and the "lake" began to be absorbed by the sewer system. Suddenly my car and my neighbors' cars emerged as from some eerie special effects movie, where unnatural steel monsters suddenly rise up from the watery terrain of earth. As the water in the streets was absorbed inch by inch, the neighborhood rose up from underwater. What remained was sandy and filthy, a lost city discovered on the bottom of a raging dirty river. We were disoriented and stunned to find ourselves in such a place. But we had no choice but to continue living in the place where we lived and we started clearing our way out at the bottom with the flooded basement.

"Where are we going to dump this amount of water? How are we going to pump it out?" I asked my wife, who just looked at me helplessly.

The basement was concrete, floor and walls, just like a swimming pool, which is what it had become. One of our neighbors urged us to go to Sears and buy a bilge pump. But my car wouldn't start after being totally submerged in water so I gave the neighbor money to please buy me a pump when he bought one for himself. When he returned, we plugged it in and began pumping the water out into the backyard using garden hoses.

It took four hours to clear the basement. We used at least seventeen towels to dry up the floor. As the extent of the damage was revealed, Rachelle and I looked at each other and burst into tears. Most of our valuables, clothes, books, my diaries, letters, mementos, gifts, photo albums and who knows what else were still packed in boxes down here since our recent move to Long Island. Whatever was in them was likely ruined, including unique and irreplaceable treasures.

We called our neighbor, the lawyer.

"You can never replace what is irreplaceable. You can only get some money back, once you report it to your insurance company."

We hunted down our insurance policies, which luckily we kept in a small waterproof safe in our bedroom closet. We called to report the disaster, estimating the damage at around $9,000. We were given a case number.

Over the next three weeks our house became a museum archive as we spread the salvaged papers all over the house, to dry in the warm air and using hair dryers. The weather was mockingly sunny outside, as if to say, *I give you rain but I also give you the sun, be grateful you are alive.* I shook my fist at the sun, useless to be angry at the God of weather, I knew, but I did it anyway. Hundreds of my rare books were wet, stuck together, covered with mud, no longer readable. The same fate befell my diaries and thousands of letters. How could I put a dollar value to this? Up and down the streets of Huntington, our neighbors were engaged in the same terrible process. Formerly cherished possessions became "garbage" left in heaps on the sidewalks for the sanitation department to pick up. I surveyed the piles and tried to recall what was said in the thousands of letters I had saved over the years from family and friends, but my memory of what was said, along with the evidence of those old relationships, were gone forever now.

Four weeks later an insurance adjuster came to assess the scene. We were prepared with a detailed list. He believed we had probably underestimated the cost of the damage, but it was too late to do anything about it as the paperwork had already been filed. Two weeks after that we received a letter, with no check enclosed. The damage was caused by a natural occurrence, rain, and was therefore, in their parlance, considered an "Act of God." We didn't qualify for coverage from them in this case. They denied our claim. We should have had special flood insurance, they said.

We were furious, first at the insurance company, then at God. Why was God punishing us like this? How can an insurance company add insult to this injury? We were fully insured. We called our neighbor the lawyer again, who asked if we'd had flood insurance. Apparently you had to pay extra for this. "A regular homeowners policy doesn't cover it," he told me, then let me in on a little secret. "You should have broken a water pipe in the basement and reported that as the cause of damage, not the flood from the rain." His advice came a bit too late, of-course.

It was hard to contain our feelings of outrage and desperation. We are supposed to manufacture a lie to be given protection? I thought we lived in "A Nation of Laws." What happened to moral citizenship? We protested but got nowhere. Most of our neighbors were compensated, I guess because they had been in this country long enough to understand how it works and they knew what to report.

Vacation in the Grand Bahamas Islands: September 18-21, 1970

While I was working as a top executive at SCM Corporation, I was notified that I and several others in my position had won the annual vacation award for excellence in the performance of our duties. My spouse and I were to be treated to a five-day, all-expenses-paid vacation in the Grand Bahamas Islands. Rachelle and I felt happy as we boarded the plane for our first significant respite since our honeymoon. We'd been busy giving birth to daughters, buying a house, cleaning up after a major flood and burglary, and making comprehensive lists of our losses! Rachelle's parents baby-sat the kids.

When we boarded the plane, I was surprised at the size of the group that was accompanying us: The getaway was not exclusive to my company, but a nation-wide event for top executives of all the major companies in the business machine industry. The plane was nearly full. Everyone on there seemed to be in a good mood and my wife and I smiled at each other, knowing we were going to have a good time.

When we arrived at our hotel we were delighted to find that it was a full-blown casino, with non-stop, 24-hours-a-day entertainment and gambling. We were advised by our organizers not to wander off on our own into town, as every minute of the trip had been planned for us in great detail.

The first day was a Saturday and we were escorted to the beach to play volleyball, swim, and take scuba lessons. I particularly enjoyed exploring the turquoise water, the magnificent ocean floor, and admiring the swirling green sea plants and uniquely enchanting and colorful schools of fish. Back on the white sand beach, we were waited on hand and foot, and served all kinds of exotic drinks and delicious food while we reclined in the shade under huge straw bungalows. Caribbean music was playing continuously the entire time we were there.

At dinner, everyone dressed up in their best clothes and we spent the evening hours singing and dancing. It was great fun introducing ourselves to people from other states and companies and exchanging business cards. One executive from IBM entertained us by regaling us with tales from his life of traveling and being on the road. He was a heavyset man, perhaps weighing over 250 pounds, at least 6'5" tall. Mr. Haggerty knew an endless quantity of raunchy jokes; they were just this side of tasteless so they could still be told in the company of ladies. We laughed and laughed and we all had a great time, very nearly forgetting that anything bad could ever happen.

Our last day, on Sunday afternoon a lavish luncheon was ours, with thankfully short speeches honoring our hard work. Somewhat reluctantly we boarded buses to the airport, checked our baggage, and boarded the plane back to New York. Everyone was in a festive mood. The stewardesses had just begun serving drinks and snacks when the pilot's voice suddenly came over the speaker with a shocking announcement: "Ladies and gentlemen, we appreciate your patronage and we hope you had a good time. We are sorry to have to report to you the accidental death of one Mr. Haggerty from IBM, who drowned during his final scuba-dive class. We truly regret this and wish to extend our sympathy to his wife and children."

We were stunned into silence. Mr. Haggerty, the funny man at our table, a man so full of life and fun, was dead?

"I guess the last joke was on him," I said, but Rachelle didn't think this was very funny.

We were silent the rest of the flight.

Chapter Sixty-Two

The Easy Life: A Boat in the Marina

At Gutzik's, Port Jefferson: July 17, 1981

I have many sad stories in my life but I can look back at my decades of marriage as good and happy times, blessed days and nights. The growing family I made, the beautiful and wise wife I married, our bright and smiling daughters, our inviting and loving home, I had all these gifts, and I treasured every minute of it.

What more could a man want? I have truly made a good life for myself here in this rich, enchanting country.

Things were working out for me in my career. I still traveled to the Orient often, which took me away from the people I love the most, my family, but this travel and work was well compensated, and no one was complaining that it meant we could afford a few luxuries.

What more could a man want?

Well, I didn't own a boat yet!

I thought I could make up for my frequent absences from home by buying us a boat. I reasoned that it would mean more "quality time" with my wife and children. And it would be a new fun challenge, the next hurrah.

The annual boat show at Long Island's Walt Whitman Mall fed my desire and enticed me to fantasize and confront the possibility that I could make my fantasy real. The salesman I met represented a dealership in Port Jefferson, named Gutzik's, and convinced me to stop by to shop.

A week later I took the 45-minute drive after work out to Port Jefferson, one of the most beautiful, exotic harbor towns on Long Island. Rachelle and I had always loved going there to walk along the harbor and admire the yachts, imagining who were the owners of these glamorous vessels, what kind of lifestyle were they leading. We were rich enough and indulged ourselves many weekends at Port Jefferson's many restaurants and unique gift shops. We especially enjoyed browsing in the art galleries.

I found Gutzik's Marine Shop on the right side of the Jericho Turnpike as I pulled off the highway into town. I walked in and asked to speak with the salesman I'd met at Walt Whitman Mall. An hour later I was the proud owner of a 22-foot Fiberform with a powerful 375 HP engine! That cute little boat could accommodate 10 people, and sleep 4, exactly suitable for me, my wife, and three girls. Yes, I drove out to the middle of Long Island one afternoon after work in Manhattan and a mere hour later, became a boat owner. The following Saturday I would return to take possession.

As I returned home that evening on the Jericho Turnpike, I pictured myself entering our house and surprising my wife and children with these pictures and brochures. Rachelle would raise her eyebrows at the expense, which is the wife's job, to keep a husband's dreams in line with the truth of his finances. But I would assure her the money was there, we had it to spend.

"Life is for living, my Rachelle. Not for denying ourselves. Let's enjoy living before we're too old to."

I spread the brochures on the dining room table already set for dinner and Rachelle reacted as I expected. Of course the girls were thrilled and could hardly contain their anticipation. I promised if they went to sleep without any fuss tonight, on Saturday when we took the boat out for its maiden voyage, they would each get a turn to steer.

Late that night, Rachelle was still frowning, wondering how can we afford this? Luckily, I was able to dissuade her from going to sleep worried with a few well-placed kisses on her collarbones and whispered reassurances in her ears as I nibbled on them and embraced all of her, secure in our love and that she would soon come around to see this my way.

Watch out for the rocks

On Saturday I took my friend named Glen along with me to help drive the boat down from Port Jefferson to nearby Huntington Harbor, to the Willis Marina, where I had reserved a slip. Glen had served in the U.S. Navy, so I assumed he had experience on the water. Because I wasn't sure what to expect, I thought Rachelle and the girls should stay home and wait for my call after a successful journey to our marina.

My new Fiberform was already in the water when we arrived. I signed some more papers, wrote another check, and then there I was, in possession of the keys. A mechanic from Gutzik's Dealership showed us around the boat and demonstrated a few steps to take in driving and maneuvering it. He explained the bilge pump and how to keep the batteries charged, and where to gas up.

"You guys have previous experience with boats, right?"

Glen said, "Not really." I looked at him, surprised by this news. He went on. "But I did serve in the U.S. Navy for three years so I know my way around water, a little."

I shrugged at my own lack of experience, then shivered. Honestly, it was the first time, as I was standing there with the keys in my hand, that I suddenly realized I knew nothing about how to drive a boat!

The mechanic studied the two of us with a smirk on his face. I could read his mind as he thought, "What a pair of jerks you two are," but said out loud, "Well, you'll learn soon enough."

He showed us a few more details, then untied the rope, climbed out on the dock, and waved goodbye as Glen started the engine.

"Watch out for rocks!" he shouted.

Glen nodded and shoved the gear into reverse, backed out of the slip, and maneuvered us into Port Jefferson Sound.

I watched every step Glen took. It seemed simple enough. We were already a significant distance from shore, headed south to Huntington.

"What rocks? What's he talking about?" I asked my friend.

"There will be rocks, some of them huge, submerged below the water. You can't see them until you're directly over them. It can be pretty scary."

Now I was worried. "So, what happens to the boat if we hit one?"

Glen laughed. "It depends. If we're lucky the boat will slide right off the rock, and we'll be fine. It depends on the angle and speed at which you hit, you see."

I grew silent and started moving from one side of the boat to the other, on the lookout for hidden rocks. My friend continued to drive.

"We should have picked up some oceanographic maps, I don't know this area well. In fact, I have never been on the North Shore. Yeah, the maps show the depth of the water and where rocks are hidden and make the journey safer."

I looked at him in bewilderment as we dashed through the rolling waters.

"Where do you buy such maps? Why didn't you mention this when we were on shore?"

"You need to go a marine supplies store, the dealers don't carry those maps. Don't worry, I'll get you to Huntington safe and sound."

Now we were miles from shore. On the far side was the coast of Connecticut. I was assured that at least we were heading south. So far, so good. I decided to relax and reached for the steering wheel.

"Hey, let me handle this for a while, you go some rest. I have to learn, you know," I said and pushed Glen aside.

Port Jefferson Harbor was behind us, no longer visible. I took over the wheel and felt like a captain in charge of his own destiny. We skimmed over the water's surface like Ahab. Until, all of a sudden, there was a loud thump on the bottom of the boat, like a collision.

Glen was drinking soda and munching on a sandwich. He jumped to his feet.

"Watch out, you hit a rock! Hold her steady."

He grabbed the steering wheel and held onto it with me as we rocked and rolled, stuck, then suddenly on our way again. It was all over in seconds.

"What was that? What happened?" I asked, shaken.

"As predicted, you hit a rock, that's what. But we're okay. Let's hope there's no damage. We'll know soon. The bilge pump will start pumping any water seeping into the hull."

Now I was scared.

"Well, is there any way to check damage before we hear the pump? Is there a chance we'll sink?" I asked frantically as old, old memories flashed before my eyes.

I can't swim! I nearly drowned twice: once in Baghdad when I was 6, and once in Caesarea when I was 11.

"No, there is no way to check, unless you want to jump in and dive under the boat to inspect it."

I stared at him. "Glen, I can't swim. I never learned. I almost drowned twice in my life."

He looked at me as if I were an idiot. "So, what are you doing buying a boat, Captain?"

I was indignant. "That's the reason I bought it. To overcome this old fear of deep water. Even the Army couldn't teach me to swim. They told me I needed hypnosis to overcome my fears and forget my near-drowning experiences."

Glen kept one hand on the wheel; with the other he patted my shoulder.

"Don't worry, Saul. We have life jackets. And if the boat should sink, the Coast Guard will rescue us. That's their job, you know."

I need two life jackets

I went down into the cabin, pulled out three life jackets, and carried them up on deck: one for Glen and two for me. I strapped one jacket in front and one in back. Glen chuckled.

"You don't need two life jackets, Man. One will hold you. Ha...Ha..."

But I felt much more secure now. "Never mind, I feel safer with two jackets."

We continued our way south until Huntington Harbor was visible on the horizon. It was late afternoon. Glen had refused to put on a life jacket, saying he didn't need it, he's a good swimmer.

"Do you know where exactly we're supposed to park this thing?" he asked.

I pulled the papers out of my leather briefcase.

"Willis Marina, slip number 173."

Glen used his old Navy skills to maneuver the boat closer in to land. We were in the harbor now. He looked at the anchored boats, hundreds of them, and tried to read the slip numbers. They were hard to see, unless you approached very closely.

"By the way," Glen noted, a little late in our journey, "you'll want to buy a pair of waterproof binoculars. They come in real handy. Remember to buy one, when you go for the maps."

After wandering a bit among the parked boats, to the disdainful looks of yachties who knew their way around a marina, Glen found my slip and maneuvered us in the general direction. It was a narrow parking space between two larger boats; I wondered how on earth I would handle this when Glen wasn't with me.

We landed, tied ourselves to the proper post, covered the boat, and left the marina, my "sea-legs" wobbling, still feeling the rocking motion in my body as if we were still on the water. My car was in the parking lot. Now I had to drive Glen all the way back north to Port Jefferson to retrieve his car, so he could go home. I expressed my gratitude for his guidance and help, and offered to buy him dinner.

"No, let's both go home, our wives are waiting for us, probably scared to death." I agreed, and suggested we call from Port Jefferson to let them know we'd safely arrived, because who knew what kind of traffic jams we'd be stuck in and how long it would take to reach home? One thing Long Island was guaranteed to have, was traffic.

Rachelle and the girls met me at the door with great enthusiasm.

"Did you get the boat, Daddy?" Suzanne asked.

"Where is it? What did you do with it?" Sandra asked.

I hugged them with a big smile. "Yes, we now have a boat. We are in the 'league' with all the rich Greek boat owners, the Long Island diner owners. We're going to have so much fun. You're going to learn to water-ski. It's a powerful engine. Glen and I drove it down and parked it in the marina."

It was too late to go back that day, already almost dark. But I promised we'd all go out tomorrow, Sunday, and have our first ride. Of course I didn't mention the damn rocks.

Mayday! Mayday! Emergency, we need help

Though Rachelle and I had a strong marriage and we both knew in our hearts that that would never change, there was always a certain amount of friction whenever I had to travel and be gone for extended periods of time. Now that we had the boat, it started to feel like the family was together more and everyone was happier. On weekends, we stocked up on soda and sandwiches and boated out into Huntington Sound, where we drove at high speed to reach places where we could leisurely drift around tiny islands and anchor in coves. We played and joked around and had a great time. Sometimes we built fires on island beaches and cooked hot dogs and hamburgers, the national cuisine of America. Sometimes we brought Taffy, our dog, and she ran all over the place, digging in the sand and happily consuming our leftovers. Other boaters joined us if we were all there at the same time and we forged some nice friendships.

Suzanne and Sandra learned to handle the boat and as they grew up, we trusted them to go out by themselves with friends from school. They had easily learned to water-ski and I had mastered the art of maneuvering along at the highest speed possible. The girls' friends came along often, which added to the fun, even though something always went wrong, each time we boarded: snaps would pop up, or the battery went dead, or we got stuck in low tides, or the weather changed drastically and we were stranded somewhere.

Once, my secretary Fran and my in-laws came along with us on one of these trips. We anchored on a beach a few miles from the marina and began the usual feasting. After a few hours of "the good life" we climbed back on the boat and began heading back. Suddenly we heard warnings on the radio: A storm was headed our way! The Coast Guard advised everyone on shore to refrain from going out. I worried.

Will we make it back before the storm hits?

Sandra was at the wheel. My in-laws were proud of their granddaughter's skillful handling as she deftly avoided rocks I was pointing out to her where the maps indicated caution. We were moving right along, but before we reached the inlet that led to our marina, torrential rain began to fall, Sandra lost control of the wheel, and the boat began to spin wildly around in circles. I took hold and calmed everyone down. They were in a panic. Sharon went down into the cabin and brought out three life jackets, put one on herself, and handed two to her grandparents. Suzanne rushed to do the same thing and brought out four life jackets. Everyone helped each other to strap the jackets in place. When it was my turn, Suzanne took over steering while I insisted on going down to find a second jacket. They were all making fun of me. Let them laugh! I simply did not trust a single jacket to keep me afloat.

The storm thickened as the sun was lost behind a dark cloud and a fierce wind blew the boat uncontrollably around on the water. I joined Suzanne to help steer, while everyone else climbed down inside the cabin, petrified. When my daughter Sandy saw the same fear in her father's normally steady eyes, she reached for the radio, the first time ever, and figured out how to use it to call the Coast Guard.

"Hello, Mayday, Mayday, come in, it's an emergency, come in…"

She repeated this call for nearly fifteen minutes, while everyone cut the tension by cracking up with laughter at how desperate she sounded. Laughing at your own fear can be a good way to forget you are in danger and feel helpless.

Finally, someone responded.

"Roger, this is the Coast Guard. What's the emergency? Report your position."

Sandy smiled triumphantly. "I knew they would eventually answer, it's their duty," she said. "Dad, where are we, what shall I say?"

"Tell them we are in the Huntington Sound, at the mouth of the harbor, and we have lost control of our boat."

Sandra relayed this information, then finished the call, saying, "Please hurry, we can't control the boat."

We waited for a reply, some reassurance, but heard nothing as I continued to struggle with the wheel but couldn't stop it from spinning and diving under the now-huge waves. I could see the lips of my in-laws down below, moving in silent prayer. I knew it wasn't time for my entire family to perish, but I felt responsible for their fear. I tried to reassure everyone on board: "This is a good, strong boat, nothing will happen to it. I promise you. And even if it should happen to capsize," I said, as a wave swept over the deck, dowsing us, "we'll be held up by the life jackets until the Coast Guard arrives to rescue us." I was telling this to myself as much as to them, as I attempted to hypnotize myself with this verbal chant, out of my ancient fear of drowning.

We were contemplating the worst, making peace with our Maker, struggling to control the dipping and spinning boat, when we heard a voice calling in our direction: "Okay, I see you now, stay put, help is on the way."

We blinked our eyes through the pouring rain and tried to locate the source of that reassuring voice, then spotted the Coast Guard vessel. Soon, some very capable hands came aboard and took over the wheel. He struggled with it for a few minutes then let out a laughing shout. "No wonder you can't steer. You're out of gas, pal."

I looked at him in disbelief, feeling embarrassed and stupid.

Another Coast Guard guy tied a rope to our boat and hauled us in the downpour back to our destination. As we were being dragged along, thunder cracked the sky and lightning lit the dark clouds in zigzag sparks. We weren't afraid of any of it, we were so relieved to feel we were safe again.

What a country! A ready Coast Guard at our service and to the rescue, no questions asked, 24/7, rain or shine. I mumbled silent prayers of thanks, feeling blessed at having been allowed to survive this challenge at sea.

We reached our slip and anchored the boat, then my wife rushed to thank the young brave men for coming out to help us in such a dangerous situation.

"It's our job," he said, as she kissed his cheek with gratitude.

The other one was writing a report of the incident, and asked me to sign it.

"It's just a formality. We have to account for our time," he assured me, so I signed it without reading it and shook his hand. I was tempted to offer a generous tip, but was afraid it wasn't proper.

On the way home we stopped, as we usually did, at our favorite Greek restaurant in the village of Huntington and enjoyed a great dinner. We were all starved, feeling like lost Navy sailors back from a tough confrontation. But we had survived the test, and now we were full of food, and thankful for how the day had ended.

In the car, we kept joking with Sandra, repeating "Mayday, Mayday..." and laughed and laughed. Except I noticed that my father-in-law, Joseph, had not uttered a word in two hours: He was still shaken by his near-death experience. I told him to thank God that everything worked out, we were back on the Jericho Turnpike, stuck in traffic as usual, but safe and sound.

A month later I received a letter from the Coast Guard, detailing the occurrences of our storm at sea. I also found enclosed a citation, for $75. My punishment for being dumb enough to run out of gas. When I showed it to Rachelle, she laughed at me. "Just a formality, huh?"

I paid the ticket. It was a small price to pay for having our lives saved.

My camera at the bottom of the harbor

On another one of our excursions on the Long Island Sound, we met up with some sailboats anchored-out next to each other. The owners were moving on and off the boats, freely jumping from one to another. They were cooking on charcoal barbecues and we were invited to put down our anchor next to them and join them to indulge in some delicious food. Their rock music was playing hard and loud, not my favorite kind of music, but I could tell my daughters would enjoy mingling with these good-looking, barely-clothed young men. Who was I to deny them these pleasures? They were growing up, and I had not forgotten my own coming-of-age years, I wasn't that old! These times, I knew, are some of the best pleasures of life!

When I agreed, my girls eagerly jumped over the railings and climbed onto the decks of the other boats, in search of other teenagers. Despite the hard rock music, we all enjoyed the most wonderful day of eating, drinking, and socializing, culminating in hours of water-skiing, with me, the great Captain, at the helm. I actually jumped into the water that day. Granted, I was wearing two life jackets to stay afloat, and I was tethered by 100-foot rope to ensure I didn't drift too far away and not be able to return to the boat. Everyone laughed at me, but I didn't care: I swam that day, for the first time in my life, and I felt safe in the deep water. To me, that was a huge accomplish-ment.

We returned to our slip, full, tired, and happy, and began carrying out the gear we had brought along with us. Sandra grabbed my camera to snap another photo of us and jumped over the ropes and as she leaped across the little space of water between the boat and the dock, I watched my camera fall from her hands to the floor of the sea.

It was my "collector's item" favorite old camera and she immediately dove in to try to retrieve it. But it was dark and murky down there, with great amounts of gasoline and oil so she had absolutely no luck, and came up really upset, tears running down her cheeks, apologizing. "I'm so sorry, Daddy. I know how much you love that camera."

I knew it was an accident, she didn't do it on purpose. I ran down the pier to the marina office to ask if there was a diver I could possibly hire to help us out. No one official was available on the weekend, but the young man in the office thought he could give it a try.

He dove under our boat and searched for a long time, coming up and diving back down several times. But, no luck: He couldn't find it. The camera was lost, including all the photos we had shot that day, of course. That camera had accompanied me for nearly twenty years of my life, all over the Far-East and the world, only to get lost at the bottom of the Long Island Sound, just a few miles from my home.

I mourned its loss for quite a long time: my camera, my loyal old trusty companion.

Identifying with Hemingway

When I was in the army I had a fair amount of free time for reading, during off-hours when the younger guys were out drinking and carousing. Especially on our long hauls across the ocean, from California, to Hawaii, to Japan, then Korea, I liked the feeling of being below-deck with a good novel. I made a point to connect with the great masters who wrote about life as a soldier, and during that time in my life, I read Hemingway's *A Farewell to Arms* and *The Sun Also Rises*. Now that I owned a boat, and was dealing head-on with the literary theme of "man versus nature" I picked up a copy of *The Old Man and the Sea* from our local library.

If I had read it as a young man, I had forgotten it. Or maybe because I was older now, I was more able to relate to the old man's emotions. I too had to learn to respect the sea and its creatures, not think that I could conquer all just because I was at the helm of a powerboat and therefore possessed some magisterial power. Being on the sea was both empowering and humbling for me, just as it was for the old man. I learned to recognize my own limitations as well as conjure forth deep reserves of strength and calm, particularly when I had others along with me, who depended on me to be the patriarch. Reading the book caused me to think about my father, the original patriarch, and all he had been through, amazed to realize that now I had assumed that role for my own wife and nearly-grown daughters. Was I an "old man" now? What rights and responsibilities went along with that position? Like Hemingway's old man, learning to trust my instincts, when to hold on and when to surrender, were among the profound lessons of manhood that being out at sea had taught me. Like Hemingway's old man, these lessons did not come easy, or without sacrifice. Losing my camera was the least thing, when I thought about how truly powerless I was, at the mercy of larger forces such as storms, waves, and fate.

Vacation in Acapulco, Mexico. Street beggars, August 21-31, 1986

In 1986 I earned a big bonus from my job and felt wealthy enough to take my family on an extravagant vacation to Acapulco. We arrived after a bumpy plane ride, tired, hungry, and grumpy. But as soon as we checked into the magnificent hotel someone at my office had recommended, we started to relax and enjoy the fact that we were on a real vacation. We stripped out of our New York clothes and dressed up in our skimpy bathing suits, heading for the beach and a midday dip in the warm turquoise ocean. We were served sour, delicious margaritas right on the sand.

The hotel accommodated thousands of guests, mostly Americans. American tourists are notoriously loud and demanding, the world over, and now I counted myself among them. The mood was decidedly festive. The sun beamed hot rays of light on our un-tanned bodies. The girls were offered rides in hot-air balloons and a wind-glider. I wasn't up for such exhilaration, especially after a few tequilas, but I had learned not to let my own fears keep my daughters from being courageous and outgoing. Rachelle and I waved to them as they drifted away, above the sand, water, and shoreline. We could see they were having a lot of fun, and we enjoyed watching them, with some trepidation, from our safe and grounded spot on the sand.

Late afternoon, we returned to our rooms to participate in the brilliant Mexican tradition of *siesta*. After an hour or two of rest, we got all dressed up for an evening "out on the town." As we were laughing and walking along, listening to the girls' stories of what it was like being up in a hot-air balloon, right outside the hotel a group of beggars approached us. About six young girls, no more than seven to ten years old, hands extended, stared at us with the most beautiful, dark, imploring eyes. They were selling flowers and other trinkets, Chiclets gum and tiny turtles with bouncing heads. They were dressed shabbily and their faces appeared not to have been washed for a while. I gave one a few coins, then three others shoved their hands up in my face. I searched my pockets for coins but found only bills, so I gave them each the equivalent of a dollar. My wife and daughters were urging me to move on, but it was hard for me to ignore their obvious poverty, while here we were, dressed in our finery, about to spend an amount of money on a single meal that would enable these children to buy enough food to last a year, or at least a few months.

At the restaurant, we put our cloth napkins on our laps and clinked glasses, making a toast to all our blessings. I tried to just enjoy this. I had earned it, after all, I deserved this luxury after the many hardships I'd endured in the course of my life. But I couldn't shake the image of these young girls in the streets. I had daughters! They could be my own daughters! Did these children attend school? Did they eat three meals a day? Did anyone ever give them a piece of chocolate? How do they feel when they see rich Americans and foreigners living it up on their country's beaches, while they are reduced to being beggars? I was disturbed and could not feel happy, though I was thankful my children had agreed to come with us on this vacation, and that my daughters were not in such dire straits.

We returned to the hotel, passing the same group of girls and indicating that I had already given them money earlier. But I decided after that experience, that I couldn't go out on the town again to face those big-eyed, hungry kids. I stayed within the hotel grounds for the rest of the week, reading on the hot beach and swimming there so I could avoid looking into those little girls' eyes ever again. Rachelle felt I was spoiling our own children's vacation. But I couldn't help it. I kept wondering: How can one of the poorest countries in the world be right next door to the richest country in the world? Where was justice? Will the Mexican people wake up one day and revolt? When they do, will the American government help the Mexican government to suppress it? Let History speaks for itself.

Vacation lifestyle

I made a decision that, if I ever went on vacation again, it would be in the United States, where I didn't have to feel guilty for my success and my desire to enjoy it. In 1992, my family and I visited Myrtle Beach, South Carolina, with our best friends, Adam (Fuad) and Roz. We all enjoyed it so much, we agreed to chip in together to buy a time-share condominium for two weeks a year, and committed to the first two weeks of August every year, when our kids were out of school and we could all go and have a good time. We had the cash, it was a good investment, plus it would force us to vacation together more often. Every time we went, we were elated that we had made this genius decision. For two entire weeks we did nothing but shop, play golf, and dine in fine restaurants, always on the lookout for "all-you-can-eat" buffets. No doubt, we all gained at least five pounds every year on these vacations. But who cares? It was worth it.

We went back to Myrtle Beach with Roz and Adam several times; other years we went with other friends. One year, we visited Roz and Adam at their home in Orlando, another time, I took Rachelle on a little visit up to the Poconos, scene of my old "couples" party weekends from when I was single. I refrained from providing her the gory details of those sexual escapades, but I savored my private memories of the days of "free love" and "make love not war." If only the world would take heed of that philosophy and never have a war again, we would all be so much happier and people wouldn't have to die in the streets in the name of God and country. History speaks for itself, but when will we ever learn from it and stop killing each other?

My friend Yeg-Al Madhala on my boat,
Huntington Harbor, NY, USA, 1976 (76)

Saul on his boat, Huntington Harbor,
NY, USA, 1990 (77)

Chapter Sixty-Three

Taffy: Our adorable dog

Our neighbor's dog gave birth to six adorable (Half Sheep/half poodle) puppies, and distributed a flyer in mailboxes all over the neighborhood, offering "Free Puppies." My daughter Sharon picked up the mail that day and begged us to let her have a dog. Rachelle and I discussed it. My wife was against it, because she knew how much work it is. So, since everyone in my family knows what a softie I am, Sharon came to me with those pretty, pleading eyes of hers, nuzzled me in the way she always uses to melt my heart, and enlisted me to help confront her mother and get her to change her mind. I wasn't so sure I wanted any part of this battle. Sharon said, "Pleeeeeeeaaaasssse, Daddy," in her most syrupy voice and promised to take on all kinds of household chores as well as total responsibility for the dog's care. (It seems I've heard that before). Before I knew what hit me, I was pleading the case to my wife. "What could be so bad," I said, "to have a small fluffy pet for the girls to play with?"

It took a few tries, but eventually I broke Rachelle down—by promising to take on all kinds of household chores and total responsibility if Sharon neglected any aspect of the dog's care. It was worth it to see how happy it made my daughter when I told her yes, she could have a puppy. She was absolutely ecstatic, gave me a giant bear hug, and ran straight over to the neighbor's house.

One particular pup caught her fancy right away: a blond, chubby little thing with huge brown eyes. Sharon carried it home in her arms and informed us she'd already given it a name: "Taffy." The whole family gathered in the kitchen and stood around in awe and pleasure as Taffy slurped up the warmed milk we gave her, and we all laughed as she chowed down on cold cuts from the fridge.

Even Rachelle came to love our new family member, as Taffy grew over the years to be a wonderful, cuddly pet who enjoyed roaming around our sprawling backyard, running along the perimeter of our fence, and jumping into the pool to cool herself off. I have to admit, I was jealous of her natural-born swimming skills. It was absolutely instinctive: she was devoid of any fear of the water.

Taffy was Sharon's dog and belonged to us all, but, frankly, she favored me: I would come home full of fatigue and tension, and she would be waiting to greet me in the driveway and jump on me, excitedly licking my face in welcome. She also got along famously with my in-laws: My mother-in-law Channah often made her famous chicken soup for us, and always kept aside some extra for Taffy. The entire family gathered most weekends for big restaurant lunches or dinners and we always brought home a "doggy bag" for Taffy, who particularly loved pungent Chinese food. Taffy was so spoiled by "people food" that she often refused to eat dog food.

Whenever we went out on the boat we always took her along. She entertained anyone who was watching, with her enthusiastic runs along the beach and her joyful willingness to be touched and petted by children. Taffy's genuine eyes, ever-wagging tail, and eager-to-please demeanor endeared her to everyone she met. She gave more than she ever took in return: All she needed was the smallest sign of your unconditional love and she was your friend for life.

Ten years of such pure pleasure, rich years when Taffy was waiting for me at the end of my weary days, the years when the girls growing up and their friends were always there, the house was full of life and laughter—and Taffy was a big part of that happiness. That little dog was a treasure for us all.

Inevitably, as with all things, the day came when Rachelle noticed she wasn't eating her food, she was limping, and we discovered a spot of blood on the blanket where she'd been lying. The vet examined her thoroughly and we were stunned at his findings: Taffy was ill with advanced-stage cancer. My daughters nearly fainted with fear and anger. At home, Rachelle was sad, maybe sadder than any of us; after her initial resistance she and Taffy ended up spending quite a lot of time together when the girls were at school and I was at the office. My wife tried her best to nurse that little dog back to health, tempting her with her favorite Channah Gertel chicken soup and veal cutlets.

But Taffy had reached that point, and wanted no part of it. We spent days and hours stroking her on the head and combing her beautiful blonde hair, but we could tell the poor thing was suffering in pain and preferred sprawling out in her carpeted corner spot alone. It was hard to keep our hands off her, to respect her privacy, to let her go.... Taffy was one of the kids. We couldn't bear the thought that we would lose her. One day Taffy was going to die, as we all do; whenever that was, it would be too soon.

It was no more than a week after the diagnosis when the vet phoned to find out how she was doing. Even he, who had dealings with many majestic animals, had fallen in love with her winning ways. We described her behavior, her lack of appetite, her general withdrawal from contact, which was so unlike the Taffy we knew. The vet was a compassionate doctor who understood how much we loved her.

"You're subjecting her to unnecessary pain, by trying to keep her alive now. For her, for the Taffy you used to know, you should put her to sleep, for her own peace. It's the right thing to do," he was sure.

We promised to think about it.

The girls implored us not to.

Sandra thought we should get a second opinion. "What if the vet is wrong? What if we put her to sleep instead of finding a cure?"

A few days later I was at work when Rachelle and the girls all piled into the car with a limp, very sick Taffy, and they schlepped her to another vet, one who knew nothing of the first opinion, only the symptoms he'd see when the patient was presented. Of course the diagnosis was exactly the same.

I'm ashamed to say I was glad I wasn't there, I was a coward who could not have borne the responsibility to make that decision. My brave Rachelle had to grant the permission to inject our beloved pet to put her down, out of her misery.

Late that night, we all stood around her corner spot that was now empty, and always would be, and Rachelle described to me the scene at the vet's.

"The doctor very slowly and quietly filled the syringe to the measuring line, and Taffy didn't put up any fight, no protest at all, not a peep. I could see in her eyes, she knew it too, that this was the right thing, the time had come. She absorbed the poison streaming through her veins, laid her little body down on the cushioned bench, barely breathing, twitching every now and then, until finally she was completely still."

The vet checked the pulse and shined light in her eyes. Nothing.

"She's gone."

"It's official."

Sharon was still trying to reason it out, how could this happen? She speculated. "Maybe the chicken soup made her sick. I never liked it."

Sandra answered, "Maybe it was all the Chinese food. It makes me sick sometimes."

We hugged them both.

"Honey, it just happened, it's what happens. Dogs get sick and die, just like people do. There's nothing anyone can do about that. It is how God intends it, we don't know why, but we must accept the fact."

Taffy's gone.

The whole family was crying, nobody was hiding it now, no one was sucking back the tears, swallowing lumps in their throats, or quietly sneaking wipes at spilled teardrops, we were openly weeping, heaving sobs, every single one of us. I realized this was the first big death for my girls, and I cried for that, and for all the deaths yet to come. I cried for all the losses in my life, but mostly I cried for the loss of Taffy, who was just a dog—but she was so much more. As our sobs settled into heaves, then gulps, then quiet dribbling and sniffling, we all swore we'd never replace her. We'd never get another dog. (Over fifteen years later, this is still true. There could never be another Taffy.)

Every day for years I pulled up my driveway fully expecting to find her there with her sweet unconditional love. But no, she wasn't there, and a small, hopeful light was gone with her forever from our lives. If there was a puppy heaven we were certain she had arrived. Taffy was being fed, groomed, and loved eternally —without the pain of this world. I knew she was better off than any of us, who had to go on with our lives somehow, without her.

Chapter Sixty-Four

My Dear In-Laws: The Gertels

Mr. Gertel's life and death in the Bronx, New York

My father-in-law, Mr. Joseph Gertel, was born in the city of Lodz in Poland on November 20, 1907, and died at a Bronx hospital in New York on May 25, 1985. I knew and loved Joseph Gertel for nearly twenty years. He was the finest of men, a loving husband and father, a willing co-conspirator as my father-in-law, and a gentle and devoted grandfather to my children.

During his years in New York, he worked every day at his profession of "sheet metal man." He commuted to Brooklyn, three hours a day by train from the Bronx. He never complained. He always said he was happy to have a job and to be able to support his beautiful family. My wife Rachelle was his only child, born into his second marriage. He and his wife Channah both lost their entire families in Auschwitz concentration camps during World War II. Joseph and Channah were spared because they were healthy and skilled professionals, useful to the German war efforts, slave labor.

Sam Gertel: Rachelle's half-brother

Joseph had a son, Sam, born to his first marriage on April 8, 1926. Sam Gertel was 13 years old when the Germans invaded Poland in September 1939 and he and his family were transported to the first of a series of concentration camps. He had to be strong and resourceful kid who witnessed grand-scale cruelty and every class of horrors, then lived to tell about it. Sam said it was his mother's death that made him the way he is: embittered but stronger, by preparing him for the harsh life still ahead of him. After his mother's death, he drew close to his father, united in their will to outlive the war. When Joseph Gertel was sick and near-death at Auschwitz, Sam mustered his courage to sneak out of the camp and do what he had to do; he stole bread, milk and potatoes from anywhere he could find it. By sheer power of will and desire, with God's help, he nursed his father back to health, so he could be put to work for the Nazi factory. To be deemed worthy to remain alive, Jews had to be healthy enough to work in the Nazi war-effort factories, as slave labor. You wouldn't think this sounds like such a great thing, unless you knew the alternative, which was, join a long line of your kin and people headed to their deaths in gas chambers.

Joseph and Sam survived by staying close, looking out for each other's backs, as they and many others were herded through several, differently horrible, concentration camps: Lidzmanstadt, Gleinwitz, Auschwitz. As they did with all their victims, the Nazis tattooed blue numbers on their arms: Sam was # B-8318, his father # B-8317. One of the first times I met Mr. Gertel, I was stunned to realize that the Nazi ID tag of a Jew was still readable after 25 years—a permanent mark indeed.

As a matter of routine, anyone in the camps could be singled out for regular beatings by the "Capo," the internal camp police, who were themselves prisoners. Sam and his father, along with countless others, suffered severe beatings at their hands and the hands of the Gestapo. My father-in-law described to me once, an especially harsh experience, when he begged the Gestapo man to stop. This man beating him senseless was a fellow human being, who had lost all sense of his own humanity. Joseph Gertel thought he didn't want to live in such a world, where one man could perpetrate such violence on another.

"Just shoot me and put an end to this suffering," Joseph pleaded.

"Jews aren't worth the cost of a bullet," the heartless officer replied, and continued to beat him without mercy.

Joseph Gertel told me he prayed as hard for the soul of the Nazi as he prayed for his own.

"What would cause a man to become so lost," my father-in-law wondered, "as to willingly participate in the mass execution of innocent people? .... I prayed for the cold hearts of Nazis to find their way back to God, the loving God of all His creatures, as I understood him."

Six years of this Holocaust, and the prisoners were finally freed by the advancing Russian Army on January 18, 1945, sadly, too late for Sam's mother. The last time Sam saw his mother alive was in Auschwitz, and for his entire life, he never forgot the date of the day he last saw her: August 23, 1944—just a few months before the war ended.

Sam told us, "Every year on that date, sharp memories of her in that scene, in that place, in that hell..." a sentence he never finished, as he paused to remember her and weep, letting his mind process those long-ago memories, as they appeared to him as clear as yesterday.

Life after the war

The Gestapo officer's refusal to shoot Mr. Gertel (even if for the wrong reasons: because they didn't want to waste a bullet) was a blessing; anytime life is given over death, potential for renewal is granted. Joseph lived, he survived the vast organized Nazi will to kill him, and went on to live a whole other life, where those times were deep in the past, not ever to be forgotten, but over.

Sam and his best friend from the ghetto, Jack Tramiel, were set free from the prisons and camps at an age when most young people graduate high school. They had "graduated" from the school of evil, having been introduced there to concepts previously unimaginable to human minds.

Jack and Sam used to talk late into the night. "How can this be happening?" one would say, every night in the camps.

"What kind of a brain does Adolf Hitler have, to think this up?"

"Do you think we'll get out of here alive?" Sam used to wonder.

"If we do, let's marry beautiful sisters and live in another country."

They made this pact as 16-year-old boys, a cheering fantasy conjured up by hopeful hearts in the dark night of World War II.

After the war the two friends reminded each other of the old pact and they smiled. They would leave Poland and live in another country. They did, they moved to Germany and, as fate would have it, they met and married two sisters: Jack married Helen, Sam married Esther. Sam eventually immigrated to the United States and fathered two daughters, Rosie and Regina.

The war over, Mr. Gertel had returned to his home in Poland grieving for his family and for the unfathomable devastation wrought by the Nazis. He was not yet certain that life was better than having to live with his memories. But life will persist on the tiniest spark of hope and somewhere in him, he could still feel it there. He came to feel profound gratitude for this spark.

He met his partner in Channah Rack, a lovely woman his same age, someone strong like him with a will to live, who had lost her whole family to the Holocaust. She had to live with this terrible fact. Channah described her memories to Joseph as "playback reels," rolling film footage of atrocities she had witnessed and barely escaped from herself.

Joseph and Channah married. Their only child, Rachelle, my future wife, was born on November 19, 1946. In the early years, they lived in a small apartment in their birthplace of Lodz.

Renewed anti-Semitism drives the Gertels to Israel

Toward the late 1950s a familiar cloud of dark air flared up again in Poland as an ancient hatred for the Jewish people remained in the hearts of individual men who carried that black teaching forward. As he sniffed this air, too-recent feelings rose in him and Mr. Gertel vowed: never again. The time had come to leave his beloved Poland. Along with thousands of Jews, from other countries as well, in 1958 Joseph, Channah, and Rachelle immigrated to Israel.

They rented a small apartment in Ramat-Gan, a province of Tel-Aviv, and Joseph's 12-year-old daughter quickly adapted to the new country, learned the Hebrew language, and grew up happy to be living in the company of people who worshipped the same God and grieved as one united larger family, the family of the Jewish people, for the suffering their family had had to endure.

Yearning for his son in New York

The Gertels stayed in Israel for two years, where, as Rachelle remembered it, her mother felt free and proud for the first time in her life. But her father nurtured a deep feeling of debt and longing for his son Sam; he owed his son his life, he said, they had been through the worst together, the long nightmare of the war, and Sam by this time was living in New York. Joseph wanted to unite his family, live in the same country. It was a hard decision: his wife and daughter wanted to remain in Israel. But Mr. Gertel persisted with his strong desire to be close to his son again, and finally convinced them to relent and go.

The Gertels landed in New York in 1960 (The same year I arrived from Brazil), and moved to the Bronx, near Sam, whom Rachelle was meeting for the first time: her half-brother. She knew the stories of what a brave and loving boy he had been in the camps, how he had saved his father's life by sneaking around to find him bread and potatoes to survive. She couldn't imagine how horrible it must have been for him to know that his sickly mother had been murdered.

Rachelle was the lucky member of the family, she knew this well; her own young life had been mercifully free of any experience of war, though she lived every day with the history, the stories. Her parents talked often of those times as the memories never ceased to rise up and demand their attention. Forty years later Mr. Gertel still suffered nightmares, waking up safe in his marriage bed in the Bronx drenched in sweat, screaming his head off as he relived old beatings at the hands of the German Gestapo.

Gold Fish in patio pool

In his old age, Joseph Gertel was able to forget those ancient nightmares sometimes, and he derived great pleasure from my buying a house in Long Island, because it gave him a focus to put his capable builder skills to use. He loved to come over and help me out with household projects. We planted trees and created a great green American lawn, erected a fence along the boundaries of my American property, and worked in the garden together. He always looked for something physical to do when he visited.

On one visit I was ready for him: I presented him with the idea of building a huge patio in the back of our house, with fish pools in the far corners. I had my floor plans all ready, like a professional architect's blueprints, and Mr. Gertel had no trouble reading them. He helped me remove the shrubs and lawn, smooth the ground, and dig ditches for the foundation. We created a finished edge all around the patio by using oil-treated railroad ties. Mr. Gertel worked very hard, perspiring profusely, taking off his shirt and baking his skin in the warm sunrays.

My vision included a small pond at the corners for exotic tropical fish to swim in. My father-in-law loved this idea. When no one else was home one Saturday afternoon, we conspired to put my plan into action. I could tell he thoroughly enjoyed shoveling the dirt out until we had created pools about two feet deep. We lined the bottom with concrete and he painted it blue, "to look natural."

When we were satisfied that the pond was ready to welcome inhabitants, Joseph came along with me to Selma's Pet Store to buy some fish. We encountered a colorful array of choices, sizes, and types. We marveled at God's exquisite sense of detail and talked about how much fun God must have had in designing some of the most extravagantly painted ones. It was hard to control our enthusiasm for life's bounty, and we ended up spending a small fortune at Selma's.

We brought our collection of swimming creatures home in a bucket filled with water. At the house, Mr. Gertel set up the water hose, filled the fishpond to the rim, and upended the bucket to set the fishes free in their new home. They eagerly scurried around the boundaries, intermingling and swimming happily in their "patio pond." We were full of smiles, and couldn't wait to show off to the women what we had accomplished in just a few short hours while they were out shopping for clothes.

When Rachelle came home with her mother Channah and the girls, she couldn't believe her eyes!

"Whose idea was this?" she asked.

"Oh, both of us," I said.

Joseph was grinning from ear to ear. "Do you like it?"

"Who is going to take care of these fish, feed them, change their water?"

Before I could answer, she scoffed, "Me, no doubt."

"No, no, I will, I will," I promised, thrilled to see my daughters' excitement, as they began pointing at various fish and giving them all names. This was a good thing we did, I thought, a fun thing. My dear wife had no choice but to let it be, she was outnumbered! And so it was that we had a pond full of beautiful and delicate tropical fish to look at all year. And the girls were willing to take on the responsibility of feeding them every day and checking their water.

Then came New York winter.

None of us had thought it through to consider what the consequences of below-freezing temperatures might be on tropical fish. From the very first snowfall the delicate creatures were "buried" in two feet of ice. We naively thought they were hibernating, like fish in the ocean will do.

Spring came around as it always does, the weather warmed up, the ice turned into water again, and we found, to our amazement, all the fish lying at the bottom of the pond, lifeless. The girls broke into tears and demanded that we replace the dead fish and start all over for another year. But we had zero support from mother Rachelle. And on this issue, she refused to back off, telling us to consider the poor fish we'd left to freeze to death in a pond of ice. From that day on, the pond was transformed into blooming flowerpots, which were nice, but there was no more happy swimming of fish to watch.

Building the Sears "ready-made" tool shed

By now I had acquired quite an array of tools and equipment that was otherwise clogging the garage and I started to covet a new storage place like those of my neighbors. A tool shed in the back yard seemed like the American thing to have. My next-door neighbor suggested that we spare ourselves a lot of work and money by buying a ready-made one from Sears, rather than build it ourselves.

My father-in-law was retired and always up for a new project. He accompanied me to Sears on a Saturday morning where we were amazed at the variety of the sample sheds in the showroom. He convinced me that only the biggest one would do, and we placed an order for a 10x16 foot shed, the biggest Sears had to offer. We returned home smiling.

"What now? What did you two do?" my wife asked, immediately suspicious.

"Nothing. We just bought a tool shed for all the gardening equipment and junk we don't have room for in the garage," I answered.

"How big, and where is it?" Rachelle asked.

Her father answered enthusiastically. "Ten feet by sixteen. It will be delivered in just two weeks."

Rachelle made a face, the familiar face she makes whenever she felt outnumbered and could do nothing to change a decision made without consulting with her.

"And where will you put it?" she conceded.

"Right there, in the corner, near the fence," I snapped. "I checked it out. It must sit at least six feet from the fence, that's the law," I said.

We waited two weeks, not thinking much about it until it arrived. First, we were surprised to receive it on time; almost nothing in life happens that way. But the bigger surprise was that it came unassembled! What's more, the Sears crew had no plans to stick around and build it: We had not contracted for that. I was in a state of shock, then I noticed my father-in-law was perfectly content. He knew all along that the tool shed would need assembling! That's what motivated him!

We opened the boxes and the plastic bags containing a multitude of parts and studied the instruction manual. There were hundreds of pieces, many steps and details. The more morose I felt, the happier my father-in-law became: It was a project that would keep him busy for weeks.

It took four weekends before it began to look anything like the tool shed in the show room. We were missing some parts, and found others duplicated beyond the need. Frustration set in for me as we had to make three more trips to Sears, explaining the shortages and returning the excesses.

On the last day of construction, Mr. Gertel was nailing the roof. He had constant trouble with bending nails. But he was smiling, as if he were familiar with the problem: "It must be *winding* today," he said, meaning *windy*.

That's cute, I thought. It's probably something he remembers from his youth in Poland.

Mr. Gertel falls ill: Parkinson's and Alzheimer's

In 1984 Mr. Gertel started to exhibit serious symptoms of illness and it took a while before doctors came up with a diagnosis of Parkinson's disease. Shortly thereafter it was clear he had Alzheimer's as well, as he could no long recognize his own wife and daughter. It's a tragic, devastating disease, horrible to watch as a fine and loving man became utterly lost, violent to the people he loved, no longer the Joseph Gertel we knew and adored. It was terribly sad to see him deteriorate daily to lower levels. One day he physically threw his wife out of the apartment and Channah called for help to get him to a hospital.

He went in and out of hospitals for a year, but as he aged and was near death, there came a time when they could do nothing more for him, and he was to remain home. This was real hardship for Channah, as Rachelle and I were busy with our own life and three daughters, and lived an hour drive from the Bronx, though we visited every week.

During his last days, Joseph Gertel asked his wife over and over, "Do you love me?"

Channah turned to us when he said this. "Look what he is questioning now, at this moment in his life, after all these years together." She turned to him, took his chin in her hand, looked hard into eyes that no longer recognized her, and a mind that had forgotten everything, the good along with the bad.

"Of course. I love you. Look around you, your family is all here. Everyone in this room loves you… just get better."

On May 25, 1985, Joseph Gertel died in his sleep.

Channah and Joseph had lived long good lives, long past the war and multiple threats to their lives. They lived to enjoy the blessings of a loving family, including five granddaughters. Mrs. Gertel is still alive, and at age 90 she brings great joy to all of us and to her four years old great-granddaughter, Danielle. She never forgot to count her blessings.

Suzanne interviews Hannah, August 27, 2000

(Note: Suzanne prepared written questions, but soon gave up, as her grandmother kept babbling away without any sequence or order).

My daughter Suzanne took on an oral history project one year, and inter-viewed her grandmother as a Holocaust survivor. She hired a professional video photographer and made an appointment with Channah Gertel, who was 86 years old at the time. Her gestures and Polish accent and wonderful, rich sense of humor made us all roll on the floor with laughter every time we watched the tape.

Here are some highlights from the stories she tells:

"My name is Hannah Gertel. I was born in Poland in 1914, in the capital of Lodz. I live in the Bronx. After the second war, I had the whole story from my life.

I was about 22 (actually 27) years old when the war started. I was not married, I married after the war. Who marries in a war?

I was the middle child. I had four sisters and one brother. The war killed everybody. We speak Polish; at home we speak Yiddish. We had very nice traditions. On Friday nights the family was together, we celebrated together, and it was very nice. The food was Jewish, like gefilte fish, potatoes, chicken soup…

Three to four years before the war, the time was not good for our people, life was hard. You want to make a living, they never want to take you. Anti-Semitism was very bad. You must work by yourself, with your parents and a sewing machine, a factory would never take you.

I remember, I was about 18, my cousin comes from France for a visit and says, "where do you want to go, you can't stay here," and my father was crying. This was in September, the New Year holiday.

They took away our houses, everything, and gave us a small place. This was the ghetto, in the same town, not far away, in Liebenstadt, with the whole family. This was wintertime, they take you from your house, and you take nothing, just what you need. We walked. They forced us. Everybody must go out from the house or they shoot you. We lived with three families in one room. It was a very bad life. In the beginning, we don't feel so bad, then after, you see what's going on, 200 people a day died. You wake up, nobody's there. In the beginning, what you can, you do. For Passover, they close the ghetto, people have no money, nothing, they give us a little monthly, marks. Once a month was a sale, with a couple of marks, from this you can buy bread for 8 days, 10 pounds of potatoes. Some people, they eat it all in one day, then they have nothing all week. Ten thousand people they took away to concentration camps. We were slaves, they could kill you for nothing. We don't have radio, we don't have nothing, nobody knows what they are going to do with us.

I remember one thing. My parents went to a cousin and the whole night I cried. This was the life, next day you are looking around for yourself, and you don't know nothing.

Our home in the ghetto was my married sister, my parents, and I. One time we went to my aunt's, she had a big room, and we started working. Germany sent us different things, we made gloves with one finger, second time with two fingers.

We had no contact with anyone outside. For this, they can kill you. Who could help us? Nobody. We lived with the hours, nobody knows what the minutes bring you. Two hundred people a day died from hunger, everything. I worked the whole week, 8 hours a day. The money you make for a whole week, you go buy soup. Every day, people don't survive. Three hundred thousand Jews when they sent us to concen-tration camp, at end then there's 5,000 left.

When you are young, you can fight with your life. When you're older, not so easy. They get a portion of food, they eat it all in one day, they don't can live. We never can sleep, we was hungry. Day by day we come home from the work. We have a potato, you make a little soup, you go to bed, you can't sleep. We were frightened for our life. You never know. When somebody dies, we listen. Tomorrow could be worse.

My father died in 1941. My mother died in 1942. They died of hunger. My brother-in-law was the first, in 1940. He can't eat, he has the bleeding ulcer in the stomach. At the last minute, I was with him. Yes, I was with my father when he died. The whole family was killed, everybody. We have a funeral every day, 200 people a day. They make a grave, the men who work in the cemetery. Germany was scared for epidemics, so they bring bread. This was the song: maybe tomorrow you will be together.

The first time we went in ghetto was September, Jewish holidays. They start shipping people to concentration camp. My brother-in-law went by himself, to have a piece of bread more, he had a third mark, for this money, he thought my sister can live with the baby. This was a time when, who can help you? Where are we going? Mama's here, sister's here. My sister said, maybe I can meet my husband in concen-tration camp. She left with her mind, maybe I can see him. Right away, you separate, kids to this side, husband to this side. This was the life. We never knew nothing.

From the factories, they take out people. When I was working, I was very sick. The lady told me, "Hannah, you are on the list. I came here with everybody. When you go, you go together with me." I went to a cousin, he was big shot. He told me, one day I want to not be hungry. I give him my bread. I hide in the roof of the attic, maybe a week. After a week, you heard, the ghetto is open, everybody must go. I want to hide, we have a piece of bread. Eight hundred people in the ghetto. From my family, nobody was left. We came with the whole family: five kids, sister-in-law, two kids, sister, one kid, five, seven, eight kids, brother-in-law, sister, baby, they never grow up at all. You don't can raise people there. I hide until the minute ghetto is open, then they send us in concentration camp. For 24 hours we are outside. We never know nothing.

After this they send us to the war in Germany. In the beginning, in Freiberg, it was okay. We were working in a factory for ammunitions. Everything was for nothing. We go on a train, we don't pay. You sit on the floor, like cows. They didn't tell us where we were going. In Hildebrand, we was working 12 hours a day, a night shift, and the daytime, 500 people in our camp. The Germans gave us the shoes of wood, in the snow, it was very bad. Some people walk miles, for hours, to work; from 10 o'clock in the night until tomorrow 12 o'clock, we eat nothing. It was impossible. You don't have schools, nothing. We had one dress. One day a week we had off, on Saturday, and everybody washed the dress. We put it on, wet.

When Russia, England and Americans go to war, it's near the end, 1945. For two weeks, we was traveling from Freiberg to Mounthassen. We could wash up. I stink. They took just men right away in gas chambers. Everybody was together outside, tables, Germans. In this place, we were for 10 days. This was the end.

When we went to Auschwitz, everybody was nudie, they take all your hair. Each other, we don't recognize. Gold teeth, rings, you take off. After this, we sit the whole night outside, some go to the gas chambers. Next day, we stay nudie. They make selection, take us to one side. We stay together, my sister, my niece. Who would expect us to be alive? Nobody. Everything was under the gun. Every minute you can be killed.

May 5, we are liberated.

At the last minute, they wanted to kill us. Most people were half-dead. "Come on, come on," I tell them, "I saw the white flag, the war is over." I start to screaming. We never know if this is the end for us.

We have no fights with the prisoners, we was all Jewish. I had here a girlfriend, German. When a German talks with me, another German can kill her.

We don't believe this can happen, gas chambers. When we get to Auschwitz, we see, we know.

We live with hope. I want to see the end. When you are young, you want to fight. You can.

I was 29 (actually 31) when the camp is liberated. After the war, we don't have a home, we have nothing. I go back with my sister, she was sick, in hospital. We go to Poland, you come to a place with no windows, no doors. I thought, what do I have left for my life? People start to ask, what happened to you?

How to meet Grandpa? A neighbor said, "listen, he is here." He goes right away to live with us. He buys me pair of shoes. He buys me underwear. He wants to buy me lots of tinks. I say one is enough. We meet in June, by six months we marry. I want to have a baby. This was my dream. I was married in 1945. In November 19 1946 I have a baby. I did everything by myself. Grandpa prepared me, helped. We named her Rachelle...Your mommy...

My situation was nice. When we are going to leave Poland, I must sign papers I will never come back. Where can I raise up a baby? I don't want to stay here. I have a cousin in Israel. He left first, he had a gun in his pocket. I went the last minute.

My place was Israel. When we go to America I fight for two years, I don't want to go. But I built a family, thank God, from one kid.

Listen, life is very short. Everything for me is short. Who expected this? It's a miracle. My daughter, the kids, my three granddaughters. For a million dollars you can't buy this.

Not just me, everybody remembers. The war touched everybody.

I take everything with love. God helped me. I built a family. Now my family must remember and say, "I have a grandma. I want everyone should know my story. The life is not so easy." She took a deep sigh.

Brother-in-law Sam and his wife Ester, USA, 2002 (78)

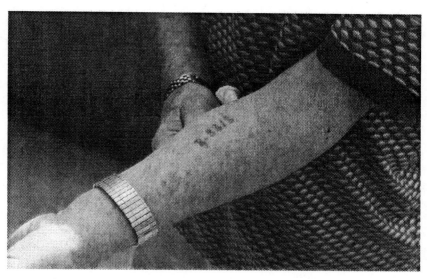

Brother-in-law Sam Gertel, "prisoner" number B-8318
complements of Auschwitz concentration camp, Poland, 1944 (79)

Chapter Sixty-Five

My Brother Yeftah

Yeftah in the merchant marines

My brother Yeftah joined the Merchant Marines after completing his service as an armored tank driver in the I.D.F. (Israel Defense Force). He traveled to ports in Europe and North Africa, carrying cargo from and to Israel.

Between ports, there was a lot of empty time on the crew's hands so they entertained themselves by playing chess, dominos, and poker. I was told years later that that was the beginning of Yeftah's addiction to gambling.

Yeftah and Edna get married

When Yeftah returned from the United States to Israel, he had already broken his engagement to an American girl. He now felt a need to find a suitable girl to marry. Within a short few months, we heard that he was engaged to a girl named Edna, who worked as the managing secretary to the mayor of Rehoboth. A few months later, they were married.

I missed Yeftah's wedding because I was on a business trip to the Far East.

After they were married, Edna and Yeftah lived in an apartment owned and gifted to them by her mother. On may 30, 1974, they had their first son, No-am, followed by a daughter they named Maya, which seemed appropriate since she was born on May 5, 1978.

Edna and Yeftah, however, had a rocky marriage from the start. He was a free spirit and continued to spend his evenings with his friends, playing cards until after midnight. Edna also had serious health issues with her liver, eventually requiring frequent dialysis treatments.

Yeftah's gambling

Yeftah's gambling's also became unsustainable. He owed huge amounts of money to his gambling buddies, who, according to rumors, threatened to kill him if he did not pay off his debts. Unfortunately, Yeftah had no money. He worked at Rhode Iron Works, making artistic fences, barriers, and railings for the builders in Rehoboth. His gambling unfortunately dissipated his earnings.

Yeftah saw only one way out of his dilemma. He determined to sell his apartment to settle his debts. Naturally, there were fights between him and his wife Edna, who tried to keep him from selling their residence, repeatedly reminding him that the apartment was actually her mother's and not his to sell. This went on for quite awhile.

In the meantime, Yeftah was getting desperate. His buddies were putting the pressure on for him to pay up. Finally, he engaged one of his lawyer friends, Mr. Tsan-ani, the strongest attorney in Rehoboth, at the time. He was able to affect the sale of the apartment, without Edna's consent, and Yeftah paid his debts in full.

Though Yeftah had saved his own life by paying off his gambling friends, he and his family were now practically homeless. Because Edna rightly blamed their status on Yeftah, she took their two children and moved back in with her mother. Yeftah came home to live with my parents. A while later, Edna filed for divorce.

Though Yeftah was ashamed of having to return to live with my parents and their tiny house, he continued to associate with his circle of friends, his fellow gamblers. This strained his relationship with my parents. They felt he had no right to have done what he had done, to turn his wife and children out into the street because of his gambling, and then to let his wife become solely responsible for raising their children.

In Yeftah's favor, he did maintain good relations with his kids. He loved them, but he didn't know how to extricate himself from his habit of gambling. This was not recognized as a disease needing treatment at this time. People attributed gambling to stupid, selfish behavior to entertain oneself. He had now lost all respect and prestige in the town, except for his narrow circle of friends. He had no car to take him places and had to send a taxi to bring his children to see him.

To compensate for his creating disruption in the lives of his family, Yeftah showered his children with candy, gifts, and other goodies and sent them back by taxi to their mother. When they grew up to be handsome teenagers and needed some pocket money, they sometimes would go all over town looking for him and would invariably find him in one of his friend's homes gambling. This embarrassed and angered him. Yeftah just tossed them a few meager coins and rushed them out of the house, saying, "We are just having a little fun betting pennies."

As unbelievable as this may sound, a year after he had come to live with our parents, Yeftah's gambling debts mounted up once more and his gambling cronies threatened him with bodily harm again. Yeftah pressured Mother to sign over her house as a gift to him, "so that he could have something of value to share with his children". Mother, feeling sorry and guilty for the suffering of her grandchildren, relented. (father had just died recently). She did not tell any of her children about this because she knew everyone would object and try to stop the transaction.

Yeftah sells mother's house to pay his debts

A while later, Yeftah engaged the same lawyer he had used before to help him affect the sale of mother's house to pay off his new gambling debts. My brother Avram and my sisters stopped talking to him. They were both angry at him and ashamed of his behavior. Mother was now forced to seek out a small rental apartment to live in. At her advanced age it was most traumatic experience.

Yeftah moved in with his young girlfriend Julia. His children, feeling abandoned by him, also harbored resentment. No-am stopped talking to him and visiting him. Maya continued to look him up and check on his health, as he was now suffering with severe diabetes.

Edna was getting sicker by the month, eventually requiring a kidney operation on January 30, 2000. She also had to endure weekly dialysis treatments at the hospital. Because of Edna's illness, her mother, Hannah, cared for her and her grandchildren, practically raising the children herself

Eventually, Edna's health worsened. She was hospitalized and placed on a dialysis machine for the rest of her life. She died on Sunday September 16, 2001. At the funeral, Yeftah tried to get closer to his children, but it was certainly too late.

He died a year later on November 21, 2002, at 6:30 am at Kaplan Hospital. Now, young No-Am and Maya were truly orphans, left in the loving care of their ninety-year-old grandmother.

One of Avram's many artistic achievements,
Israel, 1970 (80)

My brother Avram, distinguished architect
in Rehoboth, Israel, 1980 (81)

Chapter Sixty-Six

Aunt Khatoon: Her life and tragic death

Aunt Khatoon was the third-eldest of twelve children. Her father and mother died young in Baghdad, which left her responsible for the health and well being of her eight younger brothers and sisters. She was so dedicated to the work of raising all her siblings that she ended up the only one in the family without an education. She could hardly read and write in either her native Arabic or her adopted Hebrew.

Like my parents and the rest of our family, she emigrated from Iraq to Israel in 1951 when it was permitted for Jews to leave Iraq. She married a man named Akram. Whose sister married Aunt Khatoon's brother David. Both families stayed very close the remainder of their lives.

Khatoon and Akram married relatively late in life and had to rush to have children. Quite quickly, they managed to produce three sons and a daughter: Badri (now called Boaz), Ezra, Zadok, and Naomi. They all grew up to be tall, blond, and striking-looking.

When Zadok was a teenager, my aunt was diagnosed with breast cancer just like her mother had been, years earlier in Baghdad. Remembering her mother's fate, Aunt Khatoon had no illusions about her own prospects. She was convinced she was going to die—and soon. Her husband Akram had suffered a fatal heart attack three years before Aunt Khatoon had received her frightful diagnosis.

I went to visit her in Israel in 1982. She lived then in a modest apartment in Ramat-Gan. She knew I was coming so she prepared my favorite Iraqi foods. I was so touched she remembered!

"Hi, Aunt Khatoon, how are you?" I asked at her door.

She shrugged and said, "God be blessed," a barely visible smile on her cheeks. She hugged me, took my jacket, and motioned me into the kitchen, which had already been set up and waiting for my arrival with plates and utensils. Her four children, already sitting at the table, greeted me warmly as I sat down with them.

"How is your mother, Salha?" Aunt Khatoon asked. "I miss her, my dear sister."

"She is okay, as well as can be expected at her age," I replied. "But, how are you doing? Are you coping with all your load?"

"Oh, yes, my husband Akram was wonderful and supportive, and my children," she looked around at them and continued in a soft and raspy voice, "may God bless each one of them, are wonderful and strong."

They removed one breast already

I noticed that she was wearing a shirt and a sweater, even though it was hot in her place since she had no air conditioning. Her sweater was buttoned all the way to her neck, as if she were hiding something. I couldn't help but see that her left breast was much larger than her right one. She followed my eyes and explained.

"They removed my right breast already, you know, and they think I am cured," she said. "But I know better, I don't believe a thing they say"

I was at a loss for words and jerked my eyes away from her body, taking refuge in the blankness of the plate set before me. "They know their business," I tried to reassure her. "Don't worry, Aunt Khatoon"

I sat numbly at the kitchen table as she poured the aromatic Iraqi soup I remembered from my childhood. Aunt Khatoon began to serve us a four-course lunch that she had cooked.

"Eat, Saul, don't be bashful," she encouraged. "Are you still shy as you always were? After all these years and all the experiences you have had in Brazil and Korea?"

I laughed. "You remember. No, I am not bashful anymore. I have gone through hell and back several times. But now, thank God, I am married and have three wonderful girls."

It's a waste of food

Aunt Khatoon sat next to me and kept urging me to eat, while she did not touch any food herself.

"You eat, too," I suggested several times but she ignored me, offering me more and more food.

Finally, I asked, "Why aren't you eating, Aunt Khatoon?"

"What for?" she said quietly. "It's a waste of food. I know I'll soon be dead, and my children will have to fend for themselves. It's a sad fate, isn't it?"

I couldn't believe that she was going to die. I tried to reason with her. "I'm sorry you feel that way," I said, "but I believe you are wrong. Doctors treat this disease all the time nowadays. It's not a death sentence. There is hope. There is always hope. Have faith, Aunty."

Tears welled in my eyes, and of course she noticed. She turned and kissed me on the forehead and nodded in half-agreement just to please me.

"He who has no luck, even God can't help him," she told me, then added darkly. "And I have no luck"

Her four young children, who had gathered around the lunch table with us, listened, trying to understand the tragic possibility of death and also the opposing forces of faith and hope.

I got up and kissed each one of them. "Don't let your mom think this way," I said. "There is hope, believe me. You'll see." They all began to cry. "And always remember, you have a huge family, so many cousins, God bless them. Don't worry, stick together, we are always here for you."

I stood and made gestures to leave. I picked up my jacket, which had been hung behind the door.

"Why are you rushing away, Saul?" Aunt Khatoon asked. "Did I say something to make you want to leave?"

"No, no, Aunt Khatoon," I reassured her. "I must go. I am late to an appointment." In truth, I was so overcome at her hopelessness that I couldn't bear it. "Thank you for the delicious food and the wonderful hospitality. Please, have faith, no matter what," I urged her.

Aunt Khatoon laughed a little. Her children got up and follow me to the door. They all gave me hugs, and her daughter Naomi kissed me on the cheek. "May be I will see you someday, in America"

"Good-bye, everyone, and good luck," I said as I started out the door as tears began streaming down my cheeks.

Aunt Khatoon smiled and put her hand on my shoulder. "Please give my loving regards to my sister Salha. Maybe I will see her sometime soon."

Crying on the boardwalk

I left Aunt Khatoon's house, still crying. I had nowhere to go, really, so I took the bus to the Tel Aviv Boardwalk, an old favorite place of mine to stand and ponder the universe and its mercies and knives. I stood at the handrail staring at the sea and the greater distance beyond it, sobbing.

"Why, God? Why punish a good and righteous woman?" I whispered. "What purpose could that serve? She took care of her brothers and sisters, sacrificed so much selflessly. Why can't you spare her for her children?"

I petitioned God, though I knew in my heart and could feel it in my bones that I would not see my dear Aunty again.

My sad prophecy comes true

Six months later, I heard from her daughter Naomi that Aunt Khatoon had died. She rushed to explain that she had not died from cancer, however, but from blocked veins in her brain, an affliction that was normally a cause of death in much older people.

Khatoon's son Zadok was serving in the army at the time. He had seen his mother two weeks earlier, kissed her goodbye, and returned to his base. She had looked very bad to him then, and he was worried. He probably felt the same prophetic tremble himself that I had experienced at the Tel Aviv Boardwalk.

The day after he had left to return to duty, he called to ask about his mother and was told that she had been admitted to Belinson Hospital. He was urged not to worry, but his bones told him different, as mine had. His captain refused to give him a pass to see his mother again, so he left on his own and went straight to the hospital.

When Aunt Khatoon saw him, she was troubled. "Why did you come here? I didn't want you to see me this way," she said.

Just then, the doctor appeared in the room to inform the family that their mother was being discharged from the hospital, as she had little time left, and they could do nothing more for her there. Unlike many people who are seriously ill, my aunt didn't want to go home in her condition. She didn't want to put her children in the position of having to care for her in her illness or to watch her die.

All of her children and her favorite brother David convinced her it was good to go home where life was familiar and she could be surrounded by family. By this point, Aunt Khatoon was delusional, bordering on madness, drifting in and out of consciousness from moment to moment.

She was ashamed, she told them. She didn't want to be seen looking so bad, feeling so weak. Sometimes, she didn't even recognize her own children. Her sister, my Aunt Marcel, came to see her the night she was brought home from the hospital.

Aunt Khatoon's ranting and suffering went on at home for an entire week. One morning, she asked Zadok to open the window. She explained, "So my soul can find the way."

It was a cold winter morning. He didn't understand why she would want the window open on such a cold day and assumed it was one of her delusions, so he refused. He excused himself and went out of his house to be on his own to breathe the fresh cold air—and to cry privately.

By the time he returned, his mother was dead. His brother Ezra and Uncle David were there with her, watching over her as her soul flew toward the window, they said.

No one wanted to let her go because they all loved her so much. They kept her close at home in her own bed, in peace and dignity until the following morning. Only then did they notify authorities and prepare for her burial that very day. My cousins told me that as her body descended into the grave, they saw their mother's soul ascend into the blue sky, restricted no longer by the burdensome ties of life.

I wondered, *did her soul find its way?*

Chapter Sixty-Seven

My Uncle Moshe: A consummate comedian

Uncle Moshe was also my hero. During our escape from Baghdad, Uncle Moshe offered his unique sense of broad humor to make us forget our troubles and enjoy the life we were given. In a short period of time, he had gone from being a glorified bureaucrat in the Iraqi import/export office to digging ditches in citrus groves in Israel. But his innate ability to find humor in any situation helped him cope with these huge life changes and difficulties.

Eventually, he was deemed worthy of a prestigious job with Tnuva, the largest distributor of food products in Israel. Uncle Moshe trained to be a computer programmer in Tnuva's accounting department.

He married in Israel and fathered a son, whom he gave the name of Ezra, in keeping with Jewish tradition, naming his son after his dead father Ezra. The family had a nice apartment in Ramat-Gan and cultivated many friends. They liked to throw parties and keep the merriment flowing.

When Uncle Moshe's son Ezra reached the age of seventeen, near the age when all Israeli boys were required to report to serve their country, Moshe and his wife were so protective of him that they felt they could not risk sending him to the army and perhaps losing his life. They had to do something to save him. Since the Israeli army notifies all parents of eligible boys a year before they will be drafted, Uncle Moshe had to hurry: Once notification is received, the youth can no longer leave the country.

My uncle quit his well-paying, prestigious job at Tnuva, sold his apartment, and immigrated to New York, where his brother, my uncle Shlomo (Salman), was already residing. Once in New York, however, Uncle Moshe's lack of English meant he could not get a decent job in his trade, accounting. In desperation, he took a job selling fancy lingerie out of a suitcase door to door.

He was not proud of his new profession and hoped to never run into anyone he knew in the course of plying his trade as he carried his oversized suitcase from one house or store to the next. One day, he entered a women's specialty store in Queens and began to introduce his line of panties, brassieres, and flimsy under-garments, when he suddenly recognized the owner, my cousin Mary Cohen, who had taken over managing the clothing store after her husband's death from cancer. Uncle Moshe immediately closed the suitcase and scurried out of the store without saying anything. Mary certainly recognized him and sympathized with his embarrassment, though of course it isn't a shameful thing to lower your professional standard if you must, when you are the sole support of your family.

Moshe continued to sell lingerie for a few years until he gained sufficient confidence in the new language of English. Always likeable, Uncle Moshe amassed numerous friends along the way as he went about his business. People who knew him naturally admired him and wanted to help him out in his desire to regain respectability. It wasn't long before he was working again in the higher-level profession he was trained for and eventually found work as a computer programmer in the garment district of Manhattan.

Uncle Moshe at the horses

Moshe's son, my cousin Ezra, attended high school in Queens and graduated with honors. He began working right away and earning a little income, to the relief of his parents. But Ezra never forgave his parents for "ruining his life," as he put it. They had taken him out of Israel, his birthplace, to avoid service in the Army, but it meant losing the dear friends he'd grown up with.

To supplement his income, he said, but more as a diversion from troubles, Uncle Moshe frequented the horse races at Belmont Park, where he would bet a good portion of his income on horses he believed were winners. He had acquired the typical gambler's expectation that "one more roll of the dice" could change his life forever. Normally, he went with friends or cousins, but on occasion he took Ezra along, for what he thought was quality time between father and son.

On one of these bonding outings, Uncle Moshe became so excited cheering on the horse he bet on to win that he collapsed in the middle of the crowd, right in mid-shout. Ezra yelled for help, and a small area vacated around them as a trained medic attempted to revive him, using mouth-to-mouth resuscitation. Unfortunately, Uncle Moshe had suffered a serious and fatal heart attack. We were told that he was dead before an ambulance even arrived.

At the funeral, my brother Yeftah told me a story about our uncle that had stuck in his mind from the time he was twelve or thirteen. Yeftah had gone to visit him in Ramat-Gan. Uncle Moshe came home tired from his long day at work and proceeded to take off his shoes and walk around the apartment in his socks.

He handed Yeftah the shoes he had just taken off, saying, "You might enjoy smelling my shoes. I accidentally spilled some expensive ladies' perfume into them."

Yeftah was young and hadn't learned yet to be on his guard against Moshe's sense of humor and actually stuck his nose in the shoe and took a deep whiff. Within seconds, he screamed out loud in disgust and ran into the bathroom to wash his hands and face and try to remove the stench from his memory. In the midst of the sadness of a funeral, we all laughed and shared our own reminiscences of how Uncle Moshe had always known how to make light of life, even in dark times.

The funeral was an especially sad day because it marked the end of connection with Uncle Moshe and more memories that could have been shared with his family. Almost immediately after the funeral, Ezra and his mother secluded themselves from the rest of the family. We never had an opportunity to hear of other stories of Uncle Moshe or to retell our own. We had lost that link to our past. Our world had become a darker place without Uncle Moshe in it.

Chapter Sixty-Eight

A Nostalgic Visit to the Old Neighborhood: Ramah

During one of my many visits to Israel, long after I had made a good life for myself and my wife and children in the United States, I asked my sister Hannah if she would be kind enough to drive us out to our old house in Ramah, where we lived so long ago, before I left Israel on my first journey to Brazil. She was delighted to drive me, and we spend some private moments reminiscing about our common past.

As we drove south from northern Rehoboth, near the Weismann Institute, where she lived, I kept pointing to places and landmarks I recognized with nostalgic enthusiasm. We passed familiar stores in the Moshavah, crossed through the old Yemenite neighborhood called Sha-ah-ra-yim, then passed by the old ice factory on our right.

"You remember this ice factory?" Hannah remarked. "We used to get the ice from here and carry it home to cool our ancient ice box we called a refrigerator."

"Sure I do," I answered with laughter, "and how many hundreds of times I pedaled my bike here to buy a block of ice. And how many times the ice block fell down on the sand, and I had to wash it off before I brought it home in shame." We both smiled, remembering how hard life was for us at times, yet how resilient we have been after all.

Arriving in Ramah, I began to feel nervous with nostalgia. Here was Love Hill where we played 'spin the bottle', danced and sang around the fire. Here is where we experienced our first kisses. And there is the Mah-ko-lett, the one and only grocery store.

Finally, after a few more sharp turns, Hannah pointed to a house. "Here it is, Saul, that's our house. This is where we grew up. But you only lived here a couple of years before you left us."

"That's really our old house?" I asked with astonishment. "It's so old, the paint is peeling off. It's so run down." I could barely hide my disappointment.

Hannah stopped the car in front of the house and parked. "Would you like to go inside? We could ask the owner, if it's O.K." my sister suggested.

"I wouldn't want to disturb her."

"Oh, you are still the same old polite and shy boy," she teased me. "Don't worry, you are back in Israel now, where it's fashionable to have *chutzpah (daring)."*

I laughed and shrugged. "You're right. I haven't changed much. I was a polite and shy boy who had grown up to become a polite and shy man." She chuckled.

As we sat in the car and argued in fun, the owner must have noticed us and became curious. "Can I help you? Is there something you need?" she asked as she walked out onto the porch. She puffed on a cigarette.

Hannah got out of the car and walked toward her while I remained seated. "We used to live here," she explained. "This was our house many years ago. This is my brother Saul, visiting his old homeland from faraway America. He just wanted to see the place where he used to live once more."

The lady laughed and motioned me to come closer. I got out and walked up to her porch. "What's there to see? It's an old falling-apart house," she said. "Was it nicer when you lived here?"

"Not much," I answered. "But still, it was the house we grew up in. We have both good and bad memories from here."

We sat down on the porch, and the lady insisted on showing us her hospitality by serving us Israeli coffee, dark muddy coffee referred to as *Bots* (mud) in Israel. Our hostess then sat down with us and began to smoke. She took deep breaths in and seemed to enjoy it very much. By then, I had quit smoking but could remember the pleasure.

Being strangers, we didn't have much to say to each other, but Hannah and I each were able to come up with some fond stories from our time here, such as when I constructed a 'bomb' for the Israeli Navy and was almost killed, and Yeftah's "missing" dog. Ah, what I would give to reverse the clock and re-live some of those days. The lady in turn told tales of raising her family within these same walls.

After an hour or so of dwelling so pleasantly in the past, we said a polite goodbye and thanked her for sharing her time with us.

"Nonsense, you kept me company," she insisted. "It gets lonely here during the day. I can't wait till my kids come home from school and make some noise."

Uncle Yehuda: The heart-breaking hermit

On the way back, I stared intently at everything, reading the store signs aloud. They were the most varied, haphazard, and colorful advertisements I had ever seen. Self-expression surely was one of the signs of true democracy.

Hannah insisted on stopping at her favorite Yemenite falafel maker. We sat outdoors at the only table and inhaled the smells of the hot, spicy, chickpea mixture as they cooked. Then we stuffed pita bread with the fried tasty balls and all kinds of salads and hot peppers and ate until we were stuffed like pita ourselves.

We began driving north again, toward Hannah's house, when she suddenly noticed a man sitting on a bench near the bus stop and shouted.

"Look, there is Uncle Yehuda," she told me excitedly. "You see him? On that bench, the one with the cane in his hand."

I looked closer. "Is that my uncle Yehuda?" I asked incredulously.

"That's him I tell you."

"My big-shot uncle, the wealthy restaurant owner, deputy-mayor of Rehoboth?" I asked again.

"Yes, that's him, Saul. Would you like to talk to him? I can't, it might embarrass him, but you can," Hannah said.

"Sure, I want to speak to him. How old is he now?"

"Eighty-five, eighty-six, thereabouts."

She stopped the car about twenty yards away from his bench and asked me again, "Do you really want to talk to him? Will he remember you?"

"Yes, please, let me off here. I will get back to your house on my own. Don't wait for me and don't worry."

Hannah let me off on the sidewalk and went on her way home.

I approached the old man with the cane and put my hand on his shoulder gently. He was gray-haired, almost blind, and fat. He wore a wrinkled white shirt and baggy, gray, striped pants, part of an old business suit. "Hi, Uncle Yehuda, do you recognize me?" I asked the man.

He had dozed off, but looked up and straight into my eyes. "Yes, of course I recognize you. You are Avram, Salha's son," he said, mistaking me for my youngest brother.

"No, Uncle Yehuda, I am Saul, the eldest son, who went years ago to Brazil," I tried to remind him of my place in the family lineup.

"Oh, Saul, I can't believe my eyes. You grew up. I remember you as a child of sixteen or seventeen. It's been a long time," he said, and motioned me to sit next to him on the bench.

I squeezed in and turned to him. "Yes, it was thirty years ago when I saw you last. I was twenty years old. How are you, Uncle Yehuda?" I asked.

"Oh, I am old, sick and old, sick and old and broke," he chuckled, then said, "What can I do? This is life. You take what you get. Everyone plays the cards he's dealt. It's all in God's hands."

I felt sorry for him, and fell silent for a moment.

He noticed and filled the gap in conversation between us. "I come here every day. I sit on this bench and look at the people coming and going. Sometimes, I count the cars and buses going by. What else am I going to do with my time? You know, sometimes I meet your mother Salha doing the same thing, not too far from here. We sit and talk about the past, our lives here, and in Iraq. Your mother remembers everything. She has a good head. I enjoy talking to her. We laugh. We laugh a lot."

I got up and said, "Come on, Uncle Yehuda, let's go have a cup of tea."

He stood up and held my arm. "No, thank you, but if you feel like walking a little, you can walk me home. I am tired. It's time for my afternoon nap."

I nodded okay and began to walk slowly along with him. He was really leaning on his cane. I don't think he could walk without it. He had been living in the Yemenite section of Sha-ah-ra-yim ever since he escaped to Israel before the Great War. He owned a nice, spacious house where he had brought up six children. In his enormous backyard, he had also established a nursery school for needy children.

As we walked past all the homes and stores in his neighborhood, I saw that nothing had changed here for thirty years. We had to stop several times on the way so Yehuda could wave hello to his acquaintances and catch his breath and rest. When we finally reached his house, he struggled to open the door with his many keys. He called me in to the living room, which was as silent as a graveyard. His six children (Ezra, Yedida, Giorah, Mazal, Norma, and Pinkhas) were all grown up now, living on their own. Some were married. A few grandchildren. His wife Ester was gone. He pulled out some old albums that were falling apart and began pointing out his favorite pictures to me.

"You remember this? You remember that?" He asked me again and again as he turned the pages, remembering, with childish enthusiasm.

Do you know how big your father was in Baghdad?

Suddenly, I came across a picture of my family from 1951, when my parents first arrived in Israel. Yehuda was excited. "You remember this? We made a picnic in the city park to welcome your family to Israel, back to us, to the family. Oh, how your parents suffered!"

I was choking with tears. I nodded, but could not answer. "What's the matter? You miss those days?" he asked. And went on: "Yes, those were the good old days... And even better in Baghdad. Do you know how much people respected your father? They bowed to him whenever they saw him. What a lady's man he was. That was before you were born, before all the Nazi propaganda that fanned the hatred of Jews in Iraq. Don't let these memories haunt you. Let me just say, I miss Silas very much."

Then he saw that I was falling apart. I could only whisper, "Yes, I miss him too. I miss him a lot. And I feel guilty for being absent most of his life."

We sat silent for a moment.

"I see you're still sensitive. I remember that about you," Uncle Yehuda said. "I say, to Hell with the world. I say, from dust we came and to dust we shall return. Remember, son, God giveth and God taketh away. Nothing lasts forever."

Now, I was openly wiping my tears away with my ever-ready handkerchief. We hugged and my old uncle began to cry, too.

"I should go now, Uncle Yehuda. Hannah is waiting for me," I said.

I walked to the door.

Yehuda shouted, "When you see my sister Salha, tell her I miss her and her wonderful stories. I want to meet her soon again on her favorite bench. Go, my son, God bless you and your family."

As I left my uncle Yehuda, I was still wiping my eyes and cheeks. I walked back all the way to Hannah's house, ashamed that someone might see me and recognize me, crying like a fifty-year-old child. I already knew in my heart that this was the last time I would ever see my dear Uncle Yehuda alive. He would not survive until my next visit.

Chapter Sixty-Nine

Return to Kibbutz Ma'anit After 40 Years.

The search for Murdi and Malchik (1990)

I'd visited Israel many times before, to stay connected to my family who lived there, and make pilgrimages to my spiritual homeland. Once I landed in 1990, as soon as I settled down at my brother Avram's apartment, our sister Pirha called from Jerusalem to welcome me. "Saul," she said, "I am at your command. Whatever you wish to do, wherever you want to go, I will take you. No limits. No conditions."

I laughed loudly, considering all the possibilities. "Anything I want?

"Yes, Saul, just name it," Pirha answered.

I don't know why this time I suddenly wished to put some old ghosts to rest. "Don't laugh at me," I said. "But I have been thinking a lot lately about my kibbutz, Ma'anit, that's where I want to go."

Half-expecting her to think me silly, I was surprised to hear my sister agree. "Is it okay if Uri comes along?"

"You think your husband will want to spend his free time visiting my old, stinking kibbutz?"

Pirha laughed. "We will pick you up in one hour."

And so it was: I returned to my old kibbutz after an absence of nearly 40 years. On the way, in the middle of Israel in the town of Hadera, we stopped at a kiosk for a refreshing soda then continued to drive east. The old dirt road was now nicely paved, and buses came and went on a regular schedule along it. As we got closer, the smell of cow and horse manure permeated the air and I knew unmistakably we were getting close. Pirha and Uri watched my face as I was feeling so emotional, excited and near tears. We pulled by the renovated office at the entrance gate.

"Shalom," I greeted the pleasant middle-aged woman at the single desk in the office.

"Shalom, please call me Daliah," she introduced herself with a smile as she stood to face me.

I extended my hand. "My name is Saul Fathi. I was once a young member here, many years ago, before your time." I said with a faint smile.

Surprised, she said, "Before my time? I have been here over twenty years!"

"Well, I am talking about 40 years ago, 1950."

We all laughed at her gesturing shoulders. "Forty years? You're right, that is really before my time. I wasn't even born yet!"

"Yes, I know, I can tell you are a young woman," to which she blushed and shrugged. My mind flashed back to when I was a young man, and everything that had changed, in the world and in Israel, in the many decades since I was the fresh-faced and worried boy who was sent from an anti-Semitic climate of war and hatred to live in a welcoming country with his younger brother at Kibbutz Ma'anit. I remembered our fearsome journey to get here, and how, over time, this green place came to feel like a safe home, even without our parents or family around us.

Recalling the name of my dear substitute father and wise adult friend, I asked for him. "Tell me," I said. "I knew a teacher here, his name was Murdi. Did you know him? Is he still here?"

Daliah became serious. "Yes, I knew him. The best human being who ever lived. And the best *Madreekh* (teacher). But I am sorry to tell you that he is no longer with us. He died from a heart attack, over 10 years ago."

Pirha, sensing that I was about to cry, came closer and held onto my arm. With a smile she asked Daliah, "Are any of the old Haverim still around? Someone that my brother would know?"

"Who else did you know?" she asked me. I was quiet, afraid to bring up other names of old friends who might be lost to me forever. I was beginning to feel maybe it was a mistake to come here. Then a vision of my most beloved friend at Ma'anit presented itself at the front of my thoughts.

Malchik: Did you know him?

"Malchik. How about Malchik? Did you know him?" I asked with a lump in my throat

"Who is Malchik? I never heard the name. Was he also a teacher?"

"Malchik was my horse. A great little white and golden horse." I said half-laughing. I tried to describe the shape and size of him with my hands.

"A horse? That's all you can remember from your wonderful old days at this kibbutz?" She asked sarcastically.

Happy memories of time spent with this gentle creature flooded my heart with both pleasure and sadness.

"Malchik was special. He loved me, and I loved him. We worked together in the banana fields. And in the evenings, I was the one who rinsed him and cooled him off and brushed his hair, before I rode him. I was only eleven then"

My emotions were rising to the surface, everyone could see my heart swelling. I felt ashamed at my trembling and tears, after so long, after 40 years of absence.

Daliah had an idea. She opened an office closet and pulled out five or six photo albums. Placing them before us on the table, she told us, "If he was anything special, he'll be in here, I guarantee it."

I moved closer to the desk and began to look into these souvenirs of my past life and the lives of so many others who had passed through this small square of land in this small country, in this large world. There were hundreds of photographs of men, women, children, and animals, moments captured then gone. I didn't recognize anyone, except as familiar-looking members of the community of Jews who are my people. I knew them all, yet they were strangers to me, and I wanted to find an image of someone or something I once knew, and once loved. I frantically turned the pages fast, unable to dwell on photos of people I would never know, and concentrated on looking for Malchik.

"When I lived here, only Murdi had a small camera, no one else. Who knows if Malchik was ever photographed?" I realized Malchik might be relegated to the vague mist of memory, and was getting ready to give up the search. Then Pirha, who had been looking in another album, shouted, "Saul, look, lots of pictures of animals and horses. Do you recognize any?"

I took the album in my hands, turning pages slowly now as feelings I had long ago let go of consumed my heart. I began to cry uncontrollably as I zeroed in on the image in my hands.

"Malchik: A good horse"

"Here, here's Malchik. This is Malchik, my Malchik. I know him. This is my horse." I pointed to a weathered black and white snapshot. Malchik was standing in a banana grove, tied to a flatbed full of bananas, just as I remembered him.

Pirha and Daliah gathered around me. Uri put his hand on my shoulder. "Saul, you've found him. It's unbelievable." As he said this, Daliah leaned and read the writing under the picture: "Malchik. Born 1939. Died 1968. A Good Horse."

"Malchik died a long time ago, over 20 years ago. Someone else must have loved him as you did, and wanted to remember him in this album, together with all the dedicated beloved Haverim who have passed away."

I allowed myself to cry, for myself and all the long-ago loved ones now departed. I closed the book and straightened my clothing, free after the release of tears from mourning those ancient losses. I turned to leave, saying apologetically, "Thank you very much" as Pirha apologized, "He's very sensitive, my brother."

The Kibbutz food tastes good now

Daliah had moist eyes too as she said, " Don't leave yet. At least we can have lunch together. And you can tell me about the good old days."

I looked at Uri. "Why not, let's have lunch. We all have to eat." He said.

We walked the familiar and not-so-familiar 300 yards to the mess hall.

"The same old place," I whispered to myself, "same lights, same benches. Probably the same food." *But me, I am not the same. I am old, and...*

We stood in line and picked up our cafeteria trays. The food selection had definitely improved, but I could still smell the meatloaf, potatoes, string beans, and sour pickles of my boyhood meals at these tables.

We sat to eat and reminisced. Funny, how good this simple food tasted after all these years. I told Daliah the story of my arrival to Kibbutz Ma'anit. How scared and confused my brother and I were. How much we missed our parents, how it felt not to even know if they were dead or alive, for the entire one and a half years of our stay in the Kibbutz. How painful it was not to have anyone visit us on weekends, like the other children.

"Our parents finally arrived in Israel and looked for us and eventually found us in this kibbutz," I paused, thinking back to the joy of that reunion, then said, "I've often regretted allowing our parents to take us out of here, to 'unite' the family. I always wondered how different life might have been, how happily uneventful, had we stayed. That's where we left our childhood forever"

Before I had to show my sensitive side in public again, I began recounting the good feelings I felt for Ma'anit. How Yeftah and I learned Hebrew, and danced the Hora on Friday nights, right here in this mess hall. Someone always played the piano, and I described the skin-and-bones young man who played the accordion so well. Yet in the midst of this good outpouring I couldn't help recalling how sad my brother and I were for him, to know he had witnessed his own mother being gassed in the ghetto in Poland. I held my tears inside me now, and no one else could see them.

We strolled back slowly across the green grounds, fresh with new growth, alive with new generations of people and horses and thousands of chickens.

The Iraqi Army shelled the water tower

"Do you remember all this, Saul?" Daliah asked, as she was about to bid us goodbye.

"Yes, sure I do. In the distance there used to be a water tower, high up on stilts, which the Iraqi army shelled again and again during the War of Independence in 1948, and the water came crashing in on the Haverim. I wasn't here then, but, how ironic. I heard stories from Murdi, the only man with a camera to record this, with his eyes that had seen so much. He told us many of his life experiences, as he tried so hard to be a father to all of us. He was a good, dedicated man, and he especially loved my brother Yeftah. Yeftah used to make him laugh". Murdi liked to laugh. He had so little of it in his life. This pleasing memory of Murdi laughing stayed with me as we departed Ma'anit, a fond enduring remembrance of my time here.

I kept thinking: How different life would have been for me and my brother Yeftah, had we stayed there when my parents arrived in Israel from Iraq. I cherished the thought. I wished I could roll back time.

Chapter Seventy

My father Silas: His Life and Death

My Father: the great admirer of America and its people

Father visited me several times after I had become established in the United States. Once, he traveled by train on his own so he could be seated among the riders and take note of what type of people they were, these Americans.

He arrived at my home full of stories, interactions, anecdotes, and dialog he had overheard. He was a consummate eavesdropper and observer of that most curious of animal kingdom, the human being.

"I am impressed with these Americans, I really admire them," my father said.

I asked him what impressed him the most.

With a smile on his face, he told me, "Their politeness. The Americans are so polite that, even when they are outraged, mad as hell, they say 'go to Hell, please'!"

I reminded him of Theodore Roosevelt's famous quotation: "Speak softly, but carry a big stick."

My father laughed. "Yes, that's the spirit of the Americans! And remember, in World War II, they conquered half the world and made great sacrifices, yet they returned every inch and helped re-build all those enemy nations. There is no parallel in the history of the world. How soon they forget…and spit in America's face"

Driving through the Midtown Tunnel with my father: July 21, 1970

The Midtown Tunnel is over a mile long under the East River and FDR Drive, connecting Queens to Manhattan. As my father and I entered deeper into the tunnel, naturally the radio grew fainter, until there was no transmission.

Father asked, "What's going on? Why has the radio stopped?"

"Because we're going through a tunnel, under the river's floor."

He was silent for a moment. I could tell he was in deep thought.

"You said, under the bottom of the river itself?" he asked, bewildered.

"Yes, Father, under the floor of the East River, which separates Manhattan from Queens. Manhattan is an island, you know"

Father looked out the car window at the tiled walls on both sides of the tunnel, lit with yellow lights, bringing every detail into his eyes.

"But, what if the walls leaked or cracked a little, what would happen to us?" He was genuinely concerned. He tried to smile, not to reveal his fears.

"Dad, don't worry, it's well constructed and engineered. Yankee ingenuity, you know. Imagine, this was built over 50 years ago, before World War II. Isn't it amazing?"

He seemed to take comfort in my positive reassurances and said no more until we emerged on the other side of the tunnel.

From that day on, when I was with my father I took the 59th Street Bridge instead of the tunnel, to spare him any undue concern.

My father Silas, his life and unexpected death:
(Born in 1903, died on June 6, 1986)

Over a period of four months in Israel, in 1986, my father became increaseingly ill. He had trouble urinating, and when he did it was an unnatural deep orange color. Upon examination at Kaplan Hospital, Silas Fathi was diagnosed with late-stage pancreatic cancer: practically a death sentence. He was sent home with medications to alleviate the pain but Mother was told he had a few months left to live.

Father had been a lifelong avid reader so with this news he began gathering around him his many books, with a goal of trying to complete his reading of them, one by one. He settled in with the masterpieces of world literature in his room with the door locked for many hours of the day and night, coming out only to shower or eat meals. He lived during those days with a healthy sense of his own impending death, and his old acquaintance with the ancient religions of Hinduism and Buddhism sustained his spirit. He continued to practice yoga every morning, standing on his head for twenty to thirty minutes each day, and "eating like a bird," as he had always preached to us.

In another country, on the other side of the world, I was going through my own severe personal and business crisis and did not feel free to go to Israel to visit him. Illogically, I may have thought that not going there to say goodbye may prolong his life. I don't know what I was thinking. I do know that ever since his passing there has never been a day that I don't regret my actions: I should have prioritized my affairs to be there with this man, my father, in the last holy days of his long hard life.

A day before his death, I telephoned and we had a long, emotional exchange. I apologized for my long absence, for having left home so many years ago to pursue my own fate and future.

On his deathbed, my father refused to accept my apology, calling it "idle."

He said to me, "Everyone has to follow his destiny, Saul. You did what you had to do. Listen, I will overcome this illness like I have overcome many tragedies in my life....or I won't. Don't worry, my son, I have learned to trust in God."

In the silence across the invisible threads that linked us around the globe, my father and I understood each other, all was forgiven, love went unspoken but was known and felt deeply. Holding the hard receiver to our ears we cried; two grown men wept together from love, so that by the time we hung up you could hear nothing but unabashed, unleashed sobbing. Between tears we said Goodbye and Go with God in all the languages we had ever used in our lifetime: Arabic, Hebrew, English.

I lay the phone in its cradle, whispered to myself my favorite prayers for my father, then gathered my wife and children in my arms, and we cried together.

Before the next sundown Silas Fathi succumbed to death, in his own bed, surrounded by people who love him.

When Mother called we discussed my need to come to Israel for the funeral and she discouraged me very much, remembering how sensitive I am. She said, "Please do not come now. He will be buried today, before you arrive, Saul. I want you to visit on a happier occasion."

I listened to her and, regretfully, I didn't go. I remained in the United States, in my home in New York, attending to my new family and business woes, facing bankruptcy after a major break-in and burglary of my factory.

I wrote the following letter and mailed it to every member of my family:

Sunday June 8, 1986
To my wife and children
Mother-in-law, brothers- and sisters-in-law
Brothers and sisters
Nephews and nieces
Aunts, uncles, cousins
My dearest mother
And all who have known my father, loved and respected him:

This morning, my father Silas Fathi, died after being diagnosed with cancer only a few months ago. I am filled with pain, sorrow, guilt, and hopelessness, which I am certain you share with me.

At times like this one finds oneself reaching into the deep recesses of memory, groping for meaning, digging for those key moments of the forgotten past and attempting to translate and understand them in a new perspective.... But on this day of mourning, nothing is forthcoming. It appears that we must bear the pain of having lost our beloved Silas. There is no escaping death. We, too all of us—will someday die.

I remember when we lived in Baghdad as the children of Silas Fathi, a prominent Jew in his country, head of the Railroad System of Iraq. He was also an active member of the underground Zionist movement, and lived in constant fear of anti-Semitic persecution. In the early years of my youth, my father and our family were protected from harm by British Officers and high-ranking Iraqis who were his loyal friends.

Then came that fateful war when the armies of five Arab countries attacked the new-formed state of Israel, and they were defeated. At this moment in history everything turned upside down for Jews. Fabricated allegations of espionage and public hangings of wealthy, prominent Jews were carried out in the name of revenge and God. My father was among those who fell out of favor and as a family we went into prolonged hiding. In this life-and-death moment, my father made a risky decision, to save the lives of his eldest sons: Saul (me), at the age of ten, and my dear brother Yeftah, who was eight-and-a-half at the time. Father had arranged to have us smuggled across the Iranian border and eventually into Israel. At our parting in the middle of that frightening night, my father leaned upon me with utmost seriousness: "You are the firstborn, Saul, you must take care of your younger brother Yeftah, and protect him from harm. Go now, God be with you...."

There was no time to think or cry as we were bundled and hustled out into the darkness. I nodded to my father, in whom I trusted with all my heart. I gave him my smile and a firm embrace, accepting the ominous responsibility. Little did I know we were on our way to two years of danger, death, hell, and separation. During that time my brother and I were on our own, cared for by strangers in other countries, until a new Iraqi government finally agreed to release all the Jews held hostage in Iraq, and our family was re-united in Israel.

Father loved to read on every subject imaginable: history, poetry, politics, medicine, he had a thirst for knowledge of all kinds. In my teen years he introduced me to R. Tagore, Byron, Shakespeare, Plutarch, Wagner, Spinoza, Gorky, Disraeli, and so many other great writers of literature and philosophy. I have been a reader of books ever since.

My father was human to the full extent of the word. He had great strengths and terrible weaknesses; he was a product of changing environments and victim of terrible circumstances such that no man should ever have to face. He was the type of man who kept troubling matters within himself, then exploded like a volcano when he could not bear the pressure anymore. Whoever stood near him (and often it was my mother) was hurt as he lashed out at the world.

When I spoke to him last, the final things he told me were: "Don't worry about me. I am more worried and concerned about you. I have won many battles in my life, and this is just the next one. Tell everyone not to suffer over me."

Silas Fathi was positive to the end. Our lives must go on. We shall always miss him. Let us hope he has finally found his peace.

With deepest love and gratitude for life's blessings,
Saul Silas Fathi

Chapter Seventy-One

Yedida and Ezra: The Secret Promise

In early April of 1982, my wife and I were notified by my sister Yedida that her husband Ezra was terminally ill with cancer. We were shocked, as he was still so young, only 49-years old.

Just a year earlier, Ezra and Yedida had come from Israel for a visit with us in the United States. It was Ezra's first trip outside of Israel in thirty years. He seemed well and enjoyed all of the sightseeing they did along the East Coast. Ezra was especially taken by the magnificence of Niagara Falls.

Unfortunately, during their visit to Washington, DC, Ezra was mugged by a young man who snatched his camera from his shoulder and ran. Ezra ran after the young hoodlum, but could not catch up with him. This experience left an indelible mark in his memory of their visit to America.

When my wife and I received the news about Ezra's illness, we faced a dilemma because we really didn't know the medical details. We wondered about when the doctors thought his illness had begun. What stage was it now? Would his good health before contracting cancer affect his treatment or his life expectancy? How could we support Yedida and Ezra and their family if we didn't have more information?

We struggled over the uncertainties of this situation and finally decided that I should go to Israel to be with my sister Yedida and to comfort her and her three children: Itzik, Ornah, & Erez. I could also spend time with Ezra and discuss all of the medical details. I left as soon as I could get away from my business.

Upon my arrival at Ben-Gurion airport, my sisters and brothers met me. Yedida told me then that Ezra had not been told that he had cancer. She made me swear that I would not reveal it to him. "It could speed up his demise," she explained. "He is a scary cat."

I understood her own fear. A friend of mine once told me about someone he knew, a big burley man, who had been told by his doctor that he had cancer, and the big man fainted on the spot. You wouldn't have thought that there was that much power, that much fear, in that six-letter word that it would make grown men faint. There was also the possibility that Ezra just might drop into a depression and give up, letting what remaining days he had just slip away. No, I decided to honor my sister's wishes and not tell Ezra about his diagnosis.

All of my siblings and I crammed into Yedida's car and headed to her home. The mood was somber throughout the entire ride. No one spoke the cursed word *cancer*, as if the very mention of the word brought death closer, either to Ezra or to us.

When we arrived at Yedida's home, she urged us to sit and have dinner. We sat around the table and noticed that Ezra was absent. He was still at the hospital, undergoing a series of tests. He would be discharged the following day.

All evening, we sat talking about Ezra's illness, why it had happened and how; what was he told so far, and had Yedida and the children been told privately. I learned that upon returning from the United States, Ezra began to complain of a stomachache. Yedida and he suspected it was an ulcer, possibly resulting from the stress of his mugging in the United States. He was treated with the usual ulcer remedies for several months: a change in diet and antacids. But the pain continued and got worse.

Finally, Ezra's doctor put him in the hospital for tests. That was when the doctors discovered cancer in his digestive system. He began a series of chemotherapy treatments: pills and injections. Everyone was hopeful that the cancer would simply go away.

Now, after more rigorous tests, my sister Yedida was told that the cancer had spread to his brain. It was incurable. She still kept this secret from her husband. She insisted that he be permitted to spend as much time as was possible at home with her and the children. She cooked the best, most flavorful meals for him and fed him by her own hand like she had one of her children.

When Ezra was ready to come home the next day, I drove to the hospital in Yedida's car with his daughter Ornah. Ezra greeted me with a puzzled look. He was pleased to see me as always but there was also a concern in his eyes. He must have thought, *If I'm only mildly sick with stomach ulcers, why would Saul come visit me now, all the way from America?*

He did ask me if this was one of my regular visits to Israel. I tried to make light conversation and draw the subject away from the strangeness of my visit and therefore the seriousness of it.

We got into the car and Ezra insisted that it was time for his adorable daughter Ornah to learn to drive. I was delighted to see him strong enough to give Ornah a driving lesson. It was fun and also scary. Ornah was easily intimidated with every remark her father made about her driving. She would get flustered and then forget to hit the clutch or look out for a bump in the road.

We returned home quite safe but a little shaken and thrilled at the same time. We sat down and drank some hot tea, a normal mid-afternoon ritual, as if everything were quite ordinary.

One day, Ezra turned to me and said, "Saul, why don't we take a walk to the *Moshavah* (the center of town) and have some ice cream?" Then he leaned closer to me and whispered, "I haven't had ice cream in a long while."

I was surprised by the oddness of the request, but thought ice cream just might be the thing for the pain in his stomach. "Ok, I don't mind the walk," I said. "I love ice cream."

My sister gave me a stern look, as if to remind me that I promised not to tell Ezra about the cancer diagnosis. I nodded reassuringly at her.

Ezra and I left the house and walked about a mile to the *Moshavah*. There, we purchased our favorite ice cream cones and Ezra insisted on paying. "You are my guest now. You paid plenty of times when I was in America. Now let me, please."

As we walked back I could sense that Ezra was rather tense and restless, something was on his mind. "Saul, what you think of this ulcer business?" he finally asked. "Am I one who could get ulcer?"

"Well, what I've heard is it can afflict anyone," I answered calmly, hoping that my composure would reassure him. "It's caused by tension and aggravation —worries maybe. My own father underwent surgery for Ulcers years ago."

Ezra wasn't buying my answer. I had a feeling he knew better, but I had promised my dear sister Yedida not to reveal his illness. If I did, I know she would say that by my careless action I had hastened his death. I tried then to change the subject, talking about his adventures in the America.

"But, tell me," Ezra persisted, "is an ulcer so hard to cure? Is an ulcer treated with radiation?" he said logically almost in the spirit of a scholarly debate, as he continued to lick his ice cream cone. "You know, the patients next to me in the hospital are all sick with you know what—that illness."

I didn't answer. I just couldn't.

He noticed my painful silence. That was when he put his arm across my shoulders. "It's OK, Saul," he said quietly. "I am glad to see you. You should come here every year, at least once a year. Your parents are not getting any younger, you know."

By now, tears were filling my eyes and streaming down my cheeks.

"Did I say something wrong?" Ezra asked. "I am out of place. Forgive me"

"No, no, Ezra, you're right," I admitted, wiping my face with my handkerchief. "I ought to visit more often. I have deep regret and guilt for leaving my family so long ago. I wish I could come back home. Permanently"

Ezra patted my back and comforted me. What an odd turn-around this conversation had taken.

When we arrived back at Ezra's house, near the famous Weitzmann Institute, we had finished the last of the ice cream cone. Ezra took my hand and walked the few steps up to his apartment. He was really weak I noticed.

My sister was patiently waiting at the door. "Welcome, welcome back you two," she greeted us with a smile. "Just in time for a snack and tea."

The following day, I took the bus with Ezra and Yedida to the hospital. The children stayed home. At the hospital, we walked the long corridor to the Oncology department. Dozens of patients were lined up to be examined by the doctors. Some were being treated with chemotherapy. I thought, *How can Ezra not know what is happening here? How can he not know that he's afflicted with cancer like the rest of these people? Was he playing along to make it easy on my sister, his dear wife, and his kids?*

In the evening, I sat at a small table in my room and wrote a tearful letter to my wife and children. Describing my sad visit and anticipating the tragic end of my beloved brother-in-law Ezra, I cried for hours that night. In the morning, I went to the Post Office to mail my letter. I returned and began preparing for my departure the following midnight. I had barely seen the other members of my family.

At the airport, we were all tearful as we said our goodbyes. Ezra had stayed at home with the children. Yedida and my brothers and sisters spoke of the wonderful man who was about to die so prematurely, leaving my sister a widow. It was heartbreaking. I hurried to the inspection station to avoid any further agony and waved my last goodbye to them.

Six weeks later, on May 20, 1982, Ezra died in the hospital. His secret was kept to the very last moment. But I wonder whose secret was not told? Was it Yedida's that she kept from Ezra that his diagnosis was cancer and not an ulcer? Or was it Ezra's that he had kept from her all these months that he knew, just to ease her pain?

Such gifts these were that true lovers give like those in the O. Henry story, "The Gift of the Magi," about the young wife who sold her hair to buy a fob for her husband's watch that he treasured and the young husband who sold his watch to buy her combs for the hair she loved so. Ezra and Yedida were two such giving people. Example to all of us.

Saul with brother-in-law Ezra (left) at hospital just before
his death from brain cancer, Israel, 1982 (82)

Chapter Seventy-Two

Our house is burglarized: The last straw

Back then, when our basement was flooded, in the midst of the cleanup, we felt at times like we might never recover from these losses, especially emotionally. But life goes on, and as long as you have your life, anything is possible. We cleaned up our house in Huntington, let go of what was unsalvageable, and slowly regained our sense of joy and hopefulness again. As time passed, we were probably even prouder of showing off our gains and accomplishments after what we had gone through. Each year, the wild property was gradually turned into a cultivated garden, with a vast green lawn, a cement swimming pool, basketball hoop, huge patio, and over a hundred leafy shade trees. Our social life improved considerably. I was traveling much less and came to love our close-knit family life. Now we had three wonderful daughters, and we added a new family member: an adorable dog (half sheepdog, half poodle), named Taffy. We felt truly blessed.

Of course, such idylls can't last forever. I don't know why this should be so, but so it is. One Friday night, we came home from a family dinner and as usual, our youngest daughter Sharon ran ahead of us to open the house while I parked the car. As she entered she noticed right away that things were different. The wrought iron gate protecting the den was shattered to pieces, which negated the very reason for its existence: To protect us from intruders.

The rest of us were filing into the house when we heard her screaming: "Dad, Mom, we've been robbed!" We ran inside and looked around in shock: The heavy, professional gate must have been broken with a significant hammer. Rachelle checked the kitchen while Suzanne ran upstairs to the living room and looked around: The TV, stereo, and all our other electronic appliances were in place. Sandra scanned the bedrooms and thought everything was fine but then she screamed, "Mom, Dad, come quick."

We all ran upstairs where Sandra was pointing to the space in the master bedroom closet where we kept the house safe.

"There is no safe! They cut the chain and stole the safe," she repeated.

I panicked. Our most precious possessions were kept in the safe: my important papers and my wife's best jewelry, which she had taken out from our bank safe just a week earlier for an important wedding; she hadn't had time to return them yet. Rachelle sat on the edge of the bed and cried, feeling stupid and unlucky and afraid.

She looked at me for sympathy as she tallied the losses. "All the precious jewelry you bought me in the Orient is gone. And your mother's beautiful bracelet, my best gift ever, all that is gone."

"Who could have done this? Who could have known about the house safe?" we asked each other. I asked the kids, "Did you ever show any of your friends this safe? Did you ever talk about it?" They all said no and swore it was the truth.

"Well, we have to call the police and report this."

My wife jumped to her feet. "Better yet, dial 9-1-1. Maybe they can still catch them. Hurry, hurry."

I dialed 9-1-1 and began to explain.

The operator asked if anyone was injured.

I said no and she informed me, "This is not the purpose of 9-1-1. This is not an emergency. Call your local precinct."

I did, and they listened, totally unimpressed and detached. "There's nothing we can do about it, except write a report. In the meantime, make a comprehensive list of what is missing or damaged and report it to your insurance company. You will have to come over here to file a report. Here is your reference / case number."

With heavy hearts my wife and I left to drive to the precinct. We locked the house door behind us and cautioned our daughters not to open it for anyone. At the station, we filed a report and were given a copy to take home.

"We'll make some effort to find out who did this but don't expect us to catch these thieves. We are understaffed and busy with more serious crimes. The important thing is to go home and make that list I told you about on the phone."

We spent the next few days taking inventory of what was broken or stolen. We studied our insurance papers and discovered we were quite underinsured, as we had not modified the policy with each acquisition of jewelry and other valuables, for years. I had a bad taste in my mouth and Rachelle said she was sick to her stomach. For the first time, we contemplated selling the house and moving farther out on Long Island.

About six weeks later the insurance company came through with a check for $7,500 to cover a loss we had estimated at over $30,000. The police also had bad news: They had caught the thieves but the one who committed the break-in was a retarded youth, with a history of mental illness and couldn't be held responsible for his actions. As to what they stole, everything had been sold immediately, at a fraction of the value, to unknown parties.

We were disappointed with the people we paid so much taxes and monthly payments to protect us: the police and the insurance company. The jewelry was truly unique and irreplaceable, loving gifts I had bought for my wife from the best stores in Korea, Singapore, Taiwan, Hong-Kong, and Japan. We felt violated and let down. Yet, as has been proven time and again in history, "time is the great healer," and indeed we were able to survive this loss too, for we still had our health, our home, and each other.

Chapter Seventy-Three

My Three Wonderful Daughters

The story of my life would be less significant if I were to leave out a tribute to one of the best parts of it: being the lucky father of three fantastic girls. I just want to chronicle their dates of birth, schooling, and some of their special characteristics. Suzanne was first, three years later was Sandra, and seven years later we were guaranteed to have a boy when along came Sharon. They are all truly wonderful.

My daughter Suzanne

Suzanne was born on Saturday, August 5, 1967, at Queens General Hospital in Queens, New York. If you've ever been in New York in the middle of summer, you know it is a hot and humid time. My wife Rachelle has never been a complainer. Through the whole experience of surrendering her body to the care and development of this new stranger in our midst, my wife was cheerful, excited, and beautiful. However, when August came, the thermostat rose, both outside on the city streets and inside Rachelle's internal perspiration factory. The poor woman was overheated, sweating all the time, "big as a house," yet she was able to deliver a strong and healthy baby girl in a big city hospital in Forest Hills. I am forever grateful for the graciousness of her sacrifices.

Suzanne was a beautiful baby, with a sunny, perpetual smile. Being the first-born granddaughter to Joseph and Hannah Gertel, my dear in-laws, she was the very light in their eyes. Once, upon returning from a business trip to the Far East, I met my wife and baby in the Bronx, at the home of the Gertels. We decided to go for lunch at the waterfront restaurant on City Island. After that we strolled along the beach. Suddenly, Suzanne broke loose and, before we could stop her, had dashed headlong into the ocean. Rachelle and Hannah screamed, while I dropped the bag I was carrying and ran into the water after this baby girl, shoes and all, and fished her out of the waves. I was still in my business suit and tie, and I didn't hesitate for a second in knowing what to do. For a single, ponderous moment, I was presented with a life-altering experience: the fear of losing my child. Rachelle and I never forgot this day at the beach, and kept a vigilant eye on our children always.

As our little girl grew, she loved to play dress-up and enjoyed the feminine art of high heels and strutting around thinking she looked like a grown woman. Suzanne was a sociable child who played easily with friends and was always generous sharing her toys, games, and possessions. Her older cousins (Michelle, Alex, and Danny) adored her. Her aunts told us she reminded them of my sister Berta, when she was that age.

Three years later, when her sister Sandra was born, Suzanne assumed the position of mentor and guide, loving and protecting her sister at every step. She made many favorite friends at school, many of whom have stayed loyal to her to this day. She loved playing in the snow, building castles, bridges, and tunnels. One day, as her mom begged her to come in the house and warm up, she insisted on staying outside and asked for a hot chocolate. This was provided but minutes later she spilled the boiling hot liquid on her foot and suffered second-degree burns and had to be brought to the hospital for treatment.

When Suzanne was in high school, her sister Sandra called her mom one day and asked her to bring her sneakers down to the school for gym class. When Rachelle went to deliver the sneakers she was waiting in the school hallway, reading the bulletin board. To her amazement, under the caption "Missing from School," she found Suzanne's name, along with the names of her best friends. Laurie and Caroline. Rachelle was flabbergasted. This wasn't like our daughter. She delivered the sneakers and conferred with Sandra about where Suzanne might be instead of at school. Not a snitch, Sandra shrugged and denied having any idea. But on a hunch, Rachelle decided to stop at the nearby McDonald's, and sure enough, the three buddies were sitting there having French fries when they should have been in history class!

All three girls were duly grounded after Rachelle reported this incident to their parents; even though they were all good kids who made good decisions most of the time, no one wanted to give the impression that skipping school was acceptable behavior. Suzanne was an A student who had to work hard to attain high grades, and we reminded her that she needed to be in class to learn the day's lessons. Her friends were good students too. Laurie later married and worked as a teacher, while Caroline went on to graduate law school and became an assistant district attorney in Brooklyn.

One summer, Suzanne surprised us by volunteering to work as a camp counselor on a long trip to the Grand Canyon and Vancouver, guiding teenage boys and girls and sleeping outdoors in tents. That summer with her away should have prepared us, but then, before we knew it, our eldest child was old enough to go off to college. She chose NYU for all the obvious reasons: that it is a great school, not far from home, we could pay resident tuition, and the neighborhood is a thrilling place to be, Soho, especially as a young adult just launching yourself into the next phase of your life.

I sent her off with the most generous feeling of excitement for her, and a little bit of jealousy too, as I recalled my early days in Manhattan: the colorful scene in Greenwich Village during the '60s, all the poets and musicians, food from every country in the world, talking, drinking, and laughing into the night. My friends and I wrote lyrics to songs and recorded ourselves: we all wanted to be songwriters and rock stars. As I thought about my daughter leaving home, I feared the liberal attitudes of the times, the culture of marijuana and drugs. It was difficult to let go of "my baby" but I recognized this was what is supposed to happen: A child grows and gains security and independence by going off to live on her own.

I am at another chapter in my life, I thought as I drove Suzanne to her luxurious university dorm on Fifth Avenue in Manhattan, with her stuffed animals, favorite pillow and blanket, and treasured possessions piled high in the back seat of my big GTO. Sandy and Sharon came along. We drove through the Mid-Town Tunnel and parked at the door of the dorm building. After we helped unpack her belongings and set up her closet and bed, Suzanne wanted us out of the way as soon as possible. We said hello and good-bye to her roommates, and hugged and kissed Suzanne where they couldn't witness this sentimental display of affection, out in the hallway.

It was hard saying good-bye and leaving without her. But it was all for the good. She met wonderful people during her time at NYU. One of her roommates became a movie star; another moved to Israel, married and settled there; another married in Spain; one married in Turkey, another in London. Her friend Gordon became a Broadway director, and her funny friend Maxine took a sales job with a Spanish magazine and traveled to all the Arab countries to sell advertisements. To this day, Suzanne has kept in touch with these loyal friends, who now live all around the world.

She graduated from NYU in 1989 after majoring in Communications, with a minor in Art History. I had always heard her say she wanted to be a doctor. But the liberal arts influence of NYU caused her to abandon this aspiration; she had no interest in being "a money machine," she had decided. She worked as a freelancer for various TV stations in New York for a while: Channel 4, 7, 13, and others. She devoted nearly ten years honing her writing and editing skills, working nights sometimes, which left no time for social activity. When she decided to give up the challenges and uncertainty of the freelance life, she interviewed with Morgan Stanley and was hired immediately in the Corporate Communications Department, where she remains.

Suzanne was living alone in an apartment on 12th street and Second Avenue the night she fell. She was mopping the kitchen floor, slid, and fell facedown on the floor, breaking her nose. She had to have plastic surgery on the nose, and the "money machine" surgeons did an excellent job of restoring her to look like her old self.

She moved to her own apartment on West End Avenue on June 27, 2003. Her career as group manager at Morgan Stanley has gone well. Even though she is single and on her own, she was able to buy a one-room studio with a divider that has a great view of the Hudson River and city skyline. She goes through stages, trying to meet someone suitable to marry, including Internet dating—with great disappointment. Luckily, these days, women don't have to rely on men to support them or make them feel whole and happy. Suzanne appears to be a happy adult, avid reader and writer, a thoughtful person.

My daughter Sandra

Sandra was born in Queens on July 30, 1970, at the same hospital as her sister Suzanne. Another summertime baby. Unfortunately, I wasn't able to be there at the birth to encourage my wife: I had left that morning to attend an important business meeting in Manhattan when Rachelle was not in labor yet. By 11:00AM, however, she was—and had to be driven by our neighbor friend June to the hospital.

Right from the start, this new baby was a night owl who nearly always gave us a hard time when it was time to go to sleep. Every night she came up with some excuse why she couldn't go to bed: I'm thirsty, I need a drink of water, I have to go to the bathroom, I'm hungry—and all the variations. When she was around two years old we used to put her to sleep in Suzanne's old crib—but not until she was good and ready.

"No, I sleep nine o'clock," Sandra told us.

Rachelle and I had to laugh at this tiny little girl who had latched onto "nine o'clock" as the time that sounded late enough for her.

After we fed her, brought her water, and led her to the bathroom, we left her in the crib and went off to sleep in our own room. No sooner would my head hit the pillow than she'd be back up and at 'em, climbing up and over the crib rail and falling down to the floor. This went on for months and we were becoming seriously sleep-deprived and grouchy. One night Rachelle was at the end of her rope, and in desperation I took the wide-awake Sandra out to the car, strapped her in, and drove her around the block a few times. She was all bundled up like a mummy child, wrapped in blankets in the back seat. She fell asleep within minutes! Stunned, thrilled, not wishing to disturb the grace of the universe that might grant us all a night of sleep, I parked the car back in the garage, silently unraveled her from her bondage, and carried her carefully upstairs. As I laid her sweet, sleepy body down into her crib, I recognized the extraordinary beauty of sleeping children, not only because they are literally so beautiful, but also because they are asleep! This drive around the block became known in our house as "the Cure" and whenever Sandra was restless and couldn't get herself to sleep, I dragged her out and we rode off into the night, whether it was rainy, snowy, or lit by the light of the moon.

By the time she reached high school, this spirit of restlessness hadn't abated. Unlike Suzanne, Sandra didn't need to study so hard to obtain A's and she was always working at part-time jobs to earn her own money and thereby express her independence. By the time she was sixteen she had worked as waitress in a posh restaurant in Northport, a dental assistant in Huntington, a salesperson at the Gap children store, and took up a hobby to which she has remained dedicated ever since: photography. During our rich period of living "the good life," Sandra was the first to learn to water-ski behind our boat and learned to drive it and maneuver it out on the bay on her own. There was the famous day when she lost control in wild weather, and we always laughed, reminding her of her frantic call for help: "Mayday, Mayday," she cried, and in all the ruckus, ended up dropping my highly-prized, expensive camera in the harbor, never to be seen again.

Perhaps needless to say, this was a bright child, with a mind of her own and the stubborn willfulness that often goes along with high intelligence. Her exasperated teachers in high school recommended that she jump a grade and Sandra started college at NYU at age 17. After a year she felt bored, she told us, and initiated a quest for adventure. She explored possibilities, made some contacts, and came to us with a proposition.

"I'll be able to save you a lot of money if I transfer to Hebrew University in Jerusalem. I'll still be pursuing my higher education, I'll see more of our family in Israel, and it will be a great chance to have some fun in my life."

I protested. "You are too young for such an adventure."

To which she promptly responded by reminding me of my own long journey away from home in 1958. I reminded her that I was 20 when I left home, not 18. She in turn reminded me that certain 'progress' has been achieved by humanity after so many years.

I tried, but soon learned that there was no way that I would win this argument.

Sandra applied and was immediately accepted into Hebrew University, to study political science and international trade. She lived outside the university dorms in Jerusalem with a few other girls and made many friends. Particularly pleasing to us was her affinity for our extended family, especially my mother. They formed a mutual admiration society. My mother firmly believed, "This one could survive anywhere on the face of the earth."

We were all terribly proud of Sandra's achievements and were starting to relax our worries about her being so young, and about being in Israel at all, a war-zone really. Then suddenly we were notified that she wanted to take a break from her studies and join the Israeli Army!

We were scared for her. Though she was by no means a hothouse flower, I still thought of her as a delicate American girl. But, just as we couldn't keep her in her crib at night when she was a baby, we could do nothing to stop her from exercising her will. She was 18, an adult, and well aware she did not need our permission anymore.

So, my middle daughter joined the Israeli Army. I supposed that I should take it as a mark of flattery that she wanted to follow in my adventurous foot-steps. Except I knew all the dangers too, from hard-won personal experience. Plus, she was a girl! Alas, the times have changed (to update Bob Dylan) and women have proven to be as strong (if not stronger, though I hate to admit it) than many men.

Sandra excelled at basic training and was soon promoted to be a "Trainer." A year after that, she was voted "Most Promising Soldier" in her division and earned the honor of being photographed with Ehud Barak, then Chief of Staff, later the Prime Minister of Israel.

She wrote us many engaging letters home during those years, including inspired praise for this boy friend Ronen whom she met in the Army and was dating. Their wedding at Kibbutz Sereni in 1997 is among my happiest and proudest moments.

A letter to Sandra in Israel: November 26, 1988

Dearest, beautiful, intelligent, political activist, 5,000-miles far-away daughter Sandra,

Yes, I miss you very much, as you miss us. But your sense of humor is truly therapy for all of us. It provides us hopes and consoles our spirit. You are in the Promised Land, across the oceans and cultures, where written history began (and may someday end... I just hope not yet!).

Your letters and telephone calls have the curious effect of a mixed emotional reaction: happy and melancholy, sweet and sour, if you will. Which reminds me that nothing has changed (remember, I used this expression on your sweet 16th), nothing is new under the sun. You must retain your convictions and spiritual commitment to accomplish what you aspire to do. To reach high is so typical of you. I am proud of you, my daughter, keep it up.

As for your desire to stay another year in Israel, and possibly volunteer for services in the Army, Mother and I are most distressed. I hope you are not telling us what you have done already, but what you would yet like to do. Of all the decisions you have made on your own, this one will cause us the most pain. It is destined to break our hearts.

"Those who do not learn from past mistakes are condemned to repeat them." You know this saying. Sandi, please don't repeat my own mistakes: I chose to leave my family at an early age and live far away from home. At the time it seemed like the right thing to do, but the decisions of my impetuous youth came to haunt me in later years. I could never extricate myself from the guilt, which I still carry deep inside me. No matter what rewards have been obtained, it was a high price to pay.

My father's passing away brought me back down to life's reality. I can't stop thinking "what if?" And "how I wish, if I had it to do all over again." Sandi, regardless of how you rationalize your action now, you will be "accountable" later on.

I am so happy to read how close you feel to Pirha, Yeftah, Avram, Yedida, Hannah, and especially to my mother. I am glad you are enjoying the love that they have for you, love that has been stored and suppressed for so long. But I trust that you are bringing them joy, too, being the natural extension of our family. This is the experience of your life; no one can take it away from you. You will no doubt treasure these times for the rest of your life. They will keep you warm in the winter's cold, if winter nights should ever befall you (which happens to us all).

Your love for Israel and its people is understandable. I am proud of you and of those who have exerted such positive influence on you. But we want you here with us: we want you to be a happy, mature, young lady, eventually with a husband, family, and a home of your own. Trust me, we are mentally ready to be grandparents, as life is too short, sometimes shorter than we expect.

Suzanne is most excited about her upcoming trip to Israel. Robin has proven to be a high-quality, lasting friend of hers, worth of your loyalty and friendship. Show them a good time in Israel. Please try to attend Suzanne's college graduation.

Missing you very much.
From all of us,
Dad

A fax from Sandra in Israel: January 1, 1989

(Rachelle and Sharon visited Sandra in Israel while I stayed in New York to work. For the first time in many years, I found myself left alone in the house, and I'm not sure what I would have done with myself, without their "loving" communiqués from the other side of the world):

Dear Mr. Fathi,
Your wife and daughter have been kidnapped by the fanatic movement named the "Fathi Clan" (the Eastern Hemisphere faction). If you ever wish to see them on American soil again, you must come immediately to Israel, with lots of presents for your lovely daughter Sandra. When you arrive at the airport, you are to be alone (except if you care to invite your charming daughter "Sushi"). You are to inform no one of your arrival (otherwise all your crazy relatives would kidnap you and we'd have no one to demand a ransom).

One of the Fathi Clan members will pick you up at the airport and transfer you to where we are holding your dear Rachelle and "Shren." Our threat is very real. They will not be released if you do not arrive within the next 24 hours (or at least, send a fax, you negligent dad!). They love you and miss you and are waiting anxiously to see you or hear from you.

Sandra Fathi
Faithful Leader of the Eastern Hemisphere Division.

P.S.: We are waiting to hear your reply, telephone number 011-972-3-6715-920/1/2

Fax from Sandra in Israel: January 3, 1989

This page included a very elaborate drawing of me behind a desk, surrounded with paper and signs, a printer and fax.

Dear Daddy Fathi,
I called home and you're not there. I assume that you are at work, as

usual. Just thought I'd drop you a fax and remind you that I love and miss you.

Take care, don't work too hard.

Love,
Me (Sandi!)

A fax from Sandra in Israel: February 12, 1989

Imagine a drawing showing a modest home with a long driveway.

*Fathi Galactic Productions presents, for your viewing pleasure, now appearing:*Saul Fathi, Home Alone. *Coming to a neighborhood near you!!!*

He doesn't cook. He doesn't clean. He doesn't do laundry. He doesn't know where the extra toilet paper is.
How will he survive?

I love you,
Sandi!

A fax from Sandra in Israel: February 15, 1989

Hello Mr. Fathi,

I hope that you are not too lonely in that big house all by yourself. We miss you dearly as usual. Mom and Shren are very busy. They have already seen Pninah, Tziporah, Motti, Sala, Masha, Channah, Fruma, your sister Hannah, Grandma, Yedida, No-Am and Maya, Avram, and today they are on their way to visit Pirha. (It's the See-All-Your-Relatives-in-5-Days Tour).

Next week, I will be done with work and we have rented a car through my employer (got a good deal). We'll be staying at Ronen's house. He and his family can't wait to meet Mom and Shren. We'll take the car up north to the Golan and Tiberia for a few days. Maybe we'll go to the Banias or the Sachneh. Remember those places? Then, on Saturday, we'll go to the Dead Sea. Are you jealous yet? If not, there is more. When Mom leaves, Sharon and I will go to Elat! Ha, ha, ha, ha.

Don't be too upset. I promise that when you come I'll take you to all those places and more! Maybe we can even get a stopover in Alaska on the way back.

Other than that, we are all happy and healthy, but we'd be happier if you were with us.

Lots of love and kisses,
Me (Sandi!)
P.S.: Give a hug to Sushi [Suzanne's nickname] when you see her.

A fax from Sandra in Israel (on Massadah letterhead): June 30, 1989

Dear Mom, Pops & Shren,
I am working hard and trying not to go crazy. But I think it's not working. I miss you as usual, and I am impatiently awaiting your arrival. In the meantime, I can be reached at 011-979-3-...
Please call, write, or send me messages by mental telepathy. But be in touch!

Love,
Your Footon daughter, Sandra

A fax from Sandra in Israel: August 5, 1989

Dear Sushi,
My sister Sue, how I love you. When you have something in your eye and when you make me want to cry, you are the smartest, bestest, most beautiful big sister that I know. Even if it doesn't always show, I think you're a wonderful cosmopolitan babe, and who the hell needed that shitty job anyways?
I hope that the coming year will be better for you: more happiness, more romance, more luck, and more letters. For example, from Publishers Clearing House telling you you've won a million.... although we know that you're worth a billion.
Happy, happy birthday!
Wish that I could be there today. Maybe next time, maybe sooner.

Signing off,
Sandra Fathi
Galactic Connection CEO,
Eastern Hemisphere Division

A letter to Sandra in Israel (while Rachelle and Sharon are there on a visit): August 11, 1994

Dearest Sandi,
Your faxes are a great source of entertainment to me. Everyone was impressed with your considerable artistic talent on the drawing. Especially your last one: "The Kidnapping." Your argument almost makes me want to spend my last dime and come to the rescue. But, I know they are having a good time, so I am not jealous. But I am envious.
I miss you and your mom most of all, but I also miss everyone who is trying to show them a good time. You have no idea how much Mom needs it (and deserves it).
I had a wonderful dinner at the Nissan's last night. They are so warm to me. They send regards.

Suzanne and I spent the weekend together.
I don't think I will learn to cook, wash the dishes, or do the laundry this time either. Unless my dear ones stay another month in Israel.

Love and kisses,
Dad

A fax from Sandra in Israel: August 16, 1994

This one was written during my wife and daughter's visit and came with an elaborate drawing, depicting a king with tears streaming down his cheeks.

Hail to the Great King Fathi,
Ruler of his own kingdom, from the far edge of this back yard down through the rolling pastures to his mailbox. But alas, the king is alone: His queen and princess have run off to a foreign land to be with his exiled daughter Sandra.
More to come in this exciting saga....

Meantime, love and kisses,
Sandra

After completing her Army tour of duty, before returning to the U.S., Sandra and her friend Debbie took a dangerous trip to Egypt, and rode a slow boat south to the Sudan, photographing hundreds of enchanting places and faces. We worried to death for her safety: She could have been caught and executed as an Israeli spy, without any regard for her being American-born.

She came back to the United States after her service in the Israeli Army, and quickly got a job as a translator at the United Nations, and as a volunteer at the UJA (United Jewish Appeal). But she felt restless as usual, and soon decided to go back to Israel and her boyfriend Ronen.

I liked writing in my journal when I wasn't sending faxes.

February 27, 1995
Sandy left the U.S. today and returned to Israel. Her visit was short and eventful. She came and left, like a hurricane, leaving a few broken hearts behind. Or, was it a cool evening breeze?

Sandra's engagement party to Ronen, Huntington, NY: September 21, 1996

This day was surely one of those rare-in-a-lifetime celebrations, with over 150 loving guests and relatives all in the same place at the same time, to mark a happy rite of passage. I took it as a good excuse to fix up the yard, and spent countless laborious and pleasing hours pruning, mowing, and gardening in preparation. I must say, all the hard work paid off as the place provided an excellent and colorful backdrop to the photo sessions at the party. It helped that

September 21 that year was a singularly perfect autumn afternoon. Everyone was memorably happy.

Never one to miss a chance to "wax poetic" I called everyone to quiet down so I could make a toast. I took over the crowd's attention and compared my daughter Sandra to my favorite Chinese soup: "hot and sour." Everybody laughed, because they knew what I meant: that Sandra had brought us happy days as well as worried us to death.

I wished Ronen good luck in intending to marry her and in subtle and not-so-subtle ways let the man understand how I felt about "handing her over" to him.

"Every father thinks no one deserves his daughter," I said and met his eyes directly, man to man. He understood and nodded his head with a smile.

I also hinted it would please me greatly to see them living here in the U.S.

Going to Sandra's wedding:
Rachelle, Sharon, and Hannah fly to Israel, January 2, 1997

They scheduled their wedding for early January, when the weather in the part of Israel where they lived is welcoming. But in the U.S. it is important for businesspeople to tend to the future growth of their market shares during these first days of each New Year. I had always used these days in January as time to get grounded and kick off the year strong, by working with renewed energy and focus. I joined my family in Israel three days after Rachelle, Sharon, and Hannah went over. I couldn't very well miss my daughter's wedding!

One favorite memory from the wedding was listening to the stories of Saba Naji, Ronen's 96-year-old grandfather, his father's father. We laughed uproariously at his depictions of the rigorous military training he received with the Turkish Army and at the awful predicaments he found himself in while in combat zones all over the Middle East. Saba Naji took small breaks while he talked, to eat some of Ronen's mother Miriam's great food. Seeing how much we enjoyed his exciting stories, he continued to tell us one anecdote after another.

Once, he leaned forward to whisper in my ear that the Russian maid who had been employed to clean his house and wash his clothes and dishes did far more than just that. She served as his companion, even though she was some fifty years younger than he was. She was supposed to be a licensed nurse, but she wasn't, and he didn't care. He said that the second-best thing he enjoyed about her were the wonderful baths she gave him. He didn't mention out loud what was the best thing he enjoyed, because it really wasn't necessary. We laughed.

I had a great time, hearing all of Saba Naji's secrets. Then soon discovered that all the secrets he was whispering in my ears actually were well known all over town!

On January 19, 1997, our party of ten flew back on El-Al to New York, happy that we had shared such a wonderful time in Sandra's life with her and her new family. We remembered all of the wonderful people we had met and the interesting stories everyone had to tell us, especially Saba Naji and his escapades.

Sandra and Ronen visit U.S. as husband and wife: May 1997

This was a very brief visit, during which they rented a car and drove all around the United States, to show Ronen how beautiful and vast this country was; perhaps this was her way of convincing him that they might want to settle here.

On their return flight to Israel, the plane had to go through Egypt airspace. I was scared to death for their safety. At the time, peace with Israel was shaky, their government had been labeled treasonous, and Egypt wanted to appease the unhappy population by arresting and executing Jews as spies. The Egyptians were attacking and setting fire to tourist buses. Luckily, with God's blessing, their little family made it safely back to the homeland.

Grand Daughter Danielle: September 7, 2000

Our first beloved granddaughter Danielle was born at 4:18 AM, September 7, 2000, in Dallas, Texas, almost four years exactly, since the blissful engagement party in our backyard in Huntington.

At that period in their lives in Israel, Sandra had been working at a technical magazine called "People and Computers", and had been promoted to Editor. Ronen worked as a statistician for a major Israeli bank. Both began to see a limited future for themselves in Israel, and, to our great pleasure, decided to move to the U.S. They achieved that in stages, by Sandy going to work for an Israel software company with her stated ambition being to expand into the U.S. market. After three months with the company, she was offered the opportunity to join their newly opened office in Dallas.

In September, 2000, our whole family flew in to be together as our lovely Sandra gave birth to a beautiful baby girl: me, Rachelle, her mother Hannah, and my other two daughters, Suzanne and Sharon. In the first hours there was so much talking and hugging that no one was hardly paying attention to the powerful contractions and deep breathing going on in the next room. We took it for granted that there would be no complications and everything would be "full steam ahead." Then after twenty hours of labor, it was decided they would need to deliver the baby caesarean style. Now we entered a hushed realm of serious-ness as we came to truly understand the miracle that is new life, how fragile it can be, what a gift. All due respect was paid to the divine planner who determines the fate of us all, as we waited and prayed that mother and child might come through this passage whole and intact. So our hurrah was particularly raucous (out of the hushed silence) when word was given that Danielle had safely arrived!

Hallelujah. With gratitude.

In December 2000, Sandy visited us in New York with sweet baby Danielle. The pleasures of being a grandfather are akin to my early memories of fathering my daughters, but parts of it are even more exquisite. This new incarnation of the

Fathi family leads me to peer from the highest mountaintop over my domain and kingdom, the next generation pointing the way to eternal life, as I see our family line stretching off to include Danielle's future children, and so on.

The other side of that coin, of course, is it means my turn on the planet is moving toward its final orbits, and I begin to ponder my own mortality, what I have accomplished in my lifetime, what awaits me on the other side.

I brought this question to the dinner table one night when the whole gang of us were assembled to do what Jews in America like to do on Christmas Day: eat Chinese food. We were passing the rice bowl, plates of pot stickers, egg rolls, Kung Pao chicken, chow mein, the works, when I asked who at the table believed in Heaven?

"You mean, do these egg rolls make me think I've died and gone to Heaven?" Sandra said. "No, definitely not. I can get better egg rolls in Dallas."

Much discussion ensued about the relative merits of egg rolls in Chinese restaurants in the various neighborhoods where the extended arms of my current family configuration lived. But I was sitting there honestly trying to come up with a serious answer to this profound question: What happens to us after we die? Unfortunately, I remained alone in my philosophical stew, as everyone else was feeling too alive and hungry to pause in the middle of their happy lives to consider death, or any other great mysteries of the universe. Once I let go of my frustration that no one would engage in this topic of conversation with me, I joined in the raucous banter and counted my blessings that we were all alive and well, healthy, and together.

When Sandra and Danielle had to return to Dallas on December 31, I was grateful they at least lived in the States and not in Israel. But still, I left them at the airport with a heavy heart and wished that they lived even closer.

The next year on January 28 (2001), my wish was granted when Sandra decided to move to New Jersey, and rent out their large house in Dallas. She had started a new job with a Dallas-based company who had a branch in New Jersey. After a few months she asked her boss a favor: to transfer her to New Jersey "to be close to my parents." Ronen wasn't thrilled with his job in Dallas at the time, and tagged along.

Not a month after the move, Danielle fell from a swing and hurt her head. The date was February 18; I remember because it was snowing really hard that day, and Ronen had to shovel his way out to get the baby to a doctor for X-rays. She was all right, thank goodness.

In late March that year, Ronen, Sandy, and Danielle visited Israel, for a nostalgic tour of places they had lived and put in time during Army duty, reminisce at famous landscapes, and visit extended family members. I think it was also one last trip to see whether they really wanted to put down their roots in the United States, or stay in the Jewish homeland as a show of support for the country's cause for peace. I like to believe it was because they wanted to be closer to us that Sandy and Ronen ended up buying a house in Teaneck, New Jersey, on May 31, which meant they were staying a while.

That year is full of happy summer memories: barbecues, beaches, being with the three of them at Central Park Zoo in August, celebrating Danielle's first birthday in September.

The following year Sandy started her own consulting business, Affect Strategies, working from home, dealing with corporate communications and promotions, a consulting company. They managed another trip to Israel that year, April 17 to April 28.

Ronen's last day as an accounting consultant was July 3, and I was quite worried for their financial future, as I was in no position to help. When my son-in-law let me know a few weeks after leaving his salaried job that he was going to start his own business: Babyride, selling baby strollers, and other kid paraphernalia on the Internet, I admit I was skeptical and thought he should try to find a secure job with a guaranteed income. I knew from experience the challenges of running a business yourself, the whims and variables of the economy and the market. However, within a year, Babyride had reached $100,000 per month in sales, and I'll be damned if the guy didn't prove me wrong. Their little family is doing very well, and I am quite proud of them all.

Sandy and Ronen went to Dallas in July, 2002, and Rachelle and I had Danielle for a glorious, 3-day weekend. Then, on August 1, Ronen's mother, Miriam, arrived in the country and was able to enjoy the best of East Coast summertime at Fire Island with our entire family. Danielle brought everyone so much pleasure—just by being herself. We all took a little tour boat from Bayshore Marina, a 30-minute ride off into the sunset, and I was never so happy.

Miriam had to return home, but my happiness lingered when the rest of us were able to gather for Danielle's second birthday party on September 7, 2002. Then a half a year later, I was reminded of mortality once more when Ronen's grandpa Saba Naji died in Israel at the age of 97. I felt of two minds: one, I could be next; two, I am a long way from 97, maybe I can look forward to many more "golden years."

Ronen, Sandra, and Danielle flew to Israel to join his family in sitting *Shiv-Ah*. Once, on the way to Dallas airport, three-year-old Danielle, becoming increasingly wise to the ways of the world, noticed all the Texas flags and asked her father, "Aba (Daddy), when are we going back to America?" Everybody laughed, to think that this baby, who had recently learned to recognize the American flag, thought the Texas flags meant that she was in another country!

On May 7, 2004, I went to Danielle's school for a party to celebrate "Grandparents Day." I had so much fun, laughing at the sight and sound of Danielle's Chinese and Korean classmates singing our old Hebrew songs and saying Shabbat prayers. "It's a small world after all" is right.

My daughter Sharon

Sharon was born in Huntington, Long Island, on October 9, 1978, at 8:00 P.M. We all piled up in our car and drove to the hospital. I cannot deny that I was hoping for a son. We thought, "third time's the charm" and kept our fingers crossed. But you know what? I wouldn't trade my daughter Sharon for any boy. And, as things have turned out, being the sole male in a house full of women who love him has not been a terrible fate. I settled in with the vicissitudes of femininity, hormones, pink, tears, and "girl power," well aware that these were not soft women easily messed with, argued with, or bossed around. My girls clearly had minds of their own. I blame myself: I must have had something to do with that.

Sharon was a child who was always dancing and cheerleading. Many compared her to those wind-up dolls in music boxes. She loved horseback riding, which cost us a small fortune at the nearby Riding Academy. She learned French. But her true love for a while was Jazzercise, which she participated in at schools and colleges all over Long Island. Then she took up figure skating, and after that, joined several soccer teams.

During one summer camp with USDAN, she met Olivia, a bright and beautiful girl from Lloyd Harbor, with whom she remains close friends to this day. When Olivia graduated college, she went to work at Disney World in Florida, and Sharon has enjoyed several visits to this fantasy park.

This daughter of ours always had a deep love for animals: She was always coming home with dogs, frogs, turtles, parakeets. Once, she could no longer take care of this one turtle, who grew so fast she had to buy him a new cage every six months. As usual, it fell on Rachelle to take care of the pets, until one day she took the overgrown turtle beast and all the other animals and gave them as a gift to a local pet shop.

Sharon attended Albany University. The first two years she lived on campus, then moved to an apartment she shared with two girls, above a small deli owned by a Pakistani (who later refused to give her back her one-month security payment. We never found out why.).

When she graduated from Albany, May 21, 2000, we stayed at the Swiss Chalmette Motel. The graduation celebrations were grand, a rite of passage I have always enjoyed. The ceremony was held at an indoor stadium, attended by thousands. It was an exciting 48 hours, for us, our daughters, and Rachelle's mother, the proud grandmother Hannah.

Sharon returned home on May 24, 2000, and was hired by Anderson Consulting (later changed name to Accenture). She worked there until September 11, 2001, when the company suffered terrible losses at the hands of the terrorists, as the Twin Towers collapsed in an inferno of fire.

One day, Sharon was looking in the family photo album and noticed a great discrepancy: "How come there are so few photos of me, compared to Suzanne and Sandra?" she asked. "How come there are four albums of Suzanne, two albums of Sandra, and only a few pages of me?"

We felt embarrassed and didn't know exactly how to answer without hurting her feelings.

"Well, as you know, the novelty of having children wears off over time," her mother answered truthfully—and soon regretted it.

"Yes, especially because you were hoping for a boy, instead of me. I bet you were both really disappointed when I came along instead."

We assured her we wouldn't trade her for a world of boys.

Sandra as a soldier in the Israeli Army, pride
of the family, Israel, 1995 (83)

Ronen and Sandra's wedding, Israel, 1997 (84)

Saul at Sandra's wedding, Israel, 1997 (85)

Daughter Sharon at Sandra's wedding, Israel, 1997 (86)

Daughter Suzanne at Sandra's wedding, Israel, 1997 (87)

Chapter Seventy-Four

Sandra Weds Ronen in Kibbutz Sereni / Israel: January 9, 1997

Our daughter Sandra had been engaged to Ronen Twiss, a boy her age whom she had met while serving in the Israeli Army. When they set the wedding date for January 9, 1997, in Israel, we wondered how we could plan a wedding over several thousand miles away and in another country. It turned out, we had nothing to worry about. Sandra and Ronen had arranged every detail. All we had to do was show up. We bought wedding gifts and new clothes, and ten of us on the American side of the family booked an El-Al flight to Israel to attend the wedding.

Sandra, in her infinite wisdom, had rented an apartment for us in Tel-Aviv that overlooked the Mediterranean. It was most convenient. For a few days prior to the wedding, we walked around Dizingoff Square, leisurely shopping at the local boutiques and sampling the culinary delights of all of the restaurants.

On the wedding day, we traveled to Kibbutz Sereni, some 30 minutes drive south of Tel-Aviv. It was a magnificent location, perfect for a wedding, with its thousands of citrus and palm trees lining the roads and planted in neat little gardens. The foyer of the main building where the wedding was to occur was opulent. There were Italian marbled floors and walls that gave the building a palatial look.

Further inside was the magnificent wedding hall where we were greeted by the Rabbi. After introductions were made, he led us to a small, secluded room, off to one side. Here, we met Ronen's parents. The Rabbi told us of the local custom of agreeing on the *Ketubbah*, an ancient document of marriage that detailed all of the marital obligations and listed the contents of the dowry. Everything was explained and decided with the Rabbi's genial coaching. The young couple and the witnesses then signed the document.

Suddenly, the Rabbi asked, "Where are the cigars I requested?"

Sandra had telephoned us before we had left New York and requested that we bring a box of good Cuban cigars with us, which we did. But, upon hearing the Rabbi's audacious request, Ronen's father, Tzion, took the cigar box we had brought and hid it. He told us, "He is getting paid lots of shekels for the ceremony. That's enough."

We suddenly had an embarrassing dilemma on our hands. Do we give him the cigars as agreed or do we hold our ground on principle because the Rabbi wasn't humble about his extra gift? As we were contemplating our response, Tzion's brother, Shaoul, began distributing the cigars to the male guests in the hall. We realized that we had to do something because the Rabbi would be greatly offended when he saw those fine Havanas in someone else's hands.

We quickly made an excuse to the Rabbi and went out and bought him three cigars. When we returned to the hall, we gave the Rabbi his precious cigars, and he promptly tucked them away in his jacket vest. There was no visible reaction from him.

For nearly two hours, we stood at the door of the hall, greeting the guests, who had come by charted buses from all over Israel. Most of them came from the town of Afulah, Ronen's hometown in the far north.

Ronen's father was constantly saying, "This is my brother," or "This is my sister," or "This is my cousin." There was always a new relative to be greeted with enthusiasm. There were so many relatives I can't remember how many hands we shook that night. Our hands were sore.

During all of this, the music from the wedding band was blasting. It wasn't traditional music; it was something very familiar. Sandra and Ronen had chosen a small African-American band that happened to be performing in Israel that season to play for her wedding guests. They were very good and helped keep the wedding guests in a happy mood. Brothers and sisters began to arrive. Every one looked happy. Mother looked radiant, without father, of-course. We wished he could be here to participate in our happy occasion. He loved Sandra very much and always felt she will be able to survive and prosper anywhere in the world.

We danced and laughed all evening. It was great fun to be with all of the members of our new family, young and old, especially all of the cousins we never knew. But, my mother-in-law Channah out-danced all of us, even at age 83.

The food was great, too. It was especially gratifying to see my mother sitting at a table next to Yeftah, with whom she had not spoken for years. She was laughing and joking all night but would not get up and dance. She never danced in her life.

Yeftah danced, though, wiggling his buttocks from side to side to the pleasure of everyone present. And, of-course, he went on a spree of joke-telling, drawing a crowd of listeners around him as he always had. They quietly absorbed every word, and then would burst into raucous laughter; some falling to the floor in sheer merriment.

Throughout the evening, I noticed something near the door of the hall. It was a huge box, resembling a McDonald's garbage can, chained to a pole. We watched as guests stopped by the large box and slipped in money and checks for the newlyweds. At the end of the evening, the Master Of Ceremonies unchained the box with all of the grandeur of a state occasion and then dumped its content into a black plastic bag. This, he gave to Ronen's father to give to the couple.

This was the signal for everyone to go home. The wedding had been magnificent in every detail, and we had spent six hours in sheer happiness, becoming a bigger family as we met new relatives and shared the joy of our daughter and son-in-law's new life together. Now, the celebrating was done. We went to our apartment in Tel-Aviv, and Ronen and Sandra went on their honeymoon.

Saba Naji and the Turkish Army

We continued to meet with our new relatives and talk with them on the phone for the next ten days. Before we flew back to the United States, we were invited to what we thought would be a small dinner party at Ronen's parents house in Afulah. Ronen's mother, Miriam, had set up a huge table that practically moaned with all of the dishes she had prepared. It was the equivalent of a twenty-course meal! In addition to us, she had also invited a few guests and neighbors to share this feast. As we all gathered, she began serving one delicious dish after another. There was so much food and so much good will we stayed for many hours.

One of the most enjoyable parts of the evening was being introduced to Saba ("Grandpa") Naji, Ronen's father's father. Ninety years old, Saba Naji was a talkative, happy-go-lucky man with many fascinating stories in his head. His wife had died a few years earlier, and he remained in his house, alone and managed fairly well. His grandchildren kept an eye on him by visiting him two to three times a week and brought him some of their mother's delicious dishes.

Within a short time after our introduction, Saba Naji stood up and began demonstrating with a broom on his shoulders how he served in the Ottoman Army in World War I. Normally, the Jews and other minorities were exempt from service, but the Turks were having a hard time holding on to their empire, and so they began drafting non-Muslims into their ranks. These men were put in the front of the line and were used as cannon fodder, to be sacrificed for the Empire. Very few of them ever returned. Saba Naji was one of those lucky ones.

We laughed uproariously at his depiction of the rigorous training he received and at the awful predicaments he found himself in while in combat zones all over the Middle East. Saba Naji then took a small break and ate some of Miriam's great food. Seeing how much we enjoyed his exciting stories, he continued to tell us one anecdote after another. Once, he leaned forward to whisper in my ear that the Russian maid who had been employed to clean his house and wash his clothes and dishes did far more than just that. She was serving as his companion. Of-course, she was some fifty years younger than he was and was also supposed to be a licensed nurse. He said that the second-best thing he enjoyed about her was the wonderful baths she gave him. He did not mention what was the best thing he enjoyed, but it really wasn't necessary.

I was having a great time that evening, hearing all of Saba Naji's secrets. I soon discovered that all the secrets he was whispering in my ears actually were well known all over town!

On January 19, 1997, our party of ten flew back on El-Al to New York, happy that we had shared such a wonderful time in Sandra's life with her and her new family. We remembered all of the wonderful people we had met and the interesting stories everyone had to tell us, especially Saba Naji and his escapades.

Saba Naji Is mugged!

Saba Naji's daily routine was to get up at 6:00 am and go to the *shook* ("open, outdoors market"), where everyone greeted him. The vendors and customers extended their hands and shouted, "Hi, Mr. Naji." He returned their greetings. Then, with a big grin, he proceeded to buy vegetables, complaining about the merchandise or the prices or the trustworthiness of the merchants, always in good fun. When his shopping was done a few hours later, he returned home and made himself a salad. Then, he sat and watched TV, waiting for the Russian maid to come to clean up and greet him in her own way.

A few months after we had returned to New York, we heard that Saba Naji had been mugged by some teenagers, who had probably been on drugs. They had followed him from the *shook* to his house, forced the door open, and demanded that he bring out all the cash he had stashed under the carpets and anywhere else. When Saba Naji failed to produce enough cash to satisfy his assailants, they knocked him down on the floor, stepped on his head, and kicked him brutally. Then, they burned him with lit cigarettes. He was found the following day near death by one of his grandchildren.

The family then decided it would be safer for Saba Naji to live in a nursing home, surrounded by other people his age and the protection of a watchful staff. He sold his house and distributed some of his money to his seven sons and two daughters and his grandchildren. Then, he moved into a facility within an hour's drive of his sons.

Six years later, on April 23, 2003 the family was notified that Saba Naji had died in his sleep. Ronen flew to Israel sit *shiv'ah*. The *shook* certainly was a lot poorer with his death. The vendors and the customers missed being entertained by Saba Naji's antics.

We miss him still.

Chapter Seventy-Five

My Brothers and I at Kibbutz Yo-Av

During one of my recent visits to Israel on my last day before I returned to the United States, my brother Avram informed me that this day was reserved for just us three brothers. Avram, Yeftah, and I were to spend the entire day together, and I was not to let anything or anyone interfere with Avram's plan.

"We are going to have a great time," he promised.

"What do you have in mind?" I asked.

"Be ready at 8 am," he responded. Then, at my questioning face, he added. "It's a surprise you will enjoy. Don't worry."

Avram picked me up at our sister Hannah's house. He announced, "Next, we go to Ah-Keer for Yeftah. I hope he won't let us down, as he's done before."

When we got to the village of Ah-Keer, there waiting outside for us was Yeftah, smoking a cigarette. We were delighted to see him.

We drove south about an hour and turned onto a dirt road not far from the Biblical town of Ashkelon. A big sign announced *Khah-mei Yo-Av (Hot springs of Yo-Av)*. We followed the winding road, lined with palm trees on both sides, until we arrived at a gated entrance. Avram pulled out three tickets and brochures describing this unique place, Kibbutz Yo-Av.

Some years back, it was discovered that the property sat atop deep, hot streams of healing mineral water. The kibbutz designed a beautiful sanctuary that directed the water to pools where visitors could enjoy vacations there. For a time, they were freed from the stresses of everyday life, from a world full of wars, divorce, and disenchantments.

This was indeed a pleasant surprise sprung upon us by Avram. We stripped out of our tight clothes and dipped our bodies into the bubbling hot waters, slowly adjusting our skin to the warm temperature and letting our noses get used to the pungent scent of sulfur. There, immersed in healing waters, three brothers enjoyed each other's company for the first time in many years. When we had had enough of the warm pools, we rested in the shade under the dates-laden palms. We took some pictures under the gorgeous palms.

We spent the entire day, bathing. Then, we showered and ate and drank together, lingering over the food and reminiscing. Yeftah was in a good mood. He told us several very funny jokes that sent us rolling on the ground.

Yeftah's Famous Joke: The Emperor and the Samurai

One of Yeftah's jokes has stuck in my mind. There once was an Emperor in Japan who had lost his most trusted Samurai to illness and needed urgently to replace him. He ordered his people to hang posters in every town and village in Japan, announcing the search for a top-notch Samurai Warrior. Candidates were to compete among themselves, producing their own champions, who then would gather in the Emperor's Palace. These finalists were wined and dined as they competed in a last elimination challenge where only three Samurai would rise as the best in the land.

Upon reaching this point, the three Samurai were summoned before the Emperor and his entourage. The Emperor's second in command officiated in one final contest. He announced the rules of this competition. "Pay full attention, please," he said and pointed to a small wooden box. "We have here several very fast and agile bees. I will take out one at a time, hurl it in the air, and you are to use your swords to cut and dismember the bee."

The first contender stepped forward. The Emperor's man opened the box slowly and took out one bee and hurled it into the air. The first Samurai unsheathed his sword and with one thrust, cut the bee in half. The two halves fell on the floor. He bowed, satisfied that he had qualified. He stepped aside, proud.

The Emperor's man removed another bee from the box and hurled it into the air. The second Samurai immediately swung his sword and cut the bee's wings. The bee fell to the floor. The Samurai bowed happily and stepped aside.

The third Samurai looked worried. *How was he going to outdo these fantastic and successful Samurai?* He pondered this dilemma deeply. The Emperor's man then pulled the third bee out of the box and hurled it far into the air, making it impossible for the last Samurai to reach it. Undaunted, the third Samurai thrust his sword at the bee with all his might. But the bee continued to fly.

The Emperor's man brushed the last Samurai aside. "You have missed the bee and have lost. You may go home now."

The indignant Samurai answered, "Nonsense, I have not missed the bee. Examine it closely, and you will see that I have cut off his penis!"

This Samurai won the position of Chief of the Samurai Guards in the Emperor's palace.

A night visit to the cemetery

Avram and I laughed and laughed at this great joke. Then we all showered, dressed, and went on our way back to Rehoboth, in uniquely playful moods. It was dark by the time we reached town. And, Avram had another idea.

"This is your last day, Saul," he said. "Would you like to pay a visit to Father in the cemetery?"

Yeftah and I looked at each other, initially believing this to be a weird and morbid idea after having spent such a fine and fun day together. Then I considered his proposal and said, "Yes, why not?"

On the way, Avram stopped at a grocery store to buy candles. "It is customary to light candles when you visit the dead after dark," he said.

Yeftah laughed and said, "Of course! The dead have to see who is visiting at this hour."

We all laughed loudly.

Avram bumped us over the long dirt road to the outskirts of Rehoboth, and we arrived at the gate about 8:00 PM. It was already very dark. You could barely see the shadows of the tombstones.

"How are we going to find Father's tombstone?" I asked. "It's hard enough in the daytime."

Yeftah had an idea. "Why don't we drive inside the cemetery and leave the car running with the headlights on? We might get lucky and actually find our father."

Avram agreed reluctantly, as this was not usually done. But Yeftah always had a way of convincing you to do things you wouldn't normally do unless you were in his devilish company.

Avram maneuvered the car slowly, careful not to hit the tombstones, and tried to get as close to the location of Father's tombstone as possible.

"There was a tree there, one lonely little tree, about fifty yards from the tomb, I remember that," Avram asserted. "If I can find that bush, we will find Father's tombstone."

We drove around the narrow boulevards of the cemetery, looking for the famous bush and the tombstone it grew beside. I wondered, *what will anyone who sees us think, grown men negotiating a car through the darkness, amongst rows of stone monuments and crypts?*

Finally, Yeftah pointed to a squat little tree, no more than a bush. "Here it is, here is the tree," he shouted.

Then he looked at Avram, as if on a dare. "Now show me Father's grave."

Avram shrugged and got out of the car. He looked all around, walking between the headstones, making gestures to us now and then to follow. Instead, we remained near the lighted beams of the car's headlights, uncomfortable to be wandering among the dead at night.

Finally, Avram came back and announced, "I found it. Come follow ." Though the car engine was silent, its headlights lit the way. We followed Avram bout a hundred yards. Sure enough, there was our father's tombstone. It was a rather nice one, similar to many around him.

Yeftah's teary reconciliation with father

The headstone was engraved with the inscription, "Silas (Saleh) Fathi. Dear Husband, Father, and Grandfather. Born 1903, Passed Away June 6, 1986." These facts were written in English and followed by a Hebrew translation.

We stared at the stone carving for a while. Then Yeftah whispered, "I'll be damned. It's been a long time." He was looking at the tombstone as if our father had come back to life and was standing behind it.

Avram pulled out the candles and lit one for each of us, then placed them inside the little compartment in the back of the gravestone, so the wind wouldn't blow them out.

Yeftah attempted to recite a few words of *Kaddish* and, to our amazement, began to cry. *Was he repenting for some of his recent escapades? Was he reaching out to make up with Father for the years when they hadn't spoken?* I was touched and bewildered. I reached out and hugged him.

"It's all right. Cry all you want. We are here alone, just us three brothers," I told him, and tears welled in my eyes, too. Avram joined us and coughed from the depth of his chest, unable to suppress his own tears.

We stood in the dark graveyard in the candlelight, as constellations held steady in a sky that changed all the time, from night to day and back to night again, as we small humans lived and died here on this small planet in the space of a vast universe none of us could understand.

"Why did things go so wrong?" Yeftah cried. But neither Avram nor I could answer. Yeftah continued, "Our lives could have been so beautiful. So many things could have been different. We didn't need much to be happy. Do you remember those days? We should have stayed on in the kibbutz. That's where we left our childhoods behind and never found them again."

But of course, all childhoods must be left behind. We grow up, assume responsibilities, face the harsh facts of life, and live as best we can.

We brothers hugged again.

"It's getting late," Avram finally said. "Everyone must be going crazy, wondering where we could be at this hour."

He pulled us both by the arms, and we headed back to the car. It was almost 10:00 pm.

Who visits at this crazy hour?

Avram drove us out of the cemetery and headed toward our mother's tiny apartment. It was so late that we had to knock on the door at least ten times, and still she didn't answer.

I became worried. "What could have happened to her?" I asked. "Can't she hear these loud knocks?"

Avram pushed me aside. "Don't you know by now that our mother, Salha Fathi, is a very smart woman? She never just answers the door at this hour. You have to speak to her. She has to hear your voice, so she knows it's you."

Finally, in response to our shouts and hellos and begging, Mother opened her door. She seemed startled. "Who visits at this crazy hour?" she asked, forgetting to say hello to her sons. She was just in her nightgown. We reached in to hug her and apologized.

"Well, don't just stand outside in the dark. Come in, for heaven's sake," she said.

She made us sit down on the edge of her bed and began to peel apples for us. I don't know what possessed us, but someone (it must have been Avram) took pictures of us all in Mother's small living room that night. When I saw the photos later, I was surprised by how old Mother looked. Then, I realized that before we arrived she had removed her dentures before going to bed. I had never seen her without them. In the pictures, our mother is smiling without her teeth and accepting her grown sons into her home, though it was very late. You can see how she loved us in the way her eyes embraced us, and her toothless mouth turned up in pleasure.

Eventually, however, we had to separate again. We had to go.

Yeftah said, "Avram, please drop me off. I can't walk all the way home at this time of the night."

I knew that my brother Yeftah must have walked these very streets at hours later than this many times before, but he wanted, I believe, to stay with his brothers just a little longer, to extend the gift of the day. Avram nodded matter-of-factly, thinking the same thing as me, I imagine. We said our goodbyes to Mother in a hurry, before we all started crying again, and caused her to worry over her sons and the raw state of their emotions.

We waited outside until we heard the latching of her many locks. Then, we climbed into the car again.

Yeftah's home was five miles away, in the opposite direction from where I was staying with our sister Hannah. Silence overtook us on the way.

What a glorious day this had been. We three brothers had been together all day. This had never happened before or since. We rode along, deep in our own private thoughts.

I was thinking, *Yeftah is right. It could have been a beautiful life. But it wasn't meant to be. That's not our fault. There are forces larger than we are at work in the universe.*

We said goodbye to Yeftah, not imagining that it was the last time I would ever see him alive again. Avram drove me to Hannah's. To my surprise, my sister was up watching TV and waiting for me.

Chapter Seventy-Six

Memories of My Brother: Yeftah

Yeftah moves to America: August 18, 1969

In 1969, my dear brother Yeftah finally left Israel and came to live with me and my family in New York. His command of English was poor and he said he felt like a real foreigner; it was hard for him to imagine he could land a salaried job in this country. He had always been an independent sort anyway. In his first months of living with us, every day he rose from his sleep and dressed nicely to go into Manhattan to "roam the streets for opportunities," as he put it. One day he came home to us, all smiles: He had found a store in NYC, right across from Alexander's on 58th Street, selling newspapers, candy, and tobacco. He wanted to borrow money to rent that store.

Without hesitation, Rachelle and I agreed to help my brother establish himself and get on his feet. We felt it was a good omen that he had found such a store, as it suited Yeftah's personality so well. He launched himself into the business and for a while he seemed very happy. When our father came to visit, he helped out in the store, handling customers and inventory.

Yeftah is mugged in broad daylight

One late afternoon my brother was working in the store alone when two black youth walked in, pretended to buy candy, then demanded he empty the cash register and hand over all his cash. One had his hand in his jacket pocket, in a potentially lethal position. Yeftah assumed he was armed and complied with their demand. He gathered all the money into a brown paper bag and handed it over.

The boy grasped the bag of cash and ran. It took a minute to sink in, what had just happened, and suddenly Yeftah felt indignant, cheated out of his own hard-earned money. He decided to go after them. He abandoned his store, leaving it unattended, to run after them. The boys split up when they saw him approaching, and started running down both sides of the street. Yeftah concentrated on the one closest to him and caught him. He knocked the boy to the ground, stepped on his head, and kicked him in the stomach. He then sat on top of him and continued to beat him up. People gathered. The accomplice noticed what was happening and walked over to return the money to Yeftah, to spare his buddy further punishment.

When my brother told me the story later, he realized, "I wasn't thinking straight. I could have been killed. It was lucky they weren't armed. "

Instead of retreating into a cowering position, after that day Yeftah took the opposite tactic, and always walked around with a big bundle of cash in his shirt pocket, as if to say "I dare you, go ahead and try to take it."

Yeftah was Yeftah. He managed to get the money back that was stolen from him, only to lose it to his new secret addiction to horse races and poker games. We did not know of his vices until they began to take over his good sense and his life.

Night fishing with Yeftah: October 1969

Yeftah lived on his own by now but he liked to come visit us on Long Island and play with Suzanne, our firstborn. I always enjoyed our brotherly get-togethers, and he often expressed his deep appreciation to Rachelle and me for helping him to acquire the store and get started in business in America.

Tonight I had a secret plan for the two of us. I thought we needed to break out of our routines of working all the time and staying in at home. I asked Yeftah if he would like to do something unique with me.

He was curious, never one to turn down an adventure.

"What? What can we do that I haven't already done?" he asked with a smile, challenging me.

"Have you ever gone fishing?"

He laughed. "You're asking a merchant marine if he has ever gone fishing? Of course, a thousand times, and I am good at it too," he replied.

"What about night fishing?" I answered.

His eyes opened wide.

"There is such a thing? How, where?"

"There is a party boat that leaves from Popeye Dock on Long Island at 10PM, fully equipped, and comes back at 4AM. They supply the equipment and bait, you bring your own food and drink"

My brother was intrigued.

"Sounds good, when can we do this?"

"Tonight, if you want to," I said and remembered to turn to my wife and ask, "Is that okay with you?"

Rachelle laughed and agreed without hesitation.

"Go have fun together, just please don't bring me any fish here."

My wife hated cleaning up fish for cooking. And I hated eating fish.

So Yeftah and I prepared a few sandwiches and cold soda, packed them in a cooler, and left to drive about 45 minutes to the south shore. We easily found Popeye Dock and approached the young captain and asked if we could join him for some night fishing. He welcomed us and motioned us to climb aboard.

Are we fishing or playing poker?

The boat filled up with about 30 passengers, then the captain started the engine and began motoring away from shore. I had no real idea what to expect, and was rather surprised when within minutes the poker tables were set up, beer started to flow and men lit cigars and started freely tossing around profanities. Yeftah felt right at home and joined them, inviting me to do the same. I sat next to my brother but didn't play as I'd never learned the game. Most of the guys were pot-bellied and middle-aged, wearing baseball caps. My brother and I were the youngest of the bunch, besides the captain, who appeared to be in his mid-twenties.

We floated out to sea and were perhaps four or five miles from shore when the poker players excused themselves one by one and left the table to prepare their bait and cast their rods into the water. After securing the poles to the rails, they came back to resume the card playing. At some point the captain shut the engine off and lowered a small anchor, to minimize the boat's drifting.

The warm, breezy night sky was abundant with stars, and out so far from the commerce and hubbub of life on land, the air was absolutely quiet. In the distance we could see a few lights blinking on the water and we guessed they were other party boats. The card playing and beer drinking grew raucous, occasionally interrupted by someone's desire to check on the fishing rods and to yell an enthusiastic scream of excitement when a fish was caught.

The boat explodes: We're in the water without life jackets

The captain's radio was playing oldies songs and everyone was enjoying the serenity of the night and the feeling of camaraderie aboard the boat. It was approaching 3AM when the captain went down below deck and emerged with a jerry can full of diesel fuel. He unscrewed the gas cap, removed the long cigar in his left hand and tucked it behind his ear, then bent over to pour the fuel into the tank when suddenly his cigar slipped off his ear and fell into the fuel tank.

The boat exploded with such force, we were all immediately scattered in the cold water, holding whatever debris we could grab onto and screaming bloody murder. The captain was in it with us, completely disoriented, shivering: "I'm sorry, my fault, I'm terribly sorry," he kept repeating, trying to swim to the boat and salvage what he could. The men were holding on to what remained of our vessel for dear life. Yeftah was an excellent swimmer and rushed over to me, remembering that I was not. "Is everyone o.k? Is anyone hurt?" the Captain yelled again and again.

"Are you okay, Saul?" he asked me with a quiver in his voice, recalling my near-drowning experiences of the past.

"Yes, yes, but I don't know how long I can hold on."

My life was staked to a wooden bench whose legs had been blown off, but it was very buoyant. The exploded fuel tank blanketed the ocean around us with flames, and the shouting and chaos were terrifying. We swam closer and gathered around the boat, the captain murmuring to himself, counting the number of men he could see alive in the water.

Rescued by other boats

It seemed an eternity but was probably no more than minutes before other boats converged on us and fished us from the water one by one. We were divided to a number of boats and hauled back to port. We thanked our rescuers and our Maker and got into our cars, wet, with no fish, glad to be alive.

On the way back Yeftah and I agreed to keep this a secret from the family: No point in frightening them as much as we were frightened ourselves. We agreed it would be a night to remember, just between us. I noted to myself that I had just been miraculously saved from drowning, again, which was surely God's blessing, but still, I never went night fishing again.

Yeftah's costume jewelry store in Jamaica, Queens: February 1970

Winter in New York passed peacefully and it was a new decade, the seventies. My brother came and went freely and we didn't ask many questions, assuming no news was good news, as he seemed to be okay. I don't remember how we came to know that Yeftah no longer owned the store in Manhattan, but instead owned a small store in Jamaica, Queens, in a poor neighborhood of the city. He sold cheap costume jewelry in a place where he could sit all day, attend to customers when they came in, and otherwise make his own jewelry, using simple hand tools. Yeftah displayed his old talent of working with his hands, and his creations were truly artistic and inventive. Maybe, I thought, he has found a calling and can advance from this to something better.

Yeftah never explained what had happened to the store in Manhattan, and I never asked. Our father had returned to Israel and knew nothing of this. What took place in his business was his business, and I wanted to spare him embarrassment if his reasons were dubious. The situation in the new store was certainly simpler. The value of the entire inventory was less than $5,000. The average item sold for less than $5. Yeftah's customers were mostly Black and Hispanic, people he readily related to as fellow minorities, and they were happy with one another. He always felt more at home among outsider types. Rachelle and I relaxed and tried to stop worrying about "my little brother," even when I'd phone him in the store in the middle of the afternoon, and was surprised to find no one answering. If I called in the morning, he was always there.

Looking for Yeftah all over Manhattan: April 1970

He was living in Queens with a nice American girl, who loved him and wanted to marry him. After dinner one night, this girlfriend called and asked if Yeftah was with us. We were surprised, as we had not heard from him for weeks. She said he had not been home for the past 48 hours, and was worried something may have happened to him, maybe he had been mugged at the store, as the area was infested with poverty and drug addicts.

My wife and I began making phone calls to the extensive list of contacts Yeftah had cultivated and given to us from time to time. No one had heard from him lately, they said, and were all surprised to think he may have gone missing. They promised to make some calls and get back to us. By midnight and dozens of phone calls later, there was no trace of Yeftah. I decided to call the police in Jamaica and involve them in the search, but they had not heard of him or anything involving him.

Around 1:30AM we received a phone call from a friend whom we had contacted earlier. With enthusiasm he told me, "I found him, don't worry, he is at a friend's house in Brooklyn."

"Where in Brooklyn? What is he doing there? Everyone is worried to death, can you give me his phone number?"

He did hesitatingly and I thanked him and dialed the number.

When I asked for Yeftah, I heard, "Who wants him?"

"I am his brother, Saul, is he there? Can I talk to him?"

I was put on hold for a long minute before Yeftah came to the phone.

"Hello, Saul. Why are you so worried? I am just out with my friends, you know me, I hate to sleep, it's a waste of time," Yeftah said with his low laughter.

"Your girlfriend called to say you haven't been to your apartment in two days, and you don't expect us to worry? What's the matter with you?"

Yeftah was silent for a moment. "I'm sorry, this is how I live. I don't want you to worry about me, I am not a child anymore, Saul."

That was the night it became clear to us that Yeftah had a serious gambling problem. He was playing poker in Brooklyn, part of a group of players who rotated between houses. He was so hooked into the lifestyle, he didn't think he had to inform his girlfriend or family where he was or what he was doing, even when he disappeared for days at a time. I was embarrassed for him and hoped no one in the family would ever have to know that our brother had this shameful disease.

Engagement to an American girl: 1972

She was a new girl who came out of nowhere and surprised us. Rachelle and I graciously organized a party at our house and we wished them the best of good luck and happiness, but no one expected it to last. This was just another sign of my brother's desperation, his feeling that if he was going to settle in the United States, marriage to an American was the easiest avenue open to him.

Engagement to Edna in Israel: 1973

Before he ever married the sweet girl to whom he had promised his heart at my house, my brother suddenly decided he had had enough of the struggle in America. He had been living alone in a transient hotel in Queens, and one night he just decided to pack a small suitcase and depart for Israel. The landlord called us to remove his effects, mostly clothes, and my wife and I were upset with him over his abrupt departure without saying goodbye, and for his immature behavior in general.

Months later we heard he had met a lovely girl, Edna, a secretary in the municipality of our old hometown of Rehoboth. They were soon engaged and got married.

Edna (Yeftah's ex-wife) died from kidney complications: September 16, 2001

Her daughter Maya called to tell me. She suffered for over 20 years. Leaving a mother 91-years old... Imagine burying your only daughter...

Diabetes or suicide attempt?

On August 9, 2002 Yeftah's daughter Maya called to tell us her father had been hospitalized at Kaplan in Rehoboth. He was being treated for severe diabetes and was facing the prospect of having toes amputated.

"He's feeling depressed, Uncle Saul. He attempted suicide in the hospital, by swallowing a bunch of sleeping pills. The midnight nurse discovered the situation and they pumped his stomach and saved him."

I tried to offer words of comfort to my brother's grown daughter, but we were both distraught, and there was no comfort to be found in this situation. I promised to call again the next day.

No-Am makes peace with his father: August 13, 2002

Maya called again to let me know her father was now getting around by wheelchair and needed the services of a 24-hour nurse.

"My brother No-Am is here, and he's making up for lost time; they talked it all out, then they hugged and kissed and cried like babies," Maya said.

No-Am had been angry at his father for many years, for justifiable reasons in my opinion, and had been out of communication with Yeftah. Still, I had always encouraged No-Am to look upon the man with eyes of compassion and forgive him his weaknesses. My brother was no saint, but he deserved our love. That's what family provides: unconditional love, which means overlooking mistakes sometimes.

Maya thanked me for my efforts through the years to accomplish this father-son reconciliation. Of course, I had no part in it now; No-Am was a grown man and had to come to his own place of peace about his father's behavior.

I asked Maya to keep a keen eye on Yeftah and let me know of any new developments, or if she needed me to fly to Israel at any time, I would be there.

Yeftah is back in the hospital, complications of diabetes: September 9, 2002

When I was finally able to get my brother on the phone, I offered to send airline tickets, bring him here for a few months, and nurse him back to health.

"That's not possible, Saul, it's out of the question. I don't want anyone to see me this way, but thank you, you were always the generous one."

We both started crying, remembering all we had been through together as children, and as adolescents and men. We were not the same kind of person, but our love for each other ran deep and was abiding. He asked me to give warm regards to Rachelle and my daughters. And he thanked me for motivating his son No-Am to make peace with him. We were both choking back tears and could not continue to speak, so we hung up the phone and turned our attention to our separate lives, mine here in New York, with my work and my wife, my daughters and in-laws, Yeftah falling apart in a country far, far away.

Yeftah attempts suicide

In the beginning of November Maya called in tears to tell me that her father had attempted suicide again. He was still in the hospital, suffering from a new diabetes-induced infection. He had swallowed the entire bottle of sleeping pills this time, but once again was saved by a night-shift nurse who came to administer his insulin. I was shocked, and felt powerless to do anything. I asked Maya to please just be with him as much as possible, and to try to telephone me every day from his bedside, and reverse the charges.

A few days later the phone rang, and it was Maya.

"Hi, Uncle Saul, how are you?"

"I am fine, thank you. And how is my brother?"

"He is okay right now, I am here in the hospital, right beside him. Would you like to speak to him?"

"Sure, Maya, let me hear my brother's voice."

"Hi, Saul, and how is everybody there?" Yeftah asked in a weak voice, with slurred speech.

"Everyone is fine but we're worried about you. How are you feeling?"

During the long pause that followed this simple, common question, I had a strong feeling that my brother was broken spiritually. He could not express his feelings anymore; they were too dark.

He tried. "Oh, the diabetes is under control, my leg wounds are almost cured, but my head, I don't know, that's where the real problem is, like always."

He suddenly handed the telephone back to his daughter.

"Maya, please make him talk to me some more. I need to ask him a few more things."

My brother's voice came through, but it wasn't the same Yeftah I knew.

"Saul, I can't speak too long, I'm not allowed. Please don't worry about me, I'll be okay."

I would be remiss in my big brother role if I did not reprimand him, and remind him to think of others beside himself, even in his condition.

"Yeftah, I hear that you are misbehaving and causing unnecessary agony to your children, your family, and your friends. You know how much we all love you... Please don't do anything foolish, something that would darken our days forever... Have hope, you must have hope, things will turn out okay, you will see."

The cross-continental phone wires were silent but I could hear him choke with sobbing; he couldn't respond to my urging except to cry.

"Yeftah, did you hear me? Did you hear what I said? You have two wonderful children, don't cause them agony for the rest of their lives by doing something foolish. When will you be out of the hospital? I want to bring you here and nurse you until you are fully recuperated."

"Saul, I can't think about this right now, I need to feel better. You were always so generous, to me and to others. Let me get back on my feet and we'll talk another time."

There was another long silence as the phone fell from his ear and Maya came back on now, saying, "Uncle Saul, it is nice of you to offer to bring him there. My father says to tell you he really appreciates it. But, there is no way this can happen right now. He must recuperate first. He can't talk to you anymore tonight, the nurses are swarming around us, and they are going to get angry and throw me out. Let me say good-bye. I'll be in touch and keep you apprised of anything new."

That turned out to be the last time I heard my dear brother's voice.

Chapter Seventy-Seven

Brother Yeftah Dies: November 21, 2002

On November 21, 2002, my brother Avram called to notify me that Yeftah had died.

"How, from what?" I asked, in shock.

"They sent him home, he seemed okay, then suddenly he developed a high fever, 104, and they brought him back to the hospital and put him in a cold-water tub and tried to lower his temperature. But it didn't work. They said it might have been some bug, bit him in the hospital, his body was too weak to withstand it."

I could not breathe, feeling rage, anger, and an unbearable sense of loss.

I asked Avram to forgive me for a moment and I put the telephone down on the kitchen table to take a few deep breaths. I screamed "Why God, why?" I wiped the streaming tears from my eyes.

"They couldn't save him? What kind of a bug? Do you believe them? It can't be true. Tell me more." I knew I was making no sense, asking unanswerable questions, but I didn't know what to say.

"No, Saul, listen, they couldn't save him. Three doctors worked on him, but he just let go. He wanted to go, he was tired of this life, he had no strength left."

Avram didn't know I had heard about Yeftah's attempted suicide a few weeks earlier, and I didn't reveal it to him now, I couldn't say the words, I didn't want to speak such truth.

"Does Mother know? How is she taking this?" I asked with great concern.

"No, we didn't tell her yet. She will find out just in time for the funeral. It is scheduled for tomorrow, Friday, before the Sabbath," Avram said.

"Tomorrow? Why so soon? I want to be there, Avram. I don't think I can get there that fast. Can you delay the funeral by a day?"

"If we delay it, it will have to be for two days: We can't bury him on the Sabbath. It will have to be on Sunday."

"Okay, Avi, then make the arrangements for Sunday, please. I'll book the first flight I can, and inform you of the details when I have them. Take care of yourself. Give my love to everyone, especially to No-Am and Maya." (Yeftah's children).

As soon as I found some composure, I began calling airlines. Too late for El-Al, they were fully booked. But Continental came through: I would arrive Friday night. Saturday I would meet with the family and with my mother in her old-age home.

That night I said good-byes to my wife and children, and called my sisters Judith and Berta in New York with the news. I told them I would be attending the funeral and urged them to try to do the same, but Yeftah had burned bridges with them, and neither of them felt strongly enough about him anymore to attend his funeral.

I return to Israel for my brother's funeral

I arrived Friday, late afternoon, and Avram and my sisters Pirha, Yedida, Hannah, and some of their children met me at Ben-Gurion Airport. At first everyone put on a smile, as it was good to see each other. Then we began talking about Yeftah and the mood changed to somber, then teary.

My brother-in-law Haiim (Hannah's husband) drove me to their house, and we sat up late that night, talking and reminiscing over the "good old days." In the morning I began telephoning extended family members and confirming all the funeral details. The ceremony would take place in the old city cemetery, where our father Silas, and brother-in-law Ezra were buried.

On Saturday night I met with Maya and visited a printer of posters, to announce Yeftah's sudden passing and the time and date of the funeral, the following day. We went along Main Street, pasting and stapling the posters to poles. Then we decided the process was going too slow and Maya engaged pro-fesssionals to poster the town in time. We went home and continued to call relatives and friends, informing them of Yeftah's sudden passing and inviting them to the funeral. These were difficult, emotional hours, as everyone we called was shocked and reacted tearfully to the news. We were in the role of comforting everyone else, as we were trying to overcome our own sad feelings. Most people we contacted promised to make arrangement to be at the cemetery on time.

At 9:30AM Sunday I met with Pirha who drove in from Jerusalem and together we went to check on our mother to see if she was up to attending the funeral. Some relatives had suggested that we leave her to herself and not subject her to a heart-wrenching burial ceremony for her son. But when we arrived at her old-age home, we found her fully dressed and sitting at the edge of her bed, waiting impatiently for us.

"Where were you two? How come you're so late?" she reprimanded.

"It's not late, Mother, it's just the right time. Are you ready to go?" Pirha asked, with a faint smile.

"Of course I am ready, I have been ready, let's go," Mother answered.

"Are you sure you want to go? You don't have to, you know," Pirha explained.

"What kind of a question is this? Of course I want to, it's Yeftah's funeral, my son," Mother retorted.

At around 11, people began to arrive at the cemetery from all over the country. We congregated outside the cemetery gates until noon and by then nearly a hundred friends and family members were present. We greeted everyone as they arrived and received their condolences. Most men wore a *keepa* on their heads, while the women had a cut black ribbon pinned to their chest, symbolizing the idea of tearing at our clothes in grief; silk scarves covered their heads.

While waiting for the services to begin, I met some of Yeftah's friends, people I didn't know. Under the circumstances, I could not remember their names, but I do remember some of their comments: "I can't believe Yeftah is dead. He was a brother to me, a dear friend.... He was so generous, he would give the shirt off his back, holding back nothing... That's Yeftah. Everyone who knew him, loved him dearly.... His own brother and sisters never invited him to their homes in ten years... They were ashamed of him and his gambling. Gambling is not a crime, it's a disease, a terrible disease... His only son, whom he loved more than life itself, didn't speak to him for months, maybe years... Too much pain, Saul, too much pain... His nephews and nieces hardly knew they had an uncle named Yeftah. Why?... You know, the greatness of our Bible is that it describes the good and the bad, even of kings... No one is free of sin and bad deeds.... He didn't mean to hurt anyone, no! not Yeftah... He couldn't help what he was, it wasn't under his control... I'm sorry, but if he was a millionaire, in spite of his gambling, his sisters would have respected him, maybe even loved him. But he wasn't rich, he had no luck and struggled all his life...They were ashamed of him...When he was in the hospital and he tried suicide, then they all came to see him, feeling sorry for him at last, then they remembered they had a brother named Yeftah... And maybe then they realized that life is short.... Everyone deserves to be forgiven, no matter what... What have they learned from this tragedy? Nothing... I doubt they learned anything... Don't judge others, lest you be judged... That's wisdom, my friend... Anger and hatred punishes the bearer.... Remember what I say to you... He who doesn't forgive is punished the most, I always say... Forgiving is a great healer... Do you know how funny your brother was? He could tell jokes non-stop for 24 hours, non-stop... He had perfect timing, he could have been a professional comedian, I tell you... Tell me, where are your sisters Berta and Judith? They couldn't come to their brother's funeral?" I didn't answer, I listened, refusing to make excuses for them, absorbing my own guilt and complicity in the judgments, though I also knew I had tried to help him out many times in his life, and to understand my troubled brother and forgive him his ways.

I was wiping tears from my eyes and cheeks, and noticed that everyone around me was doing the same. I couldn't respond to Yeftah's friends and their observations. I just touched each one on the shoulder with sympathy and acknowledged their feelings. The Rabbi appeared at the cemetery gate then, and called on everyone to follow him. We entered a large entry room where the open casket rested on a wooden stand at the center. Everyone filed in and formed a circle around the box, staring at the body of Yeftah, wrapped in white linen, at peace in death, inside.

The Rabbi opened a folded sheet of paper and read the name of the diseased: "Yeftah Ben Saleh Fathi (Yeftah, son of Saleh Fathi). May God have mercy on his soul. Is that right? Could you identify him please?"

He pulled the linen off Yeftah's face and I turned away, feeling sharp pains in my chest. Maya was the brave one that day; she looked at her father closely and nodded her head, whispering, "Yes."

The Rabbi presented us with a death certificate to sign, and we signed it, then the ceremony began.

The Rabbi recited the Prayer of the Dead, then relayed a short account of Yeftah's life. Everyone was sobbing out loud. I stood near my mother, held her arm, and rested my head on her shoulder.

"What kind of life did he live?... A dog's life is better than man's... He suffered a lot... He lived for his friends... His friends were his world... What is a mother to do? I wish it was me instead of him... I have lived enough... Seen enough. " Mother murmured.

My poor mother, no woman should ever have to bury her own child, no matter at what age.

The Rabbi motioned us to follow him again as Yeftah's coffin was placed on a four-wheel open flatbed carriage, and the assistants began to wheel him toward his tomb. We walked a winding road, among hundreds of buried people, young and old, of all denominations. At the end of the procession we stopped near Yeftah's designated resting ground, the grave freshly dug and ready for him. We gathered around, encircling him once more.

Again, the Rabbi read a prayer for the dead, while we each laid flowers on top of the casket, and whispered private words to Yeftah. The Rabbi's assistant jumped into the tomb, standing on an inside ledge, and Yeftah's body was handed over, wrapped in white linen. The throngs let out cries and some pounded on their hearts and called his name: "Yeftah... Yeftah, why did you go so soon?" We circled closer, standing at the edge of the tomb, looking in on death, sobbing uncontrollably.

The Rabbi gave the prayer book to No-Am, Yeftah's son, who was trembling from the stream of his tears. He read the prayer slowly, breaking down to cry every few words, as deep pain enveloped us. I looked at my family, my friends and Yeftah's, then I walked around to shake their hands, thanking everyone for coming. I gave each person a weak hug, then rushed over to my mother who was surrounded by my sisters, wiping tears from their eyes. I thought once again, what a terrible thing it is to have to bury your own child. I held her close to me, encircling my strong and loving arms around her fragile, tiny body, bending so she could rest her head on her son's shoulder.

The Rabbi motioned the man to begin shoveling earth back into the hole, covering Yeftah in his permanent home. Members of his immediate family and his close friends began to do the same. The grave was slowly filling with dirt and the Rabbi asked if anyone would like to say anything for the last time.

"I'm sorry, I failed to protect my little brother"

I felt the urge to speak. I raised my hand and walked to stand at the very edge of Yeftah's grave. All eyes were upon me.

"Some fifty years ago, while attempting to flee the hatred of Jews in Baghdad and come to our safe home in Israel, my father gave me the onerous responsibility of protecting my younger brother Yeftah as we escaped in the night. He said to me, 'Look after your younger brother, you are the eldest, protect him from harm.' I was ten years old. Yeftah was eight-and-a-half. I did my best to protect him then and we survived a long and hard journey. Now, fifty years later, light-years from those terrible days, I feel ultimately I failed to protect my little brother. I promised my father to protect him, but I failed. And now I can't go back and correct my shortcomings. I'm sorry. My only hope is that all of you who loved him to the end, will remember him, and pray for him to find some peace...." I couldn't continue, my whole body was shaking, everyone was weeping. My mother whispered something no one could hear.

To feel useful, I began shoveling dirt and gently throwing it over my brother. His friends joined me, crying quietly now. When the hole was filled to the top with soil, loved ones tossed in roses and other flowers. Some placed small rocks as a lining around the edge of the grave, as if to protect the soul within. Slowly we walked away from Yeftah to visit other deceased family members: Silas, my father, Ezra (Yedida's husband), and Edna (Yeftah's ex-wife, mother of No-Am and Maya). A sad thought nagged me, "These children are truly orphans now."

We returned to Yeftah's gravesite, thanked the Rabbi, and said good-bye to all who attended, a process that lasted over an hour.

A sense of humor till the very end

I was standing in the cemetery parking lot apart from everyone, trying to absorb everything that had just happened, when my sister Hannah came close to give me a light hug, as if to say, "I know how you feel, my dear brother." She wanted to soften the harshness of reality with her considerable sense of humor and tell me something about Yeftah that was fun and humorous, to bring a smile to my face.

"You know, Saul, only a few days ago our brother was resting in the hospital hallway and looking over all the young nurses passing by. He said, 'Look, Hannah, not one of them is worth looking at, there's no life in them, they're like mannequins, I can't even get a smile from them now and then.' "

I tried to suppress my laughter, thinking it somehow disrespectful to be laughing at such a solemn occasion, but when Avram let go to laugh, so did I. It was the first laughter we had shared in weeks, and it felt good to remember the best things about Yeftah.

Sweet memories of other times and places

On the way to bring mother back to her old-age home, I left the car window open so I could take in the familiar sweet scent of the citrus trees lining Israel's roads. I began to remember so many anecdotes from the past. How Yeftah and I ran away, hitchhiked north, and ended up in the kibbutz. How we stole oranges to have pocket money, and sold them to Uncle Yehuda. How Yeftah left his wife and went to live with a 16-year-old, Julia, who stood by him and supported his actions unquestionably, dedicating her life to him, denying herself the joy of marriage and motherhood. Like plants, we were uprooted so many times. My mother sat in the passenger seat next to me, pondering her own memories, some we shared, others of her own, that no one could know. I looked out of the corner of my eye at this frail 90-year-old woman, my mother, who endured so much hardship and travail in the nine decades of her life. She has survived everything that tried to kill her along the way, and raised eight children, and now she has just been forced to bury her beloved son. No religion or philosophy could explain her anguish, her utter silence as she leaned back with her eyes closed, murmuring things no one could hear or understand. Why was this saintly woman, this fragile soul, bestowed with such a punishment? I knew that none of us is spared, but my mother didn't deserve this terrible event at this late stage of her life. No, not even God himself could give me a satisfactory reason. She had loved her Yeftah unconditionally, as only a mother can. I asked myself: How long will she last after this? Will she ever adjust to accept this cruel fate?

I parked at her place and escorted her in to her bed. Now it was the end of this day, and my mother removed the shawl from her head, took off her shoes, and lay down. I kissed her on the forehead and promised to be back in the morning to pick her up for the *Shiv-ah*, which is the way that Jews mourn for the dead, by sitting for seven days and nights together.

Sitting Shiv-ah for Yeftah

On Sunday November 24, 2002, I moved my suitcase and things from Hannah's house to Yedida's, where the *Shiv-Ah* was being held. My sisters and brother and I sat till after midnight, talking quietly and reminiscing. This is one good thing about occasions like these: we are forced to be with one another, to pause and assess our lives, and to remember.

I couldn't sleep all night. I had a million thoughts to process and many emotions to set square as the cars and trucks passing by on the busy roads outside my window kept me awake. I could picture perfectly what the rest of the week would be like. The family will sit at home and receive myriad guests and relatives in a continuous stream, at all hours of the day and night. We will serve food and drinks and conduct long conversations about our life in years past. We will talk especially of Yeftah, the meaning of his life, what we should take from it and keep, where was he now, what does death offer? We will be both sad and happy when *Shiv-ah* ends, seven days later, when we will rejoin the world's pulse and breathe in the fresh air of being alive.

After the funeral: Now I am a tourist

Monday December 1, 2002: After breakfast Yedida suggested that we "get out of the house" for a few hours, and I agreed enthusiastically. The two of us piled in the car and drove to Yafah, bought hot bagels and cold drinks, and climbed the slippery rocks of the old Port of Yafah (Jaffa), built in the days of the

Ottoman Empire. We sat and ate, drank and talked, just Yedida and me; we had never had a similar occasion to be alone together in our lives. It was truly a treat to remember because it was so ordinary and calm, yet so special.

We headed to Or-Yehuda that afternoon and ate an early dinner at Entebbe, a magnificent meal with over twenty varieties of food. We visited the unique Iraqi Museum in Or-Yehuda and bought some books and souvenirs. Then Yedida dropped me off at a mall in northern Tel Aviv, where I met with No-Am, my nephew. We sat and sipped gourmet coffee and ate sweet doughnuts, when suddenly I realized my jacket was gone from behind my seat.

We rushed to the management office.

"If it doesn't show up here in Lost and Found in ten minutes, forget about finding it," the manager said, from experience. It was never found but such losses are minor in the grand scheme of possible losses.

Monday December 2, 2002: Yedida and I drove south this time, to the old city of Ashdod. We toured the Moroccan Pavilion, shopped, and pondered the view from an outdoors restaurant while we ate a delicious lunch. We looked over the beautiful beaches of the Mediterranean; in the distance numerous cargo ships had been moored for months, because of striking port workers.

Mother: "What is man? No better than a dog"

In the evening, Avram and Pirha and I went to visit Mother, who was so glad to see us.

Avram began telling her about our sister Berta in New York. She had recently been diagnosed with uterine cancer.

Mother began to cry. "Tell her not to worry. Tell her if she had to get cancer, it should be this type. No one dies from this cancer."

She took a deep breath and grew silent.

"I can't sleep lately," she said. "I am exhausted and can't sleep. I pray for my dear son Yeftah and for all of my children. Now I will pray especially for Berta. Tell her to have courage, not to be afraid."

She was silent for a time again, then concluded, "What is a man? No better than a stray dog. Even a dog is better. What can we do? Each one has his fate, we can change nothing, everything is pre-ordained, believe me."

The magnificent Baha'I Shrine

Tuesday December 3, 2002: Haiim and Hannah drove their son Gai to school and I went along for the ride because it was halfway between Rehoboth and Bilu. My sister was pleased with the school, it was a nice place to learn and work in the shop, for her son to develop mechanical skills and dexterity.

That afternoon, Yedida and our cousin Mikhal and I drove north all the way to the Port of Haifa, where we strolled the magnificent gardens of the Baha'I Shrine, on the slopes of Mount Carmel. A female guide explained the fundamentals of this uniquely moral religion emanating from Persia. We had a great time. I got to know my cousin Mikhal much better. I admired her friendship with my sister Yedida and her utter dedication to my mother and the family.

That evening No-Am and I went to see a movie: *The Tuxedo* with Jackie Chan. It was so bad, we left in the middle of it.

Visiting Aunt Marcel (Nava)

Wednesday December 4, 2002: Pirha, Yedida, Mikhal, and I went to Hertzelia, a beautiful town on the Mediterranean Sea, in the middle of Israel. We had lunch at its exquisite marina and explored a private museum with a collection of sculptures from around the world. On our way back we paid a visit to our ailing Aunt Marcel (Nava). She lived in a modest apartment, attended by a full-time, sleep-in, Filipina maid. Aunt Nava was elated to see us, and apologized for not being healthy enough to have been at Yeftah's funeral. She loved him so, and she had many stories to tell about him and his exploits.

Over the course of the afternoon Aunt Nava's stories reminded me that she was the most educated of Mother's sisters, a revered tutor of the children of two Iraqi Prime Ministers: Salah Jabber and Nuri Al-Saiid. The pictures hanging crooked on the wall attested to her history and connections. Her son Ezra had been Mayor of her town, Hod-Ha-Sharon. She was so proud of him.

We ate and talked and laughed a bit then bid her good-bye.

"Give my regards and love to my sister Salha, don't forget. Please tell her I will visit her as soon as I feel better."

After the touring, the talking

Thursday December 5, 2003: I moved back into Hannah's house with my little suitcase that now contained new books, souvenirs, and photographs to develop inside my camera. I missed my wife and daughters, but it had been a meaningful opportunity to be back in this country, among my kin and country-men. I enjoyed many conversations with my dear brother-in-law Haiim, who also loves to study history and talk about the cycles of war and peace, so we always got along famously.

Late afternoon, I took a train to Tel Aviv and met Ronen's family for dinner. I went with him, his parents Tzion and Miriam, and their son Meeko and his girlfriend to a fun, fancy restaurant named "Mamma Miyah." We had jolly conversations and consumed a wonderful Italian dinner. Exploiting the wonders of cell phone technology, we telephoned my daughter Sandra from there and spoke to my grandchild Danielle in the US. It was the "frosting on the cake" to hear her sweet baby voice over the miles.

Then we drove to Meeko's apartment in north Tel Aviv, where his girlfriend had parked her Vespa scooter and now she mounted it and rode it home. The rest of us scoured the local mall and helped me select gifts to take back to New York.

Friday December 6, 2002: Yedida, Hannah, and I saw Mother and told her we had visited Aunt Marcel.

"Oh, how is she? How is her sugar?" Aunt Marcel suffers from severe diabetes. "She is well, Mother, considering her age. But she has some leg wounds that refuse to heal, and she passes out sometimes," Hannah said.

"Thank God she has that Filipina caregiver, she really takes good care of her," Yedida added.

"She sends you her regards, Mother, she said she will visit you as soon as she can," I said, speaking louder into her bad ear.

Mother was deep in thought. "Did my sister Ruth ask about me? Does she know Yeftah has passed away?" she inquired, feeling pity for herself.

"Yes, Mother, we spoke to her. She is very sad for Yeftah. You know how much she loved him," Yedida said. "She sent condolences, she is sorry she couldn't come."

The head nurse walked into Mother's room to include us in urging the patient to take better care of herself. "Your dear mother has not been eating or sleeping well lately. She has too much in her head. Talk to her, tell her she has to go back to her normal life, there's nothing she can do about her son's death." She urged in heavy Russian accent.

Hannah promised to talk to her, but the nurse continued to share her philosophy of life with us. "Your mother told me about her dear son Yeftah. What a tragedy. But, what is a mother to do? This is how life is. She has become too quiet, not talking to anyone here. She used to talk incessantly," the nurse continued. She moved closer to Mother and gave her a light hug, then left.

"When will I see you again, Saul?" she asked me.

Before I could reply, she asked again, "When will you go back to America?"

I sat close to her ear so she could hear me. "I am leaving in two days, Mother. I will come to see you again tomorrow."

Mother turned to Hannah now. "You look good, Hannah-leh, you lost a lot of weight," she said with a smile. Then she turned to Yedida. "You should do the same, it will become you." Yedida of course resented this remark and gave her a dirty look.

"Hannah, I need you to clip my toenails, I can't do it myself anymore. The nurses here only have scissors. I hate scissors."

"All right, leave it to me, I will come here after Saul leaves to go home to New York, and help you bathe and I will cut your nails," Hannah said with a smile. "I will make you so pretty you will be ready for a honeymoon."

Mother laughed. So did we. Hannah always knew how to make her laugh.

"How are Suzie and Sandy? Do they have boyfriends?" my mother asked me, grinning.

"What about Sharon, Mother, did you forget Sharon?" Yedida asked.

"No, God forbid, I didn't forget her. But she is young. I'm concerned about the older ones. It's time they found someone." She forgot that Sandra was married.

We laughed. "Mother, don't you have enough to worry about? Don't worry about my girls, they will find someone when the time comes," I assured her.

We hugged her tiny frame and kissed her cheeks, and went on our way. The sun was still out and it was a beautiful day.

That evening we had dinner at the beach in Rishon Le-Tzion, where we ran into Avram with his sons Itai and Yoni, daughter Aliza, and his wife Rutti. We had the owner push some tables together and we shared a modest and subdued but tasty dinner.

Yeftah: Our own Zorba the Greek

I couldn't help believing that Yeftah died young as some kind of punishment for being less than perfect. But no one possessed more humanity than him. He loved life, even while he endured most of its cruelest pains; he loved all life's pleasures, a true Zorba. His wife Edna had passed away young too, a year ago, and I wondered if his guilt over how he had treated her had anything to do with his premature death? Were they able to love each other despite all they endured? I sought answers, but none were forthcoming that night, and I knew I would spend the rest of my life searching for meanings, sorting things out, trying to understand what this life is all about.

As I flew home, I could not forget Yeftah for a minute: his lively demeanor, his love of fun, his open-hearted generosity, his tragic addictions to gambling.

A favorite Christina Rossetti poem resonated in my head:

Remember me when I am gone away
gone far away into the silent Land;
when you can no more hold me by the hand.
Yet, if you should forget me for a while
and afterwards remember, do not grieve;
better by far you should remember and be sad....

Chapter Seventy-Eight

With Mother In the United States

At the New York World's Fair: 1964

Salha Fathi had been the witness to many tumultuous changes during the course of her 20th-century life. Seeing her son grow up to be an American was but one among many unforeseen futures God seemed to have in store for us. That she would one day fly across the ocean to land in New York and visit the Statue of Liberty and Ellis Island—places she'd long admired as beacons of openness when the world seemed most closed—this, she could only believe with her own eyes. Rachelle and I had escorted my mother around the city as if leading a blind woman who could suddenly see, as she encountered each new sight with fresh awe and wonder. The vending machines at Horn & Hardart, subway tokens, neon signs, buildings 100 stories tall, millions of people crowding the streets, all this was unimaginable when my mother was a young girl growing up in Iraq. In her own lifetime, the Old World had given way most strenuously and not without fights, to the New World. Nothing symbolized that better than New York City. In 1964, the opening of the New York World's Fair in Queens signaled this new world's dawning inventions.

From our home in Queens, we had been reading news of an upcoming, exciting, historical event to be held at Flushing Meadow. The times we lived in had already been coined by the media as "The Space Age" and the World's Fair was being advertised as "Man in a Shrinking Globe in an Expanding Universe." Over a period of months and years, over 646 acres were converted on the old site of the 1939-40 World's Fair to serve as host to 140 pavilions. The exhibits were being designed as homage to the vast industrial and technological innovations of the decades since the end of the '30s. U.S. industry wanted to showcase its mid-century achievements to the world and provide an invigorating antidote to the horrors of the century's wars. Major national corporations such as General Electric, Ford, General Motors, Chrysler, IBM, Bell Telephone, U.S. Steel, Pepsi Cola, Dupont, RCA, and Westinghouse were all represented, along with 21 state pavilions and 36 other countries. More than a billion dollars was spent to construct entertaining attractions to lure new masses of buyers to American products. During two seasons from April 1964 to October 1965, they say 51 million people visited the World's Fair, 7 million during its final three weeks alone, setting a new record for international expositions.

Among those hordes were the Fathi's, a family who was willing to embrace the best aspects of this modern industrialized world. Despite Kennedy's assassination a year before, the times were optimistic and even my skeptical and modest mother could not help but be dazzled at the scope of promises being offered. We could fly to the moon one day! We could transmit live images around the globe in an instant! We would all be connected by miles of thin wires threaded throughout the landscape! Soon, we will be communicating on Picture-Phones!

My mother took everything in, as wide-eyed as a child eagerly learning new language.

"Saul, did you ever imagine in your life that you could talk with your mother in Israel and you on the other side of the world, and now we will be able to see each other as if we are sitting together in the same parlor! "

My mother was speaking out loud, even using my name, but when she started philosophizing and speculating, I had learned she was speaking to herself primarily, and it was my role to simply listen as she let her mind wander freely over the wonders of life.

Afterlife and reincarnation: I remember her vision of life after death

Years later, late at night, after our day of touring then slogging home in traffic along with seemingly everyone else in New York, my mother was tired but wide awake and talkative. I drifted in and out of the conversation between her and my wife as they covered so many subjects at a rate of chatter that only women seem to have mastered. During that visit, ever since she got there, my mother had been remarking on how well we fed and cared for our dog Taffy, and now as she watched Rachelle brush Taffy's soft fur then offer her bone-shaped biscuits for being "such a good doggie," my mother said, "Oh, to be a dog in America."

After awhile, I heard Rachelle bring up the subject of reincarnation.

I heard her ask my mother, "Mother, do you believe in the afterlife or reincarnation?"

Where'd that come from? I thought.

I was even more surprised by my mother's answer: "Sure, I believe. Saul's father Silas believes in it, too. And we are not the only ones; millions of people have faith that there's life after death."

I decided, as I often did, to stay out of this dialog, and let them resolve these weighty matters on their own. But I kept half an ear tuned, because I was curious too.

Rachelle asked, "So mother, if you are reincarnated, what would you like to come back as?"

I opened one eye long enough to see my mother's short hesitation, then a big smile came across her face.

"In the next incarnation, I wish to come back as a dog."

Why would she want to be a dog? I wondered.

"But only as a dog in America," she said, with Taffy curled up on her lap, warm, well fed, and well loved. We all laughed.

Ah yes, being a dog in America is not so bad.

Mother visits Disney World in Florida: August, 1967 and December, 1977

Salha Fathi was a grown woman in her fifties the first time, and a bona fide senior citizen when we returned ten years later, but the extravagant imaginative world of Disney brought out the innocent child in her. Perhaps only in her later years was she finally free to feel like a child, as her own childhood had been consumed by pogroms, wars, and being uprooted again and again.

If New York City was a marvel of the American will to build higher and denser than anywhere else in the world, Florida's Disney World was a true fantasyland, artificial paradise of the most sophisticated kind. As we passed through the turnstiles into the park at Disney World a sign told us that we had just entered "The Most Magical Place on Earth" and for that day, the Fathi's believed in magic. We rode little boats through "It's a Small World," an attraction that featured dancing dolls dressed in the costumes of the various cultures of the world as the song played over and over (a song that doesn't leave your brain even after the ride is over). "It's a small world after all, it's a small world after all, it's a small world after all, it's a small, small world...." These lyrics used to pop into my head from time to time after that, on my way to work, stuck in traffic, or reading the daily newspaper; I guess because the words are true.

On the plane, I forced my mind not to latch onto these lyrics so I wouldn't be stuck with them for the whole rest of the flight. I focused on recalling the great joy my mother took from shaking the white-gloved hand of Mickey Mouse and the wonderful lunch we ate in one of Disney World's many theme restaurants. Mother got a real kick out of watching the children's star-struck responses to the colorful cartoon characters.

At the end of the day our daughter Suzanne had asked, "Grandma, what impressed you the most at Disney World?"

Mother looked at Rachelle for help in translating the question to Hebrew, then replied, "It is just so unique. Everyone on the face of the earth should experience it at least once in a lifetime. Like the Hajj to Mecca," she said as tears of joy welled in her eyes.

On the Circle Line Cruise, New York Harbor: July 24, 1987

In her seventies, Salha Fathi remained open to new experiences that would take her to places she'd only heard about, as well as places she'd been before but never from the vantage point of uncynical wisdom that age provides. New York Harbor's Circle Line Cruises were the perfect kind of "magic realism" for someone like my mother, who came to appreciate having a little bit of magic in the midst of life's harsher realities.

I remembered the day clearly.

We left from Pier 16 at the South Street Seaport for the two-hour narrated cruise up the Hudson and East Rivers. The big boat glided slowly past a skyline we had only seen from our car before. To see the Empire State and Chrysler Building, the Brooklyn Bridge and the Colgate Clock from the water offered us a new perspective on the stately grandeur of Manhattan and the broad scope of its imposing sprawl.

I took thirty-six photos that day, jumping all over the boat like a kid in a candy store, posing my mother along the rails with various famous backgrounds to frame her. We felt excited to send these images back to our relatives in Israel, to let them know how good we had it here, to show off America. Well, as with some of my other well-intentioned plans, the photo verification of our good life didn't work out either, as when I went to rewind the film to develop the prints, I discovered to my amazement, there had been no film in my camera! The numbers had continued to go up as if there was film, a definite shortcoming in the camera's design, which I still do not understand.

After docking on Ellis Island, we learned that Lady Liberty stands nearly 151 feet tall and weighs 225 tons. The inscription on her tablet reads July 4, 1776 in Roman numerals, the date of America's Declaration of Independence from Britain. There are 25 windows in her crown, from which the views are naturally spectacular. The day we were there was perfectly clear.

I looked over at my mother as she stared out at the sweeping vista and saw there were tears streaming down her face.

"Mother, what is it? Are you all right?" I asked.

"America, America, you feed the world, yet everyone spits in your face," she had said as she pondered my translation to Hebrew of the words on the plaque with Emma Lazarus's famous 1883 sonnet inscribed on it:

Give me your tired, your poor,
Your huddled masses yearning to breathe free,
The wretched refuse of your teeming shore.
Send these, the homeless, tempest-lost to me,
I lift my lamp beside the golden door…

These words became an inextricable part of American culture; they are part of a famous Irving Berlin show tune and stand as a global call for immigrant rights. My mother was crying because Emma Lazarus was one of the first successful Jewish American poets, part of the late nineteenth century New York literary elite. Emma Lazarus wrote many other poems and essays protesting the rise of anti-Semitism and called on Jews the world over to unite and create a homeland in Palestine long before the word *Zionist* had made it into the dictionary. She died very young.

"God willing, Saul, in your lifetime, you will see that freedom and tolerance will simply be the way of the world."

Sadly, Mother, we are not there yet, even as I write this book five years after the turn of the New Millennium.

Mother spent four days in a coma at South Shore Hospital

Years later, during another visit, my mother was dividing her time among the homes of all her children who had made their way to the States. At the moment she was staying with my sister Judith. One night around 11PM we got a frantic call.

Judith cried into the phone. "Mother fell down the stairs! She is not responding. We think she is in a coma. Can you come over quick, please? I don't know what to do."

I wanted to panic as my heart leaped up in my shirt, but I was being called upon to be calm.

"Call the ambulance, right now. Call 911. We'll be there as soon as we can. Don't wait for us. Just do whatever the paramedics say."

When we arrived around midnight at my sister's house, her daughter Ronit met us in the driveway.

"They took Grandma to the hospital. Mom went with her."

I asked for details of what happened.

"Mom thinks she must have gotten up to go to the bathroom, and she made the wrong turn and fell down the stairs to the basement. She hit her head hard on the concrete floor."

I kissed Ronit and told her not to worry, everything would be all right. We rushed to South Shore Hospital Emergency Room and asked after Salha Fathi.

After showing some id's and signing some forms, we were directed to the Intensive Care Unit.

"That's not good," I said to Rachelle.

"She is still alive, so there is hope, Saul," my wife had assured me, squeezing my hand in prayer as we negotiated the long hallways with its harsh lighting, beepers and alarms, and disinfectant smells.

That time, in the eerie light of the ICU we found my sister standing over Mother's bed, calling to her with a pleading voice, "*Eemah* ('Mother' in Hebrew), can you hear me? Please answer if you can hear, just blink your eyes."

Rachelle and I hugged Judith and she collapsed into tears of guilt.

"I'm so sorry, Saul. She got up dazed in the middle of the night and walked right over to the staircase and fell."

"Shh, it's not your fault, Judith. Don't worry, no one blames you," I said.

We joined our voices to the effort to revive mother until a nurse came in and told us to keep the noise down.

"You are disturbing the other patients. Please. Your mother is in coma. She had a serious trauma to the head. The doctors examined her and took X-rays. They've concluded there is nothing to do but wait. She will wake up when she is ready."

I sat there for a while then needed to feel a little bit useful. I went out to the hallway pay phones to call our sister Berta, who arrived within the hour to join in our quiet bedside chorus to communicate with Mother and keep her here among us. Throughout the rest of that night, then the next day and the day after that, we took turns going to the bathroom and to the cafeteria, so as to never leave her alone.

Those days I remember as four days of absolute terror.

What will become of us without our dear mother, always there looking upon us with her eyes of love?

That time, on the fourth day, Mother opened her eyes!

"Where am I?" she asked. We broke into a loud laughter.

Surprised, as we had begun to settle into the stillness and uncertainty of the coma situation, we all hugged each other. At Mother's startled look, we had to laugh as we began to explain what had happened. She appeared confused, could not remember a thing.

She stayed in the hospital for observation a while longer, then Rachelle and I brought her home with us.

But she was anxious to go back home, to Israel.

We didn't think it was a good idea to travel so soon after such a huge trauma but we could not oppose her wishes, so we arranged for new flight tickets to allow her early return.

At the airport we had gathered around her frail shoulders to embrace her and bid her good-bye.

"I hope this unfortunate experience won't discourage you from getting back to visit us in the U.S. again, Mother," I said.

"When I die, I want to die in Israel," she stated.

"Don't speak that way. You are not going to die anytime soon."

"I'm just letting all of you know, for the future. I want you to know"

A bill from South Shore Hospital: You owe us $ 10,500

Three weeks after we had put Mother on the plane back to Israel, I was flabbergasted when I opened the invoice from the hospital. $10,500!

I called Judith and Berta with the information.

Judith said she couldn't help at all, she was barely getting by as it was.

Berta's first reaction was indignance. "Don't pay it, Saul, what can they do to you?"

Meanwhile, I visited the hospital to confront the accounting office face to face. The clerk proceeded to bring forth proof that the invoice was correct and justified.

"You signed right here, see? You agreed to bear all costs associated with your mother's treatment. She had no insurance. Someone had to do this for her."

"What choice did I have? My mother needed urgent medical attention. She was in a coma."

"Of course, you're her eldest son. I would do the same for my mother." The clerk tried to convince me that I had indeed done the right thing. But there was nothing she could do to change the numbers. I went home disappointed and worried about how we would ever come up with that kind of money.

A week later I spoke to Mother on the phone.

"How are you feeling?" I asked.

She was in good spirits but she could hardly hear me, I had to shout into the receiver. She was still quite confused in her mind, unable to account for the days she'd lost.

When I mentioned the amount of the hospital bill, she let out a scream.

"What are you saying? Ten thousand dollars? For me? For four days in the hospital? How can that be? Let them go to hell," my mother spoke, using the kind of language I rarely heard her use. This was an unimaginable amount of money in a socialized-medicine country like Israel.

"It's okay, Mom, I don't want to upset you. Forget it. I'll deal with it."

I tried to calm her down and suddenly her voice turned completely lucid and accommodating.

"No, my son. Why should you pay? I bought health insurance through the travel agent when I came to visit. Send me a copy of the bill. I will take it to him. They have to cover me."

I was shocked. How did she know to buy insurance? Who advised her?

I laughed into the phone. "Mother, you always surprise me. You are the smartest mother in the world. I'll go ahead and send the invoice. If we're lucky, they'll at least cover part of it."

I put the bill in the mail to her and waited to hear from her. Periodically the hospital accounting officers called to ask for payment. I was practicing Berta's suggestion of seeing what they'd do if I simply didn't pay. At one point they seemed to suggest that they would have to take legal action against me, and I shook with anger. Then I heard my mother's voice: "Let them go to hell!"

Three months later, unbeknownst to me, the hospital received a check for the full amount of $10,500. My mother's last-minute purchase of travel insurance had covered the entire bill. Leave it to my mother to cover all her bases. She is a self-reliant woman who never asked for help or charity from anyone.

My mother turns lemons into lemonade

Among other lingering effects of her tumble down the basement stairs, however, Mother had lost her hearing in her left ear. As was typical of her, she refused to wear a hearing aid. She didn't like the way it raised the volume of all the sounds in the world; there were many things she didn't want or need to hear, she said.

Whenever I called her in Israel, before I could say one word, Mother began to babble away non-stop. I thought she might have been suffering selective dementia until I realized that she kept on talking because she could hear nothing that I said. I'd call, she'd talk on and on, then she would hang up. Sometimes I'd finally get through across all the long-distance connections that needed to be made, I'd wait impatiently while the phone rang and rang, and when she at last picked up, all I could hear was, "I can't hear you, whoever it is, I'm sorry, I can't hear you." Then she would hung up.

What I would give to hear her babble at me again.

Chapter Seventy-Nine

On El-Al to Israel: Is This the End?

My sister Berta and I took a memorable El-Al flight to Israel in the early 1990s. The food was bad as usual, the service negligent, and the attitude of the flight attendants unpleasant, but these were not the worst things. A few hours into the flight, high over the Mediterranean Sea, the pilot suddenly silenced the movie and the soundtracks to announce that we would be encountering some turbulence. Not to worry, he said, he would simply climb higher to avoid them. Instead, within minutes the plane dropped fifty feet, and we were all jolted violently from side to side.

I looked at Berta, who was shaking and seems to be praying. She reached out to hold my hand, "What is going on? Is this the end?" she asked in a quivering voice. Her face was stark white and her eyes were open wide.

"This happens all the time up here," I tried to comfort her. As I did so, another great jolt caused this giant jet to rock back and forth, loose altitude, then rise up again. It was as if we were on a huge roller coaster, but there certainly was no fun in it.

The passengers looked at the only flight attendant in the cabin for reassurance as the pilot came on the intercom. "We are safe," he said. "Don't worry. We'll climb a little more and avoid the force of the storm."

Climbing, however, made no difference. The storm was massive. Its turbulent air extended into the highest reaches of the earth's atmosphere. For the next four hours, we battled the elements. We prayed; some passengers vomited; others cursed out loud in fear and trembling. Trapped in the great metal beast in the middle of the vast dark sky and at the mercy of forces beyond our control, we each pondered our fates, our worthiness for heaven, and whether we had lived life well enough to be willing to leave it on this night.

We shook. We rose and fell. We bounced up and down. We held on tight. "Oh God, not now. Not like this" Berta screamed, begging mercy. I felt a sudden, unique sense of bonding with Berta I had never felt before. Is it possible we are destined to die together, falling some 40,000 feet from the sky? When we finally touched ground at Ben-Gurion Airport, no one burst out in song or gave thanks to God or to our pilot. Our terror was too fresh, too real, too tangible, to easily put behind us.

Members of our family met us at the airport, fresh-faced and unaware of what we had just been through. My sweaty palm was a clue as I shook hands all around and Berta's fierce embrace of each relative was a clear indication that something untoward had happened.

Instead of being bustled out to our relative's home, Berta asked to sit a moment in the airport cafeteria so that we could catch our breaths. Safely on the ground with our loved ones around us, we recounted the stark terror of our flight and the horrific thunderstorm. But, as with many such stories, we did not receive the sympathy we felt we deserved. No one believed it was as bad as we said it was. As the time passed, we had no choice but to calm our beating hearts and surrender to the normality of life around us. We had survived, after all.

After our reunion with our extended family, they went off in various directions to carry on their daily activities. Berta and I went home with our brother Avram and our sister Yedida.

Chapter Eighty

With Mother at Entebbe Night Club:

A taste of Iraq in the middle of Israel

On Friday, during one of our visits to Israel, my sister Hannah called everyone and suggested that we go to Or-Yehuda, a suburb of Tel-Aviv, for dinner at Entebbe, a well-known Iraqi restaurant. It would be like returning to Baghdad in happier times. We picked up Mother, and other family members followed in another car.

At Entebbe, the restaurant was packed with customers, including high-ranking military officers in uniform. To accommodate all of us, two tables were set up back to back in front of the stage. Mother was seated between Berta and me, her sweet face radiating joy. Everyone was smiling, anticipating our great meal and the entertainment that went along with it. We were not disappointed. Before we even ordered the meals, over twenty appetizer plates tempted us with their delicate flavors and luscious textures, along with plenty of soda, fine wine, and dark beers.

A small band played Iraqi music, and a singer sat with them, waiting for his signal from the owner to start singing his lyrics. Next to him, a beautiful young belly dancer tempted us with her transparent silk shawl and skirt.

Mother and Berta ordered their favorite fresh fish, barbecued and smothered with the fragrant spices of our original homeland. Avram and I ordered an assorment of shish kebabs with beef, lamb, chicken, and three types of rice.

The band started fingering their instruments and the singer was introduced by the owner as a famous Syrian who specialized in Iraqi music. Familiar melodies filled the air. As the Syrian sang, many guests joined in, once again enjoying the poetry of these old songs.

Some of the elders among us, my mother's age, grew melancholy. The rhythms of Iraq brought forth memories in them that had been suppressed for decades. But when the songs ended, they stood and clapped with enthusiasm.

The Syrian was an excellent singer. He asked if anyone had a favorite song he or she wanted to hear. People shouted requests all at the same time. When he sang again the songs of their youth, memory, and history, the audience threw money on the stage to show their immense appreciation. Mother was silent, staring up at the stage with glazed eyes.

"What's the matter, Mom?" Berta asked, "Aren't you enjoying this great show?"

Mother looked at us. She seemed to be trying to remember something. Then she said, "I am thinking of a song, an old song. None of you has ever heard it. Let's test this Syrian. Let's see if he knows it. He is old enough."

"Mom, what song is that? What's the name of it?" I asked.

She smirked, as if to say, there is *no* way this man could know this song. She spelled the title out for Berta, slowly. "It's an old Bedouin love song," Mother said.

Berta began to write the name of the song in Hebrew on a piece of paper.

Mother snatched the pen and paper from her hands, and wrote in Arabic: *"ALF-LAYLA-WA-LAYLA /Um Kalthum."* ("1001 Nights" by Um Kalthum).

Berta approached the stage and handed the paper to the singer, saying, "This is important to my mother. I hope you know it."

He looked at the note carefully and smiled knowingly. He motioned with his head toward my mother as if to convey his joy at her request.

Mother: "There is no happiness without tears"

The Syrian began to sing, pressing his hand against his temple and right ear. "ALF LAYLA WA LAYLA... "

My mother listened intently. This was an ancient song, known only in the Arab world to its senior members. *How did he know it? Will he know the whole song? Will he sing it to the end?* The singer knew the song well and sang the beautiful song to its very last note.

I turned to look at my mother, but she no longer had a smiling, radiant face. She was crying. She pulled a handkerchief out of her purse and wiped her tears. We all looked on and tried to understand her emotions.

"I don't know why I am crying," she seemed to apologize. Thinking a moment, she explained. "It reminds me of a life we once lived in Baghdad. For a time, it was the Garden of Eden. If only the Arabs didn't hate us so much, we could have lived nicely together. Our ancestors were buried there, including my father and my mother. You are too young to know how good our lives were once."

The singer could see from a distance the effect the song was having on my mother. Afterwards, he came by our table to shake hands with us. Tenderly, he reached over and kissed Mother on the forehead. "I understand how you feel," he said, in his heavy Arabic accent. "Believe me, I understand." Quickly, he returned to the stage.

By now we were all crying, holding onto our mother and rubbing her arms to express our love for her and to try in some small way to console her over the loss of her culture and her tragic disconnection with the past.

At the end of the long feast of food and emotions, Hannah reminded us, "We came here to laugh and enjoy being together. I hope the sad songs and the tears didn't spoil it for you all."

Mother looked into our eyes and assured us,

"I am very happy. There is no happiness without tears. Remember that."

Chapter Eighty-One

My Daughters Interview My Mother

During another trip, on one of our more pleasant visits to Israel in 1997, on the occasion of my daughter Sandra's wedding, my daughters got together at their Aunt Hannah's house to interview my mother. They encircled mother, who looked happy to be flanked by her many grandchildren. Sandra was the one who knew her best and asked the first question.

"Grandma Salha, how did you meet Grandpa Silas?"

Mother smiled and hesitated.

"It was in Basra. My sister Ruthi went to visit my brother Yehuda, who worked for Silas…"

Mother proceeded to tell the whole story of their introduction. It was classic "love at first sight" for both of them, according to her.

My daughter Suzanne asked, "Do you remember what you wore at your wedding?"

Mother enjoyed their inquisitiveness and loved this question in particular.

"Oh, I wore the most exquisite, long, white lace dress anyone ever saw. My mother, may God bless her soul, bought the material, and she and all my sisters took turns designing and sewing it. It took weeks to finish. At the wedding, everyone asked, 'Where did you buy such a magnificent dress?" Mother's eyes sparkled.

My daughter Sharon piped up. "Grandma, who came to your wedding? How many people?"

My mother enjoyed the attention of her granddaughters and her children, and she relished the act of remembering. This was something she had always done very well. She had always kept track of the past and its details and the feelings that went with each story.

"Oh, many, many came. As you may know, in Iraq you don't just invite the parents, like you do there in America. They would be insulted. You invite the whole family, including their children. Sometimes, on their own, the guests invite their neighbors too. But no one ever thought it was too much. The more, the merrier.

"Silas had so many friends my family didn't even know: Indians, British, prominent Muslims. They all came and they brought expensive gifts.

"I was the first to marry in my family. My mother and father were so happy to let me go. They hoped I'd 'open the door of luck' for the rest of my brothers and sisters. And, for a while it was a good life. But it only lasted a few years."

My daughters were fascinated with the image of their old grandmother as a young, hopeful, and beautiful bride in a magnificent, hand-sewn, lace dress.

The soon-to-be bride (within hours) Sandra asked, "What did you learn from all your experiences, Grandma? From all of the eight children you mothered?"

Mother frowned and became serious, no longer giggling as she recounted her memories.

"Oh, I tell you, it's no good to bring so many children into the world. The fun they bring you lasts very short. As they grow older, then begin the problems. And when you're old, you are all alone, as if you had no children. No one visits. No one cares. This is how life is. You can't change a thing. Nothing ever changes."

Sandra's face showed she was confused by this revelation of the hardships of life and the challenges of raising children on this night, the eve of her wedding.

"You don't recommend having children, Grandma Salha?" she asked, puzzled, reconsidering the vision she had for herself and her future as a wife and possibly a mother.

At this suggestion that her granddaughter should do without children of her own, my mother practically jumped to her feet. She was unaware that her words had had such a profound effect. "No, who told you that? I didn't say that. You didn't understand me. You have to have a few children. A family without children—what good is that? Have children! But, not too many." We laughed. Sandy gave her a gentle hug. Mother began to laugh again.

The gentle, persistent probing of Grandma Salha's mind for advice and reminiscences went on for several more hours. My sisters, my wife, my daughters, and I all laughed, sometimes rolling on the floor with laughter at the things my mother said and the way she put things. Her devilish sense of humor and her long-held convictions that sometimes seemed so old-fashioned came through her recollections. How we cherished her!

Mother was in rare form that night and in such a good mood. So were we all. No one got mad at her for saying, "no one visits, no one cares," for we knew we had done our parts and were good, attentive children. She just forgets sometimes. We also knew that complaining gave old women some mysterious pleasures. Why deny them?

Chapter Eighty-Two

You Will Find Your Mother Sitting on a Bench

On another of my many trips to Israel, I went straight to Hannah's. After resting a bit and sipping on the exotic tea of that country, I wanted to visit Mother, to walk the same old half-mile to her apartment.

After Father's passing, Mother had moved to a tiny, one-bedroom apartment in Rehoboth, a few blocks from the old bus station. The kitchen was part of her sleeping/living quarters, with a bath and shower to the side. A convertible sofa was her bed. No more than four people at a time could fit in her apartment. The kitchen stove, refrigerator, and television all sat together in the one main room.

I arrived and knocked, but there was no answer. I knew that she was hard of hearing, since her fall in the US, so I knocked repeatedly, harder, but Mother didn't answer. I began to worry and was about to leave and telephone my sister when my mother's neighbor opened the door.

"I thought I heard someone knocking. Who are you?" she inquired.

"I am Saul, Salha's son from America. Do you know where she is?"

The woman smiled. "You will find your mother sitting on a bench in front of the bank. She likes listening to that crazy Russian play his violin."

I was startled. *My own mother sitting on a bench in the street? Which bank? There is a bank on every corner in Rehoboth*!

The old lady noticed how perplexed I looked. "Look, just go down this street, past the pizza store, past the shoe store, past the El-Al office, and you will be there. You can't miss it. You will hear the violin player."

I thanked her and bowed as you do in Japan.

She probably thought, "By God, he knows nothing, the son from America."

I walked briskly toward the center of the town, "the *Moshavah*," they used to call it. On the way, I began to feel lost as I bumped into people on the sidewalk and had to apologize more than once. I felt dazed, out of my element, no longer a local of this place. I passed pizza stores, the El-Al travel office, several shoe stores, more than one bank, but no Mother in sight. I finally stopped and asked a woman behind a falafel counter.

"Excuse me, could you please tell me where a Russian is playing the violin?" I asked.

She laughed and waved her hand. "Which one? There are so many. They play very well, but you can't earn a living that way. Not here in Israel."

"The one who plays in front of a bank," I replied, to narrow it down.

"Oh, no problem. Just go a few blocks further down, on the other side of the street. That's where you will find the fiddler."

I walked faster, passed a hundred little stores. When the traffic light changed to green, I crossed the street. Lo and behold, I began to hear music. Someone was playing the fiddle, indeed. I ran toward the source of the music, bumping into more people. Finally, I arrived breathless in front of the bank. The Russian had his violin case on the ground with a respectable amount of coins and Shekels in it. Mother was sitting on the bench as predicted, listening, munching on an apple.

Sitting down beside her, I tried to embrace her. "Hi, Mom. What are you doing here?"

She looked at me for a long moment, appearing surprised and confused. She looked me over, feeling my face with her wrinkled hands, the softest hands on the face of the planet.

"Ha, *Shaoul,* (Saul in Hebrew), when did you get here?" exclaimed finally. "Nobody told me you were coming."

"I just came in from the airport a couple of hours ago. How are you, Mom?"

She lifted her face up to the sky and pointed her fingers to the heavens. *"Barookh ha-shem* (May God be blessed). I am alive, no?" she said.

I hugged her harder. "Yes, you are. I am glad you are. And what are you doing here by yourself?" I asked.

She smiled, her old charming and all-knowing smile. "I am here, listening to the music. It's nice, no?" (She did not wait for my answer). "I come here every day. I sit on this old bench, listen, and think about years gone by. What else do I have to do? It's free of charge."

I knew she wasn't asking a question. She was making a statement, and I sensed there was more.

"I am all alone," she continued. "Nobody pays me any attention. I brought eight children into this world, and where are they now? Do I see them? No, I am left here like a dog. So I go to the mall, sit there, and watch people come and go. Everyone knows me there. They wave hello or stop to ask if I need anything. Yes, people are nice to me. They love me, like they loved your father. Silas was a good man. They don't forget."

Sometimes, to make a point, she used to swear to us, "by the graves of my mother and father." These parents of hers were buried in the 2,000-years old Jewish cemetery in Baghdad, a place we shall never returned to. None of us knew if it still existed or whether it had been bulldozed over. I felt for my mother. How horrible it must have been for her, to suffer that disconnection from her past and ancestry, to have to live in exile from the land where her parents were buried. The Russian kept playing his classical music.

Mother cupped my face with her hands again and said softly, "It's nice, this music. Isn't it? And it's free. All you have to do is throw some coins in occasionally. Listen. See how talented these Russians are? I don't know why they came here to Israel. There are no jobs. They can't feed their families. And they are so talented."

I looked at my watch, took out a couple of shekels, and put them in the violin case.

"No, that's too much," Mother said. "What are you doing? You are spoiling him. Don't spoil him."

"It's okay, Mother," I said. "I'm paying for all the times you have been entertained by this poor fellow, and forgot to tip him.'"

I helped Mom to her feet and held her under her arm. *She is skin and bones*, I thought. *How fragile she is!* Skin was hanging under her chin and under her arms. Her hair had faded to gray. However, her cheeks were rosy, hopeful, and defiant. Her face was the face of all humanity.

"Mom, let's take a taxi. It's too far to walk back," I said.

She pulled her arm away and faced me. "No, don't you dare. I walk this every day and more. I need to walk. And by the way, you've put on a lot a weight, Saul, my son. You should exercise more. And eat less." As she was uttering these words, she pulled me in the direction of her apartment.

Yes, I felt ashamed, even lazy, and I was reminded of how my father loved to walk and would refuse a ride offered to him by anyone.

When we finally arrived at my mother's apartment, she opened the refrigerator, took out some fruit, and peeled it. Then she took out three kinds of yogurt and some half-stale bread.

"Eat, my son, eat! You must be hungry," she urged. "And by the way, how did you find me?"

"Your nice neighbor opened the door and told me where to find you."

Mother laughed heartily. "This *majnoonah*? (This insane woman?) I hope she didn't mislead you. She can't remember anything. Her brain is too small"

"No, Mom, she explained it to me perfectly. I found you, didn't I?"

She laughed some more. I didn't dare tell her that I had gotten lost with the woman's directions.

My mother bent down to look on the lower shelf of the refrigerator. She took out a small pot and opened it. "Should I warm this rice for you? I just cooked it yesterday."

I gently asked her to sit down next to me on the sofa, remembering what a poor cook she had become. "No, please, I am not hungry. Don't warm anything up."

Mother watches silent TV

My mother then decided to turn on the TV and sat on the edge of the sofa bed next to me. I could not hear the TV because the volume was set too low. "Mom, how come there is no sound? I can't hear a thing," I remarked.

She smiled and said, "Oh, my son, what's the point of increasing the sound? I am almost deaf. I understand the stories from watching, not from hearing."

She got up and found the remote control. "Here, try with this thing. I never use it. I don't know how it works."

I raised the volume so that I could hear and understand. The TV was broadcasting a romantic movie from Amman, Jordan, in Arabic. It was very professionally done.

"Mom, how come you're watching a program from Amman? Do you under-stand Arabic still?" I wondered.

She waved a hand in front of my face as if I were the most ignorant of men. "Of course I understand. It's a continuation *(serialization)*, twice a week. I can tell you every episode in minute detail, nothing to it. It's all about love. It's always about love and betrayals. Nothing new." (I knew she meant, "Nothing is changed.")

Chapter Eighty-Three

Memories of My Mother

Mother is mugged by a teenager

I was at home in New York the day my sister Pirha called me from Jerusalem to tell me bad news. Mother had been mugged by a teenage girl as she walked home after her daily ritual of roaming the local mall and sitting on a public bench.

At her door when Mother reached for the keys in her purse, the girl hit her on the head with her own purse, knocking my mother to the ground, and snatching her bag. The mugger left the poor woman on the ground, screaming for help. By the time anyone noticed her and helped her back up on her feet, the perpetrator had fled the scene.

My brother Avram had been summoned. He wrote a lengthy report at the police station but was told not to expect an arrest. The girl was probably an addict, and the police were powerless to pursue such criminals. They were under-staffed.

"Sorry, just go home and comfort your mother," the police officer told Avram.

Mother recovered physically from the scrapes, but she was deeply shaken emotionally. Ever after, she felt no sense of security or trust, even among her own people. She would continually look around her to see who was behind her when she walked anywhere.

Mother: "Saying goodbye is the way of the world"

On a Friday afternoon, October 24, 2003, my sister Pirha called me in New York to inform me that our mother had been taken to Asaf Ha-Rofeh Hospital in Tel Aviv. "It's serious, Saul."

In 2003, my mother was ninety years old. The story Pirha told me was that she was eating lunch at her old-age home when she suddenly had difficulty chewing the chicken they served her. When she tried to swallow, a piece became lodged in her throat. During the few minutes while she was choking and attempting to expel the obstruction to her breathing, apparently she fell into a coma.

"The nurse on duty looked at her chart and saw that Mother is diabetic so she assumed she passed out because of low blood sugar. You remember, this happened once before? Mother was lying there unconscious, Saul, and the nurse tried to force her to eat jam and drink orange juice!"

My sister's voice was increasingly distraught but I urged her to finish telling me the story.

"After an hour of failed efforts, this nurse finally decides to call an ambulance. Mother was taken to Asaf Ha-Rofeh Hospital, a 30-minute ride away. They admitted her immediately and put her in Intensive Care. At this hospital, Saul, the ICU employs only Russian immigrants; the doctors and nurses speak broken Hebrew with the patients. Among themselves, they speak Russian and I can't understand a word they say."

"Pirha," I said quietly, trying to calm her down, "what is the diagnosis?"

"I'm not sure what the outcome will be. The doctors haven't been able to wake her from the coma but she's being fed intravenously and she is alive, thank God."

She urged me to come to Israel as soon as possible.

On the plane with a heavy heart

On Saturday, October 25, I kissed my wife at Kennedy Airport and boarded an El-Al plane that would land in Israel on Sunday afternoon. For the entire flight I was painfully aware that the last time I'd been in this airport I had foreseen this return trip and that it would be for this reason: to face the possibility of my mother's death.

I had never been able to globetrot back and forth to Israel as often as I might have liked, to visit my mother and relatives in our Jewish homeland. I had my work and my home, and daughters to raise. This made the times when I could visit, that much sweeter and meaningful. As the plane lifted off the runway I leaned my seat back and thought about my last visit, in 2002.

At 8:30 in the morning, my sister Hannah had gone to pick Mother up at her old-age home and bring her over for breakfast at her house. That day, Mother greeted Hannah with uncommon enthusiasm.

"How often do I get the opportunity to avoid institution food?" Mother said, in explanation for her happiness as they drove along the citrus-scented dirt road. When they arrived back at the house, Mother kissed everyone, and kissed me twice: "one for the road," she told me.

She looked particularly radiant that morning, in a smiling good mood, I remembered.

Hannah whisked her in to the bathroom to trim her toenails and remove some long whiskery hairs from her chin, at Mother's request. They were in there awhile but she came out smiling. We had a nice, hearty breakfast and Mother ate with a big appetite as we gathered outside in my sister's backyard, overlooking the vast green fields and industrial buildings across the main highway. The air was crisp, and Mother wore a light blue hand-knitted sweater that I remembered from years ago and it made me so nostalgic for times that would never come again. Only the sweater remained from those times; we were all changed, older, the world was different, but we had the present moment, and we had reminisced and laughed about the old days.

We ate, we drank, we were merry. We covered all topics of discussion, it seemed, the past, the present, the future, then we drove Mother back to her place of residence, which she mocked as her "gilded cage." We parted with kisses.

"May God bless you all," Mother said, as she waved us good-bye.

I saw her a few more times on that visit, but at other times she was prayerful and worried about Berta, who was having surgery in New York, or she was anxious about one thing or another.

As the plane reached its highest altitude now, for the long flight across the sea, I understood in my heart that the visit to Israel last year might turn out to be the last time I saw my mother, Salha (Ani) Fathi, alive and well. I allowed myself to close my eyes and picture her as she was in Hannah's backyard that day: radiant in her hand-knitted sweater, talking eloquently and blessing us all with her smile and her love.

A visit to ancient Caesarea

On my next to last afternoon, Haiim and Hannah drove me to Caesarea, one of the most picturesque towns in Israel. We visited Museum Ralli, which was exhibiting magnificent contemporary art from Latin America. The museum had been established and fully funded by a wealthy Israeli banker/industrialist, Mr. Harry Recanati, a Jew born in Salonica, Greece. He built branches of his museum in other countries as well. Most impressive, in the outdoor garden, dozens of freestanding sculptures stood erect in the fresh air against the tantalizing background of the deep blue Mediterranean Sea.

We had lunch at the high-class Indian restaurant Tambouri, managed by a Hindi woman, who came by our table in her authentic costume to say hello and welcome us. Somehow the background music brought memories to me of Baghdad and my father's Indian Club, which he frequented when I was a boy, and I had to spend most of the meal fighting back tears so no one would accuse me of being "too sensitive" as they always did when I became weepy in public.

Nostalgia for Chalghi Baghdad

We returned home tired from the long and stimulating day. Haiim reminded me not to accept any invitations for tonight, as the special musical show he spoke to me about would air on television at 9:30PM. It was called *Chalghi Baghdad* (Baghdad Concert) and we decided to record it on video so I could copy it and take it back to the United States. A good idea as it turned out, since it later mesmerized about eighteen of my closest friends and family members to whom I gave copies.

The ensemble consisted of nine Iraqi musicians who were famous in the old days in Baghdad. They had graduated from different music schools. One of them had been born blind but played regularly for the Iraqi people, broadcasting from the Baghdad radio station. The first part of the two-hour program showed interviews with the musicians; these nine were the only ones left alive out of a total of eighty who had arrived in Israel in 1950-51. Each one had a unique, emotional story.

Once arriving in Israel, they had struggled like everyone else coming to a new, poor, constantly threatened country. They managed to form a band based on their shared love of music and played for *Kol Yisrael,* (The voice of Israel), the only broadcast station in Israel at the time. But over time their Arabic ways were phased out in an effort to require immigrants to Israel to adopt the unified language of Hebrew, and leave their foreign past behind. By the time of these interviews, the musicians were in their late seventies, early eighties, including one woman, Hanan, the only woman vocalist in the group.

The second hour of the program featured examples of favorite Arab music, some originally composed by these musicians. I telephoned my sister Yedida to alert her to this program, but she was already aware of it and listening intently to the music.

Honoring my father's influence in our early years of living in Israel, I had worked hard to abandon my knowledge of the Arabic language and its music, seeking to erase from memory all the pain and atrocities our people had suffered at Arab hands. But now, at age 64, I was listening again, and unexpectedly feeling a deep longing for my childhood in Baghdad. The typically sad songs made me recall the simpler, innocent lives we lived in the days before the Jews were forced to leave their native land. I thought about the night of our escape from Baghdad and my brother Yeftah's recent passing and I began to cry. Several times during the broadcast I had to leave the room and walk out to the backyard, to breathe fresh air and be alone with my tears. I kept thinking: Yeftah would have loved this music, he always did.

By the time the show was over, we were all crying. As we went off to our separate beds we knew there would be no restful sleep tonight, just the solitary processing of emotional thoughts and ancient memories.

Tomorrow, I will be leaving Israel yet again, to return to my family in the U.S. It will be a long day, I had thought as I lay there wide awake and feeling so many feelings. Perhaps my heart was so heavy because I knew I would be back too soon, to hold my mother's hand as she was dying.

Mother's prayers were answered

As I was packing to leave in the morning we heard from Berta that her initial operation went well; she was okay. We all breathed a sigh of relief.

Then Pirha came and picked me up to visit my niece Maya, Yeftah's daughter, at her nursery. She was busy decorating the place, as babies and tod-dlers crawled all over the carpeted floor. We helped out a little but we couldn't stay long.

From there, we had one last stop to make before I was on my way, and that was to see Mother once more. She was cheerful, or pretended to be, to make it easier on me. We sat outside on the bench, holding hands, eating nuts and talking.

"Mother," Pirha told her, "we heard from Berta. She is okay, the operation went well. She sends her regards, and she thanks you for your prayers."

Mother's eyes opened wide and with her winning smile she said, "You see, I told you so. I told her not to be afraid. God listens to my prayers, sometimes."

Time to say our good-byes

Saying good-bye was always sad and cumbersome for me. Mother knew this morning was our last visit before I flew back to New York.

Who knows if we will see each other again? I was thinking as I did whenever I had to part ways, but this time turned out to be prophetic.

"Mother, I have to go now. I have a lot of little details to arrange," I said.

She knew this was true, but she said, "So soon? Are you leaving today? Can't you stay a few more days?"

I was hesitating to answer then she saved me from my struggle by saying, "It's all right, Saul. Go back home to your family. They must miss you. Give them my regards and my blessings. I want you to know that I am always praying for Susie to get married and settle down and have children of her own. Goodbyes are the way of the world, my son, there's nothing we can do about that."

I was on the verge of sobbing then Mother made a gesture with her hand, up to the sky. I understood.

"Thanks, Mom. I'll tell Susie she should get married soon, so you can come and dance at her wedding. You take good care of yourself and stay cheerful. Like you just said, Goodbyes are the way of the world."

She kissed me on both cheeks, my face in her bony warm hands.

"Go, Saul. May God bless you and help you arrive safely in America."

Driving back to my sister's house I thought: Mother is of the "old school." She believes everything in our lives is pre-ordained. I always wanted to argue with this philosophy, for if it is all pre-ordained, then it follows that we have no choice of action. Therefore, how can we punish anyone committing infractions or sin? I always grappled with this dilemma and never found any answers.

I spent the afternoon running around and making last-minute arrangements. I was on the phone a long-time, saying goodbye to everyone I knew in Israel. At 9:30PM Haiim. Hannah, and Gai took me to Ben-Gurion Airport. We sat in the cafeteria and shared cold drinks. I thanked them for their hospitality and thanked Haiim for the videotape of *Chalghi Baghdad.* We said goodbye once more and I entered the passenger terminal.

I passed the rigorous security inspection then sat for hours before boarding the plane. Luckily, I had a good book of poetry to pass the time: my all-time favorite companion, Rabindranath Tagore. On the plane, for the entire flight I couldn't shake the feeling that this was the last time I would see my mother alive. I tried to divert my thoughts from this morbid feeling. I had to sit belted in my seat with the reality of my foreboding portent, and now here I was, flying back to face its truth.

Our individual lives are no more than sand castles on a beach, I thought, always threatened with obliteration by the next wave. Finally, we live on only in the memories of those we leave behind, and only for a while at that. How many of us get to build pyramids to offset this fear?

I kept thinking about how many times I had made this flight, how often I have been uprooted, and what was in store for me when I landed this time. I recalled all the times she had come to see us in New York. She was so proud of my success.

Chapter Eighty-Four

Mother in the old-age home: A gilded cage …

As Mother aged, my sisters and brothers arranged for her to live in a beautiful old-age home in Rishon Le-Zion, a town just a few miles from Rehoboth, where she had lived for many years. Her tiny apartment was rented to a college student, and her private possessions were either given away or thrown out. Among them, all my father's books and correspondence. They all thought Mother would be safer and less lonely in this place with nurses to look after her and people her age to talk to.

When I visited her in early 2003, I could sense that she was unhappy. She had raised eight children, and she should not have ended up this way, she believed. When I commented how beautiful and serene the place was, Mother said, **"Yes, it may be a gilded cage, but it is still a cage."**

I understood what she meant, and I hugged her. She had that same, familiar, illuminating smile on her face. She was happy to see me, but unhappy where she was.

"You know, I miss my daily walks to the mall and the supermarket," she said. "I can't leave here without written permission from one of my children. Just think about that. They want me to be happy here. But I can't have a cup of tea in the afternoon. I can't peel my own apple. I can't hang any pictures on my walls. And I hate the food they cook here for us. Otherwise, it's okay."

I hugged her again because I truly understood her frustration about her lack of independence and being surrounded by the things that were most familiar to her. Then, an idea came to me. "Mom, would you like me to take you to the mall?" I asked.

Her eyes lit up. "Can you? Will they let you?"

I could see how much that meant to her. "Yes, mom. Let me go talk to the head-nurse."

I walked to the reception desk and asked if I could take my mother to the mall for an hour. I promised to bring her back. "You will have to sign a form indicating your relationship, and how you intend to take her there and bring her back."

I looked the nurse in the eye. "I am her eldest son. I live in America. I will call a taxi, both ways. I just want her to be out of the cage a little." I signed the form on the dotted line.

The nurse called a taxi, which appeared within minutes. Mom and I were waiting at the gate, which was patrolled by a security person. I helped her get seated in the taxi, and we headed to the mall, a few minutes ride. There, we sat in a cafeteria and ordered cake, with tea for her and coffee for me. Music was playing from hidden speakers, and throngs of shoppers passed busily before our eyes. Mom was happy. She was part of the outside, free world again.

About an hour later, I asked her if she'd had enough. I told her the nurse was expecting us back by now. Mother nodded, accepting the new rules. We left the mall, and our same taxi was there waiting for us. I helped her get in and get seated, and in a few minutes we arrived at the facility where she lived.

The one-way ambulance

But Mother didn't want to go inside the building just yet. The residents would be getting ready to have their daily game of dominos or be expected to draw with crayons. We sat on a bench in the shade of the trees on the nursing home grounds and looked up into the branches at some magnificent multi-colored blackbirds. I had a camera with me and snapped some photos of my mother.

Some movement drew our eyes to the side of the building. We both watched as an ambulance approached. *Is someone sick? Does Mom know the person?* I wondered.

Mother didn't speak until the patient was brought out and slid into the ambulance, which took off with a familiar wail. "You see that ambulance?" she asked as if I had never noticed it. **"Anyone that goes away in it never comes back,"** she said cryptically.

Was this a prophecy? I wondered. Is she trying to tell me something?

I gave her a tiny hug. "Mom, don't talk like that. Be positive. This is a wonderful place."

Less than a year later, I was back in that 'wonderful' place, but this time the one-way ambulance had come for her. It was my turn to attend my mother's funeral.

My wife Rachelle and her mother Channah,
USA, 2001 (88)

Grandaughter Dannielle, age 4 and son-in-law Ronen,
USA, 2004 (89)

Sister Judith and nephew No-Am in
NY, USA, 2003 (90)

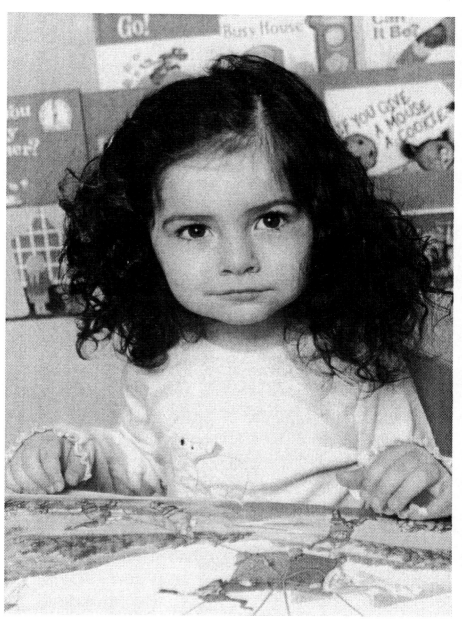

Grandchild Danielle (Sandra's daughter),
USA, 2003 (91)

Sandra and Danielle visit my mother in nursing home,
Israel, 2002 (93)

Last picture of my mother, Israel, 2002 (93)

3 brothers, Avram (l), Yeftah (c) and Saul (r),
at Kibbutz Yo-Av, Israel, 2002 (94)

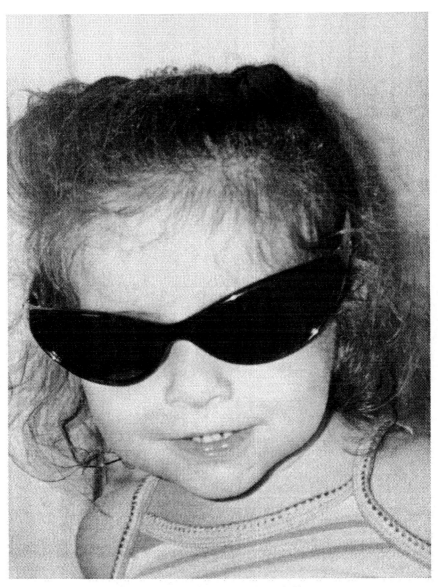

First grandaughter Danielle
age 3, USA, 2003 (95)

Chapter Eighty-Five

Mother: Will she survive this ordeal?

I landed in Israel, October 26, 2003

My fondest memories of my mother had safely carried me through a long and painful plane ride, and now I had to deal with what the present moment would ask of me. I smiled at my seatmate, who had no idea I hadn't been listening to a word she said, and we slowly made our way down the crowded aisle and through the airport. I waited impatiently for my bags to come up then took a taxi straight to the hospital. There, I was directed to "H" department.

I kept all the best memories of Salha (Ani) Fathi in my mind as I walked the long hallway with its smells and bad lighting then found the room. It was full of family, my sisters Pirha and Hannah and my brother Avram, all busily rubbing Mother's arms and legs, talking to her, hoping for a response.

I came close to her bed and kissed her on the forehead.

Hannah shouted in mother's ears, "Mamma, here is Saul. Say hello to him."

Mother didn't respond, not at all. IV tubes ran in to her veins, her eyes were closed, and she was covered with a white bed sheet and light blanket. We stood around her bed and took turns trying to wake her up.

Suddenly she moved her head slightly, opened her eyes, seemed to know that we were all here with her, and she smiled. "Oh God, she's awake !" We shouted with excitement.

Pirha ran to inform the nurse and begged her to come do whatever she could for our mother. But the nurse shrugged and warned us, "Please don't get too excited. Don't get your hopes up. This happens all the time." She was ice-cold.

Mother closed her eyes and went back to "sleep." We continued to visit her at different hours for the next three days, but noticed no progress. The doctors merely provided medication to alleviate pain and monitored her vital signs, which were excellent. We were frustrated that none of the doctors seemed to have a plan to revive her to consciousness. We asked to speak to the head of the department, who promised to take X-rays to further his understanding of what was taking place.

A log of my Mother's last days: Asaf Ha-Rofeh hospital
Sunday, November 3

The head nurse approached us with a big smile to say that the X-rays revealed, to their surprise, that a piece of chicken had been stuck in her throat all along. They had summoned a surgeon who inserted an instrument to extract the pieces one by one.

"Now," they said, "if she hasn't suffered brain damage, she should wake up from her condition, anytime."

They also said they had found "big masses" in her intestines. But they would attend to that later, after she wakes up.

We were all furious.

"A person is brought to the hospital in a coma and they don't do an X-ray for four days?" Pirha said.

"How is that possible?" I wondered.

When we expressed our dismay, the head doctor became indignant.

"There is nothing more I can do. Your mother is very old. She might make it and wake up, but don't count on it. She may be too weak."

Tuesday November 4

Our sister Judith arrived from New York and joined us in department "H" in the ICU. She massaged Mother's legs, which had grown to twice the normal size with fluid, and turned black and blue. Yedida applied moist warm towels to her face, and tried to talk to her. There was no response. We kept looking at the instruments monitoring her vital signs, all of which indicated okay—except she wasn't.

Wednesday, November 5

The hospital nurse called Avram at night and told him Mother's vital signs had deteriorated drastically. They didn't think she would last the night. She asked him to inform the family, so we would have the opportunity to visit while she was still alive.

We drove in from four directions of the country and met up at Mother's room. We stayed till 4 AM, there was no change in her status. Then we decided there was no logic in staying, and went home to catch some sleep.

"No one knows how long this process might take; it may be hours, it may be days, even weeks," we were told.

Thursday, November 6

I visited my cousins Pninah and Tziporah, who expressed their love and concern about my mother. I saw Tziporah's son Oren and met his wife and infant son for the first time, blessed symbol of the ongoing continuity of generations: as one dies, another is born.

Later that day, Pninah and her husband Yitzhak picked me up and took me to dinner at their son's restaurant in Ramat Ha-Sharon. We had a magnificent meal and I was brought back to Rehoboth.

Friday, November 7

I called the hospital and found that everything regarding my mother remained the same: she is in a coma, she has not recovered, no one can tell when or if she will awaken or die.

I decided to take this opportunity to visit Ronen's parents in Afulah, and update them about my mother's condition. I took the train to the port city of Haifa. About two thirds of the passengers were soldiers, men and women in uniform, with machine guns on their laps. I felt secure, yet newly aware of the ever-present threat of acts of sabotage by Arab suicide bombers that Israelis lived with every day.

When I arrived at the train station in Haifa, Ronen's father Tzion picked me up. We had dinner in his brother Shaoul's backyard, which was very pleasant. Their children were there and we shared loose conversations about all topics. Shaoul picked fresh fruits from his extensive garden and served us platefuls. I was encouraged to sleep over and spend the next day with them. They enticed me with, "Let's go to the Golan Heights in the morning, breathe some good air, and forget our troubles for a while." I agreed that this sounded like a good idea.

Saturday, November 8

Shaoul's wife Hannah, and children Sagit and Oren, walked over to Ronen's house, some 100 yards away, to join us on the trip to the Golan Heights. We took fruits, sandwiches, and cold drinks for the road. The winding roads and view of the cultivated fields were magnificent and brought a flood of fond childhood memories from Kibbutz Ma'anit. I felt a bit melancholy yet also grateful for all the blessings life had provided me. I said a silent prayer for my mother in her hospital bed.

As we climbed the mountainous Golan Heights and passed various security checkpoints, I kept reading plaques commemorating fallen soldiers in the war with Syria, Israel's archenemy. At the top, we took a tour that chronicled the war of 1967 and stood and marveled at the huge gliding eagles circling the mountain-top. I wished I could soar like these free-spirited eagles.

On the way back we stopped at a Druze restaurant for a lavish early dinner at 3PM. We took photos of the captivating view of the valley bellow and of us as a group.

When we returned home we shared one more light snack and I thanked my hosts for her wonderful hospitality and the few hours of relief from the burden of our mother's predicament. They encouraged me to be hopeful, and stay strong.

Then Ronen's father Tzion and his brother Shaoul drove me back to the train station in Haifa. On the way, they telephoned the railroad company to ask about the scheduled trains for the Sabbath, and were told that I had just missed the last train to Tel Aviv.

Not to take defeat lightly, the men decided to race against the train by driving me halfway back, to the city of Hadera. Shaoul drove like a maniac and got me there just as the train was pulling into the station.

We had no time for goodbyes. I ran inside as the train pulled up and then I rode away across the dark Israeli night.

Upon arriving in Tel Aviv, I grabbed a cab directly to the hospital. Nothing had changed in my mother's condition during the past two days. Frustrated, I joined Pirha and traveled to Jerusalem to sleep the night at her house.

We had dinner with Pirha's son Roii and his lovely wife Il-Il, then we sat in the basement and listened to classical music. I particularly enjoyed a long stretch of Beethoven's Symphony #8. At about 10:30 we turned in to go to sleep. That is, attempted to sleep, for I could not. I lay wide-awake with a bad feeling about Mother's prospects, and worse feelings about her incompetent doctors. I selected a book from my sister's extensive library and began to read, just to tire my eyes.

Saturday, November 8

Late that night we got a telephone call from the hospital, advising us that Mother's breathing had become very strained and shallow, her vital signs were failing, and she might not make it another night. Pirha knocked on my door and was surprised to find me awake. She passed the hospital message on to me and asked me if I thought it appropriate to call everyone to meet again at the hospital. While we were making phone calls, we heard from Yedida, who was at our mother's bedside.

Mother passed away at 11:23PM.

Yedida insisted there was no need to drive all the way in from Jerusalem at this hour, since there was nothing we could do. She suggested that we meet at the hospital in the morning.

Sunday, November 9

I met with Avram at the hospital at 8 in the morning. The administration office gave us a piece of paper confirming that our mother had passed away, including the date and time of her death, but no reason was specified.

When I asked the reason for death, I was told, "Your mother died of complications brought about by her coma and old age."

I wasn't satisfied, but I said nothing.

When death finally comes, there is nothing more to do.

Mother's funeral arrangements: Hevrah Kadisha

Avram told me, "We must go see Hevrah Kaddisha to arrange for burial later today."

I accompanied him and we parked outside their office in Rehoboth. The Rabbi in attendance was an intelligent, sympathetic young man.

"We want to find a grave location close to my father, Mr. Silas Fathi, who died 17 years ago, and is buried in the old cemetery," Avram said.

The Rabbi punched the keyboard of his computer, scouring an extensive, surprisingly professional map of the cemetery.

"I'm terribly sorry. Here is where your father is buried, may God bless his soul. But you see, there is no space available anywhere near him. You should have reserved the space at the time when your father was buried."

Avram was getting nervous and agitated, then I had an idea.

"Rabbi, can you check another spot? We buried our brother only a year ago in the same cemetery. Can you please search for a space nearby him?" I asked, in a pleading tone.

"I doubt that very much. Did you reserve a spot at the time?"

"No, but please try."

"What's his name?" the Rabbi asked.

"Yeftah Ben Silas Fathi," Avram snapped.

The Rabbi studied the map of thousands of graves, going back to the British Mandate. Suddenly his eyes lit up.

"Here he is. I can't believe it, it seems impossible," the Rabbi said.

"What? What did you find?" we asked him in one voice.

He stiffened. "Here is your brother, and I can't believe it, there is an empty spot right next to him. How is that possible, after a year's time?"

We looked at the map and confirmed this was Yeftah's grave. To his right, there was an empty spot surrounded by other tombs claimed by others but this space had been inexplicably left open, and was available.

"A miracle," the Rabbi confirmed. "Your mother must have been a saint... she must have loved her son very much...."

At the cemetery: November 9, 2003

By 3PM we were standing outside the cemetery gates in the parking lot waiting for the gathering to assemble. We had notified everyone we could think of who knew our mother, and people who had heard of her passing from others also began to arrive. Each of my mother's children was approached with a hand-shake and warm condolences. The women had silk scarves on their heads, while most of the men wore *yarmulkes*. There were many people I did not recognize, and Avram and Hannah had to properly introduce me to them: "Please meet my brother Saul, from America."

When about 65 people had congregated outside the cemetery, the assistant to the Rabbi motioned us inside the same sun-lit room where just a year ago my brother Yeftah was mourned. I thought about my poor mother, who had to live long enough to bury a son. No one should have to bury their own child. I mourned my mother's passing, but this was the natural order and I understood the sacred truth of this fact as we drew a circle of acceptance around Salha Faith's coffin.

Heads down, the Rabbi began to read the prayers for the dead.

"Amen, Amen," we responded.

There came a moment when he motioned my brother Avram and me aside and he whispered, "You must formally identify the body now, then sign this document."

He pulled the white drape from Mother's face. Then he slipped a hand under her neck to support the head and began to unwind another cloth from her head and face.

Avram and I looked at our mother's sweet familiar face for a second and bravely nodded like men, without crying, "Yes, that is Salha Fathi."

The Rabbi quickly re-wrapped the head and covered the body with the linen cloth. We signed the certificate matter-of-factly but I felt weak at the knees, barely able to stand. I held on to the podium so no one could see me trembling.

More prayers were read, heads looking down at the floor, handkerchiefs in hand, voices replying "Amen."

Then the assistant to the Rabbi wheeled out the carriage where the coffin rested, through the door of the room, through the doorway of life to the open field of death, along the winding walkways among the graves. The grieving throng followed.

We stopped next to Yeftah's tombstone. A space had been cleared beside him, to enfold my mother in the earth to the right of her son.

Reading of the Kaddish

Again we surrounded the coffin with our love and prayers of remembrance. The Rabbi read, then handed the book to Avram to read the *Mourner's Kaddish:*

"Glorified and sanctified be God's great name throughout the world, which He has created according to His will. May He establish His kingdom in your lifetime and during your days, and within the life of the entire House of Israel, speedily and soon; and say, Amen. "Amen"

May His great name be blessed forever and to all eternity. "Amen"

"Blessed and praised, glorified and exalted, extolled and honored, adored and lauded be the name of the Holy One, blessed be He, beyond all the blessings and hymns, praises and consolations that are ever spoken in the world; and say, Amen. "Amen"

"May there be abundant peace from Heaven, and life, for us, and for all Israel; and say, Amen. "Amen"

"He who creates peace in His celestial heights, may he create peace for us and for all Israel; and say, Amen. "Amen"

Then the assistant stood on the steps to the grave as two men lifted the body down from the carriage and slowly lowered Mother to his hands. I cringed as the linen-draped figure was revealed: the body was so flexible, soft and bending. The assistant hugged the body close to him to hold her firmly as he lowered her to her grave. Then he climbed the steps back up and began shoveling in the dirt to bury her.

A huge collective sigh was released as women stepped forward to toss flowers into the grave, while others took turns with the shovel. It took fifteen minutes to fill the hole to the top.

The Rabbi recited some final prayers and asked if anyone wished to speak.

My sister Yedida had suffered a lifetime of "issues" with Mother, and as she tried to make her final peace she sobbed out loud, still feeling hurt that Mother had not distributed her love equally to all of us.

"She always loved Yeftah the most. Look, to the very end she doesn't let go of him. She is sleeping forever now, next to her beloved and favorite son, Yeftah."

A loud cry went up from the crowd, all wrestling with their individual feelings about Salha and how she had treated them.

Yeftah's children, Maya and No-Am, came close and hugged me from both sides. No-Am whispered, "I love you, Saul, you are my favorite uncle." He was trying to be strong, to be a man, but his voice was breaking.

We are truly orphans now

I stepped forward and asked permission to speak.

"First, I want to thank each and every one of you for coming today to pay last respects to our dear mother Salha Fathi. Some of you don't know me or have forgotten who I am. I am the eldest son, Saul, who left Israel a long time ago; I live in America."

I began to choke with guilt, but continued because this was not about me but about my mother.

"Mother was an independent woman who lived life on her own terms. She took good care of all of her children, and lived to see us all marry and settle down. She loved her many grandchildren without reserve. Throughout her life and into old age, my mother made sure never to be a burden on anyone. She loved us all, and yes, we all knew she loved Yeftah the best, perhaps because he needed her the most. Now they are united, together again in death. And we are truly orphans now...."

I could not continue, as my grief rose to block the air in my throat.

Avram stepped up to finish.

"Just look. How is it that an open space was left here for Mother, right next to Yeftah? We didn't reserve it at the time of his death and the Rabbi told us this is a miracle. So here we are, witness to a miracle, a mother and her son, together in death as in life. Thank you all for coming. We will be sitting *Shiv-Ah* all week at Yedida's house. Please join us there for food and a celebration of life."

Paying respect to other graves

The Rabbi put the prayer book under his arm and bid us goodbye and God bless, and left to lead services for another burial. We were following him out when Pirha suggested that we visit Yeftah's wife Edna's grave, a simple, elegant piece of earth. Maya and No-Am flanked me, holding my hands as we silently read the words carved on her tombstone. Maya bent down to brush away fallen leaves and wind-blown dust. No-Am found a small glittery stone and placed it on his mother's grave as a marker that he had been here to show his eternal love and pay his respects. So did I.

Yedida asked, "Should we go ahead and visit Ezra's and Father's grave, as long as we are here?"

We walked about 150 yards and found Ezra's grave. Yedida lit a candle and placed it in the little compartment behind the marble stone.

"Look, the writing is fading. I need to get someone to fix this," Yedida said, pointing to the shadowy outlines of old letters.

Other family members joined us at Father's grave, another 50 yards down the row. I was remembering the night, not so long ago, when three brothers, Yeftah, Avram, and I, stood right here in the dark, aided by car lights, and did this very same ritual together. Yeftah made his peace with Father that night, after so many years, and broke down crying. I had witnessed the pain and deep agony in his eyes, followed by the sense of relief that comes when forgiveness is truly offered. Now my brother was buried here in this cemetery too, and today his mother has finally come to be near him in death. She understood him as no one else did and always forgave him, no matter how big the offense.

Hannah lit a candle for Father and placed it in the back of the stone, whispering a prayer that he might rest in peace. Then we walked among the thousand graves of our Jewish kindred spirits praying for blessings on all their souls. When we arrived at the exit we washed our hands, according to Jewish custom, and walked out into the light of the rest of our lives as motherless children.

Sitting Shiv-ah: (Seven days of mourning) for mother
Sunday, November 9

My watch said it was 5:30 PM as we drove to Yedida's apartment to begin preparations to receive well-wishers and face life without our beloved mother. Tables were set with platters of food and a selection of drinks; on others, prayer books and *kappa's*. Photo albums were placed around the room so we could sit together and look back over Mother's life. In the corner, about twenty folding chairs had been stacked after being brought up from the basement and we unfolded them one by one as guests and relatives began to arrive at the house. Already, some of the day's earlier, more raw sadness was dissipating from their eyes, their faces less mournful. People smiled and greeted each other as we always had at family gatherings, helped themselves to drinks and catered goodies, and made small talk as if it were just another party.

We reminisced about Mother, sad and funny anecdotes, and some of us were able to manage a little laughter. Naomi and Tzadok, my aunt Khatoon's children, sat next to me and I realized I didn't know them very well, as I had left Israel so long ago. I sat in the midst of "the path not chosen," a life in Israel, and pondered how different my life might have been had I chosen to stay. Naomi and Tzadok were beautiful and polite, highly sympathetic toward my mother, whom they called "Dear Aunt Salha." I liked these people very much; had I stayed, we would perhaps have become good friends, participating closely in each other's lives. As it was, since I had chosen a different path, they were comfortable strangers who happened to know some of the same people I did.

Opposite us were two other people I barely knew: my uncle David's wife Flora and son Ezra.

Flora noted, "Now only Salman is still alive, out of six brothers. They all died young. Terrible diseases that run in our family killed them."

I asked what diseases ran in our family, so I could prepare myself for possibilities.

"Diabetes, heart attack, and cancer."

"Guess that covers the big ones, eh?" I said, thinking, I don't stand much of a chance with that kind of genetic inheritance.

Monday, November 10

I woke early, not sure if I had slept at all. We sat for breakfast, which Yedida overcooked as usual. At least she made a decent cup of coffee.

We were surprised to begin greeting visitors as early as 8:30 in the morning, and people continued to stream in all day, until 9:30 that night.

My aunt Ruthi's daughter Mikhal insisted on washing dishes and serving food, and would not yield to my sister's request that she sit down with the rest of the guests.

Yedida's childhood friend Leah came and was very pleasant and sympathetic. I was surprised that she recognized me immediately, after nearly fifty years. "Berta is not here? She actually neglected to come to her mother's funeral," she said in a way that invited me to participate in gossip and open old family wounds. I chose to ignore the comment and asked her how she'd been in the forty-five years since we'd last seen each other.

The telephone did not let up for ten minutes. Aunt Marcel (Nava) called several times to express condolences, remind us how much she loved Mother, and apologize that she could not attend the funeral, for health reasons. She couldn't walk at all anymore, she said, and apologized again for her son Ezra, who was too busy to bring her. Aunt Nava cried on the phone and insisted on talking to me and to each of my sisters, one by one, then repeating the same thing to every single one. We were exasperated, rolling our eyes, but no one could be angry with her, as she was obviously well meaning.

In the afternoon Marcel's son Ezra arrived, unannounced—a welcome surprise. He asked us to keep the visit a secret from his mother who could not function or walk at all anymore. Sadly, he relayed that besides the physical strain, it would have been too much of an emotional drain for her to attend the funeral.

"She loved your mother most of all," he said, then paused to ponder the reality of what he was about to say next. "She is devastated, because she is contemplating her own death these days."

The tombstone carver arrived late in the day to sit down with Avram and agree on the details.

Tuesday November 11

In the morning I eagerly accepted an invitation from Pirha's son Roii to take me on an outing for a few hours, to Jaffa and Tel-Aviv. We had a great time catching up on many years of intrigue and the changes life had brought us both. We ate lunch in a nice restaurant in north Tel-Aviv then he brought me back to Yedida's in the late afternoon.

My cousin Jamil's wife Simkhah came in, greeted me with her perpetual smile, and gave me a strong, long hug. I learned again what I already vaguely knew about her, but had forgotten, or not thought about very much: Her husband Jamil had been dead for several years, her children were grown and married, she has beautiful grandchildren, but she was alone.

"But I have no complaints," Simkhah said. "I accept life's verdicts without hesitation, because I have faith in God's will... Who am I to question anything?"

I listened, simply enjoying her beauty as she told stories of how she used to meet Salha walking in the mall or sitting on the bench in the Moshavah. She told me some things I didn't know about my mother, and she made me laugh.

Hours later a Yemenite woman showed up, who introduced herself as "your mother's helper and adopted sister."

Yedida brought her to me. "Saul, this nice woman was Mother's helper when she lived alone in her apartment. Do you remember? I know that Mother loved her, even though she gave her plenty of grief. You know how independent mother was."

We laughed, in acknowledgement of how tough our mother could be when she set her mind to something.

The Yemenite said, "Your mother was very smart, one of the smartest women I have ever met. So never mind the aggravations I had with her. I learned a lot from her, and I loved her like a sister."

Then she remembered something and began to laugh.

"She called me *Majnoonah* (insane lady), when I told her that I was looking for a young man to marry, because the last one I married was old and he had "broken tools". Your mother said I was crazy to marry again. *Majnoonah,* she called me. And you know what? She turned out to be right!"

We all laughed. We needed this.

People kept coming in droves. We greeted each one, served food and drink, initiated polite conversations, listened to their stories of how they knew our mother, and comforted their grief. It was heartwarming, but tiring.

That evening, Avram took me to a synagogue where we listened to a sermon from a Rabbi on the story of Sodom and Gomorrah. He tried to draw comparisons to today's sinful youth of Israel, but I disagreed with his harangue, because I could see the goodness in the next generation, who had inherited such a difficult world and were doing their best to cope and be responsible citizens. I was bored by his approach and upset by his accusatory and negative tone. At the conclusion Avram and I dropped a few coins in the donation box but returned to Yedida as fast as we could get away.

Wednesday November 12

I took a long walk with No-Am and we had ice cream cones at the Moshavah. We spoke about politics and the future of Israel in the age of suicide bombers. His views were aggressive and extreme right, supporting Sharon 100 percent.

When we returned to Yedida's, new guests had arrived from Afulah: Ronen's parents, his uncle Shaoul, wife Hannah, and son Oren. They brought food, as was the custom for Moroccan Jews.

Hannah came by in the afternoon with her husband Haiim, son Gai, and beautiful infant granddaughter, Le-Or. We enjoyed watching this newest member of our family crawl all over the floor and smile at everyone's shoes. Le-Or caused me to be homesick for my family in New York, as she brought forth my feelings for my own lovely grandchild Danielle at home waiting for my return to America.

Thursday, November 13

Thursday was lighter than the other days. We were able to truly sit, relax and talk, just the brothers and sisters. A few visitors came but they didn't stay as long as on the other days, which were marathons. We caught up with a lot of family matters, and I began to feel we were on our way to healing. I suppose this is why *Shiv-Ah* is a seven-day process, to allow for time to pass so we can come to accept the concept that we can proceed into our futures without our dear departed, much-loved mother.

Friday, November 14

Shiv-Ah will end before the Sabbath sunset. We decided to make a car trip to the port city of Ashdod in the south of the country, on the Mediterranean Sea. We found a restaurant in the marina, took in the brisk clean air, and basked in the sun's rays. I took photos of everyone and of the sights, including one of a beautiful bulldog walking by unattended. New high-rise apartment buildings were being constructed everywhere we looked. The future felt hopeful and it was a wonderful day out with the family.

Saturday, November 15

I enjoyed a leisurely breakfast with Yedida, Judith, Pirha, Hannah, and Avram, all of us except Berta and Yeftah. Now that *Shiv-Ah* was over, we felt free to talk about business and other less-than-sacred matters. We discussed the details of Mother's modest inheritance, which Avram had prepared in minute detail. She had left us $75,000, to divide as we saw fit. We agreed to include Yeftah in splitting the sum into eight parts, and give Yeftah's portion to his children, No-Am and Maya.

That afternoon Maya and I went out to a local movie. It was so bad, we walked out in the middle. But we were together, talking and laughing, and that was the most important thing to us. She reminded me of some fun stories about her father and we were able to laugh at some of his ways. I felt so close to her; I wanted to be her best uncle and compensate for lost years when we were apart, and for some of my brother's more unfortunate behavior.

Later we visited Hannah. Haiim suggested we go out for dinner in Tel Aviv. There was no resistance from me; Tel Aviv was one of my favorite cities on earth. Haiim, Hannah, Gai, and I dined at a unique restaurant attached to a gas station, called "Ass." We sat in the backyard (the parking lot, really) and ate shish kebab and Israeli salads, pita bread, hummus, and other Mediterranean style foods. The time was most enjoyable, and we did not even smell the emissions as cars pulled into the gas station beside us to fill up.

As we were eating, many anecdotes in connection with Yeftah came to our minds: his many love affairs, how many "conquests" he had, how he was the "James Dean" of the family, as they were both handsome men who were a little bit reckless and died young. At the end, Yeftah had lost his desire to live because he was ashamed of the dire condition he had brought himself to and did not want anyone to see him that way. Of course, we all agreed, any one of us would have been more than willing to help him out; being dead was much worse than being in trouble and needing the help of family.

At the public park in Ramat-Gan we took a series of photos and felt lucky to be alive and healthy, with our plentiful futures still ahead. Lots of dogs were running around, with and without leashes. We shared a small picnic there, then went to "Old Tel Aviv" where we continued our eating spree. Hours later, we returned to Hannah's house in Rehoboth and watched videotapes of the comedian Yossi Bannai and the comedy group Ha-gah-shash. We laughed as we never laughed before.

Sunday, November 16

We gathered the entire family and returned to the cemetery to visit Mother's grave, to perform the *Ah-liy-yah lah-keh-ver* ritual, where we read the *Kaddish* and *Yeskor*. We didn't dwell there long, as mourning too long is just as inappropriate as rushing the process.

As I was taking pictures of all the graves of family members, near Yeftah's grave a man in a captain's uniform drew close and asked if I knew Yeftah Fathi.

"Yes, he was my brother."

The man introduced himself. "I am the son of Yo-av Shar-ah-bi, one of your brother's closest friends. Yeftah used to come to our house to play cards with my father, at least weekly. He would stay for dinner and tell jokes non-stop for hours. We learned a lot from him, he was very smart. I miss his brilliance and his jokes. I still can't believe he is dead."

"Nor can we," I assured him, and thanked him for sharing that story with us. "It means a lot to know that others were able to appreciate his sense of humor and devilish spirit of fun."

Taking a break from misery and mourning

Within an hour we were on our way to Jaffa. I composed some artsy photos of the city's old, narrow streets, beautifully cultivated gardens, and its magnificent view of the ocean. Then we ate lunch at Abu-El-Afya. The tasty meal was complimented by the fresh-smelling air that carried wafts of new life and *joie de vivre* over the waves of the Mediterranean Sea. A stray cat came and sat next to me. I gave her cheese and some of my Coke, and she seemed to like both. Then another cat came along, but this one was finicky and refused to eat any of the leftover food I offered. Bashful, picky, or simply not hungry? Oh well, his problem, not mine.

On the way back, Yedida was still focused on resolving Yeftah's death for herself.

"Do you really believe he died from a bug bite?" she asked, perhaps hoping that I could shed light on the matter or engage in speculation that he had committed suicide.

I wasn't interested in indicting my brother, or in answering questions I was not equipped to understand.

Instead I looked up toward the sky and replied in a soft voice, "Who knows what was in Yeftah's heart at the end, Yedida? Only God knows."

We drove in silence the remainder of the way, absorbing the mystery.

Monday, November 17

I spent the day with Pirha and Yedida then moved my baggage over to Hannah's. Someone still needed to visit Mother's *Beit-Avot* (old-age home), so we agreed to take on this task together.

The head nurse had been notified by the hospital of Mother's passing, and she expressed her regrets and condolences, with a faint Russian accent.

"Your mother still has clothes and some other private possessions here. Would you like to take them with you now?" she asked.

She led us to Mother's room and opened the closet. Her familiar dresses and nightgowns still hung neatly on the hangers. In the drawers we found a few pocketbooks and some jewelry. We also found at least twenty beautiful silk scarves, some still in their original gift boxes, and a few hand-knit sweaters, including the blue one she really loved. I had been doing all right up to that point, but seeing that sweater brought tears to my eyes as I remembered the day I last saw Mother radiantly alive and wearing this sweater, eating and talking happily in Hannah's backyard.

"Do you mind if I keep this sweater?" I asked my sister.

"Of course not, Saul, take whatever you want. I have no use for these old clothes."

In the bottom-most bureau drawer, we found a box containing dozens of photos, some going back over fifty years. Hannah and I sat on the bed and looked through them, marveling at the emotions and memories that these small black and white reminders could conjure up, and we cried openly yet again, to think we would never again see our sweet mother alive.

We asked at the nurse's office for some big plastic bags to put all the clothes in, then asked her, "Please, donate these things to the needy poor," which she agreed to do.

"Thank you for taking care of our mother in her last year," Hannah said.

When we left, we couldn't help but stop at the benches where Mother used to sit in the shade. I took some photographs of them, and thought about my children coming upon these strange images among my belongings after my passing. *What will they think about these abstract pictures of empty benches? Will they mean anything?* I decided that it didn't matter what my children would think, the photos mean something to me, and I am not dead yet.

We drove to Caesarea and visited our favorite museum again, had lunch, walked on the beach, and on the way back, we called our cousin Ezra Benyamini, Marcel's first-born son. He and his wife Carmella greeted us warmly, and we passed the afternoon in their lovely backyard sipping tea and eating cookies. Trees surrounded a deep blue swimming pool, and it appeared to me that probably no one ever swam in it.

We drove back through Petakh-Tikvah and shopped at a factory that manufactured specialty Iraqi food and treats. We bought some, planning to take it home and share it, but then we couldn't wait to get home. We sat in the car and ate it all until we were nearly sick we were so full, licking our fingers hungrily.

At Hannah's house, I agreed to take some sleeping pills from Haiim as I had barely slept since my arrival in Israel.

Tuesday, November 18

The sleeping pills didn't help, I could not fall asleep, knowing that the next day would be my last day in Israel. Late that night I would board a plane and go back to New York. Who knew when I would ever be here again, now that both my parents had died? I hoped there would not be another funeral to attend for a long time to come.

At 8 in the morning, tired of pretending to sleep, I walked downstairs for a cold drink in the kitchen and found Hannah's grandchild Le-Or sleeping in a stroller in the living room. Her father Asaf had dropped her off on his way to work, around 7 o'clock. I sat on the couch looking at that beautiful sleeping baby, jealous that sleep came so easily to her, then allowed her gentle, peaceful breathing to lull me to sleep on the living room sofa.

Around 11 AM Avram came in and found me still in my pajamas, sound asleep in the middle of the rest of the household going on about its business. Hannah had found me there when she came in to check on the baby, and covered me with a blanket, which had added to my feeling of comfort and enabled me to blank out the world for a few hours at last.

Avram felt it was urgent to go to the bank and sign papers regarding the inheritance before I left the country. Hannah and I went along and signed the necessary forms. I gave Yedida Power-of-Attorney to receive the money in my name, then forward it to me in New York.

Then Haiim and Hannah drove us south to Bee-lu to pick up their son Gai and to stop for falafel in Sha-Ah-Ra-Yim. We took some more photos of each other smiling and eating.

We stopped at Yedida's, who informed us, "Aunt Nava called three times. She insists on speaking to you, Saul. Please remember, she is not to know that her son Ezra stopped by, and certainly she mustn't know you visited him at his house."

I was silent, not wanting to get involved in lies, even if only lies of omission.

Yedida continued. "Aunt Nava says she has been cooking for two days for you, and that you must go to her, who else is going to eat all that food?"

I was so stressed out, I didn't have the time or strength, let alone desire, for any more visiting. It was my last day in Israel and I wanted to spend it with my immediate family. *Who knows when will I be back again?*

I telephoned my aunt and apologized, telling her it was impossible to visit today, as I was leaving the country that night.

"So, to whom do you want me to give all this food? I worked two days to prepare it for you special. Shall I throw it all in the garbage?"

I had no good answers. "Sorry *Dodah* (my aunt), do what you must with the food. Thank you for preparing it and thinking of me, but I can't come visit you today and I must go now," I said and hung up before she had time to torture me any further. I had disappointed people in the past by having to leave, and here I was doing it again. But as my mother used to say, "Saying goodbye, that's the way of the world."

Tell us everything, Dad, everything

So once again, I found myself at Ben-Gurion airport, waiting for a long flight across the ocean. Avram and his wife Rutti and I sat in the cafeteria for an hour and said our good-byes, without too much emotion, as we had spent our allotment already in these last hard days and weeks together.

On the plane my whole life flashed before me: the happy years of our childhood in Baghdad, the challenging years of settlement in Israel, the years of separation from family and friends, and now, a new phase: being an orphan, a man without parents.

I started to think about how little fun my mother truly enjoyed in her ninety years of life. As I was feeling sorry for her and for myself, I remembered some lines from one of Tagore's poems:

Mother, I shall weave a chain of pearls for thy neck with my tears of sorrow
Wealth and fame come from thee and it is for thee to give or to withhold them
But this my sorrow is absolutely mine own
And when I bring it to thee as my offering
Thou rewardest me with thy grace.

When I finally arrived in New York, my wife and children met me at Kennedy Airport.

My daughter Suzanne welcomed me with a warm hug:
"Tell us everything, Dad, everything."

The End

History: Supplementary companion, sold separately. (see details)

Printed in the United States
49729LVS00001B/8

9 780977 711727